COMPREHENSIVE GUIDE TO

FACTORY LAW

Important

The main text must always be read in conjunction with the up-dating supplement at the back of this book. Information given in the supplement may sometimes over-rule that in the main text. Readers are therefore advised to note in the main text where an item is also treated in the supplement.

COMPREHENSIVE GUIDE TO FACTORY LAW

A classified guide to the requirements of the Factories Act and other legislation, including the Health and Safety at Work Act 1974, affecting factories and allied premises, including construction sites, docks and offices

Sixth edition with supplement on
The Health and Safety at Work Act 1974

ROBERT MCKOWN

Sixth edition revised by
John Parris LLB, PhD

GEORGE GODWIN LIMITED
The book publishing subsidiary of the Builder Group

First edition published by Chantry Publications Limited, 1954

Second edition 1961

Third edition, revised and enlarged, published by
George Godwin Limited 1965

Fourth edition 1968
(Reprinted with minor revisions 1969)

Fifth edition 1974

Sixth edition revised with supplement 1976
published by
George Godwin Limited
2-4 Catherine Street
London W.C.2.

ISBN 0 7114 3312 7

Printed in Great Britain by WATMOUGHS LIMITED, Idle, Bradford; and London.

Contents

Introduction to the Sixth Edition

The Health and Safety at Work etc Act 1974

The *et cetera* in the title gives the game away. The Health and Safety at Work etc. Act 1974 is a ragbag of legislation into which has been thrust a number of different subjects making it, as William Henry Duke of Gloucester said, 'another damned, thick, square book'. 'An Act to make further provision for securing the health, safety and welfare of persons at work . . . for preventing the unlawful acquisitions of explosives . . . for controlling emissions into the atmosphere . . . and to amend the law relating to building regulations' runs part of the preamble. All it omits is legislation to determine how many persons can sleep in one bed or angels dance on the point of a needle.

But that is the modern fashion. Important amendments to the Sale of Goods Act, about the right to reject goods, are contained in a statute called The Theft Act, just so everybody will know where to find it.

The Health and Safety at Work etc Act empowers the Secretary of State for Employment to repeal or amend, at his discretion, the whole or part of no less than 31 earlier Acts of Parliament and all the regulations made under them. To Lord Hewitt it would have seemed the ultimate triumph of *The New Despotism*. He must be gyrating in his grave like a spinning top. But I suppose we ought to be grateful. There were 3,480 Acts of Parliament in force in 1974, and Parliament has been increasing the statute book at the rate of 1,500 pages a year.

But these are constitutional issues with which we are not here directly concerned.

What is of more relevance is the manner in which the minister (that is, his civil servants) has chosen to exercise the powers that Parliament has bestowed on him.

If there is one subject on which legislation should be clear and explicit, so that the foreman on the building site or the manager on the factory floor may know exactly what his duty is, it is safety precautions. It is equally important for magistrates who, as the Lord Chief Justice reminded them recently, have the untrained minds of jurymen. What then is Bill Bloggins, whether on the floor or the bench, to make of delegated legislation which purports to repeal 'subsections (1) to (4) of Section 146 of the Factories Act 1961, except for the purposes of Section 148'?

Are sub-sections 146 (1) to (4) repealed or are they not repealed? Are they amended and, if so, in what words?

Or are they consigned, by some new Manichaeism, to a purgatory from which they can return to haunt us?

It is extremely difficult to find out what regulations are repealed and what are still in force and in this the Department of the Employment and the new Health and Safety at Work Commission are less than helpful. They don't know either.

I do not therefore, and cannot, warrant that the law as stated herein is that in force on the 1st January 1976. After many hours of ill remunerated labour, all I can say is that I hope it is.

John Parris

January 1976

General Introduction

This book, now in its sixth edition, is intended as a comprehensive guide to the obligations placed on factory occupiers by the Factories Act and other relevant legislation, such as the Petroleum Acts, the Explosives Acts, etc., and by the numerous codes of regulations made under them. It contains references to all statutory requirements affecting safety precautions, environmental conditions, health and welfare of employees, hours of work, and legal formalities such as the reporting of accidents. It also includes the requirements for offices (including factory offices) introduced under the Offices, Shops and Railway Premises Act, Contract of Employment Act, 1972, Truck Acts, Employment Medical Services Act, 1972 etc. A supplement at the back of this book details new legislation passed under the Health and Safety at Work Act 1974.

Supplement to the 6th Edition: The Health and Safety at Work Act

The intention of the Health and Safety at Work Act is that certain statutes, together with the statutory instruments made under them, should be repealed and progressively replaced by a system of regulations and approved codes of practice.

Since the fifth edition of this book, published prior to the passing of the Act, a number of regulations have already been made. However the process is far from complete and is still very much an on-going one.

In order to enable people in industry to keep well up-to-date with new legislation it has been decided to revise this book more regularly by means of up-dating supplements. *This sixth edition gives details of new legislation up to 1st January 1976.*

Important: The main text must always be read in conjunction with the supplement, since information given there may sometimes over-rule that given in the main text. Readers are advised to add a note in the main text where an item is also treated in the supplement.

Arrangement of Contents

As in previous editions, the various legal requirements are arranged according to subject, irrespective of the Acts or regulations in which they occur. For instance, requirements regarding heating and ventilation are contained in the main Factories Act and in various codes of regulations, including the Food Hygiene Regulations and the Thermal Insulation Regulations; in this book all these are grouped under one heading.

Readers should also consult the supplement for details of recent revisions to legislation passed under the Health and Safety at Work Act. Information in the supplement is arranged according to the same item numbers as the main text.

The book is divided into chapters under such general headings as Factory Buildings, Machinery, Electrical Equipment, and so on; it is thus a simple matter to see the scope of the legislation in respect of each subject. A comprehensive index and a system of cross-references ensures that no legal requirement need be overlooked.

Many industries and processes are subject to special regulations, over and above the requirements of the main Acts. Where such a process is in common use (e.g. woodworking, construction work, docks, etc.) the relevant legislation is often quoted in full. Where the process is confined to a single highly-specialised industry (e.g., herring curing and patent fuel) a brief outline only has been given, in order to save space, but this is sufficient to tell the reader whether his own factory is likely to be affected and he can then refer to the appropriate published regulations for full details.

Legal References

Every legal requirement quoted is followed by a reference to the Act or regulation in which it occurs. To save space, the titles of the Acts and regulations are generally given in abbreviated form; thus *FA: 13(1)* refers to the Factories Act 1961, Section 13, Sub-section 1. These abbreviations are explained in the Appendix but it will be convenient to keep in mind that the Factories Act 1961, to which frequent reference is made, is abbreviated to *FA*.

In a few places the legal reference is not to a statutory requirement but to a legal decision made by a judge when interpreting the law. In such circumstances the reference is the title of the case, e.g. *Brophy v. J. C. Bradfield and Co., 1955*; under these titles the reports of the cases will be found in the published volumes of law reports and other legal works.

Meaning of Terms Used

Many terms have not been legally defined, either by statute or by the courts. The meaning of such terms must therefore remain a matter of interpretation, based on full consideration of the particular circumstances and on the apparent intention of the Acts concerned. Some terms (or expressions) are defined under Interpretation in the Acts and regulations, e.g., *FA: 176. ABW: 3,* etc. Other expressions are referred to as they occur.

Common Law Liability

In addition to the statutory duties placed on factory occupiers by the various Acts, every employer has certain duties at Common Law. These are mainly concerned with providing a safe system of working and otherwise taking reasonable general precautions for the safety of employees. These obligations are dealt with in a special chapter.

Official Forms and other Publications

Throughout the book reference is made to various official factory forms and other publications issued by the Ministry of Labour,* and Department of Employment. Some of these must be obtained in order to comply with the law (e.g. the prescribed abstract of the Factories Act which has to be displayed in every factory) but others consist of advisory leaflets, memoranda, Health and Safety Booklets etc., the obtaining of which is not obligatory but which will be found very helpful in carrying out the requirements of the law. All factory occupiers are advised to obtain a copy of Government Publications Sectional List No. 18, which contains particulars of all these publications, including certificates of exemption and approval. Sectional List 18 is available free of charge from H.M. Stationery Office, 49, High Holborn, London, W.C.2, or from the other branches of the Stationery Office in Birmingham, Bristol, Cardiff, Manchester, Edinburgh and Belfast.

The Annual Report, now issued by the Health and Safety Commission, contains information on current health and safety problems, accident statistics, etc. and the Department of Employment Gazette lists new and proposed legislation.

H.M. Factory Inspectorate also issue free of charge Technical Data Notes (T.D.N.) on machinery guarding and health problems. Details of these may be obtained from the district inspector of factories. The T.D.N.'s are also listed in Sectional List 18.

In the British Standards Year Book will be found British Standards and Codes of Practice covering industrial safety and health matters.

Membership of the Royal Society for the Prevention of Accidents (industrial division), or the British Safety Council will enable firms or individuals to obtain information on current matters, safety training courses, etc.

The Indexes

In the indexes, and in all cross-references, the figures given refer to the number of the *item,* not the number of the page. This is designed to increase the ease with which the desired information is found, as most items occupy less than a page and are therefore more quickly searched through.

The opportunity has been taken to add to new indexes to the sixth edition. These are an Index to Statutes and an Index to Statutory Instruments. The Index to Statutes will also show the reader what statutes are to be repealed or have already been repealed or amended under the Health and Safety at Work Act.

In using the general index, reference should first be made to the actual machine, plant, process, etc., about which information is required. If it does not appear in the index it means that it is unlikely to be mentioned by name in any relevant legislation, and reference should then be to the general heading appropriate to the subject (e.g., machinery) or to the nature of the hazard involved (e.g., dust). It must be remembered that comparatively few types of machine, items of plant or substances are mentioned by name in any factory legislation, and then only in connexion with special requirements. For instance, it will be found that the only actual reference to guillotines by name is in connexion with the training of young workers; everything else connected with them is dealt with by general requirements—their guards under the requirements for guarding machinery, any electrical equipment under the requirements for electricity. Similarly mercury is only referred to in connexion with reporting of industrial diseases (item 296), everything else is dealt with by processes producing dusts and fumes (item 117).

---

* The title of the Minister of Labour has now been changed to that of Secretary of State for Employment. Throughout this book all references to the Minister and his department should be read accordingly.

Chapter I

Premises Affected

Except where otherwise stated, the legal requirements quoted in this book apply to all factories as defined by Section 175 of the Factories Act, 1961. Some provisions of the Act also apply to employment in electrical sub stations, docks, warehouses, ships in wet docks, building operations, etc. The effect of these definitions is outlined below.

1 - General Definition of a Factory

Premises, whether under cover or in the open air, constitute a factory if persons are employed in manual labour for *any* of the purposes mentioned in the Act, provided that the work is carried on by way of trade or for the purpose of gain, and provided also that the employer has the right of access or control. These purposes are:—

(*a*) the making of any article or of part of any article;

(*b*) the ornamenting or finishing of any article;

(*c*) the altering, repairing, cleaning or washing of any article;

(*d*) the breaking up or demolition of any article;

(*e*) the adapting for sale of any article;

(*f*) the slaughtering of cattle, sheep, swine, goats, horses, asses, or mules, or the confinement of such animals elsewhere while awaiting slaughter (except when the place of confinement is part of a market or is maintained mainly for agricultural purposes);

(*g*) the special purposes mentioned in item 2 below.

It should be noted that the term "adapting for sale" has been given a very wide meaning by the Courts. It has been held to include, for instance, the arranging of sweetmeats in ornamental boxes, the making of wreaths and crosses in a florist's shop, and the sorting of town refuse into saleable and unsaleable portions. Whether any particular process is "adapting for sale" is a matter of fact to be decided separately in each individual case (See *Hudson Bay Co. v. Thompson 1959*).

For the premises to be a factory there must be employment in manual labour. Employment denotes the relationship of master and servant, thus a technical institute was held not to be a factory in the case of *Weston v. L.C.C. 1941*. Manual labour is not defined but it has been held that some kinds of manual labour require little strength and much labour. In the case of *J. & F. Stone v. Haygarth 1968*, it was held that a radio and television repair engineer was employed in manual labour. Also the words used are for trade *or* gain. See *Stanger v. Hendon Borough Council 1948*.

In the earlier Factory Acts a distinction was made between premises in which mechanical power was used and those in which it was not used. This distinction was abolished in 1937, so far as the general definition of a factory was concerned: if premises come within the definition quoted above they constitute a factory irrespective of whether mechanical power is used or not. *FA: 175*

2 - Special Definitions

Premises in which persons are employed in manual labour for any of the following purposes are also classed as factories, even though they are not covered by the general definition quoted in item 1 above.

(*a*) the sorting of articles as a preliminary to the work carried on in a factory or incidentally to the purposes of a factory; (see *Hudson Bay Co. v. Thompson 1959*).

(*b*) washing or filling bottles or containers incidentally to the purposes of a factory. (In the case of *Sedgwick v. Watney Coombe Reid and Company 1931* it was held that a bottling store was a factory even though the beer being bottled was brewed elsewhere);

(*c*) the packing of articles incidentally to the purposes of a factory;

(*d*) the construction, reconstruction or repair of vehicles, locomotives, or other plant used for transport purposes, when ancillary to a transport undertaking or other industrial or commercial undertaking. Certain premises (except those of a railway undertaking) used for housing vehicles and locomotives, where only running repairs or minor adjustments are done, are not deemed to be factories. (Running repairs have been held as the repair of defects which arise in a vehicle in the course of its ordinary running but do include repairs following a collision.) *FA: 175(2)(f) and 175(10)*

(*e*) the use of mechanical power in the making or repair of articles of metal or wood incidentally to any business carried on by way of trade or for the purposes of gain. (This is one of the few occasions on which the use or non-use of mechanical power still makes a difference);

(*f*) printing by letterpress, lithography, photogravure, or other similar process, if carried on by way of trade or for the purposes of gain, or incidentally to another business so carried on;

(*g*) bookbinding carried on by way of trade or for the purposes of gain, or incidentally to another business so carried on;

(*h*) laundering carried on as ancillary to another business, or incidentally to the purpose of any public institution. (Laundries carried on for ordinary commercial purposes are cleaning articles by way of trade or for purposes of gain, and are therefore covered by the general definition quoted in item 1);

(*j*) the making or preparing of articles incidentally to any building operation or work of engineering construction (except when done on the premises where the actual operations or works of engineering construction are being carried on);

(*k*) the storage of gas in any gasholder with a capacity of 5,000 cu. ft. or more;

(*l*) the hooking, plaiting, lapping, making-up or packing of yarn or cloth;

(*m*) the making, adapting or repairing of scenery, costumes and properties for theatrical or film purposes carried on by way of trade or for the purposes of gain. (This does not include the occasional repairs or adaptations done on the stage or in a dressing room);

(*n*) making or mending nets incidentally to the fishing industry;

(*o*) the production of cinema films by way of trade or for the purposes of gain. (It should be noted that actors and their dressers, etc., are not persons "employed" for the purposes of the Factories Acts);

(*p*) shipbuilding, ship repairing, and ship breaking (see item 7).

Any workplace in which, with the permission of the owner, two or more people carry on any work which would bring the workplace within the definition of a factory if the persons working there were employed by the owner or occupier is considered a factory for the purposes of the Acts, even though the persons working there are not actually employed persons *FA: 175(5)*

3 – Factories belonging to the Crown, municipal and public authorities, institutions, etc.

Although premises belonging to the Crown, to a local authority, or to a public undertaking may not be carried on by way of trade or for the purposes of gain, they will be classed as factories if they fulfil the other terms of the definitions quoted above. Thus, a naval dockyard is legally a factory even though it is not carried on by way of trade or for the purposes of gain. *FA: 173(1) and 175(9)*. Atomic Energy Authority premises are deemed to be Crown premises by the Atomic Energy Authority Act 1954.

Charitable institutions, reformatories etc., may come within the scope of the Factories Acts if any of their inmates or employees are engaged in manual labour in making, altering, repairing, ornamenting, finishing, washing, cleaning or adapting for sale any articles. *FA: 124 and 179*

Under the Visiting Forces and International Headquarters (Application of Law) Order 1965, premises occupied by the armed forces of other countries while stationed in Great Britain are in the same position as Crown premises so far as responsibility under the Factories Act and other legislation is concerned.

4 – Railway Lines and Running Sheds

Railway lines and shunting yards belonging to a railway undertaking are not covered by the Factories Act but any line or siding which is not part of the public railway system and which is used in connexion with a factory will be considered as part of that factory. If the same line or siding is used by several different factory occupiers it will be considered as a separate factory. *FA: 175(3)*

Sheds of a railway undertaking in which repairs to locomotives are carried out (including running repairs and minor adjustments) are factories within the meaning of the Factories Act. See item 2.

Buildings (other than locomotive repair sheds and electrical stations), used for the purposes of a railway undertaking and situated in the vicinity of the permanent way are railway premises within the meaning of the Offices, Shops and Railway Premises Act and are subject to the requirements set out in Chapter XV.

Locomotives are subject to the Clean Air Act as regards the emission of smoke. See item 135.

Special requirements for rails used in connexion with building operations or works of engineering construction are given in item 179.

5 – Electrical Stations

Premises in which persons are regularly employed in generating, transforming, converting or regulating electricity are classed as factories, if the electricity is supplied by way of trade or for the purposes of any transport undertaking or other industrial or commercial undertaking. The same applies if the electricity is supplied for the purposes of a public building or public institution or for streets and other public places. *FA: 123(1)*

Electrical stations in which no persons are permanently employed but which are large enough to admit the entry of a person (e.g., transformer cubicles) are subject to only a few parts of the Act.

If, however, such stations stand on premises which are factories by general definition they should be considered as part of the factory in which they stand. *FA: 123(2)*

Office premises forming part of an electrical station are subject to the Offices, Shops and Railway Premises Act (see items 264 to 279) except that first aid requirements are covered by the Factories Act (see item 277).

6 – Mines and Quarries

Mines and quarries are subject to separate legislation and are not covered by the Factories Acts so long as the only processes carried on are ancillary to the getting, dressing or preparation for sale of minerals. If any other process is carried on (e.g., the mixing of stone with bitumen to make road-surfacing materials) the premises will become subject to the Factories Acts unless the Minister of Labour agrees otherwise. *FA: 174 and Mines and Quarries Act 1954, Section 184*

7 – Other Special Premises

Docks, Wharves, Etc.—Docks, wharves and quays, if not forming part of a factory as defined above, are subject only to such parts of the Factories Act as are mentioned in Section 125 of the 1961 Act. However, they are subject instead to special statutory regulations, quoted in items 138 to 151.

Warehouses—Warehouses forming part of a factory are covered by the main Act, like any other part of the factory premises. Warehouses belonging to a dock or wharf and all other warehouses in which mechanical power is used are subject to such parts of the Act as are mentioned in Section 125 of the 1961 Act. These include the provisions for guarding and operating machinery (items 43 to 68), hoists and other lifting appliances (items 78 to 81), floors, passages and stairs (items 12 and 13), steam boilers (item 84), the keeping of registers (item 297), the reporting of accidents (item 296), the display of notices (item 298) and certain administrative matters.

Warehouses which are not part of a factory, dock, wharf or quay, and which do not use mechanical power, are outside the scope of the Factories Acts.

Warehouses in which a wholesale dealer or merchant keeps goods for sale are shops within the meaning of the Offices, Shops and Railway Premises Act. (See Chapter XV.)

Testing Establishments—It has been held in Court that the premises on which a firm tests its own products is a factory, even though the products may be made on other premises, because the testing is incidental to or part of a manufacturing process carried on by the occupiers. See *Acton Borough Council v. West Middlesex Assessment Committee, 1949*.

Where premises are used for the testing of other people's products or plant, as part of a service, such premises will not normally be regarded as a factory. But if such testing involves any manufacturing process, such as forging a new chain link to replace one cut during the test or making concrete cubes in order to test the strength of the mix, this is sufficient to make the testing establishment a factory. See *Grove v. Lloyds British Testing Company 1931* and *Stanger v. Hendon Borough Council 1948.*

SHIPS AND SHIPYARDS—Yards or drydocks in which ships or vessels are constructed, reconstructed, repaired, refitted, finished or broken up are subject to the full requirements of the Acts. They are also subject to the Shipbuilding Regulations and to certain other special regulations. (See item 244.)

Work carried out on ships in harbour or public wet docks is subject only to such parts of the main Factories Act as are mentioned in Section 126 of the Act. Work in a private wet dock forming part of a shipyard is subject to the whole Act. All work in harbours and wet docks is subject to the special regulations already referred to. See item 244.

BUILDING WORK AND ENGINEERING CONSTRUCTION—Building operations and works of engineering construction carried out on factory premises are subject to all the provisions of the Factories Act and also to the various Construction Regulations set out in items 152 to 188. When such operations are carried out elsewhere than on factory premises they are subject to the regulations and to certain sections only of the Factories Act; what these sections are is explained in Chapter XII.

BUILDINGS UNDER CONSTRUCTION—A building which is under construction but has not been taken into use does not constitute part of a factory even though it forms part of factory premises; it will, however, be subject to the special regulations for Building Operations, mentioned above. The same applies to a factory building which has been temporarily taken out of use and handed over to builders for reconstruction, etc.

If part of a building is taken into use for factory purposes while the rest is still under construction or reconstruction, the part that has been taken into use is treated as a factory. *Barrington v. Kent River Catchment Board 1947.*

8 – Division of Premises into Separate Factories

If the Chief Inspector of Factories agrees, any part of a factory may be treated as a separate factory for the purpose of the Acts, and two or more separate factories may be considered as one factory. *FA: 175(4)*

If part of a factory is used solely for some purpose other than the processes carried on in the factory it will be considered to be a separate premises and, if it comes under the definition of a factory quoted above, will be classed as a separate factory. For these conditions to apply, however, the work done in the part concerned must be quite unrelated to that done in the rest of the factory. For example, a shed used solely for the repair and maintenance of machinery used in the factory was held to be part of that factory and not a separate premises. *FA: 175(6) and Thorogood v. Van den Berghs and Jurgens, 1951*

Where part or parts of a building are let off to different occupiers, each part so let will constitute a separate factory. In such circumstances some of the responsibilities under the Acts will fall on the owner and not on the occupier. (See item 10, below.)

The Minister of Labour has power to make regulations whereby different branches or departments of work carried out in the same factory are treated as being carried out in separate factories. *FA: 175(8)*

9 – Offices, Canteens, etc.

Parts of a factory which are not used in connexion with the actual manufacturing processes may or may not be part of the factory for purposes of the Factories Act.

OFFICES—Factory offices, whether within the curtilage of the factory or completely separate from it, are subject to the Offices, Shops and Railway Premises Act. The requirements of this Act are summarised in Chapter XV.

CANTEENS—A works canteen, used by those working on the actual manufacturing processes, is considered to be part of the factory if it is within the curtilage, and is therefore subject to the Factories Act. *Luttman v. Imperial Chemical Industries, 1955*

A staff canteen, used wholly or mainly by the office staff, is not part of the factory for the purposes of the Factories Act but is part of the office for the purposes of the Offices, Shops and Railway Premises Act; this applies whether or not the canteen is actually part of the office premises. *OSRA: 1(5)*

All canteens are subject to the Food Hygiene Regulations. See item 136.

SHOPS, SHOWROOMS, ETC.—Any building, or part of a building, used for the purposes of retail trade or business is a shop within the meaning of the Offices, Shops and Railways Premises Act. This would include any showroom in which the products made in the factory were demonstrated to potential retail customers. See item 264.

REPAIR SHOPS—Premises on which articles are repaired by way of trade or for the purpose of gain are factories within the meaning of the Act (see item 1); that part of a building to which members of the public resort in order to deliver goods for repair is a shop within the meaning of the Offices, Shops and Railway Premises Act. See item 264.

A repair shop used for the repair of machinery or other equipment used in the factory itself would be considered part of the factory since the work is ancillary to the actual manufacturing process.

DRAWING OFFICES, ETC.—Drawing offices are covered by the Offices, Shops and Railway Premises Act. So are places used for calculating by means of a machine; this would include computers. See item 264.

10 – Responsibility for Carrying Out the Acts

With the few exceptions mentioned below, the occupier of the factory is responsible for seeing that the law is complied with. He cannot delegate this responsibility to a manager or other servant and if a breach of the law occurs he cannot escape conviction by pleading that it was the fault of an employee unless he himself has used all due diligence to enforce the law. See item 299.

Generally speaking, the occupier's responsibility includes that of making the factory safe for every person employed or working therein, and not only for his own employees. For instance, his responsibility for providing safe access (item 12) applies irrespective of whether the persons working in a particular location are his own employees or those of a contractor.

If part of a building is leased off as a separate factory, or as a tenement factory, the responsibility for certain parts of the Factories Acts will rest upon the owner instead of on the various occupiers. Full details will be found in Sections 121, 122, 123 and Schedule 2 of the Factories Act 1961.

If the employees of a building or civil engineering contractor are working in a factory, the responsibility for carrying out the Construction Regulations will rest on the contractor. The occupier, however, will still have his own responsibilities under the main Act, unless the part of the factory in which the contractor's men are working has ceased to be used, for the time being, and is not entered by anybody other than the contractor's men. See item 153.

If a machine used in a factory is owned or hired by someone other than the occupier the responsibility for guarding it rests, to some extent only, on the owner or hirer instead of on the occupier. See item 43.

When ships or other vessels are being loaded or unloaded, responsibility is divided between the occupier of the dock, wharf or quay and the owner or master of the vessel. See item 139.

When radioactive substances or apparatus for producing ionising radiations are used in factories the responsibility for carrying out the appropriate regulations may sometimes rest with the owner of the apparatus, etc., and not the occupier. See items 249 and 259.

Persons employed have certain legal responsibilities (see item 293) but their failure to comply with the law does not absolve the occupier from his own responsibility.

Local authorities, doctors, etc., have various duties which are summarised in items 301 and 302.

CHAPTER II

Factory Buildings (Design, Construction and Maintenance)

Except where otherwise stated, the requirements quoted in this chapter apply to all factory buildings, whether newly erected or not. New factories, and additions or structural alterations to existing factories, are subject in addition to the requirements applied to all new buildings under the Public Health Acts, London Building Acts, etc. and to any conditions imposed by the local town planning authority under the Town and Country Planning Acts. Since January 1st, 1959, new factory buildings have also been subject to special requirements respecting thermal insulation (see item 31).

11 – Alterations to Leasehold Factories

If the terms of a lease, or other contract, prevent the owner or occupier of a factory from making alterations which are necessary in order to comply with the law, application may be made to the County Court or, in Scotland, the sheriff, asking for such restrictive covenants to be set aside. *FA: 169*

If factory premises have to be altered in order to comply with the law, and if the occupier and the owner cannot agree as to who should bear the cost, either party may ask the County Court or sheriff to make an order apportioning the cost between the parties. *FA: 170*

A similar provision for structural alterations is made under the Offices, Shops and Railway Premises Act. See item 279.

12 – Passages, Stairs and Means of Access

So far as is reasonably practicable, there must be a safe means of access to every place at which any person has at any time to work. This means of access must be maintained in good repair and in an efficient state. Attention is drawn to the phrases, "any person" and "at any time"; the fact that the occupier's own employees do not have to reach a particular part of the factory, or that they only have to do so on rare occasions, does not absolve the occupier from the duty of providing safe means of access. The means of access may, however, be a temporary one (e.g., a ladder) so long as it is available when required and is adequate for its purpose. *FA: 29(1)*

Special mention is made of safe access to crane cabins and other parts of lifting machinery (see item 79). More detailed requirements regarding safe means of access have been laid down for building operations and works of engineering construction (item 156), docks (items 140 and 141) and shipyards (item 244). Access to underground sub-stations is dealt with in item 75.

The maintenance of safe access in the proximity of railway tracks is dealt with in item 20 (general) and item 179 (construction sites).

STAIRS—All stairs must be of sound construction and must be properly maintained. They must also, so far as is reasonably practicable, be kept free from any obstruction and from any substance likely to cause persons to slip. *FA: 28(1)*

Dirt must be removed daily, and staircases must be whitewashed, painted, or otherwise treated at regular intervals. See items 28 and 29.

All stairs inside buildings, and all stairs affording a means of exit from buildings, must have a handrail. If the staircase has an open side the handrail must be on that side and there must also be a lower rail or other effective means of preventing falls. If there are two open sides, handrails, etc., must be provided on both sides. Stairs which, owing to their construction, condition, or other circumstances, are particularly liable to cause accidents must also have a handrail on both sides, whether the sides are open or not. *FA: 28(2) and (3)*

Stairs used in building operations are subject to additional requirements. See item 159.

All stairways must be adequately lighted. See item 30.

LADDERS—All ladders must be soundly constructed and properly maintained. In the absence of any legal decision to the contrary it must be assumed that this applies to all ladders used on the premises, whether they belong to the occupier or to an outside contractor such as a window cleaner. *FA: 28(5)*

Ladders used for building operations are subject to more detailed requirements (see item 158). These requirements do not apply to ladders used otherwise than for building operations but they might influence the Court in deciding whether a ladder was "soundly constructed" for the purposes of the main Act. It is therefore advisable to adopt the requirements quoted in item 158 as a voluntary standard for *all* ladders.

Ladders used by certified machinery attendants must be fixed, lashed, or held in certain circumstances. See item 68.

Ladders used in connexion with the loading and unloading of ships and other vessels are dealt with in items 141 and 142. Ladders used in shipyards are covered by the Shipbuilding and Ship-repairing Regulations; see item 244.

PASSAGES AND GANGWAYS—All passages, steps and gangways must be of sound construction and must be properly maintained. They must also, so far as is reasonably practicable, be kept free from any obstruction and from any substance likely to cause persons to slip. *FA: 28(1)*

All passages must be adequately lighted. See item 30.

Dirt must be removed daily, and passages must be whitewashed, painted, or otherwise treated at regular intervals. See items 28 and 29.

Openings in the floors of passages must be securely fenced, except when the nature of the work makes fencing impracticable. *FA: 28(4)*

Gangways and pouring aisles in foundries are subject to additional requirements. See item 132.

Passageways of electrical switch boards are subject to requirements. See item 72.

STAIRS, LADDERS AND GANGWAYS OVER SUMPS, ETC.—If a stair, ladder or gangway is over or inside a fixed vessel, structure, sump or pit containing a scalding, corrosive or poisonous liquid, it must comply with the additional requirements quoted in item 18.

OFFICES AND SHOPS—Passages, stairs, etc., in offices and shops are subject to the same sort of requirements as those in factories. See item 267.

13 – Walls, Ceilings, Floors, Windows and Doors

WALLS AND CEILINGS—All inside walls, partitions and ceilings must be whitewashed, painted, or otherwise treated at regular intervals. See item 29.

WINDOWS—All glazed windows and skylights used for the lighting of workrooms must be kept clean and free from obstruction, both inside and out, so far as is practicable. It is permissible, however, to whitewash or shade windows and skylights in order to reduce heat or glare. *FA: 5(4)*

Windows of humid sheds in cotton cloth factories must face between N.E. and N.N.W. and must not be at an angle of more than 30 degrees to the vertical except when placed in flat concrete or brick roofs (unless built before 1912). *CCF: 7*

Windows for lead compound stoves are subject to special requirements. See item 96.

In rooms where wet grinding of metals is done, windows must be properly glazed and kept clean, and must have a total area equal to at least one-sixth of the floor area. *GM: 5*

DOORS—Doors affording a means of exit from the factory for persons employed therein must open outwards, unless they are sliding doors. (In buildings used as factories prior to July 1st, 1938, these requirements apply only to doors opening on to stairs and passages from rooms in which 10 or more are employed, and to doors at the foot of a staircase in buildings where more than 10 are employed above the ground floor where such doors are not kept permanently open.) *FA: 48(2) and (3)*

While any person is within the factory, no exit doors must be locked or fastened in such a way that they cannot be easily and immediately opened from inside. *FA: 48(1)*

Doors and other exits affording an emergency exit in case of fire must be so marked, unless also in ordinary use as exits. The marking must be done by a notice in letters of adequate size. *FA: 48(6)*

Teagle openings and other doorways used for hoisting or lowering goods or materials must have secure hand-holds on each side and must be fenced except when hoisting or lowering is actually being done. *FA: 24*

FLOORS—All floors must be of sound construction and must be properly maintained. They must also, so far is as reasonably practicable, be kept free from any obstruction and from any substance likely to cause persons to slip. *FA: 28(1). See Jenkins v Allied Iron Foundries Ltd. 1969* (obstruction) and *Dorman Long (Steel) Ltd. v Bell* (substances likely to cause persons to slip).

Opening in floors must be securely fenced except to such an extent as the nature of the work makes this impracticable. See item 17.

Effective means of draining must be provided if the process is liable to make the floor so wet that drainage would remove the wet. (A similar requirement appears in the regulations for spinning flax and tow, etc., quoted in item 239, but this is largely superseded by the wider scope of the general requirement quoted here.) *FA: 6*

Special drainage is required to remove petrol from aircraft testing rooms. See item 191.

Floors of workrooms must have accumulations of dirt removed daily and must be cleaned at least once a week by washing or some other effective and suitable method. *FA: 1(2)*

Floors round woodworking machines must be kept in a good and level condition and must not be allowed to become slippery. They must be kept as free as possible from chips, and other materials. *WWM: 4*

Floors of rooms, or parts of rooms, in which dry grinding of metals is done must be maintained in a smooth and firm condition so as to permit of proper sweeping or cleaning. *GM: 10*

Floors round horizontal milling machines must be maintained in a good and even condition and clear of loose materials. Effective steps must be taken to prevent them becoming slippery through the splashing of suds or otherwise. *HMM: 1*

Special requirements regarding the construction and maintenance of floors apply to the following processes: chromium plating (item 94). file cutting by hand (item 190), lead processes (item 96), manufacture and decoration of pottery (item 203), manufacture and repair of accumulators (item 205), vitreous enamelling (item 134), spinning and weaving of flax and tow (item 239), unsealed radioactive substances (*IRUS: 37*), abrasive wheels (*ABW: 17*), patent fuel (item 226), lead smelting (item 199) and refractory materials (item 224).

OFFICES AND SHOPS—Floors in offices and shops are subject to the same sort of requirements as those in factories. See item 267.

PLACES WHERE FOOD IS HANDLED—In canteens and other places where food is handled or where food containers, etc., are cleaned, the walls, ceilings, floors, doors, windows, and woodwork must be kept clean and in such good order, repair and condition as to enable them to be cleaned effectively and to prevent, so far as is reasonably practicable, any risk of infestation by rats, mice and insects. *FHR: 25(1)*

14 – Workrooms and Other Workplaces

SAFETY—So far as is reasonably practicable, there must be safe means of access to every place at which any person has at anytime to work and every such place, must, so far is as reasonably practicable, be made and kept safe for any person working there. *FA: 29(1)*

This general requirement is in addition to more specific requirements mentioned in connexion with floors (item 13), prevention of falls from heights (item 17), fencing of sumps and pits (item 18) and fire precautions (item 26).

Where overhead cranes are used, steps must be taken to protect persons working near the crane track. See item 79.

OVERCROWDING—The permitted number of persons allowed to work in a workroom at any one time depends on the amount of cubic space; there must be at least 400 cu. ft. for every person. *FA: 2(2)*

In calculating the amount of space in any room, no space more than 14 ft. from the floor must be taken into account.

If the room contains a gallery, the latter must be treated as a separate room for this purpose. *FA: 2(5)*

It may happen that, owing to the nature of the process or for some other reason, the maximum number calculated as above cannot be employed in a workroom without danger to health. In such circumstances a smaller number must be employed. *FA: 2(1)*

A notice showing the permitted number must be displayed in every workroom, unless the District Inspector of Factories otherwise allows. *FA: 2(6)*

The local fire authority, in issuing a certificate specifying the means of escape in case of fire (see item 26) will also specify the maximum number that may be employed in the whole factory and may specify the maximum number for each room. *FA: 40(6)*

Where persons are employed in file cutting by hand (item 190), accumulator manufacture or repair (item 205), vitreous enamelling (item 134), or wool-sorting (item 238), the amount of space per person must be increased to that specified in the appropriate regulations. Where explosives are manufactured or handled the Chief Inspector of Factories has power to amend the space per person by special certificate. *FA: 2(3)*

A workplace which is so overcrowded as to be detrimental to health constitutes a nuisance within the meaning of the Public Health Acts. So far as workrooms covered by the Factories Act or the Offices Act are concerned these provisions of the Public Health Acts are virtually redundant but they must be kept in mind in connexion with any parts of the factory not covered by these acts.

DIMENSIONS—Workrooms in which wet grinding is done must be at least 10 ft. high and must have a window area equal to at least one sixth of the floor area. *GM: 5 and GC: 7*

In cotton cloth factories, all humid sheds erected after April 1st, 1912, and all other weaving sheds erected or taken into use after May 15th, 1929 must have an average height of at least 14½ ft. The height of the valley gutter from the floor must be at least 12 ft. *CCF: 7 (a)*

ARRANGEMENTS OF CONTENTS—The contents of a room in which persons are employed must be so arranged that, in case of fire, everyone has a free passage-way to a means of escape. *FA: 48(10)*

Additional requirements have been made regarding the arrangement of the contents of foundries. See items 24 and 132.

There are few statutory requirements regarding the spacing of machinery and plant. Care must be taken, however, to ensure that machines are not so placed as to prevent the safe means of access required by law. See item 12.

Woodworking machinery must be so positioned as to leave adequate working space to ensure safety. *WWM: 3*

If the traversing part of a self-acting machine runs over a space where anyone is liable to pass, the machine must be so positioned that neither the traversing part nor the material on it can come within 18 ins. of any fixed structure. This requirement applies to *(a)* all factories built since 1895, *(b)* factories or parts of factories built in 1895 or earlier but reconstructed since July, 1937 and *(c)* extensions or additions made since July, 1937. (See item 54 for special application to self-acting mules.) *FA: 19*

Grindstones used for grinding cutlery (item 189), stocks used for file cutting by hand (item 190) and working positions in pasting rooms for accumulator manufacture and repair (item 205) must be spaced in accordance with regulations.

In potteries the number of tile presses permitted for a given floor area is restricted by regulations. See item 203.

In active areas where radioactive substances are used benches and tables must have unobstructed working spaces. *IRUS: 37*

SEATING—If employees have, in the course of their work, reasonable opportunities for sitting down without detriment to their work, suitable and sufficient sitting facilities must be provided and maintained. *FA: 60(1)*

If a substantial proportion of the work can be done sitting, each person so employed must be given a seat of suitable design, construction and dimensions. If necessary, a foot-rest must also be provided. The seats must be properly and adequately supported. *FA: 60(2) and (3)*

There are no statutory requirements regarding the actual design of seats but official recommendations are given in the Department of Employment Booklet No. 45, *Seats for Workers in Offices, Factories and Shops.*

WORK-BENCHES—Accumulations of dirt and refuse must be removed daily from all work-benches by a suitable method. *FA: 1(2)*

Under the Ionising Radiations (Unsealed Radioactive Substances) Regulations 1968, benches and tables used for luminising or other work involving the use of unsealed radioactive substances must, so far as is reasonably practicable, have impervious surfaces and be capable of being easily and effectively cleaned.

Work-benches in potteries (item 203), in places where wool or hair is sorted (item 238), in places where accumulators are made or repaired (item 205) and where asbestos is handled (*AS: 9*) are also subject to special requirements.

LIGHTING, TEMPERATURE AND VENTILATION—All workrooms must be adequately lighted and ventilated and must be kept at a reasonable temperature. See items 30 and 31.

FOOD ROOMS—Rooms in which food is handled are subject to the Food Hygiene Regulations, 1960. See item 136.

SEPARATE WORKROOMS FOR CERTAIN PROCESSES—Each of the following processes must be carried out in a workroom set apart for that purpose and for no other: the testing of aircraft engines, carburettors and fuel pumps (item 191), film-stripping (item 193), certain operations in foundries (item 132) the use of ionising radiations (*IRSS: 41*), the willowing of wool or hair (item 238), working in a slip house (*P(HW)R: 28*), and the sorting and disinfection of horsehair (item 236).

The application of luminous compounds, and other work which involves the use of unsealed radioactive substances, must be done in special areas complying with the Ionising Radiations (Unsealed Radioactive Substances) Regulations 1968 (SI 1968: No. 780).

OFFICES—The requirements for offices, under the Offices, Shops and Railway Premises Act, are given in items 267 to 270.

15 – Underground Rooms

For the purposes of the Factories Act, an underground room is one in which any part is so situated that more than half its height is below the surface of the ground adjoining or nearby. *FA: 69(5)*

No work may be done in any underground room (other than one used only as a store) if the District Inspector of Factories has certified it as being unfit for the purpose. *FA: 69(1)*

Before an underground room is taken into use as a workroom for the first time, notice must be given to the District Inspector. The form the notice must take is laid down in the Work in Underground Rooms (Form of Notice) Order, 1946. *FA: 69(3)*

If a factory occupier is aggrieved by any decision made by the District Inspector in connexion with an underground room, he may appeal to the Courts within 21 days. *FA: 69(4)*

Rooms having any part of the floor 3 ft. or more below ground level must not be used as bakehouses unless they have been so used since before July 1937 and have been certified as suitable by the district council. See item 214.

Under the India Rubber Regulations 1922, a fume process must not be carried on in any room if any part of the floor is below the surrounding ground (item 200).

The Minister of Labour has power to prescribe processes of a hot, wet or dusty nature, and processes liable to give off fumes, which must not be carried out in an underground room. So far no such processes have been prescribed. *FA: 69(3)*

16 – Storerooms

A storeroom should be regarded as a workroom and the requirements quoted in item 14 should be considered applicable.

Adequate lighting must be provided for all storerooms (see item 30) and the requirements for safe means of access (item 12) apply to storerooms as to workrooms.

If the storeroom and its contents are so arranged that persons may have to work more than 6 ft. 6 in. above the ground or floor, all reasonable precautions must be taken against falls. See item 17.

Storerooms in which any of the following are kept must be constructed in accordance with the appropriate regulations for such materials: petrol and petroleum mixtures (item 101), calcium carbide (item 106), celluloid and films (items 192 and 193), explosives (item 111), clay dust in potteries (item 203), wool and hair (item 238), radioactive substances (items 204 and 255), asbestos (item 228), and highly flammable liquids and liquefied petroleum gases (item 130).

The bulk storage of material and residues in foundries is subject to special regulations. See item 132.

Fuel stores in which fuel is kept for sale are subject to the Offices, Shops and Railway Premises Act. See item 265.

17 – Locations from which persons may fall

The following precautions must be taken whether the persons concerned are employed by the occupier or by some other person.

When persons have to work in places from which they may fall more than 6 ft. 6 in. their safety must be ensured as far as is reasonably practicable by the provision of secure handhold and foothold, by fencing, or by some other means. *FA: 29(2)*

All reasonably practicable steps must be taken to protect persons against falling while on their way to or from any place at which they have to work. *FA: 29(1)*

Stairs must comply with the requirements set out in item 12.

Hoistways must be enclosed and fitted with gates, and teagle openings must be fenced. See items 78 and 80.

Gantries carrying a line of rails should be securely fenced (*LR: 4*).

Openings in floors must be securely fenced except in so far as the nature of the work makes it impracticable.

An excavation in a sand bed of a foundry was held to be an opening in a floor—see *Harrison v. Metropolitan Vickers Electrical Co. Ltd. 1954*.

Persons engaged in building operations, including the painting and repairing of buildings, and works of engineering construction must be protected against falls by additional means laid down in the appropriate regulations. See items 156 to 164. There are also special requirements for guarding against falls during the loading and unloading of ships and other vessels (item 140) and shipbuilding and ship-repairing (item 244).

18 – Sumps, Pits, Vats, etc.

Fixed vessels, sumps and pits containing scalding, corrosive or poisonous liquids must be securely covered or else securely fenced to a height of 3 ft., unless the edge is at least 3 ft. above the highest part of the adjoining ground or platform. If the nature of the work makes such fencing or covering impracticable all practicable alternative steps must be taken to prevent any person from falling in. *FA: 18(1)*

Where any fixed vessel, structure, sump or pit contains any scalding, corrosive or poisonous liquid and is not securely covered, no ladder, stair or gangway must be placed above it, across it, or inside it, unless the ladder, stair or gangway in question is at least 18 inches wide, is securely fixed, and is securely fenced on both sides to a height of at least 3 ft. The fencing must consist either of sheet fencing or of upper and lower rails and toe-boards. *FA: 18(2)*

Where two or more fixed vessels, structures, sumps or pits containing scalding, corrosive or poisonous liquids adjoin one another, and have between them a space that is less than 18 in. wide or is not securely fenced on both sides to a height of 3 ft. or more, secure barriers must be erected to prevent persons passing between them. *FA: 18(3)*

In chemical works, open fixed vessels containing dangerous materials must be fenced to a height of 3 ft. unless the edge is at least 3 ft. above the adjacent ground or platform. Any plank or gangway placed across such vessels must be at least 18 in. wide and must be securely fenced to a height of 3 ft. Any passage way between two adjoining vessels must be closed by barriers unless it is more than 18 in. wide and is securely fenced to a height of 3 ft. *CWR: 1*

Kiers used for boiling textile materials are subject to additional requirements. See item 97.

19 – Outdoor Workplaces

Accommodation for shelter during wet weather must be provided for all persons employed in building operations. See item 184.

Electrical apparatus exposed to the weather must be constructed or protected in such a way as to prevent danger arising from such exposure. See item 76.

The law contains few references to work in the open air, see fume process (*IR: 4*) and breaking of pitch (item 226). However, all relevant legal requirements (e.g., those for safe access, safe place of work, lighting, guarding of machines, etc) apply to outdoor parts of the factory premises as well as to indoor work places. *FA: 175 (7)*

When an outdoor workplace includes or adjoins a railway track, precautions must be taken to ensure that persons working or passing have adequate space for safety. See item 20 (general) and item 179 (construction sites).

Works yards in potteries must comply with special requirements as to surfacing and maintenance. See item 203.

Kiln workers at clay works must be provided with shelters unless the messroom or other accommodation is available and conveniently accessible. See item 230.

20 – Railway Lines and Crane Tracks

RAILWAY LINES—Sidings and other lines of rails on which wagons are moved by locomotive or mechanically operated capstans must have point rods and signal wires covered or otherwise guarded if these are in such a position as to be a source of danger. *LR: 1*

Ground levers operating points must be so placed that men working them are clear of adjacent lines. They must be placed parallel to adjacent lines, or else in such a position and of such form as to cause as little obstruction as possible. *LR: 2*

Lines of rails and points must be periodically examined and kept in efficient order, having regard to the nature of the traffic. *LR: 3*

Gantries carrying such lines of rails must be properly constructed and be maintained in proper repair. They must have properly fixed structures to act as stop-blocks at every terminal point. *LR: 4*

At every point on a gantry over 6 ft. high where persons have to work or pass on foot there must be a suitable footway. A footway which is between the rails and the edge of the gantry must, so far as is reasonably practicable, be securely fenced at such a distance from the line of rails as will permit a person to pass safely between the fence and any locomotive, wagon, or load. *LR: 4*

Efficient lighting, either by handlamps or stationary lights, must be provided in certain circumstances. See item 135.

The above requirements do not apply to lines of rails less than 3 feet in gauge, nor to those which are not worked by mechanical power in any form. Nor do they apply to buildings in course of construction; lines outside the factory premises and used for running purposes only; lines on docks, wharves and quays which are outside the factory; or premises which are subject to the Coal Mines Acts, the Metalliferous Mines Regulations Act, the Quarries Act, or the Regulation of Railways Act.

The operation of lines of rails in factories is dealt with in item 135. The use of railway lines in connexion with building operations and works of engineering construction is dealt with in item 179.

CRANE AND TRANSPORTER TRACKS—Rails on which travelling cranes move, and tracks on which the carriages of transporters or runways move, must be of proper size, adequate strength, and with even running surfaces. Such rails and tracks must be properly laid, adequately supported, and properly maintained. *FA: 27(3)*

Tracks for cranes used in connexion with building operations or works of engineering construction are dealt with in item 165.

21 – Docks, Wharves and Quays

All places at which ships, barges or lighters are loaded or unloaded must comply with the Docks Regulations. See items 138 to 151.

22 – Highly Flammable Liquids

Workrooms, cabinets and enclosures in factories, warehouses, docks, building operations, etc., where highly flammable liquids are present should be constructed in accordance with the Regulations (item 130).

CINEMATOGRAPH FILM—There are requirements for rooms used for manufacture and stripping of film containing nitro-cellulose or other nitrated products (item 193).

ASBESTOS—Buildings in factories, warehouses, etc, where scheduled processes are done must be constructed to comply with the regulations (item 228).

23 – Boiler Houses

Furnaces, chimneys, etc., must be designed to prevent the emission of excessive smoke. See item 82.

Boilers and boiler flues must be constructed in accordance with the requirements quoted in items 83 and 84.

In most cotton cloth factories, boiler houses and engine rooms must be separated from the weaving sheds by an alley at least 6 ft. wide and either open to the outside air or provided with louvre or roof ventilation, the ventilator being equal to one fourth the floor area of the alley. Boiler flues in such factories must not pass under any weaving shed. *CCF: 7.*

24 – Foundries

GANGWAYS AND POURING AISLES—Any part of an iron foundry or steel foundry in which molten metal is transported or used must (if constructed, reconstructed, or converted after October, 1953) have sufficient main gangways. These must be clearly defined, with a hard and even surface, and they must not be of sand, nor must they have more sand on them than is necessary to avoid risk of flying metal from accidental spillage. Their minimum widths must be as follows:—

(*a*) if they are not used for carrying molten metal .. 3 ft.
(*b*) if used for molten metal in truck ladles but not otherwise .. .. .. 2 ft. wider than the ladle
(*c*) if used for molten metal carried in hand shanks by not more than two men .. .. 3 ft.
(*d*) if used for molten metal carried in hand shanks by more than two men .. .. 4 ft.
(*e*) if used for simultaneous travel in both directions by men carrying hand shanks .. .. .. 6 ft.

In foundries not constructed or reconstructed since October 1st, 1953, the gangways must comply with the above requirements as far as is reasonably practicable. *ISF: 6(1)*

All foundries must have sufficient pouring aisles, which must be properly maintained, have a firm and even surface, and be kept free of obstruction as far as is reasonably practicable. They must be at least 18 inches wide, and must be wider still if a greater width is necessary to prevent danger to persons carrying or pouring molten metal. In foundries constructed or reconstructed after October 1st, 1953, the pouring aisles must have a surface of hard material and must not be of sand nor have more sand on them than is necessary to avoid risk of flying metal from accidental spillage. (These requirements for pouring aisles do not apply to any room or part of a room where, by nature of the work done, the floor has to be of sand.) *ISF: 6(2)*

RACKS, BINS AND BUNKERS, ETC.—Racks, bins, or other receptacles must be provided for gear and tools, and bins, bunkers or other receptacles must be provided if sand, fuel or other materials are stored in bulk. *ISF: 4*

BATHS AND CHANGING ROOMS—Every iron and steel foundry must have adequate and suitable facilities for taking shower or other baths, with suitable arrangements for privacy and accommodation for dressing, undressing, or changing clothes. These changing rooms must adjoin every room in which baths are situated. *ISF: 9(1)*

Lockers or other suitable accommodation for clothing must be provided near to the changing rooms. *ISF: 9(1)*

BLASTING ENCLOSURES—Blasting enclosures are subject to special regulations. See item 93.

OTHER REQUIREMENTS—Requirements affecting the carrying out of operations in foundries are dealt with in item 132.

25 – Electrical Stations and Fittings

Electrical equipment, fittings, wiring, etc., including substations on the consumer's side of the consumer's terminals, must comply with the Electricity Regulations. See items 69 and 77.

Office premises forming part of an electrical station are subject to the Offices, Shops and Railway Premises Act (see items 264 and 288) except that first aid requirements are covered by the Factories Act (see item 277).

26 – Means of Escape in Case of Fire

Every factory in which more than 20 people are employed must have a certificate from the fire authority* specifying the means of escape, the maximum number of employees, etc. This certificate must be attached to the general register. *FA: 40*

Factories employing fewer than twenty persons must also have a certificate if any of the following conditions apply: (*a*) if explosives or highly flammable materials are stored or used in or under the factory, (*b*) if the factory was constructed before July 1937 and more than 10 persons are employed above the first floor of any one building or more than 20 feet from the ground, or (*c*) if the factory was constructed after July 1937 and more than 10 persons are employed above the ground floor of any building. *FA: 40 and 45*

If some parts of a building are used as a factory and other parts are used as offices or shops, the total number of persons employed in all such parts must be included when deciding whether the building comes within any of the classes mentioned above. *Factories Act (Extension of Section 40) Regulations, SI 1964 No. 762*

The form in which applications for a certificate must be made is prescribed by the Factories (Fire Certificate Application) Order 1965 (SI 1965: No. 1293). The application must give the address of the factory, the name of the occupier and the owner, the maximum number of persons to be employed at any one time, the nature of the work to be carried out, and the nature and maximum quantity of any explosive or highly flammable materials stored or used in or under the premises. The application must also state whether any part of the premises is subject to the Offices, Shops and Railway Premises Act and, if so, how many persons are employed in that part.

Once an application for a certificate has been made in the prescribed form, the factory may be used while the occupier is awaiting the granting of the certificate. *FA: 40(2)*

A factory forming part of a building which complies, as regards means of escape, with Part V of the London Building Acts (Amendment) Act 1939 is entitled to receive a certificate, so long as no changes have been made which affect the adequacy of such means of escape. *FA: 44*

If the fire authority refuses to grant a certificate, or attaches conditions which the occupier considers unreasonable, an appeal to the magistrate's court may be made within 21 days. *FA: 43*

If, after the certificate has been granted, it is proposed to extend or alter the factory materially, or to increase materially the number of employees, notice must be given to the Fire Authority. This also applies if it is proposed to begin or extend the storage or use of explosives or highly flammable materials: *FA: 41(3)*

Guidance to fire authorities in the granting of fire certificates is given in Form SHW 2031, published by the Stationery Office.

PROVISION OF MEANS OF ESCAPE—The following requirements apply to all factories and are irrespective of any additional conditions that may be made by the Fire Authority in its certificate or by the district council in its byelaws.

In factories constructed or converted after July 1938, all doors affording a means of exit must either open outwards or else slide. *FA: 48(2)*

In factories constructed or converted before July 1938, the foregoing requirement applies only to (*a*) doors opening on to stairs or corridors from rooms in which more than 10 are employed and (*b*) doors which are not continuously open and which are at the feet of stairs affording means of exit from buildings where more than 10 are employed above the ground floor. *FA: 48(2) and (3)*

The Chief Inspector of Factories may grant exemption from these requirements, with or without conditions, if he is satisfied that in a particular case compliance is inappropriate or undesirable. *FA: 48(5)*

All doors, windows and other exits affording a means of escape must be conspicuously marked by a notice in letters of adequate size, but this does not apply to the doors or other openings which are in ordinary use as exits. (The law formerly required the letters to be in red, but this requirement has now been revoked.) *FA: 48(6)*

While persons are in the factory, no doors affording means of escape must be locked or fastened in such a way that they cannot be opened from inside, easily and immediately. *FA: 48(1)*

All means of escape must be properly maintained and kept

---

* In county boroughs the Fire Authority is the borough council; in Greater London it is the Greater London Council; elsewhere in England and Wales the Fire Authority is the county council. In Scotland the Fire Authorities are the City of Glasgow and the joint committees controlling the ten fire areas into which the rest of Scotland is divided.

clear of obstruction. *FA: 41(1)*

The contents of any room in which persons are employed must be so arranged that everybody in the room has a free passage to a means of escape. *FA: 48(10)*

The Minister of Labour has power to make regulations imposing further requirements as to means of escape. A requirement as to maintaining adequate means of escape is included in the regulations for celluloid (item 192), cinematograph film manufacture and stripping (item 193), the testing of aircraft engines (item 191) and highly flammable liquids and liquefied petroleum gases (item 130).

Local fire authorities have power to make byelaws regarding means of escape in factories, so long as these do not conflict with any regulations made by the Minister of Labour and so long as they are confirmed by the Minister of Housing and Local Government or, in Scotland, the Secretary of State. *FA: 46*

INSTRUCTION OF EMPLOYEES—In factories in which more than 20 persons are employed above the first floor of any building, or more than 20 feet above ground level, effective steps must be taken to ensure that all persons so employed are familiar with the means of escape and the routine to be followed in case of fire. The same requirement applies, regardless of the number employed, where people work in a building in which explosives or highly flammable materials are stored or used.

The Minister of Labour may make regulations prescribing the means by which this instruction is to be given, and may extend the requirements to include factories not covered by the above description. So far no regulations of this kind have been made. *FA: 49(3)*

27 – Other Precautions against Fire

CONSTRUCTION—Every hoistway or liftway in a building constructed after July 1938 must be completely enclosed with fire-resisting materials, except at the top. All means of access to such hoists or lifts must be fitted with fire-resisting doors. The tops of these hoistways and liftways must be of some material easily broken by fire or else must be provided with a vent. The Chief Inspector of Factories may grant an exemption from these requirements where he considers that compliance would be inappropriate or undesirable. *FA: 48(4) and (5)*

In buildings designed or constructed after January 1st, 1959, the materials used to secure the standard of heat insulation required by the Thermal Insulation (Industrial Buildings) Regulations must be such as will satisfy the standard of fire resistance laid down in those regulations. See item 31.

Workrooms, cabinets and enclosures must comply with the HFL and LPG Regulations (item 130).

Factories in which cinematograph film is made, repaired, stripped, etc., are subject to special requirements respecting construction. See item 193.

The Minister of Labour may make regulations regarding the internal construction of any factory or type of factory, and the materials to be used in its construction. *FA: 50(1)*

Other matters concerning construction are normally covered by the local authority's byelaws and by any conditions which may be imposed by the local fire authority in granting the certificates referred to in item 26.

FIRE ALARMS—All factories mentioned in the first two paragraphs of item 26 as requiring certificates from the Fire Authority must also have fire alarms capable of giving audible warning throughout the premises. Such fire alarms must be capable of being operated without exposing anyone to undue risk. *FA: 48(7)*

Fire alarms must be properly maintained and must be tested or examined at least once in every three months and at such other times as the factory inspector may require. The results of such tests or examinations must be entered in the general register. The Minister of Labour may make regulations prescribing the method of test or examination to be used for any particular type of alarm, and may vary the intervals at which tests and examinations must be made. *FA: 52*

The Minister of Labour may modify these requirements, or grant complete exemption from them, in cases where they appear to be unnecessary or unreasonable. He may also apply them to factories which would otherwise be outside their scope. *FA: 48(8) and (9)*

FIRE-FIGHTING EQUIPMENT—All factories, unless granted exemption, are required to provide and maintain appropriate means of fire-fighting, so placed as to be readily available for use. The Minister may specify particular means of fire-fighting for particular types of factory; in the absence of any special requirements the occupier must provide what he considers appropriate and must be prepared to justify his choice if called upon. *FA: 51*

In addition to the above general requirements, several codes of regulations specifically require the provision of fire-fighting equipment. They are those for celluloid (item 192), keeping petrol (items 99 and 102), testing of aircraft engines (item 191) and use, etc. of highly flammable liquid sand liquefied petroleum gases in warehouses, building operations, docks, etc. (item 130).

FIRE HYDRANTS—Schedule Three of the Water Act 1945 makes provision for local water undertakings to provide convenient fire-hydrants when so requested by a factory owner or occupier. Provision is subject to practicability and must be at the expense of the occupier or owner of the factory.

PROHIBITION OF SMOKING—Smoking must not be allowed in any room or place where the following processes are going on: the grinding of magnesium or the handling of magnesium dust, sludge or scale (item 128), the manufacture, storage or use of celluloid (item 192), the generation of acetylene for purposes connected with shipbuilding or repairing (item 244), any chemical process involving risk of explosion from gases, vapour or dust (item 247), film making and film stripping (item 193). There are restrictions on smoking under the HFL and LPG Regulations (item 130) and Testing of Aircraft Engines Regulations (item 191).

Smoking by persons handling food is prohibited by the Food Hygiene Regulations 1960 (see item 136) which, for reasons of hygiene, forbid the use of tobacco in any form. The prohibition also applies to persons cleaning equipment used in any food business.

Apart from these special processes, it is an offence for an employee to do, wilfully and without reasonable cause, anything likely to endanger himself or others. This would include smoking in locations where it was unsafe to do so, if the employee were aware of the danger. *FA: 143(2)*

FLAMMABLE OR EXPLOSIVE DUSTS—If any grinding, sieving or other process gives off a dust liable to explode on ignition, all practicable steps must be taken to prevent an explosion. These steps may include the enclosure of the plant. See item 117.

FLAMMABLE VAPOURS—Special precautions must be taken when opening plant that contains flammable gas or vapour under pressure. See item 121.

Welding, bronzing and soldering operations on plant and vessels that have contained flammable or explosive substances are subject to special requirements. See item 122.

During the demolition of buildings, all practicable steps must be taken to prevent fire or explosion occurring through the release of flammable gas or vapour. *CGP: 41(4)*

For additional precautions with highly flammable liquids with flash point below 32 degrees Celsius see item 130.

ELECTRICAL EQUIPMENT—All electrical equipment must be installed and maintained in accordance with the Electricity Regulations. The requirements include the provision of flameproof apparatus for explosive atmospheres. See items 69 to 77.

PETROL AND EXPLOSIVES—Petrol, petroleum mixtures, and explosives must be used and stored in the manner prescribed by the appropriate acts. See items 99 to 112.

OTHER HIGH FIRE RISKS—Special precautions against fire are required when the following processes are carried on: storage and use of calcium carbide (item 106), grinding of magnesium (item 128), testing aircraft engines, etc. (item 191), manufacture and use of celluloid (item 192), manufacture, use and stripping of film (item 193), distillation of tar and turpentine (item 232), the use of oxy-acetylene equipment in shipbuilding (item 244), chemical processes giving off flammable or explosive gas, vapour or dust (item 247), dry cleaning (item 243) and the use, storage, etc. of highly flammable liquids and liquefied petroleum gases (item 130).

RADIOACTIVE FIRE DETECTORS—If radioactive types of fire detectors are used, the loss of any such detector must be reported to the Ministry of Housing and Local Government. If a detector contains more than 100 microcuries of all radio nuclides present it must be registered under the appropriate Act. See items 260 and 261.

REPORTING OF FIRES—Under the Dangerous Occurrences Regulations certain fires must be reported to the factory inspector even if no one is injured. See item 296.

OTHER REQUIREMENTS—Under Section 50 of the Factories Act 1961 the Minister of Labour has power to make special regulations for the prevention of fire or the limitation of the spread of flame and smoke. See HFL and LPG Regulations (item 130).

OFFICES AND SHOPS—Fire precautions required in offices and shops are given in items 274 and 275.

DUTIES OF FIRE AUTHORITIES AND FACTORY INSPECTORS—The duties and powers of fire authorities and factory inspectors in regard to fire precautions are dealt with in items 300 and 301.

28 – Cleaning of Buildings

Every factory must be kept in a clean state, and free from effluvia arising from any drain, sanitary convenience or nuisance. *FA: 1(1)*

STAIRS AND PASSAGES—Accumulations of dirt and refuse must be removed daily by a suitable method. Walls, sides and tops must be washed, limewashed or colourwashed at intervals shown in item 29. *FA: 1(2)*

So far as reasonably practicable, stairs and passages must be kept free from any substance likely to cause persons to slip. *FA: 28*

WINDOWS—Glazed windows and skylights used for lighting of workrooms must, so far as practicable, be kept clean both inside and out. This requirement does not prevent the whitewashing of windows and skylights to reduce heat or glare. *FA: 5(4)*

WORK-BENCHES AND OTHER FIXTURES—Accumulations of dirt and refuse must be removed daily from all work-benches, by a suitable method. *FA: 1(2)*

Benches used for the vitreous enamelling of metal or glass must be cleaned daily and kept free from collections of dust. *VER: 2(b)*

Work benches must be kept clean and free from asbestos dust. *AS: 9*

Work benches, tables and seats in active areas must have impervious surfaces and be capable of being easily cleaned. *IRUS: 37*

See also Accumulators (item 205) and Pottery (item 203).

In rooms where certain grinding processes are carried on, all fixtures must be properly swept at stated intervals. See items 129 and 189.

Waste and scrap from rooms where cinematograph film is manufactured, handled or stripped must be collected at frequent intervals during the day and removed from the workroom daily. See item 193.

WALLS AND CEILINGS—Like all other parts of the factory, walls and ceilings must be kept in a clean state. They must also be whitewashed, colourwashed, painted, or otherwise treated as shown in item 29. *FA: 1(3)*

FLOORS—Floors of workrooms must be cleaned at least once a week by washing or, if it is effective and suitable, by some other method such as sweeping. *FA: 1(2)*

In rooms where the cleaning or smoothing of castings is done, all accessible parts of the floor must be swept or otherwise cleaned every day. *GM: 10(b)*

In rooms where the vitreous enamelling of metal or glass is done, floors must be cleaned daily and kept free from collections of dust. *VER: 2(b)*

See Pottery (item 203), Asbestos (item 228) and Refractory Materials (item 227).

So far as reasonably practicable, floors must be kept free from any substance likely to cause persons to slip. *FA: 28*

ROOMS IN WHICH FOOD IS PREPARED—In rooms where food is handled, or in which equipment used in a food business is cleaned, the walls, floors, doors, windows, ceiling, woodwork and all other parts of the structure must be kept clean. *FHR: 25(1)*

In such rooms no refuse or filth must be allowed to accumulate, except so far as may be unavoidable for the proper carrying on of the business. *FHR: 26*

ROOMS IN WHICH MAGNESIUM IS GROUND—Dust, sludge and scale deposited in scrubbers must be removed weekly and disposed of as required by the relevant regulations. Steps must be taken to prevent the accumulation of any magnesium dust not collected by exhaust apparatus. See item 129.

ROOMS IN WHICH CELLULOID IS MADE OR USED—Celluloid waste must not be allowed to accumulate on the floor of the workroom but must be collected as created, or at frequent intervals. When work ceases for the day, all waste must be removed from the workroom. *CEL: 3*

OTHER PROCESSES WITH SPECIAL REQUIREMENTS—Special requirements are in force respecting the cleaning of rooms in which any of the following processes are carried on: file cutting by hand (item 190), manufacture, use and stripping of film (item 193), lead smelting and the manufacture of lead compounds (item 199), manufacture and decoration of pottery (item 203), active areas where radioactive substances are used (*IRSS: 37*), manufacture and repair of accumulators (item 205), manufacture of patent fuel (item 226), drying of silica bricks (item 227), the use of Chinese, Siberian or Russian horsehair (item 236), tinning of hollow-ware (item 197), processing of asbestos (item 228), wool sorting (238), and the storage of protective equipment used during the blasting of castings (item 133).

OFFICES AND SHOPS—The cleaning of offices is dealt with in item 269.

29 – Painting, Limewashing, etc.

Except where otherwise stated, all walls and partitions (up to a height of 20 feet from the floor) and all ceilings, must be treated in one of the ways specified below. (This requirement includes the walls and tops of passages and staircases.) *FA 37: 1(c) and the Factories (Cleanliness of Walls and Ceilings) Order, 1960. (SI 1960: 1794)*

SMOOTH IMPERVIOUS SURFACES—These must be washed, at intervals of not more than 14 months, with hot water and soap or other suitable detergent, unless the district inspector approves some other method of cleaning.

PAINTED SURFACES—These must be repainted at intervals of not more than 7 years by the application of a suitable paint in such a manner as to produce, over the whole treated surface, a compact continuous film capable of being washed. Surfaces must be repainted, in whole or in part, more frequently than once in 7 years if this is necessary to maintain a compact continuous surface of the kind described.

Painted surfaces must be washed, at intervals of not more than 14 months, with hot water and soap or other suitable detergent, unless the district inspector approves some other method of cleaning.

VARNISHED SURFACES—These must be revarnished at intervals of not more than 7 years. All or part of the surface must be revarnished more frequently than once in 7 years if this is necessary to maintain a compact continuous film.

Varnished surfaces must be washed at intervals of not more than 14 months unless the district inspector approves some other method of cleaning.

OTHER SURFACES—Surfaces other than those mentioned above must be whitewashed or colourwashed at intervals of not more than 14 months.

EXCEPTIONS—In the following places the requirements for painting, limewashing, etc., apply only to messrooms, cloakrooms, lavatories, sanitary conveniences, engine houses and maintenance shops:—

(*a*) Parts of a factory which are used mainly for storage and in which no process is regularly carried on;

(*b*) Electric generating or transformer stations;

(*c*) Saw mills, including re-saw mills;

(*d*) Blast furnaces, melting shops and rolling mills, and any sintering, crushing and screening houses used in connexion with them;

(*e*) Brick and tile works in which unglazed bricks and tiles are made;

(*f*) Parts of a factory where lamp black, carbon black, charcoal or graphite is manufactured, or where any of these materials are used in powder form to a substantial extent;

(*g*) Parts of cement works in which dry materials are handled or manufactured;

(*h*) Parts of a factory in which lime, limestone or chalk is crushed and ground;

(*j*) Control rooms and pump houses in chemical works, tar distillation works and gas works, or used in connexion with coke ovens;

(*k*) Retort houses and purifier houses in gas works;

(*l*) Platers' sheds, prefabrication sheds, blacksmiths' shops, coppersmiths' shops, anglesmiths' shops, and plumbers' shops if such sheds or shops are in shipbuilding yards.

In print works, bleach works and dye works, the ceilings of rooms in which steam is evolved are exempt from the requirements but the walls and partitions, up to the prescribed height of 20 feet, must still be given the appropriate treatment.

See The Factories (Cleanliness of Walls and Ceilings) Order 1960 (*SI 1960 No. 1794*).

In factories where no mechanical power is used and where fewer than ten persons are employed the requirements quoted in this item do not apply unless the district inspector of factories so directs. *FA: 1(4)*

ADDITIONAL REQUIREMENTS FOR CERTAIN PROCESSES—In rooms where file cutting is done by hand, all painted, varnished and glazed walls and ceilings must be cleaned weekly. Other walls and ceilings must be limewashed once in the first six months of every year and once in the second six months. *FCR: 7 and 8*

In rooms where the opening, sorting or willowing of wool is carried out, all walls, partitions and ceilings must be limewashed at least once a year and cleaned at least once in every six months. *WSR: 13*

The roof windows of weaving sheds in cotton cloth factories must be kept whitewashed inside and out, from May 31st to September 15th. The outside of the rest of the roof must also be kept whitewashed during this period. *FA: 5(4) and CCF: 8*

Chapter III

Environmental Conditions, Welfare, etc.

The requirements quoted in this chapter are supplementary to those in Chapter II. They consist of matters which must be taken into consideration when a factory building is designed or taken into use and which must be kept under constant supervision and review thereafter to ensure that the standards are maintained.

30 – Lighting

Sufficient and suitable lighting, either natural or artificial, must be maintained in every part of the factory where persons are working or passing. It should be noted that this requirement is not confined to the indoor portion of the premises; yards and other outdoor places within the curtilage of the factory must be illuminated when persons are working or passing. *FA: 5 and 175(7)*

All glazed windows and skylights used for the lighting of workrooms must, so far as practicable, be kept clean and free from obstruction both inside and out. This does not prevent windows and skylights from being whitewashed or shaded to reduce heat or glare. *FA: 5*

In all rooms where food is handled, or in which equipment used in a food business is cleaned, suitable and sufficient means of lighting must be provided. This applies to all such rooms, whether or not they are part of the factory. *FHR: 22*

Requirements for the lighting of docks, wharves and quays are given in item 140.

Requirements for the lighting of excavations, tunnels, etc., made in the course of building operations or works of engineering construction are given in item 177. General requirements for lighting during building operations and works of engineering construction are given in item 183.

Standards of Lighting for Factories—Standards were laid down by The Factories (Standard of Lighting) Regulations 1941 (*SRO 1941 No. 94*). These standards apply only to factories where persons are regularly employed for more than 48 working hours a week or in shifts. The prescribed illumination is 6 foot-candles where persons are regularly employed and 0·5 foot-candles where persons pass. These standards are without prejudice to additional illumination required by the nature of the work.

Exemptions subject to conditions are given for some industries. There are requirements to deal with glare, reflection light and shadow. *SLR*

Electric lighting Fittings—All electric lighting fittings, connexions, etc., must comply with the Electricity Regulations. See items 69 to 77.

Special Lighting for certain Operations—Special requirements affecting lighting are included in the regulations for woodworking machinery (item 126), horizontal milling machines (item 127), locomotives and wagons (item 135) and vitreous enamelling (item 134).

When shipbuilding or ship-repairing operations involve working in places where flammable vapours may be present, approved types of flame-proof lamps or torches must be used. See item 244.

Offices and Shops—Lighting for offices and shops is dealt with in item 268.

31 – Heating and Ventilation (General)

A reasonable temperature must be maintained in every workroom. The term " reasonable temperature " has not been legally defined but a Factory Department memorandum gives the following guidance: in deciding whether or not a temperature is reasonable, important considerations are the nature of the tasks performed (i.e., whether heavy or light) and the extent to which the workers move about from one place to another. It should also be borne in mind that effects of low temperatures may be counter-balanced by heat from manufacturing operations or plant affording warmth by direct radiation. *FA: 3(1)*

If a substantial proportion of the work is done sitting and does not involve serious physical effort, the temperature after the first hour must be at least 60° F. At least one thermometer must be kept in a suitable position in every workroom to which this applies. (The choice of a suitable position for the thermometer must be governed by circumstances but the position recommended for most workrooms is in the centre of the room at a height of about 5 ft. from the floor.) *FA: 3(2)*

Prevention of Heat Losses—Factory buildings erected since January 1st, 1959 (including any extension made since that date to an existing building) must be safeguarded against loss of heat by having the standard of thermal insulation prescribed by the Thermal Insulation (Industrial Buildings) Regulations, 1972 (*SI 1972 No. 87*). All materials used to obtain this standard of thermal insulation must have the degree of fire resistance laid down in the same regulations.

Methods of Heating—Workrooms must not be heated by any method which allows injurious or offensive fumes to escape into the air of the room. In chemical works, stoves must not be used to heat places in which there is danger of igniting gas, vapour or dust; and steam pipes and radiators must have at least 2 in. between them and the wall and must be protected by a wire screen. *FA: 3(1) and CWR: 4 (c)*

Heating apparatus in petrol stores must not burn petrol as fuel unless specially constructed. See item 99.

The use of open fires in foundries is restricted by the regulations. See item 137.

Temperature Requirements for Special Processes—Messrooms provided under the special regulations for certain industries must be warmed while in use (see item 36).

Shelters provided for kiln workers in clayworks must be sufficiently warmed. *CLW: 3*

In laundries, effective steps must be taken to regulate the temperature in ironing rooms. Employees must be protected against the heat from stoves used for heating irons. *FA: 71*

Any part of a room in which woodworking machinery is being used must be kept at at least 50° F., except where the construction of the room and the necessities of the business make this impracticable. *WWM: 8*

Specific temperatures are also laid down for the following processes: drying of films (item 193), manufacture and decoration of pottery (item 203), spinning and weaving (item 239) and wool-sorting and combing (item 238).

GENERAL VENTILATION.—Adequate ventilation of every workroom must be provided by the circulation of fresh air. *FA 4(1)*

Sufficient and suitable ventilation must be provided and maintained for all rooms in which food is handled or in which equipment used in any food business is cleaned. (This does not apply to humidity-controlled or temperature-controlled chambers.) *FHR: 23*

All factories must be kept free from effluvia arising from any drain, sanitary convenience, or nuisance. *FA: 4(1)*

Petrol stores must be effectively ventilated to the open air. See item 99.

Special requirements for the general ventilation of workrooms are contained in the regulations for the following processes: file cutting by hand (item 190), manufacture and decoration of pottery (item 203), manufacture and repair of accumulators (item 205), spinning and weaving (item 239).

VENTILATION OF CONFINED SPACES—Tanks, vats, chambers, pits and other confined spaces in which persons may have to work are subject to special requirements. See items 119 and 120.

Ventilation of places used to store radioactive substances is dealt with in items 204 and 255.

VENTILATION OF BOILER ROOMS—It has been decided by the Court of Appeal that a boiler room is not a workroom within the meaning of Section 4 of the Factories Act 1961 and that fumes given off by a furnace used for a central heating plant are not generated in the course of a factory process within the meaning of Section 63. (*Brophy v. J. C. Bradfield and Co., 1955.*) There is thus no statutory duty to provide either general or local exhaust ventilation but the observations of the Court in the case quoted made it clear that there is a duty at Common Law to ensure that boiler rooms and plant are so designed and operated as to safeguard employees against dangerous fumes. (This distinction between statutory obligations and Common Law obligations is explained in item 280.)

OFFICES—Heating and ventilating of offices is dealt with in item 268.

32 – Dust Control, Humidity, etc.

The following requirements are additional to the general requirements for ventilation quoted in item 31, and apply to certain processes, conditions, etc.

PRECAUTIONS AGAINST FUMES, DUST, ETC.—If the work carried on in a workroom or other workplace produces any fume, dust or other impurities liable to be injurious to health, all practical steps must be taken to render them harmless. In *Ebbs v. James Whitson and Co. Ltd., 1952*, the Court of Appeal decided that to render fumes or dust harmless within the meaning of the Act it was sufficient to provide adequate ventilation and that there was no obligation to render fumes or dust harmless by other means, such as chemical treatment, filtering, etc. *FA: 4(1)*

If any dust, fume or impurity given off by a process is likely to be injurious or offensive, all practicable measures must be taken to protect employees against inhaling such dust, etc., and to prevent its accumulation in any workroom. Where the nature of the process permits, local exhaust ventilation must be provided as near as possible to the point of origin of the dust, fume, etc. (Employers are expected to keep up to date in their knowledge of the dangers arising from industrial dust, etc.) See item 117 and *FA: 63(1)*.

Exhaust ventilation is specifically mentioned in the regulations for the following processes: grinding of magnesium and other metals (items 128 and 129), chromium plating (item 94), blasting of castings (item 93), grinding of cutlery and edge tools (item 189), testing of aircraft engines, carburettors, etc. (item 191), tinning of hollow-ware (item 197), bronzing (item 198), lead smelting and other lead processes (item 96 and 199), indiarubber manufacture (item 200), paint manufacture (item 201), spray-painting of vehicles (item 202), manufacture and decoration of pottery (item 203), vitreous enamelling (item 134), casting of brass (item 224), manufacture of patent fuel (item 226), processing of refractory materials and making of silica bricks (item 227), processing of asbestos (item 228), handling of Chinese, Siberian or Russian horsehair (item 236), wool-sorting and combing (items 237 and 238), jute spinning and weaving (item 239), the heading of yarn by lead compounds (item 239), certain operations in foundries (item 132), and use of radioactive substances (item 204).

GASES FROM I.C. ENGINES—When a stationary internal combustion engine is used, provision must be made for conducting the exhaust gases into the open air. Except when undergoing tests, such engines must be partitioned off so as to prevent fumes entering any other part of a workroom. *FA: 63(2)*

SMOKE CONTROL—Under the Clean Air Act 1968 it is an offence to allow dark smoke to be emitted from any industrial or trade premises, unless it can be shown that such emission was inadvertent and that all practicable steps had been taken to prevent it or minimise it. (For emission of smoke from chimneys, see item 119.)

STEAM, FUMES AND VAPOUR—In laundries, steps must be taken to carry away the steam from wash-houses and no gas-irons emitting noxious fumes may be used. *FA: 71*

The regulations for the spinning and weaving of hemp or jute include provision for the removal of steam and vapour. See item 239. The regulations for the manufacture of patent fuel require measures for removal of excess steam at heaters, coolers and pugmills (item 226).

HUMID FACTORIES—Artificial humidity produced in connexion with textile processes is subject to special requirements under Section 68 of the Factories Act 1961 and the regulations for the textile industry. See item 239.

33 – Noise Abatement

The Factories Acts make no statutory requirements relating to the reduction or prevention of noise. But if a noise is of such a nature as to do harm to employees—e.g., by causing deafness or by having a serious effect on the nerves—this may lead to an action for damages at Common Law. Also, if the safety of any employees depends on their being able to hear warning signals, etc., the occupiers must obviously satisfy themselves that there is no danger of the warning being rendered inaudible by other noises. See *Berry v. Stone Manganese Marine Ltd.* (1971), *Noise and the Worker*, No. 25 by the Department of Employment, and the Code of Practice for reducing exposure of employed persons to noise, (H.M.S.O.).

Under the Noise Abatement Act 1960, any noise or vibration which is a nuisance to the occupiers of neighbouring premises becomes a statutory nuisance within the meaning of the Public Health Act 1936, the Public Health (London) Act 1936, and the Public Health (Scotland) Act 1897. This means that the local authority can serve a notice on the factory occupiers requiring them to abate the nuisance and if the local authority itself does not take action the aggrieved neighbours may lay a complaint before a magistrate. In any proceedings under these Acts, it will be a sufficient defence for the factory occupier to prove that he is using the best practicable means for preventing, and for counteracting the effects of, the noise or vibration.

The Minister of Labour has power to make regulations for protecting workers in offices and shops against the effects of noise or vibration. *OSRA: 21*

34 – Washing Facilities

Adequate and suitable washing facilities must be provided and maintained for the use of persons employed. These facilities must include clean running hot and cold or warm water and soap and clean towels or other suitable means of cleaning and drying. These facilities must be conveniently accessible and must be kept in a clean and orderly condition. *FA: 58(1)*

The District Inspector of Factories has power to grant exemption from this requirement if the provision of running water is not reasonably practicable or if accommodation for washing facilities in the factory is restricted and facilities with hot and cold or warm running water are conveniently available elsewhere. *Washing Facilities (Running Water) Exemption Regulations 1960 (SI 1960: 1029)*

The scale on which washing facilities must be provided is not legally laid down, so far as factories in general are concerned.

In *Reid v. The Westfield Paper Company 1957* the Scottish Court of Session decided that an employee who had contracted dermatitis through the firm's failure to provide adequate washing facilities was entitled to damages.

For many processes, including the handling of food in canteens or elsewhere, there are requirements laid down in statutory regulations and welfare orders. These are shown in the table opposite. Requirements for washing facilities in offices and shops are given in item 271.

REQUIREMENTS FOR WASHING FACILITIES IN SPECIAL PROCESSES

Where any of the following processes are carried on, the washing facilities must comply with the requirements shown in column 2, as well as with the general requirements already quoted.

Dyeing by chrome solutions.* **Fruit preserving.*** **Glass** bottle manufacture.* **Gut scraping and tripe dressing.** **Laundries.** **Oil cake manufacture.** **Sack cleaning and repairing.** **Sugar** manufacture. **Tanning** by chrome solutions.* **Tanning** by other methods. **Tinplate** manufacture.*	Facilities must include a sufficient supply of clean towels, and must be under the charge of a responsible person. In processes marked (*) the facilities must be part of the equipment of the messroom (see item 34) and will therefore be in charge of the person responsible for that room. (In laundries there is no statutory obligation to appoint a responsible person but such a course is obviously advisable to ensure that the facilities are kept in the clean and orderly state required by law.) Facilities for those engaged in hot, dirty or sticky processes in the manufacture or refining of sugar must include baths.
Lead processes in which women and young persons are employed.	As above, with the additional requirement that nail brushes must be provided.
Casting of brass. **Bronzing.** Chromium plating.† Handling of hides and skins. **Handling** undisinfected horsehair. Hollow-ware mfr. (certain processes). Lead processes in indiarubber manufacture. Paint manufacture.‡ Painting of vehicles.§ Vitreous enamelling. Yarn heading.	Facilities must be under cover. They must consist of either lavatory basins or troughs, with a sufficient supply of clean towels (renewed daily), soap and nail brushes. They must be kept clean, orderly and in good repair. If troughs are provided they must be of such length as to allow 2 ft. for every 5 persons employed. They must have a smooth impervious surface, must be fitted with a wastepipe without a plug and must have a constant supply of warm water from taps or jets placed above the trough at intervals not exceeding 2 ft. If basins are used there must be at least one for every 5 employees. Each basin must either have a waste pipe and plug or must be placed in a trough with a waste pipe.
Lead smelting and the manufacture of certain lead compounds. (See item 199.)	As above, with the additional requirement that bath accommodation (douche or otherwise) must be provided, with hot water laid on, unless the other facilities are so arranged that a warm douche for arms, face and neck can be taken. For persons employed in the manufacture of lead compounds there must also be facilities for washing out the mouth and all washing facilities must be in charge of a responsible person.
Chemical works (certain processes only: see item 247).	As above, with the addition of bath accommodation for workers in certain specified processes.
Bakehouses (employees handling dough). Biscuit manufacture.	One basin to be provided for every 10 employees, with a sufficient supply of warm water, soap, nail brushes and towels. Wherever practicable, the supply of water must be laid on to the basins. Basins must have a smooth impervious surface and a wastepipe, and must be at least 7 in. deep and 20 in. long. Fixed basins installed in bakehouses before May, 1927, or in biscuit works before December, 1927, will satisfy the requirements if, regardless of their dimensions, they are large enough to enable the hands and forearms to be readily washed.
Other processes involving the handling of food (including canteens).	Facilities must consist of basins, not troughs, and must include nail brushes. They must be used solely for personal cleanliness; not for the washing of containers, etc.
Building operations and works of engineering construction.	Facilities for washing the hands must be provided adjacent to every messroom. For employees liable to come into contact with lead compounds or other poisonous substances, the facilities must include nail brushes, soap and towels.
Work in compressed air.	Washing facilities must include soap and clean towels.
Painting of buildings.	One bucket or basin must be provided for every 5 persons liable to come into contact with lead paint (not counting employees who are only occasionally employed in such work). A sufficient supply of water, soap, nail brushes, and towels must be available.
Docks.	See the Docks and Harbours Act, 1966 for welfare amenities.
Iron and Steel Foundries.	In addition to the washing facilities prescribed by the main Act, showers or other baths must be provided. See item 24.
Clayworks (item 230). File cutting by hand (item 190). Glass bevelling (item 223). Herring curing (item 219). Jute spinning, etc. (item 239). Lead processes in accumulator manufacture or repair (item 205). Radioactive substances (item 204). Patent fuel manufacture (item 226). Pottery manufacture (item 203). Wool sorting (item 238).	For all these processes there are various requirements. For details, reference should be made to the appropriate statutory regulations.

* Washing facilities for these processes must be part of the equipment of the messroom.

† Wash basins for this process must be at least 7 in. deep and 20 in. long, and ointment must be provided as well as soap, unless issued individually to each employee concerned.

‡ Facilities for this process need not be under cover. § Daily renewal of towels is not compulsory for this process.

35 – Messrooms and Canteens

There is no general obligation to provide messrooms or canteens but the regulations and welfare orders for certain industries and processes contain the requirements shown below.

Industry or process	Requirements
Tanning by chrome process. Dyeing by chrome process. Glass bottle manufacture. Tinplate manufacture. Herring curing in Norfolk and Suffolk.	Messrooms, separate from cloakrooms, must be provided for all employees remaining on the premises at mealtimes. They must have (*a*) sufficient tables and chairs, or benches with back-rests, (*b*) adequate facilities for boiling water and warming food and (*c*) suitable washing facilities comprising sufficient clean towels, soap, and warm water. Messrooms must be kept under the charge of a responsible person, kept clean, and warmed when in use.
Oil-cake manufacture. Fruit preserving.	As above, except that facilities for heating food and boiling water need not be provided if there is a canteen on the premises which serves hot meals.
Tanning, other than by chrome process. Manufacture of certain lead compounds (see item 199). Handling of hides and skins. Lead and fume processes in indiarubber manufacture.* Lead processes in the repair and manufacture of accumulators.*	Messrooms, separate from cloakrooms, to be provided for all employees remaining on the premises during meal-times. They must have (*a*) sufficient tables and chairs, or benches with back-rests and (*b*) adequate facilities for boiling water and warming food. Messrooms must be under the charge of a responsible person, kept clean, and warmed when in use. (The requirement regarding warming does not apply to processes marked (*).)
Laundries. Gut scraping and tripe dressing. Cleaning and repairing sacks. Lead processes in which women or young persons are employed.	As above, except that facilities for heating food and boiling water need not be provided if there is a canteen on the premises which serves hot meals. (In lead processes the messroom need not be separate from the cloakroom but must be separate from all workrooms.)
Cement works. Sugar manufacture.	Messrooms to be provided for all employees except workers on continuous processes. They must be furnished with sufficient tables, chairs or benches, and facilities for boiling water and heating food. A responsible person must be in charge and the room must be warmed when in use.
Certain processes in chemical works (see item 247). Scheduled processes in potteries (see item 203).	Messrooms to be provided for all employees. They must be furnished with sufficient tables, chairs or benches with back-rests, and facilities for boiling water and heating food. In chemical works there must also be facilities for washing crockery and utensils and in potteries there must be arrangements for employees to store food. Messrooms must be separate from any room in which a process is carried on. They must be in charge of a responsible person, kept clean, and warmed when in use.
Wool-sorting (certain processes only). Handling of horsehair. Vitreous enamelling. Hollow-ware manufacture (certain processes only). Lead smelting. Painting of vehicles.	Suitable meal-rooms, separate from workrooms, must be provided. No definite requirements are laid down regarding seating accommodation, heating facilities, etc., but the requirements for other processes, quoted above, may be taken as a guide to what is considered suitable.
Paint manufacture. Yarn heading by lead compounds.	Suitable messrooms, separate from workrooms, to be provided unless all employees leave the factory at meal-times.
Building operations and works of engineering construction.	Suitable accommodation for meals, protected from the weather, must be made available. It must have sufficient tables and seats or benches, with facilities for boiling water and adjacent facilities for washing hands. If this accommodation is provided in a separate building it must not also be used for the deposit or storage of material if this would interfere with its proper purpose.
Clayworks (item 230). Flour mills (item 213). Jute spinning, etc. (item 239). Patent fuel mfr. (item 226).	For all these industries and processes there are different requirements. For details, reference should be made to the appropriate statutory regulations.
Use of lead, arsenic, or other poisonous substances in such a way as to give rise to dust or fume.	Provision must be made for meals to be taken elsewhere than in the room where these substances are used.

As explained in item 9, works canteens are legally part of the factory and are therefore subject to all the requirements of the Factories Acts. In addition, canteens are subject to the Food Hygiene (General) Regulations 1970. See item 136. Canteens provided in connexion with offices and shops are subject to the Offices, Shops and Railway Premises Act. See item 273. For docks see the Docks and Harbours Act 1966.

36 – Water Supplies

DRINKING WATER—An adequate supply of wholesome drinking water must be provided and maintained at places conveniently accessible to all persons employed. The supply must come either from the public main or from some other source approved in writing by the district council. *FA: 57(1)*

If the water is not laid on from the mains it must be kept in suitable vessels and must be renewed daily. All practicable steps must be taken to preserve the water and vessels from contamination. *FA: 57(2)*

Except where the water is delivered in an upward drinking jet from which persons can conveniently drink, one or more suitable cups or drinking vessels must be provided at each point of supply. There must also be facilities for rinsing the cups, etc., in drinking water. *FA: 57(3)*

The requirements for chromium plating (item 131), baking and biscuit making (item 214), glass bottle making (item 223), laundries (item 234) and chemical works (item 247) specify that each supply must be clearly marked "Drinking water". The district inspector may, at his discretion, apply the same requirement to any other factory. *FA: 57(2)*

On construction sites each supply must be marked "Drinking water" unless it is patently intended for that purpose. See item 184.

In offices and shops the requirements regarding drinking water are similar to those for factories. See item 273.

WATER FOR WASHING—With certain exceptions, hot and cold running water must be provided for washing. See item 34.

WATER FOR CANTEENS AND OTHER FOOD ROOMS—In all premises subject to the Food Hygiene Regulations 1970 (see item 136) there must be a supply of water sufficient to enable the Regulations to be carried out. The water must be clean and wholesome and the supply must be constant (if the provision of a constant supply is reasonably practicable and is in accordance with good practice in premises used for businesses of a similar class). *FHR: 17*

A cistern supplying water to a canteen or other food room must not also supply a sanitary convenience except through an efficient flushing apparatus. *FHR: 15*

SOURCES OF WATER SUPPLY—As mentioned above, drinking water must come from either the public main or some other source approved by the district council.

Water used for food processes must be clean and wholesome but need not come from any specified source.

Under the Water Resources Act 1963 a licence from the local river authority is normally needed before water is drawn from any river or other source, including a newly-sunk well. A licence is not necessary if the quantity drawn does not exceed 10000 gallons and is not drawn as part of a continuous process. ,

37 – Accommodation for Clothing

GENERAL REQUIREMENTS—Adequate and suitable accommodation must be provided for clothing not worn during working hours, and such arrangements as are reasonably practicable must be made for drying clothing. *FA: 59*

Many codes of regulations for particular industries contain a similar requirement, but as these are now made redundant by the above general requirement of the main Act they have been omitted here, except for those which contain additional requirements over and above the general provisions of the Act. Such additional requirements are mentioned below.

It has been held in the Court of Appeal that the accommodation provided must give protection against theft *McCarthy and others v. Daily Mirror Newspapers (1949)*. In factories subject to the Patent Fuel Manufacture Regulations (item 226) there is a definite obligation to have clothing kept under lock and key.

ADDITIONAL REQUIREMENTS FOR CERTAIN PROCESSES—When protective clothing is supplied under statutory regulations it may be necessary to provide separate accommodation for such clothing. See Appendix III.

Suitable and sufficient locker or cupboard accommodation must be provided for clothing and footwear not worn during working hours by canteen workers and others engaged in handling food. *FHR: 20*

Changing rooms in foundries must have lockers for clothing and other personal belongings. See item 24.

When lead paint is used in the painting of buildings or vehicles, arrangements must be made to prevent the clothing taken off from being soiled by lead paint. *LPR: 5 and PVR: 7*

In factories subject to the Lead Smelting Regulations (item 199) the cloakroom must be so placed as not to be exposed to dust or fumes from any manufacturing process. *LSR: 11 (b)*

Cloakrooms provided under the Compressed Air Regulations (see item 246) must have adequate and suitable facilities for changing.

In factories subject to the following regulations, the cloakroom must be separate from the messroom: manufacture of lead compounds (item 199), manufacture of indiarubber (item 200), manufacture and decoration of pottery (item 203), manufacture and repair of accumulators (item 205), and the handling of hides and skins (item 235). Cloakroom accommodation in potteries must also be outside any room in which certain scheduled processes are carried on.

In the factories subject to the following regulations, the cloakroom must be in the charge of a responsible person: tinplate manufacture (item 195), manufacture and use of lead compounds (item 199), oil-cake manufacture (item 209), sugar refining and manufacture (item 215), gut scraping, etc. (item 217), fruit preserving (item 220), glass bottle manufacture (item 223), cleaning and repairing sacks (items 229 and 233), laundries (item 234), tanning (item 235), handling hides and skins (item 235), cotton cloth factories (item 240), dyeing by chrome solutions (item 241) and chemical works (item 247).

More detailed requirements for cloakrooms are given in the regulations for jute spinning and cotton cloth weaving (item 239), building operations (item 184) and work in compressed air (item 246).

Accommodation for clothing in offices and shops is dealt with in item 273.

38 – Sanitary Conveniences

In all factories, sanitary conveniences must be provided, maintained, and kept clean. Where both sexes are employed there must be separate conveniences for each sex, unless all employees are members of the same family. *FA: 7(1)*

NUMBER REQUIRED—In all factories where females are employed there must be one suitable convenience for every 25 females. *SAR: 2*

In factories where not more than 100 males are employed there must be one convenience, other than a urinal, for every 25 males. In factories where more than 100 males are employed, and where there is sufficient urinal accommodation, the scale of conveniences other than urinals must be 1 for every 25 males up to the first 100 and one for every 40 thereafter. *SAR: 3*

If a factory employs more than 500 males, and has not been built, enlarged or converted since June 1938, it is sufficient to provide one convenience for every 60 males, so long as there is sufficient urinal accommodation and so long as the Medical Officer of Health has issued a certificate of approval. *SAR: 3*

In calculating the number of conveniences required, any odd number of persons less than 25, 40 or 60 should be reckoned as a complete 25, etc. *SAR: 4*

ARRANGEMENT—The conveniences must be so arranged as to be readily accessible to employees at all times, *SAR: 7*

Urinals must be so placed or screened as not to be visible from other parts of the factory where persons work or pass. *SAR: 6*

Conveniences other than urinals must be under cover, partitioned off to secure privacy, and must have proper doors with fastenings. *SAR: 6*

Where conveniences have to be provided for both sexes, those for each sex must be indicated by a suitable notice and must have separate approaches. They must be so arranged and screened that the interiors are not visible from any place where members of the opposite sex have to pass. *SAR: 8*

LIGHTING AND VENTILATION—Effective provision must be made for lighting all conveniences. *FA: 7(1)*

Every convenience must be sufficiently ventilated and must not communicate with any workroom except through the open air or through an intervening ventilated space. (Workrooms in use prior to January, 1903, are exempt from this requirement if they are mechanically ventilated in such a way that air cannot be drawn into the workroom through the convenience.) *SAR: 5*

Factories must be kept free from effluvia arising from any sanitary convenience. *FA: 7(1)*

SPECIAL REQUIREMENTS FOR FOOD PREMISES—In canteens and in other places where food is handled the following additional requirements apply.

No cistern for the supply of water to a room where food is handled must supply a sanitary convenience, except through a flushing cistern or some other apparatus equally efficient and suitable for the prevention of contamination of water supplies. *FHR: 15*

Sanitary conveniences must be so placed that no offensive odours therefrom can penetrate to any room where food is prepared or handled. *FHR: 16*

No room which contains a sanitary convenience must be used for the handling of food. No room communicating directly with a room or other place containing a sanitary convenience must be used for the handling of open food or for the cleaning of equipment used in the handling or preparation of food. *FHR: 16*

Every sanitary convenience provided for persons handling food must have a clearly legible notice requesting users to wash their hands after using the convenience. *FHR: 16*

Sanitary conveniences must be kept clean and in efficient order and every room or other place containing a sanitary convenience must be suitably and sufficiently lighted and ventilated. *FHR: 16*

OFFICES AND SHOPS—The scale and standard of sanitary conveniences for office workers and shop workers is given in item 272.

OTHER PREMISES—All the requirements quoted as applying to factories apply also to electrical stations of the kind described in item 5. *SAR: 1*

Sanitary conveniences for building sites and works of engineering construction are dealt with in item 184.

DISCHARGE OF SEWAGE—Sewage must not be discharged into a stream or other water course without the consent of the local river board. See item 39.

39 – Drainage and the Disposal of Waste

DRAINS—Factories must be kept free from effluvia arising from drains. *FA: 1*

The fresh air intake of a ventilation pipe included in the soil drainage system must not be situated in any room where food is handled. *FHR: 14*

If any inlet into a soil drainage system is located in a room where food is handled it must be trapped. *FHR: 14*

All practicable steps must be taken to prevent petrol from flowing into any drain or sewer. See items 99 and 102.

Drainage from alkali works is subject to restrictions under Section 3 of the Alkali, etc., Works Regulations Act 1906. See item 247.

SEWERS—Except where the local council has given consent under the Public Health (Draining of Trade Premises) Act 1937 it is an offence to discharge into sewers: (*a*) any matter likely to injure the sewer or to interfere with the flow or to affect prejudicially the treatment of the sewage; (*b*) any chemical refuse, waste steam, or liquid above 110° F. which might be dangerous, a nuisance or prejudicial to health, either alone or in combination with the contents of the sewer; (*c*) petroleum spirit or carbide of calcium, including crude petroleum, petroleum oil, and petroleum mixtures giving off a flammable vapour at less than 73° F. *PHA 36: 27*

Trade effluent which does not violate the above requirements may be discharged into a public sewer if effluent of the same nature or composition, in the same quantities and at the same rate of discharge, was being discharged during the year ended March 3rd, 1937. If it is intended to begin the discharge of other or additional trade effluent, notice must be given to the local council two months before such discharges are to begin and during those two months the local council may lay down conditions under which the discharge will be permitted. *Public Health (Draining of Trade Premises) Act 1937*

Under Section 7 of the Rivers Pollution Act 1876, local authorities must give factory occupiers facilities for discharging liquids into the public sewers, provided that this can be done without overloading or prejudicially affecting the sewers.

POLLUTION OF RIVERS AND OTHER INLAND WATERS—Under the Rivers (Prevention of Pollution) Act 1961, no trade or sewage effluent may be discharged into a stream, river, watercourse, etc., without the consent of the local river authority. Applications for consent must give the nature and composition, maximum temperature, maximum daily quantity, and highest proposed rate of discharge. The river authority, in giving consent, may impose appropriate conditions. (No consent is needed for the discharge of water raised or drained from the underground part of a mine.)

Under the Rivers (Prevention of Pollution) (Scotland) Act 1965, similar restrictions now apply to Scotland.

POLLUTION OF TIDAL WATERS—Under the Clean Rivers (Estuaries and Tidal Waters) Act 1960, the powers of river boards to control the bringing into use of new or altered outlets for trade effluent are extended to include tidal waters and such parts of the sea as are specified in the schedule to the Act.

PROTECTION OF FISH—If a river or other water contains fish it is an offence under the Salmon and Freshwater Fisheries Act 1923 and the Salmon Fisheries (Scotland) Act 1862 to discharge any liquid or solid into it to such an extent as to make the water poisonous or injurious to fish or spawning grounds. The same restriction applies to tributaries of such rivers, etc., even if the tributaries themselves do not contain fish. (Certain exceptions may be made as regards discharges which have been going on since 1923.)

Under the Sea Fisheries Regulations Act 1888 and the Sea Fisheries Regulations (Scotland) Act 1895, local fishing boards and fishery committees may make local regulations governing or prohibiting the discharge of injurious solids or liquids into the waters of a sea fishing district.

POLLUTION OF WATER SUPPLIES—Under the Water Act 1945 and the Water (Scotland) Act 1946 it is an offence to do anything liable to pollute a well, spring, etc., which provides water for human consumption, domestic purposes, or food manufacture.

DISCHARGES FROM GAS WORKS—The discharge into rivers, etc., of waste products from gas works may be restricted under Section 68 of the Public Health Act 1875 and the Third Schedule to the Gas Act 1948. Under the Water Act 1945 and the Water (Scotland) Act 1946 restrictions may also be imposed when water supplies are likely to be contaminated.

RADIOACTIVE WASTE—Radioactive waste must not be disposed of without authority of the Minister of Housing and Local Government or the Secretary of State for Scotland except in certain circumstances covered by certificates of exemption. See items 260 and 261.

ALKALI WASTE—Alkali waste must not be deposited or discharged in any way without the best practicable means being used for preventing any nuisance therefrom. This is a general requirement of the Alkali Works Regulations Act, 1906, and is in addition to the restrictions already mentioned in connexion with rivers and sewers. *AWRA: 4*

Work in which any liquid containing acid or other substances capable of liberating sulphuretted hydrogen from alkali waste or drainage therefrom must be so carried out that the liquid cannot come into contact with the waste or drainage. *AWRA: 3*

CREATION OF NUISANCE—Nothing done in connexion with the disposal of waste or rubbish must be allowed to constitute a nuisance to local inhabitants, or to prejudice their health. *PHA 36: 92*

40 – Provision of First Aid Facilities

Every factory must have a first aid box or cupboard containing the prescribed contents shown in this item. If more than 150 persons are liable to be working in the factory at any one time there must be an additional box for every additional 150 persons or fraction thereof. *FA: 61(1)*

Each box or cupboard must be in charge of a responsible person, who must always be readily available during working hours. There must be a notice in every room, showing the name of the person in charge of the box provided for that room. *FA: 61(4) and (5)*

Every box provided since May 5th, 1938, must be plainly marked with the words " First Aid ". Earlier regulations requiring boxes to be marked with a white cross on a red ground are no longer in force. *FAB: 3(2)*

Nothing except first aid requisites and appliances must be kept in any first aid box or cupboard. *FA: 61(3)*

TRAINED FIRST-AIDERS—In factories where more than fifty people are employed the person in charge of a first aid box must be either a registered nurse or an enrolled assistant nurse within the meaning of the Nurses Acts or else must be recognised as qualified by the St. John Ambulance Association, the St. Andrew's Ambulance Association, the British Red Cross Society, or some other organisation approved by the Minister. (Organisations so far approved are given in Certificate of Approval No. 5 (General) Form 2337 issued under number 2 of the First Aid (Standard of Training) Order 1960 *SI 1960 No. 1612.*) A certificate issued by an approved organisation is not valid for purposes of the regulations unless it has been issued within the previous three years. *FA: 61 and First Aid (Standard of Training) Order 1960 as amplified by subsequent certificates of approval.*

An occupier can escape conviction for failure to have a trained first-aider in charge of a box if he can satisfy the Court that he made every attempt to comply with the law but was unable to do so. *FA: 61(7)*

Where trained first-aiders are required under the Act, an entry must be made in, or attached to, the general register showing the names of such personnel, the nature and date of their qualifications, and the date on which the evidence of their qualifications was inspected by the occupier. *FA(ST)O: 4*

CONTENTS OF FIRST AID BOXES—Materials for dressings must reach the standard prescribed by the British Pharmaceutical Codex, including all supplements thereto in force on May 21st, 1959, or subsequently approved.

The prescribed contents of first aid boxes and cupboards vary according to the size of the factory, and there are additional requirements for certain special industries. The quantities shown below represent the absolute minimum for each size of factory; if a box is liable to be in frequent use it may be necessary to increase the quantities so as to ensure that there is always an adequate supply at any given time.

Contents	Quantity Required		
	1 to 10 employees	11 to 50 employees	Over 50 employees
Factory Department leaflet No. 1008	1	1	1
Small sterilised unmedicated finger dressings	6	12	24
Medium sterilised unmedicated dressings for hands or feet	3	6	12
Large sterilised unmedicated dressings for other parts of the body	3	6	12
Adhesive wound dressings of the type approved in Factory Form 695	12	24	36
Triangular bandages of unbleached calico with one side at least 51″ and the others at least 36″ ...	2	4	8
Sterilised eye-pads in separate sealed packets	2	4	8
Rubber bandage or pressure bandage	1	1	1
Adhesive plaster, absorbent sterilised cotton wool in ¼ oz. packets, safety pins, and 60-grain tubes of sulphacetamide eye ointment complying with the requirements of Factory Form 693	A sufficient supply.		

Construction Sites—The requirements for first aid facilities on building sites and for workers engaged in works of engineering construction are covered by the Construction (Health and Welfare) Regulations 1966. See item 185.

Docks—First aid boxes on premises covered by the Docks Regulations (see item 149) must have the same contents as boxes in a factory with a comparable number of employees. *DR: 4 (a) and Docks (First-aid Boxes) Order 1959*

Additional requirements for certain industries—In addition to the above requirements, first aid boxes provided for canteen workers or other persons handling food must include waterproof dressings and an antiseptic. *FHR: 17*

Waterproof adhesive dressings (in assorted sizes) and waterproof adhesive plaster must be provided for workers engaged in the following processes—chromium plating (item 131), gut scraping and tripe dressing (item 217), herring curing (item 219), fruit preserving (item 220), aerated water manufacture (item 221), laundries (item 234), tanning (item 235), handling of hides and skins (item 235), dyeing by chrome solutions (item 241) and chemical works (item 247).

Other matters connected with First Aid—Exemption from some or all of the above requirements may be granted to factories having an adequate ambulance room, but it is necessary to obtain a certificate from H.M. Chief Inspector of Factories. *FA: 61(8)*

First aid requirements for offices and shops are dealt with in item 277.

Wall charts showing the treatment of electric shock must be displayed in all premises where electricity is used at voltages of over 250 DC or 150 AC. *ER 29 and Home Office Order of March 18th, 1935.*

Persons handling food must have any open cuts or abrasions covered with a waterproof dressing if they are on exposed parts of the skin. *FHR: 10*

Persons handling hides and skins must report any cuts or sores to the foreman and must have them treated before proceeding with the work. See item 235.

41 - Ambulance Carriages and Ambulance Rooms

Ambulances—Ambulances must be provided for construction sites where more than 25 persons are employed and there is no means of summoning an ambulance by telephone or radio. They must also be provided for docks and wharves where more than 50 persons are employed and no arrangements are in force for obtaining an ambulance quickly. See items 149 and 185.

In chemical works there must be a person or persons responsible for summoning an ambulance or other means of transport when needed. The same applies when more than 500 persons are employed in blast furnaces, copper mills, iron mills, saw mills, and factories making wooden articles. *Chemical Works Ambulance (Amendment) Regulations 1961* and *Blast Furnaces and Saw Mills Ambulance (Amendment) Regulations 1961*

Section 1 of the National Health Service (Amendment) Act 1957 provides for ambulances to be made available by the health authorities where industrial undertakings have a legal obligation to make provision for them.

Ambulance Rooms—Except in the special industries and processes mentioned below, there is no legal compulsion to provide an ambulance room in a factory. As explained in item 40, however, the provision of an ambulance room may save the occupier from having to provide and maintain first aid boxes, always assuming that the Chief Inspector of Factories gives his approval. *FA: 61(8)*

Ambulance rooms *must* be provided if 250 persons are employed at any one time in processes covered by the Chemical Works Regulations (item 246) or if more than 500 are employed in any blast furnaces, copper mills, iron mills, foundries, metal works, saw mills, factories in which articles of wood are manufactured, or in the manufacture of oil cake (items 225, 126 and 209).

Ambulance rooms are also compulsory on certain construction sites (item 185), shipyards (item 244), clayworks (item 230) and certain places where herring curing is carried on (item 219).

Contents of Ambulance Rooms—If an ambulance room is provided in lieu of first aid boxes the Chief Inspector of Factories, in giving his approval, may specify the minimum equipment to be provided.

Ambulance rooms provided for the special industries and processes mentioned above must contain a glazed sink with hot and cold water always available, a table with a smooth top, means for sterilising instruments, a couch, a stretcher and a supply of suitable dressings, bandages, and splints. Ambulance rooms for clayworks must also have a footbath, and on construction sites there must also be a footbath, blankets, and hot water bottles.

Supervision of Ambulance Rooms—Ambulance rooms provided under statutory regulations must be in charge of a qualified nurse or other person trained in first aid, and such person must always be readily available during working hours. A record must be kept of all cases of accident and sickness treated in the ambulance room.

The supervision of an ambulance room provided in lieu of first aid boxes is a matter on which the Chief Inspector of Factories may lay down requirements in granting the necessary certificate.

42 - Employment Medical Services Act 1972

The provisions of The Factories Act, 1961, relating to the medical examination and certification of young persons under 18 (i.e. *FA: 118* and *99(4)*) were repealed by the above Act. Also sections *10A* and *119A* were added to the Factories Act, 1961. Appointed factory doctor duties have been taken over by employment medical advisers and so *FA: 151* and *152* (relating to their appointment and fees) have also been repealed.

The effect of the above Act is as follows:

(i) The yearly examination of young persons under 18 is no longer required under *FA: 99* now repealed.

(ii) *FA: 10A* added by the 1972 Act enables an employment medical adviser to examine any person employed in the factory, in construction work, etc. (*EMSA: 3*)

(iii) If the occupier of the factory, etc takes a young person into employment, he must, within seven days, send particulars to the local careers office, giving name, address, date of birth and the name of the school of the young person.

(iv) Medical examinations required by certain special regulations are now to be done by the employment medical adviser (see next section).

OTHER MEDICAL EXAMINATIONS—Those who are employed in the following processes must be examined at the intervals prescribed in the appropriate regulations: vitreous enamelling (item 134), tinning of hollow-ware (item 197), manufacture and use of lead compounds and other lead processes (item 199), lead processes in the manufacture of indiarubber (item 200), certain processes in the manufacture of paints and colours (item 201), scheduled processes in potteries (item 203), ionising radiations (items 204 and 249), lead processes in the manufacture or repair of accumulators (item 205), patent fuel manufacture (item 226), yarn heading (item 229), mule spinning (item 239), diving operations (item 245), chrome processes or nitro or amido processes in chemical works (item 247) and work in compressed air (item 246). Workers covered by the regulations for biscuit making (item 214) must be inspected periodically for signs of dermatitis.

Employees engaged in the painting of buildings or vehicles must also be examined periodically if the Chief Inspector of Factories so directs. *LPR: 6 and PVR: 9*

See the Employment Medical Advisory (Factories Act Orders, etc.) Order, 1973. *SI 1973 No. 36*

MEDICAL SUPERVISION—The employment medical adviser has power to inspect the general register.

The Minister of Labour and the Chief Inspector of Factories have power to make requirements for medical supervision of the employees in any factory or class of factory. Except where special directions are given under these powers there are no legal requirements for medical supervision, other than the compulsory medical examinations mentioned above. *FA: 11(1)*

DUTIES OF DOCTORS—Any doctor whose patient is suffering from anthrax, toxic jaundice, epitheliomatous ulceration from pitch, etc., or from lead, phosphorus, arsenic, mercurial, carbon bisulphide, benzene, aniline or manganese poisoning, and who believes the disease to have been contracted in a factory, must notify the Chief Inspector of Factories unless satisfied that notice has already been given. *FA: 82(1)*

See also the Factories (Notification of Diseases) Regulations, 1966 (*SI 1966 No. 1400*).

Chapter IV

Machinery (Design and Construction)

This chapter deals with the design, construction and fencing of machinery. Requirements affecting use and maintenance will be found in the next chapter—items 63 to 68.

43 – Responsibility for Guarding Machinery

When machinery is owned or hired by the occupier of the factory, he is responsible for seeing that it is guarded in such a way as to satisfy the law. It is not sufficient for him to plead that the machine is as supplied by the makers.

When a machine or implement moved by mechanical power and used in a factory belongs to, or is hired by, someone other than the occupier (e.g., a contractor) the owner or hirer is responsible for guarding it, so far as the safety of his own employees is concerned. If, however, such a machine is brought into a factory unguarded, the occupier is responsible for seeing that *his* employees, and those of any third party, are not endangered by it. *FA: 163*

It should be noted that mechanical power is not defined by the Act.

Anyone who sells, or lets on hire, a machine covered by Section 17 of the Factories Act 1961, Regulation 43 of the Construction (General Provisions) Regulations 1961, or Regulation 27 of the Jute Regulations 1948, is responsible for seeing that it is guarded to the extent required by such legislation. The failure of the seller or hirer to comply with the law does not, however, release the occupier from his own obligations to see that the machine is adequately guarded.

44 – Meaning of "Dangerous Part"

Except where special requirements are laid down for particular types of machinery or parts of machines—e.g., transmission machinery, circular saw blades—the duty of fencing machinery is summed up in the general requirement (quoted in item 48) that every dangerous part of a machine must be securely fenced unless it is in such a position or of such construction as to be as safe as if it were securely fenced.

In deciding whether a particular part of any machine is dangerous, the Courts normally follow the test laid down by Mr. Justice du Parcq in the leading case of *Walker v. Bletchley Flettons Ltd., 1937:* "In considering whether machinery is dangerous it must not be assumed that everybody will always be careful. A part of a machine is dangerous if it is a possible cause of injury to anybody acting in a way a human being may be reasonably expected to act in circumstances which may reasonably be expected to occur."

Once it has been decided that a part of machinery is dangerous the duty to provide secure fencing is absolute. See *Summers v. Frost, 1955,* which also considered the meaning of "secure fencing" and held that if the provision of secure fencing makes the machine unusable it does not affect the duty. The absolute nature of the duty to provide secure fencing can be modified by *FA: 76(2)*. See *ABW 2(2)*, item 53.

It is therefore no defence in law to say that a machine is safe if the employee is careful, or if he does as he is told. The occupier is expected to guard against the employee's acts of carelessness or disobedience, so far as such acts are reasonably foreseeable. Thus, it would not be considered sufficient to provide a power-press operator with tongs and then leave the tools unguarded, because such a machine would only be safe so long as the operator used the tongs provided and it is easy to envisage circumstances (e.g., the jamming of a component) in which the operator would discard the tongs and put his hand into the machine if there were no guard.

In the case *Uddin v. Associated Portland Cement Manufacturers Ltd., 1965* it was held that the section *FA: 14(1)* was intended to secure safety for every person employed or working on the premises. The word employed does not mean that one should exclude acts done on a frolic or not within the scope of employment.

It should be noted that the Factories Act specifically refers to dangerous parts of the machine itself and does not, in general, make any reference to the guarding of materials or components which are being worked on a machine; the only exceptions are the guarding of stock-bars on lathes (see item 52) and the guarding of bottle-filling machines (see item 57).

The Courts have also held that there is no statutory duty to guard against part of the machine being ejected. There was formerly some doubt on this point, as there was about the fencing of materials carried on the machines, but the matter has now been settled (pending the passing of any new legislation) by the decision of the House of Lords in *Close v. Steel Company of Wales, 1961.*

Remarks made by the then Lord Chief Justice in the case just quoted imply that if a machine has a known tendency to eject either parts of materials worked on it or loose parts of the machine itself, there may be a duty at Common Law (see item 280) to take appropriate precautions.

45 – Safety by Position or Construction

It will be seen that some of the requirements set out in this chapter do not apply to parts of machinery which are safe by position or construction. As this matter is one about which there has been considerable misunderstanding it is desirable that factory occupiers should clearly understand the legal position.

A dangerous part of a machine is safe by position or construction, "if it is in such a position or of such construction as to be as safe to every person employed or working on the premises as it would be if securely fenced." It is for the occupier to ensure that this state of affairs really does exist. For example, if a length of shafting 15 ft. from the ground is left unfenced because it is considered safe by position, steps must be taken to ensure that no one ever approaches it while it is in motion (with the possible exception of authorised maintenance men carrying out the operations mentioned in items 65, 66 or 68). There have been numerous occasions on which painters, electricians, etc., have had to work near moving machinery normally regarded as safe by position and have thus met with accidents. When such accidents have been followed by legal proceedings it has generally been held that the dangerous parts were not, at the time of the accident, safe by position or construction.

Two further points should be noted. One is that the posting of a warning notice telling people to keep clear of moving machinery does not make such machinery safe by position. The other point is that the occupier's liabilities in this matter are the same whether the machinery is approached by one of his own employees or by someone else who is employed or working on the premises. When a contractor's men are working in a factory it is therefore necessary to ensure that they do not endanger themselves by approaching machinery normally considered safe by position.

46 – Construction and Maintenance of Guards

All fencing and other safeguards must be of suitable construction and must be constantly maintained in an efficient state, efficient working order, and in good repair. *FA: 16*

Whether a guard is of suitable construction is a question of fact to be decided in the light of the circumstances; the general principle, as laid down in the leading case of *John Summers & Sons Ltd. v. Frost, 1955*, is that it must give complete protection against the danger contemplated (except where, as with certain types of woodworking machinery, abrasive wheels, etc., special regulations prescribe a less stringent form of guarding).

Guards must be kept in position at all times when the dangerous parts are in motion. The only exceptions to this rule are when certain woodworking operations make the use of a guard impracticable (see items 49 to 51) and when authorised machinery attendants are doing certain types of maintenance work (see items 65 to 68).

47 – Prime Movers and Transmission Machinery

The term Prime Movers covers every engine, motor, or other appliance which provides mechanical energy derived from steam, water, wind, electricity, the combustion of fuel, or other source. *FA: 176*

Electric Motors, etc.—All parts of electric generators, motors, and rotary converters, and every flywheel directly connected with them, must be securely fenced unless in such a position or of such construction as to be as safe for everyone employed or working on the premises as if securely fenced. *FA: 12(3)*

Electric generators, motors and converters must be so installed as to comply with the Electricity Regulations. See items 69 to 77.

Water-wheels and Water-turbines—Every moving part of a water-wheel or water-turbine, including the head and tail race, must be securely fenced. *FA: 12(1) and 12(2)*

All other Prime Movers—Every moving part of the prime mover, and every flywheel directly connected to it must be securely fenced. This applies whether or not the prime mover or flywheel is situated in an engine house. *FA: 12(1)*

Prime movers used during building operations and works of engineering construction are subject to the requirements of the Construction (General Provisions) Regulation 1961. See item 172.

Transmission Machinery—The term Transmission Machinery includes every shaft, wheel, drum, pulley, system of fast and loose pulleys, coupling, clutch, driving belt or other device by which the motion of a prime mover is transmitted to, or received by, any machine or appliance. *FA: 176*

Every part of the transmission machinery must be securely fenced unless it is safe by position or construction. *FA: 13(1)*

Transmission machinery is deemed to be dangerous and does not have to be proved as is the case of a "dangerous part of machinery," (items 44 and 48). It includes machinery not driven by mechanical power (*Richard Thomas and Baldwins v. Cummings, 1955*).

Belts used in continuous processes listed in item 68 must, if they are ever mounted with the machinery in motion, comply with the special requirements quoted in that item. (Belts used in other processes are not affected, as they must *never* be approached with the machinery in motion.)

In every room or place where work is carried on (including places in the open air) there must be an efficient device for cutting off the power from all transmission machinery in that place. *FA: 13(2)*

Driving belts must not be allowed to rest or ride on any revolving shaft which forms part of transmission machinery. *FA: 31(3)*

Driving belts must not be moved to and from fast and loose pulleys except by means of suitable striking gear or other efficient mechanical appliances. Such gear and appliances must be so constructed, placed, and maintained as to prevent the belt from creeping on to the fast pulley. *FA: 13(4)*

Transmission machinery which has been left unfenced because it is considered safe by position or construction must not be approached while in motion, except by a certified machinery attendant carrying out certain necessary operations mentioned in items 65 to 68.

48 – Other Machinery (General)

The following requirements apply to all machinery used in a factory, apart from prime movers and transmission machinery, except where more detailed requirements have been made in special regulations for certain parts of particular machines. (See items 49 to 57.) The requirements for guarding machinery do not apply to machines which have been constructed in the factory and are intended for sale, even though they may be in motion for purposes of testing. See *Parvin v. Morton Machine Co. Ltd., 1952*.

Basic General Requirements—Every dangerous part of any machine, whether power driven or not, must be securely fenced, unless it is in such a position or of such construction as to be as safe as if it were securely fenced. For the test to be applied when deciding whether a part is dangerous see item 44; for notes on safety by position see item 45. *FA: 14(1)*

Other General Requirements—If the nature of the operation makes it impossible to fence a dangerous part by means of a fixed guard, it is sufficient to provide an automatic device which will effectively prevent the operator of the machine from coming into contact with the dangerous part. (The most familiar example of such a device is the automatic guard often fitted to power presses.) It should be noted that this concession applies only when the use of a fixed guard (including an interlocked fixed guard) is impossible. *FA: 14(2)*

The following additional requirements apply to all power driven machinery constructed after July 1937: every set-screw, bolt or key on any revolving shaft, spindle, wheel or pinion must be so sunk, encased or otherwise guarded as to prevent danger and all spur or other toothed or friction gearing must be completely encased unless it requires frequent adjustment while in motion or is safe by position. It is an offence for anyone to sell or let on hire a machine which does not satisfy these requirements but this does not absolve the occupier from liability if he accepts a machine which does not comply with the law and allows it to be used in that state. *FA: 17*

Additional detailed requirements for the fencing of certain parts apply to machinery which has to be approached while in motion by a machinery attendant. See item 66.

49 – Band Saws

The following requirements affect all band-saws used for cutting wood, if the cutting edge moves in a vertical direction (except log-saws or band re-sawing machines.)

Both sides of the bottom pulley must be completely encased by sheet metal or other suitable material *WWM: 12(a)*

The front of the top pulley must be covered with sheet metal or other suitable material. *WWM: 12(b)*

All parts of the blade must be enclosed or otherwise securely guarded except the portion between the bench table and the top guide. The guard must be so adjusted as to enable the work to be done without unnecessary risk. *WWM: 12(c) and 21*

A band-saw will be exempt from these requirements if it can be shown that alternative safeguards have been provided and maintained which make the machine equally safe. *WWM: 22*

The requirements quoted for the guarding of the pulleys and blade replace the general requirements for the guarding of dangerous parts laid down in Sections 14 and 17 of the Factories Act and quoted in item 48. All other dangerous parts of the machine must, however, be guarded to the full standard quoted in item 48.

Every band-saw must have an efficient stopping and starting device, so arranged as to be readily and conveniently operated by the person in charge of the machine. *WWM: 1*

The floor around the band-saw must be level and unobstructed. Artificial lighting, where necessary, must be so arranged as to prevent glare. *WWM: 3, 4 and 6*

Band-saws must not be used by anyone other than trained workers or persons working under adequate supervision. Occupiers and operators must ensure that the saws are used in conformity with the Regulations. See item 126.

Extension of Regulations—Under new regulations which are proposed, the regulations quoted will probably be extended to include band-saws used for cutting fibre-board, plastics, and similar materials, instead of being limited by definition to those used for cutting wood.

It is expected that the new regulations will also be extended to include straight line edging machines, which will have to have anti-kick-back fingers and other adequate means of protecting operators.

50 – Circular Saws

The following requirements apply to all circular saws working in a bench (including a rack-bench) for the purpose of ripping, deep-cutting or cross-cutting wood. They do not apply to swing-saws or other saws which are moved towards the wood.

Guards for Saw Blades—The part of the saw that comes below the bench must be guarded by plates of metal, or other suitable material, placed one on each side of the blade and not more than 6 in. apart. Beaded metal plates must be of a thickness equal to at least 20 gauge; unbeaded plates, at least 14 gauge. The plates must extend outwards from the axis of the saw to at least 2 in. beyond the teeth. *WWM: 10(a)*

A riving knife must be fitted behind the saw and in a direct line with it. It must be strong, rigid and easily adjustable and must have a smooth surface. The edge of the knife nearest the saw must be shaped to form an arc of a circle with a radius no greater than that of the largest saw used on that bench. For saws with a diameter of 24 in. or over this part of the knife must extend upwards at least 9 in. above the bench; for smaller saws the knife must extend to within 1 in. of the top of the saw. *WWM: 10(b)*

The riving knife must be kept as close as practicable to the saw, having regard to the nature of the work being done at the time. At bench level the distance between the front edge of the knife and the teeth of the saw must not exceed ½ in. *WWM: 10(b)*

The top of the saw must be covered by a strong and easily adjustable guard, with a flange at the side of the saw farthest from the fence. The guard must be kept so adjusted that it extends from the top of the riving knife to a point as low as practicable at the cutting edge of the saw, with the flange extending below the roots of the teeth. *WWM: 10(c)*

Alternative methods of guarding the blade will be accepted if they make the saw as safe to use as if the prescribed guards and riving knife were fitted. *WWM: 22*

The guards provided must be kept in position, properly adjusted, whenever the saw is in motion—except when the nature of the work makes this impracticable. *WWM: 21*

Guarding in General—The requirements quoted for the guarding of the saw blade replace the general requirements for the guarding of dangerous parts laid down in Sections 14 and 17 of the Factories Act and quoted in item 48; the effect of this is that if the blade cannot be guarded to the absolute standard normally required for fencing dangerous parts it is still permissible to use the machine so long as the guarding of the blade is as effective as practicable. All other dangerous parts, however, must be guarded to the full standard quoted in item 48.

Push Sticks—A suitable push-stick must be kept available for use at every circular saw fed by hand. *WWM: 11*

Stopping Devices—Every circular saw must have an efficient stopping and starting device, so arranged as to be readily and conveniently operated by the person in charge of the machine. *WWM: 1*

Other Requirements—The floor around a saw-bench must be level and unobstructed. Artificial lighting, where necessary, must be so arranged as to prevent glare. *WWM: 3, 4 and 6*

Circular saws must not be used by anyone other than a trained sawyer or someone working under his supervision. Occupiers and operators must ensure that the saws are used in conformity with the Regulations. See item 126.

EXTENSION OF REGULATIONS—Under new regulations which are proposed, the regulations quoted will probably be extended to include circular saws used for cutting fibre-board, plastics and similar materials, instead of being limited by definition to those used for cutting wood.

It is probable that these new regulations will also include requirements as to the sizes of blades that can be used on the same spindle.

51 – Other Woodworking Machinery

GUARDS FOR CHAIN MORTISING MACHINES—The chain of every chain mortising machine operating on wood must have a guard which encloses the cutters as far as practicable. The guard must be so adjusted as to enable the work to be carried on without unnecessary risk and must be kept in position whenever the machine is in motion unless the nature of the work makes the use of a guard impracticable. *WWM: 20 and 21*

All other dangerous parts must be guarded as indicated in item 48.

GUARDS FOR PLANING MACHINES—Every planing machine used for the overhand planing of wood must either be mechanically fed or else must have a cylindrical cutter block. In either case it must have a bridge guard capable of covering the full length and breadth of the cutting slot and this guard must be easily adjustable both horizontally and vertically. *WWM: 13 and 15*

Every planing machine used for thicknessing, except a combined machine for thicknessing and overhand planing, must have an efficient guard for the feed roller. *WWM: 16*

All guards must be maintained in an efficient state and must be constantly kept in place while the machine is in motion unless the nature of the work renders this impracticable. *WWM: 21*

Alternative methods of guarding will be accepted if they make the machine as safe to use as if the prescribed guards were provided. *WWM: 22*

All other dangerous parts of a planing machine must be guarded as indicated in item 48.

GUARDS FOR VERTICAL SPINDLE MOULDERS—When practicable, the cutter of every vertical spindle moulder operating on wood must be provided with the most efficient guard that can be used for the particular work being done. The guard must be so adjusted as to enable the work to be done with the minimum of risk and must be kept in position while the machine is in motion, except when the nature of the work makes this impracticable. *WWM: 17 and 21*

All other dangerous parts must be guarded as indicated in item 48.

For work that cannot be done with the cutter efficiently guarded, suitable jigs and holders must be used if practicable. *WWM: 18*

A suitable spike or push-stick must be provided for every spindle moulding machine. *WWM: 19*

STOPPING DEVICES—Planing machines, vertical spindle moulders and chain mortising machines must have an efficient stopping and starting device, readily and conveniently operated by the person in charge of the machine. *WWM: 1*

OTHER REQUIREMENTS—The floor around any woodworking machine must be level and unobstructed. Artificial lighting, where necessary, must be so arranged as to prevent glare. *WWM: 3, 4 and 6*

No woodworking machine must be used by anyone other than a trained operator or someone working under his supervision. Both occupier and operator must ensure that the machine is used in conformity with the Regulations. See item 126.

EXTENSION OF REGULATIONS—Under new regulations which are proposed, the regulations quoted will probably be extended to include woodworking machinery used for cutting fibre-board, plastics, and similar materials, instead of being limited by definition to those used for cutting wood.

Among the machines to be specifically brought within the definition of woodworking machinery will probably be chain saws, grooving machines, wood-turning lathes (both automatic and semi-automatic), tenoning machines and trenching machines.

The regulations for planing machines will probably be extended by the inclusion of specific requirements covering the design and mounting of bridge guards. Another proposed requirement is that every planing machine used for thicknessing must, on the operator's side of the feed roller, have a suitable device to contain, as far as practicable, any workpiece accidentally ejected by the machine. A period of grace will probably be allowed during which machines already in use can be adapted to meet any new requirements imposed.

52 – Lathes

Any part of a stock-bar that projects beyond the head-stock must be securely fenced unless safe by position. *FA: 14(5)*

In view of the many accidents that have occurred when people have had to pass near unfenced stock-bars, the bar should never be regarded as safe by position unless it is quite impossible for anyone to get dangerously close to it.

All dangerous parts of the lathe itself must be guarded as indicated in item 48.

WOOD-TURNING LATHES—Under certain new regulations it is proposed that lathes used on wood, wood products, fibre-board, plastics or similar materials shall be classed as woodworking machinery and subject to the regulations applicable to such machines. These will probably include the provision of guards for cutters, etc., efficient starting and stopping devices, the provision of sufficient space around machines, the maintenance of floors surrounding machines, and the maintenance of a prescribed minimum temperature.

53 – Abrasive Wheels

The Abrasive Wheel Regulations 1970 (*SI 1970 No. 535*) came into force in 1971.

The Regulations define abrasive wheels (*ABW 2(2)*) require a Cautionary Notice (Form 2347) to be affixed, speeds of wheels to be marked (*ABW 6*), and wheels to be mounted by an appointed, trained and competent person (*ABW 9*). The training is prescribed in the Schedule to the Regulations.

FA: 14(1) (see item 48) does not apply to an abrasive wheel as defined but the following requirements apply. The wheel must be properly mounted and suitable so as to reduce risk of injury. The wheel must have a guard, designed and constructed to contain every part of the wheel in the event of a fracture so far as is practicable. The guard must be maintained and secured, and must enclose the whole of the wheel except the part necessarily exposed for the purpose of the work. A wheel rest must be adjusted as close as practicable to the wheel. The diameters of tapered flanges are prescribed.

See Certificates of Exemption granted in respect of certain wheels and discs.

Abrasive wheels used for grinding metals must be fitted with exhaust ventilation satisfying the requirements of the Grinding of Metals Regulations (item 129), the Magnesium Regulations (item 128) or the Grinding of Cutlery and Edge Tools Regulations (item 189) as the case may be.

54 – Milling Machines

The cutter or cutters of every horizontal milling machine must be fenced by a strong guard enclosing the whole of the cutting surface except such part as is necessarily exposed for milling. Except when face milling is being done, the guard must either (*a*) be provided with an adequate side flange or else (*b*) must extend on each side of the cutter to the end of the arbor, or to the arbor support, or to a distance equal to at least half the diameter of the cutter. *HMM: 3*

The guards so provided must be kept properly adjusted whenever the machine is in motion, except when the toolsetter is setting up the machine. *HMM: 3 and 6*

All dangerous parts other than the cutters must be guarded as indicated in item 48.

Every horizontal milling machine must have an efficient starting and stopping device, so arranged as to be readily and conveniently operated by the person using the machine. *HMM: 4*

Suitable means must be provided for removing swarf, and when suds or other cutting lubricants are used there must be suitable arrangements enabling the operator to apply them or to adjust the supply pipe. *HMM: 5*

The floor surrounding a horizontal milling machine must be in good and even condition and must be kept clear. Arrangements must be made to prevent suds making the floor slippery. *HMM: 1*

Artificial lighting, where necessary, must be so arranged as to prevent glare. *HMM: 2*

Young persons under 18 must not use horizontal milling machines except after adequate training and supervision and every person using such machines must use the guards provided. See item 127.

Exceptions—When the following operations are being carried out the cutter or cutters need not be guarded in the manner prescribed above but must be so guarded as to satisfy Section 14 of the Factories Act, 1961 (see item 48): internal milling, end milling other than face-milling; automatic gear cutting, hobbing or profiling; thread milling; and the making of tools, jigs and gauges for use in the factory, or similar accurate operations where the operator can at any time manipulate those parts of the machine that control the position of the work and the cutter.

Cutters used on a spindle exceeding 2½ in. in diameter, or an arbor exceeding 2 in. in diameter at the place where the cutter is mounted, are also exempt from the specific requirements of the Regulations but are subject to the general requirements of Section 14. See item 48.

55 – Self-Acting Machines

Traversing parts of self-acting machines, and material carried on those parts, must not be allowed to run within 18 in. of any fixed structure if people are liable to pass between the machine and the structure. *FA: 19(1)*

These requirements are modified slightly in respect of self-acting mules, the carriage of which may run to within 12 in. of the headstock of another such machine. *FA: 19(1)*

In factories erected before December 31st, 1895, the above requirements apply only to such parts of them as may have been added, extended or reconstructed since July, 1937. *FA: 19(1)*

All practicable steps, including instructions to the person in charge of the self-acting machine, must be taken to ensure that no person is in the danger area between the fixed and traversing parts, except when the machine is stopped with the traversing part on the outward run. *FA: 19(1)*

All dangerous parts of self-acting machines must be guarded as indicated in item 48.

56 – Power Presses

For the purpose of these regulations, a power press is a press or press brake which is power driven, embodies a flywheel and a clutch mechanism, and is used wholly or partly for working metal by means of tools or for die proving. The regulations do not, however, apply when a press is used for working hot metal or is out of use and will next be used for hot metal. *PPR: 2 and 3*

Every power press, and every safety device used for protecting the tools of a power press, must be clearly marked with some means of identification. *PPR: 9*

Every power press constructed after July 20th, 1966 must be plainly marked to show the direction and maximum permitted speed of the flywheel. *PPR: 10*

A power press which has been newly installed (even if it has previously been used elsewhere) must not be used in its new location until it has been thoroughly examined and tested by a competent person. Thereafter it must be examined and tested every 12 months if the tools are fenced exclusively by fixed guards and every 6 months if the tools are protected by other means, such as an automatic guard. A report of each examination and test must be made on Factory Form F 2197 and attached to the general register within 14 days. *PPR: 5*

Every safety device for fencing or otherwise safeguarding the tools of a power press must be tested and examined by a competent person after being installed on the particular press on which it is about to be used, and the press must not be used until the examination and test have taken place. A report of the examination and test must be made on Factory Form 2197 and attached to the general register within 14 days. *PPR: 5*

If the person making the examination and test of a power press or a safety device discovers a defect which makes the press or device dangerous to use he must inform the occupier as soon as possible. If the defect does not make the press or device dangerous for the time being but may become a source of danger later on, the person making the test must state the maximum period for which the press or device may be used without remedying the defect. The form for reporting defects is Factory Form 2198; after the defect is remedied the fact must be recorded either on the same form or on a document attached to it. *PPR: 6*

Where the occupier has been informed under this Regulation of defects, a copy of the report required by Regulation 5(4) above should be sent to the district inspector of factories. See the Power Presses (Amendment) Regulations 1972 (*SI 1972 No. 1512*).

In addition to the above specific requirements, power presses are subject to the general requirements for guarding machinery set out in item 48.

Requirements for the setting-up of power presses and the installation and adjustment of guards are given in item 67.

57 – Tile Presses in Potteries

Presses used in potteries for the making of tiles by compression must have the control handle placed as near as possible to table level. In no circumstances may the handle be above the shoulder level of the operator. *P(HW)R: 22(a)*

The number of tile presses permitted for a given floor area is specified in the appropriate regulations. See item 183.

All dangerous parts of such presses must be guarded as indicated in item 48.

58 – Other Special Factory Machinery

Machines used for filling bottles or syphons with aerated water must be so constructed, placed and fenced as to ensure, so far as possible, that persons cannot be struck by fragments of bursting bottles or syphons. The operation of such machines is subject to special requirements. See item 221.

In the manufacture of patent fuel, machinery and plant must be enclosed to prevent escape of dust (item 226).

All machinery used in the spinning or weaving of jute, or the calendering or cropping of jute cloth, is subject to the general requirements set out in item 48. Any such machinery constructed after January 1st, 1949, is also subject to additional and detailed requirements set out in the schedule to the Jute (Safety, Health and Welfare) Regulations, 1948. See item 239.

These machines, like all others, are subject to the general requirements for guarding set out in item 48.

All machinery used in building operations and works of engineering construction, whether power-driven or not, is subject to the requirements of the Construction (General Provisions) Regulations 1961. See item 172.

59 – Internal Combustion Engines

Stationary internal combustion engines must not be used in a factory unless provision is made for conducting the exhaust gases from the engine to the open air. Except when such engines are under test, they must be so partitioned off from any workroom or part of a workroom as to prevent injurious fumes from entering the air of such rooms. *FA: 63(2)*

Precautions against fumes must also be taken when internal combustion engines are used in pits, excavations, or other confined spaces in connexion with building operations or works of engineering construction. See item 183.

Compressed air plant used for starting internal combustion engines may be subject to the requirements for air receivers. See item 89.

All internal combustion engines used in a factory are prime movers within the meaning of the Factories Act, 1961. Every moving part, and every flywheel, must therefore be guarded. See item 46.

60 – Electrically Driven Machines

All electrically operated machines, whether fixed or portable must be so constructed and installed as to satisfy the Electricity Regulations (see items 69 to 77). Dangerous parts of such machines must be guarded in the same way as mechanically-driven or hand-operated machinery of the same type.

61 – Machines requiring Exhaust Ventilation

Abrasive wheels and grindstones subject to the Grinding of Metals Regulations (item 129), the Magnesium Regulations (item 128) or the Grinding of Cutlery Regulations (item 189) must be fitted with exhaust ventilation satisfying the requirements of those regulations.

Exhaust ventilation is also required for machinery used in the following processes, unless there is some other means of suppressing harmful dusts: bronzing (item 198), vulcanising (item 200), crushing of refractory materials (item 227), processing of asbestos (item 228), extracting dust from East India wool (item 238), the manufacture of patent fuel and the grinding or crushing of caustics in chemical works (item 247).

Section 63 of the Factories Act 1961 requires that employees should be protected against any harmful or offensive dusts, fume, etc. See item 117. To comply with this general requirement it may be necessary to fit exhaust ventilation to machines other than those covered by the regulations mentioned above.

62 – Other Machinery

Factory machines not mentioned by name in this chapter have not been made the subject of any special requirements as regards guarding; they are subject to the general requirements quoted in item 48.

Lifting appliances, including cranes and hoists, are subject to certain constructional requirements dealt with in items 78 to 80, but so far as guarding is concerned they are covered by the general provisions of the Act as outlined in item 48. The same applies to the various items of plant dealt with in items 82 to 98.

Machines used in offices or shops, or on railway premises as defined in the Offices, Shops and Railway Premises Act, are dealt with in item 276.

Requirements affecting the *use* of machines are dealt with in the next chapter.

Chapter V

Machinery (Use and Maintenance)

Before any machinery is put into operation it must be checked to ensure that it is properly equipped with the guards and other devices dealt with in Chapter IV. The requirements quoted in the present chapter apply to the actual use of the machinery, including its cleaning and maintenance.

63 – Use of Machinery (General)

Guards provided under the Factories Acts must be kept in position whenever the machine is in use, unless a certified machinery attendant removes it for the purposes mentioned in items 66 to 68.

If any employee removes or interferes with a guard, without reasonable cause, he is liable to prosecution. This fact, however, does not free the employer from his legal obligation to see that guards are maintained in position. *FA: 143 and 155*(2)

Except for operators of woodworking machinery (item 126), the setting-up and testing of power presses (item 67) and the mounting of abrasive wheels (item 53), there are no statutory requirements regarding the training or supervision of adult machine operators. But see items 170 and 179 for lifting appliances and vehicles on construction sites. However, if an employee meets with an accident owing to insufficient training or supervision it may be held that the employer has failed in his obligations at Common Law. See item 280.

Young persons under 18 must not work at certain types of machinery unless they have been fully instructed concerning the dangers and about the precautions to be taken and unless they have either (*a*) received sufficient training in the work or (*b*) are under adequate supervision. The machines to which this condition applies are guillotines and platen printing machines (whether hand operated or power operated); and wire-stitching machines, semi-automatic wood-turning lathes; other woodworking machinery; power presses (including hydraulic and pneumatic presses); brick and tile presses; milling machines used in the metal trades; dough mixers and dough brakes; pie and tart making machines; meat mincing machines; worm pressure extruding machines; loose knife punching machines; corner-staying machines; carding machines and gill boxes used in the wool textile trades; machines used for opening and teasing in upholstery and bedding works; and calenders, garment presses, hydro-extractors and washing machines used in laundries. Except for hand-operated guillotines and platen printing machines, only machines operated by mechanical power are affected. *FA 21, DMO*

Similar restrictions apply to the use of certain machines by young workers in offices and shops. See item 276.

64 – Use of Machines covered by Special Regulations

Special regulations are in force affecting the use of power presses (item 67), woodworking machinery (item 126), horizontal milling machines (item 127) and abrasive wheels and grindstones (items 53, 128, 129 and 189).

65 – Cleaning of Machinery

If machinery is cleaned while in motion all guards provided for dangerous parts must be kept in position. *FA: 16*

Women and young persons must not clean machinery, whether moving or stationary, if the work would expose them to danger either from the machine being cleaned or from any adjacent machine. *FA: 20*

In no circumstances may women or young persons under 18 clean any part of moving prime movers or transmission machinery. *FA: 20*

66 – Examination, Lubrication and Adjustment

As a general rule, it is an offence to allow an employee to approach any dangerous part of a machine while that part is in motion and unfenced. The examination, lubrication, and adjustment of such parts must therefore be done with the machinery at rest or with the guards in position.

It is realised, however, that there are occasions when examination, lubrication or adjustment must be done with the machinery unfenced and in motion. To cover this contingency, the Factories Act provides for the appointment of certified machinery attendants who *in certain circumstances only* may carry out this work. *FA: 15 and 16*

APPOINTMENT OF MACHINERY ATTENDANTS—Every certified machinery attendant must be a male of 18 years or over. He must have been given sufficient training in the work he has to do and must be acquainted with the dangers arising from it. *OUM: 3*

The appointment must be made by an entry in, or attached to, the general register and each machinery attendant must be given a certificate. At the discretion of the occupier, the attendant may be authorised to carry out all operations covered by the Operations at Unfenced Machinery Regulations or he may be restricted to certain operations only; if he is so restricted this must be stated on the certificate. *OUM: 2*

The certified machinery attendant must be familiar with the Operations at Unfenced Machinery Regulations and must be given a copy of the prescribed Factory Department leaflet (Factory Form 280). *OUM: 4*

A male employee of 18 or over who is not a certified machinery attendant may carry out the duties of one on any special occasion for which he is given written authority by a responsible member of the management. Such written authority, however, can apply only to the one occasion. *OUM: 5*

OCCASIONS ON WHICH A MACHINERY ATTENDANT MAY ACT—Even a certified machinery attendant may not lubricate, examine or adjust unfenced moving machinery on every occasion. The circumstances in which he may do so are restricted to the following:—

(*a*) if it is necessary to examine part of the machinery, and this examination cannot be carried out with the machinery at rest or with guards in position;

(*b*) if examination shows that lubrication or adjustment is immediately necessary and such lubrication or adjustment cannot possibly be done with the machinery at rest or with guards in place;

(*c*) if it is necessary to lubricate transmission machinery used in one of the scheduled continuous processes mentioned in item 68 and such lubrication cannot be postponed until the machinery can be stopped without detriment to the process. *FA: 15*

PRECAUTIONS TO BE TAKEN BY MACHINERY ATTENDANTS—Every certified machinery attendant, when approaching unfenced moving machinery, must wear a close-fitting single-piece overall, without external pockets other than a hip pocket and fastened by some method which has no exposed loose ends. This overall must completely cover all loose ends of other clothing and must be in good repair. The regulations do not require the occupier to *provide* such overalls; whether they are provided by employer or employee is a matter for arrangement between the two parties. The employer is, however, legally responsible for seeing that such overalls are worn. *OUM: 5(b) and 12*

While the machinery attendant is at work a second person must be available within sight or hearing and this person must know what to do in an emergency. *OUM: 5(c)*

Every ladder used by a machinery attendant must be securely fixed or lashed, or else must be firmly held by a second person. *OUM: 7*

Every set-screw, bolt or key on any revolving shaft, spindle, wheel, or pinion; and all spur and other toothed or friction gearing in motion must be securely fenced if it is in such a position that the attendant is likely to come into contact with it. (This does not apply to parts which have been necessarily exposed for the purpose of lubrication, examination or adjustment.) *OUM: 6*

Steps must be taken to prevent any person other than the machinery attendant from being in a position where he or she is exposed to danger from the machinery. Where appropriate and reasonably practicable, the steps taken must include the erection of a barrier. *OUM: 5(d)*

If the machinery is moved only by hand, or by a barring engine or a proper inching device, the only one of the above precautions which need be taken is the securing of ladders. (This concession does *not* apply when the machinery is being inched by means of the ordinary starter button.) *OUM: 1*

Machinery attendants must make proper use of any appliances provided for the safe carrying out of their work. *OUM: 12 and FA: 143*

The Chief Inspector of Factories may vary or modify any of the above requirements if he considers that they are unreasonable or inappropriate in respect of any particular factory or machinery. *OUM: 13 and 14*

67 – Setting-up of Machines

A tool-setter or other skilled mechanic authorised to set up a machine must be registered as a machinery attendant if he has to do any part of his work with dangerous machinery unfenced and in motion. He must be given a machinery attendant's certificate, as described in item 66, but need not wear the prescribed type of overall nor have a second person available. *OUM: 1 and 2, and Nash v. High Duty Alloys Ltd., 1947*

Every set-screw, bolt or key on any revolving shaft, spindle, wheel or pinion; and all spur and other toothed or friction gearing in motion must be securely fenced if it is in such a position that the tool-setter is likely to come in contact with it. (This does not apply to parts which have necessarily been exposed for the purpose of the work.) *OUM: 6*

The tool-setter must make proper use of any appliance provided for the safe carrying out of his work. *OUM: 12 and FA: 143*

The tool-setter must not work with the guards removed and the machinery in motion except when it is impossible to do his work in any other way. If part of the work (e.g., the trial of the machine after setting up) can be done with the guards in position they must be replaced before that part of the work is done. *FA: 16*

POWER PRESSES—The setting, re-setting, adjusting and trying out of the tools on a power press must (except during training) be done only by a person who is over 18, has been adequately trained, is competent to carry out the duties in question, and has been formally appointed by the occupier to carry out such duties in respect of that class of press. The appointment must be recorded by a signed and dated entry in a special register, or by a signed and dated certificate attached to the register. *PPR: 4(1)*

The training given to the person so certified must include suitable and sufficient practical instruction in the following matters, so far as they are applicable to the type of press in respect of which the certificate is given: power press mechanisms (with particular reference to their bearing on safety; the nature and function of clutch mechanisms, flywheels, brakes and ancillary equipment; the causes and prevention of accidents, with special reference to power presses; safe methods of working; lubrication; co-operation with the press operator; tool design in relation to safe methods of working; and the functions of each type of safety device and the methods of installing, inspecting, testing and detecting faults in respect of safety devices. *PPR: 4 and Schedule*

The installation or adjustment of fencing or other safeguards provided for the tools of a power press must also be done by a trained and certificated man satisfying the above requirements in so far as they affect the type of safety device in question. *PPR: 4*

Persons who are under 18, or who do not satisfy the other requirements quoted, may do the work described if they are undergoing training under the immediate supervision of a certificated person. The fact that such training is being given must be entered in the register, or on a certificate attached to the register, the entry being signed by the person giving the training. *PPR: 4(4)*

After the setting, re-setting or adjustment of tools, the power press must not be used until the safety devices have been inspected and tested (while in position on the press) by a competent person duly appointed as described above. (This requirement does not apply if the setting, etc., has been done without altering, adjusting or disturbance of the safety device and if the latter remains in working order.) *PPR: 7(1)*

After the fourth hour of the working day or shift no power press may be used unless every safety device for protecting the tools has been given an inspection and test since the last time it was used. *PPR 7(3)*

After every inspection and test of a safety device a certificate must be completed giving the date and time, the number of the press or other means of identification, and certifying that every safety device on the press is in working order. Certificates must be kept available at or near the press until superseded by a later certificate and must then be retained in the factory for 6 months. *PPR: 7(5)*

ABRASIVE WHEELS—The mounting of an abrasive wheel must be done by a trained and competent person appointed by certificate (Form 2346). See item 53.

68 – Belt Mounting

As a general rule it is illegal to handle belts at a moving pulley for the purpose of mounting or shipping them. Belts must therefore be mounted with the machinery at rest, unless it is possible to use a belt mounting device which permits the belts to be mounted on moving pulleys without any danger.

It is recognised, however, that certain continuous processes cannot be stopped without detriment to the process and product. In these processes, which are listed below, a certified machinery attendant may mount belts on running pulleys subject to certain conditions.

PRECAUTIONS TO BE TAKEN—Where the law permits a certified machinery attendant to handle belts at a moving pulley he must take all the precautions listed in item 66. *OUM: 5 to 7*

The belt must comply with the following requirements: it must be less than 6 in. in width (except in flour mills), it must already have been used on the pulley on to which it is being mounted, it must have a joint which is either laced or flush with the belt or is secured by a method approved by the Chief Inspector of Factories. *OUM: 10 and Certificate of Exemption No. 5 (Form F 2322)*

The belt, including the joint, and the pulley rim must be in good repair and there must be reasonable clearance between the pulley and any fixed plant or structure. *OUM: 10*

Secure foothold and, where necessary, secure handhold must be afforded. *OUM: 10*

All belts which may have to be handled at a moving pulley must be inspected daily by a competent person, with a view to ascertaining whether they require repair or replacement. If such an inspection is made with the belt, or any adjacent machinery, in motion it must be made from a safe position. Any repair or replacement found to be necessary must be carried out as soon as practicable. *OUM: 11*

SCHEDULED CONTINUOUS PROCESSES—The continuous processes referred to in this item and in item 66 are set out in the schedule to the Operations at Unfenced Machinery (Amended Schedule) Regulations, 1946. They are as follows:—

All processes in the manufacture of beet sugar, flour from wheat, sulphur dioxide, inlaid linoleum, paper and paperboard, sodium hyposulphite and sodium sulphoxylate, viscose transparent paper or film, provender and compound foodstuffs for animal feeding, sodium carbonate made by the ammonia soda or Solvay process, and caustic soda made by the ammonia soda or Solvay process or by continuous causticising.

All processes in the milling of cereals, seeds or nuts.

All processes in the extraction of oil or other similar products from cereals or seeds.

The filtering process in the manufacture of sulphate of ammonia.

The phosphate reaction pumping process in the manufacture of concentrated fertiliser.

The electrolytic process for the manufacture of metallic sodium, as regards the dredging of sodium cells.

The electrolytic process for the manufacture of caustic soda.

Any manufacturing process in which a mixture of nitric and sulphuric acids is employed and where risk of fire or explosion would arise if the transmission machinery were stopped.

The reducing, volatising and decomposing process in the production of nickel.

Any process in the manufacture of phosphorus halides directly from phosphorus if it involves the risk of considerable rise in temperature and of the evolution of toxic gases if the transmission machinery is stopped.

The process of enamelling wire, including re-winding after enamelling.

The kier process in the manufacture of aluminium from bauxite.

PROCESSES NOT SCHEDULED—If the process is not one of those included in the list given above, even a certified machinery attendant is not permitted to handle a belt at a moving pulley.

URGENCY OF BELT MOUNTING—Even in a scheduled process, belts must not be handled at moving pulleys if it is possible, without detriment to the process, to postpone the mounting of the belt until the machinery can be stopped.

Chapter VI

Electrical Equipment (Design, Construction, Use and Maintenance)

The requirements given in this chapter apply, with a few exceptions, to all electrical equipment in factories, electrica stations, docks, shipyards, building sites, and works of engineering construction. The few types of electrical equipment which are entirely outside the scope of these requirements are listed in item 77.

Requirements marked with an asterisk (*) do not apply to electrical systems in which the pressure does not exceed 125 volts A.C. or 250 volts D.C. nor to certain low pressure systems in public supply generating stations and sub-stations.

For information additional to that given below see Form SHW928, Explanatory Memorandum—Electricity Regulations (H.M.S.O.).

69 – General Requirements

All apparatus and conductors must be sufficient in size and power for the work they have to do, and must be so constructed, installed, protected, worked, and maintained as to prevent danger so far as is reasonably practicable. *ER: 1*

* All conductors must either be covered with insulating material and further protected where necessary to prevent danger, or else must be so placed and guarded as to prevent danger so far as is reasonably practicable. Where one of the main conductors of a system is bare and uninsulated, such as the bare return of a concentric system, no switch, fuse or circuit breaker may be placed in that conductor or any conductor connected to it, and the bare conductor itself must be earthed. (This does not prevent the use of a fuse or circuit-breaker to break the connexion with the generators or transformers supplying the power, so long as the connexion between bare conductor and earth is not broken.) *ER: 2 and 10*

Every electrical joint and connexion must be of proper construction as regards conductivity, insulation, mechanical strength, and protection. *ER: 6*

* Adequate precautions must be taken to prevent any metal other than conductors from being electrically charged, if such a charge would create danger. The precautions may consist either of earthing or of some other effective means. *ER: 21*

70 – Fuses, etc.

Efficient means must be provided to protect all parts of the system from excess of current which might cause danger. The means must be suitably located. *ER: 8*

Every fuse and automatic circuit-breaker must be so constructed and arranged as to interrupt the current before it becomes so excessive as to be dangerous. Fuses and automatic circuit-breakers must be so constructed—or so guarded or placed—as to prevent any danger from over-heating, arcing, or the scattering of hot metal or other substance. *ER: 5*

Fuses must be so constructed, or so protected by switches, that the fusible metal can readily be renewed without danger. *ER: 5*

* Fuses and circuit-breakers must not be placed in any bare conductor, or any other conductor connected therewith. (This does not prevent the use of a fuse or circuit-breaker to break the connexion with the generators or transformers supplying the power, so long as the connexion between the bare conductor and earth is not broken thereby.) *ER: 10*

71 – Switches and Circuit-breakers

* There must be some means of cutting off all pressure from every part of the system, so as to prevent danger. Such means must be suitably located. *ER: 7*

* Every switch, switch fuse, circuit-breaker and isolating link must be so constructed, placed or protected as to prevent danger. It must be constructed and adjusted so that it makes and maintains good contact accurately, and must be provided with an efficient handle or other means of working, such handle or other means being insulated from the system and so arranged that the hand of the operator cannot inadvertently touch live metal. Switches, etc., must be so constructed and arranged that they cannot accidentally fall or move into contact when left out of contact. *ER: 3*

* Switches and circuit-breakers must not be placed in any bare conductor, or any other conductor connected therewith (This does not prevent the use of a switch or circuit-breaker to break the connexion with the generators or transformers supplying the power, so long as the connexion between the bare conductor and earth is not broken thereby.) *ER: 10*

* If one conductor of a system is connected to earth, no single-pole switch must be placed in that conductor or any branch of it. (This does not apply to a link used for testing purposes or a switch used in controlling a generator, nor to certain switches and cut-outs in generating stations.) *ER: 9*

* Every switch intended for breaking a circuit, and every circuit-breaker, must be so constructed that it cannot be left in partial contact if proper care is used. This applies to each pole of a double-pole or multipole switch or circuit-breaker. *ER: 4*

* Every switch intended for breaking a circuit, and every circuit-breaker, must be so constructed that an arc cannot be maintained accidentally. *ER: 4*

72 – Switchboards

The general arrangement of every switchboard must, so far as is reasonably practicable, satisfy the following requirements: (*a*) all parts which may have to be adjusted or handled must be readily accessible; (*b*) it must be possible, where necessary, to trace the course of every conductor readily; (*c*) conductors not arranged for connexion to the same system must be kept well apart and, where necessary, must be readily distinguishable; and (*d*) all bare conductors must be so placed as to prevent danger from accidental short circuit. *ER: 14*

* If a switchboard normally has bare conductors exposed so

that they can be touched, it must be fenced or enclosed unless it is in an area accessible only to persons authorised to attend the switchboard. *ER: 15*

* All switchboard apparatus that requires handling must, so far as practicable, be so arranged that it can be operated from the working platform of the switchboard. All measuring instruments and indicators must, so far as practicable, be so placed that they can be observed from the working platform. If it is essential for any apparatus to be worked or observed from any other place, adequate precautions must be taken to prevent danger. *ER: 16*

* If bare conductors are liable to be exposed in such a way that they may be touched, when live, by persons using the switchboard platform or switchboard passage-way, the platforms and passage-ways in question must be so designed as to afford clear and unobstructed passage of ample width and height, with a firm and even floor. *ER: 17*

* Adequate means of access, free from danger, must be provided for every switchboard passage-way. (For the purpose of these regulations, a switchboard passage-way is any passage-way or compartment large enough for a person to enter, and used in connexion with a switchboard when live.) *ER: 17*

* The following additional requirements apply to switchboard working platforms and switchboard passage-ways constructed after January 1st, 1909, unless all bare conductors are protected against danger by divisions, screens, or other means.

If the voltage is 650 or less, platforms and passage-ways must have a clear height of at least 7 ft. and a clear width, measured from bare conductor, of at least 3 ft., and bare conductors must not be exposed on both sides of a passage-way unless those on one side are guarded or the width of the passage-way is increased to 4 ft. 6 in.

If the voltage is over 650 the height is increased to 8 ft. and the width to 3 ft. 6 in., with a width of 8 ft. if there are bare conductors on both sides of a passage-way.

These measurements do not apply to certain operating desks and panels working at a lower pressure than the rest of the board. *ER: 17*

ADDITIONAL REQUIREMENTS FOR SPECIALLY HIGH VOLTAGES—The following additional requirements apply to switchboards used for voltages above 650: (*a*) conductors in passage-ways or within reach of the platform must be so placed or protected as to prevent danger, unless they are working at less than 650 volts; (*b*) the metal cases of all instruments working at over 650 volts must be earthed or else completely enclosed by insulating covers; (*c*) metal handles of switches working at 650 volts or over must be earthed, and other metal gear for working the switches must also be earthed if they would otherwise be dangerous; (*d*) when work is done on the switchboards, the latter must be made dead unless it is so arranged that the work can be done without danger or unless the section on which the work is done is made dead and is isolated or separated from the rest of the board. *ER: 18 and E(FA)R: 4*

73 – Fixed Apparatus

* Every motor, converter and transformer must be protected by efficient means suitably placed and must be so connected that all pressure can be cut off from it. If, however, one point of the system is connected to earth there is no obligation to break the connexion on that side. *ER: 11*

Every electric motor must be controlled by an efficient switch or switches for starting and stopping, so placed as to be easily worked by the person in charge. In every place where electric motors are used to drive machines, there must be a means of switching off the motors or stopping the machines if necessary to prevent danger. *ER: 12*

* Adequate precautions must be taken to prevent the metal parts of fixed apparatus from becoming electrically charged, if such charge would be a source of danger. *ER: 21*

* Adequate working space and means of access, free from danger, must be provided for all apparatus which has to be worked or attended to by any person. All parts of the premises in which there is any apparatus must be adequately lighted to prevent danger. *ER: 25 and 26*

All parts of generators, motors, transformers, or other similar apparatus, if working at more than 650 volts and within reach of any place where persons are working or passing, must be so protected as to prevent danger so far as is reasonably practicable. *ER: 19*

Motors, generators, and all other apparatus which has dangerous moving parts must be securely fenced or safe by position, as described in items 43 to 48.

74 – Portable Apparatus

If any portable apparatus is operated by alternating current of any voltage or by direct current above 150 volts, the flexible wires belonging to it must be connected to the system by permanent joints or properly constructed connectors. *ER: 13*

If the person handling portable apparatus would be liable to get a shock if the metal work of the apparatus became charged, such metal work must be efficiently earthed. The flexible metallic covers of conductors must also be earthed and must not themselves be used as the only earth connexion for the apparatus.

This does not apply to apparatus working below 150 volts direct current nor to all-insulated or double-insulated apparatus certified for the purpose of the regulations by the British Standards Institution and marked to this effect. *ER: 13; the Electricity Regulations (Portable Apparatus Exemption) Order 1968; and Certificate of Approval No. 1 (Factory Form 2332)*

Lampholders of portable lamps must not be in metallic connexion with the guard or other metal work of the lamp. If there is any danger of shock should the metal work become charged, the apparatus must be earthed. *ER: 13*

All portable apparatus working at more than 250 volts must have its metal work earthed independently of any flexible metal cover of the conductors, and such flexible covers must be independently earthed. All such apparatus, and its conductors, must be controlled by an efficient means, suitably located and capable of cutting off the pressure. *ER: 13*

75 – Sub-stations and Transformers

* Every sub-station must be substantially constructed and must be so arranged that no unauthorised person can obtain access otherwise than by the proper entrance or can interfere with the apparatus or conductors from outside. *ER: 30*

* Sub-stations must be ventilated and kept dry. *ER: 30*

* Every sub-station must be under control of an authorised person appointed by the occupier (or a contractor under contract to the occupier) and competent to carry out the work in question. Only the authorised person, or someone under his immediate supervision, may enter any part of the sub-station where there may be danger. *ER: 31*

Underground sub-stations must be provided with adequate means of access. Unless other easy and safe means are available, the means provided must consist of a door or trap-door with a staircase or securely fixed ladder. Ladders and stairs must be so placed that no live part of any switchboard, or any bare conductor, is within reach of persons ascending or descending. Where any person is regularly employed in the sub-station, other than for inspection or cleaning, a doorway and staircase *must* be provided, and the same strict rule applies if the sub-station contains moving machinery (other than ventilating fans) or apparatus working at over 3,000 volts. *ER: 32*

If current above 650 volts is transformed for use at a lower pressure, or if current at a low voltage is transformed for use above 250 volts, precautions must be taken to prevent danger arising through the lower-voltage circuits being accidentally charged with the higher voltage. *ER: 20*

76 – Miscellaneous Requirements

* Insulating stands, screens, boots, gloves, and other suitable means of preventing danger must be provided and used when necessary, and must be examined periodically by an authorised person. *ER: 24*

* Where necessary, insulating stands or screens must be kept permanently in position and maintained in a sound condition. *ER: 23*

Conductors or apparatus exposed to weather, wet, corrosion, flammable surroundings, or explosive atmospheres must be so constructed or protected as to prevent danger arising from their use in such circumstances. Precautions must also be taken if apparatus is used for any special purpose that might create danger. (Details of electrical apparatus officially approved for use in certain specified atmospheres may be obtained from H.M. Factory Inspectorate.) *ER: 27*

No one but an authorised person, or someone under his immediate supervision, must undertake any work in which technical knowledge or experience is required to avoid danger. *ER: 28*

Any repair, alteration, extension, cleaning or other work which might be dangerous to an inexperienced person, or one without technical knowledge, must be done only by an authorised person or a competent adult of 21 or over working under the immediate supervision of an authorised person. Such work must not be done unaccompanied. Where the danger to be avoided is under the control of the occupier, the authorised person must be appointed by the occupier. If a contractor is employed and has control of the danger, it is for the contractor to make the appointment. (The stipulation that those working under the supervision of the authorised person must be over 21 has been waived in the case of persons between 18 and 21 who have either completed an approved apprenticeship or studentship course or are in the third year of such a course.) *ER: 28 and Electricity Regulations (Competent Persons Exemption) Order 1968 (SI 1968 No. 1454)*

Where overhead power lines or other live conductors might provide a source of danger during building operations or works of engineering construction, appropriate precautions must be taken. See item 173.

Electrical apparatus used in rooms where aircraft engines are tested must comply with special requirements. See item 191.

Lamps and torches used when shipyard workers have to work where flammable vapours may be present must be of an approved type. See item 244.

* When persons are working on any conductor or apparatus, adequate precautions must be taken to prevent its becoming charged. There is no legal definition of "adequate precautions" but it may safely be said that it is not sufficient to give verbal warnings to other employees. The removal of fuses, or the padlocking of switches in the OFF position, is the least that is likely to be accepted. *ER: 22*

Instructions for the treatment of persons suffering from shock must be posted up in all premises where electricity is used at over 250 volts D.C. or 125 volts A.C. Wall charts for this purpose can be obtained from H.M. Stationery Office and from various commercial publishers. *ER: 29, amplified by Home Office Order of 18.3.35*

Electrical equipment used in places where cinematograph film is made, repaired, stripped, etc., must comply with additional requirements. See item 193.

77 – Electrical Equipment not subject to Regulations

Electrical equipment in certain rooms with insulated floors is exempt from the requirements of the Electricity Regulations. For this exemption to operate, the only electricity used in the room must be for lighting by means of incandescent lamps at a voltage of 250 volts or less, the floor must be of wood or be otherwise insulated, the room must be free from machinery or other earthed metal with which a person handling unearthed lighting fittings may come in contact, no live conductor must be normally exposed, and no process which makes the floor wet may be carried on. *Exemption Order dated July 28th, 1909*

The following types of equipment are also exempt from the Electricity Regulations:—

(*a*) service lines and apparatus on the supply side of the consumer's terminals, and the chambers containing such lines and apparatus, so long as no live metal is exposed so that it can be touched and that the supply is given from outside the premises and under Board of Trade regulations.

(*b*) Apparatus used exclusively for electro-chemical or electro-thermal or testing or research purposes, so long as the processes are so worked and the apparatus so constructed and protected as to prevent danger.

(*c*) Fixed apparatus which is part of the permanent equipment of a building or ship outside the scope of the Factories Acts, even though such apparatus may be temporarily used during building operations or works of engineering construction or work on the ship.

Certain underground sub-stations in Greater London, specified in an order of May 20th, 1911, are exempt from some of the requirements.

The Minister of Labour has power to exempt other equipment from some or all of the regulations if he thinks fit.

Chapter VII

Lifting Appliances (Design, Construction, Use and Maintenance)

The requirements quoted in this chapter are laid down under the Factories Act, and are for the protection of persons employed. When a lifting appliance is used on or near a public highway, so that members of the general public may be endangered by swinging or falling loads, the occupier has a duty at Common Law to take precautions for the safety of the public and may also have such obligations under local byelaws.

78 – Hoists and Lifts

The following requirements apply to factory hoists in which the movement of a cage or platform is restricted by a guide or guides. The term "hoist" includes lifts. (Hoists used on building sites or in connexion with works of engineering construction are dealt with in item 171.) *FA: 25(1)*

Every hoist must be of good mechanical construction, sound material, and adequate strength and must be properly maintained. *FA: 22(1)*

Hand-operated hoists, and all types of continuous hoist, must be examined by a competent person every 12 months. All other hoists must be examined every 6 months. A report of the examination must be entered on Factory Form 54 and attached to the general register within 28 days. If the examination shows that the hoist cannot be used with safety unless certain repairs are carried out the person making the examination must send a report to the factory inspector within 28 days. *FA: 22(2) and (3) and 25(2)*

Every hoist, except a continuous hoist or a drop-pit hoist used in connexion with railway rolling stock, must be marked conspicuously with the safe working load and must not be used for any heavier load. *FA: 22(8) and HEO*

Hoists used for carrying persons, either with or without goods, must have efficient automatic devices to prevent overrunning. *FA: 23(1)(a)*

If a hoist used for carrying persons, either with or without goods, has a platform or cage supported by ropes or chains. there must be at least two ropes or chains—each separately connected and each capable of supporting the maximum working load. There must also be effective devices to support the fully loaded platform or cage if the ropes or chains fail. (This requirement applies only to hoists constructed or re-constructed after July 1937.) *FA: 23(3)*

Hoistways and Gates (General)—The following requirements apply to all hoists and hoistways in factories, except for the special types mentioned in the table overleaf.

Hoistways must be protected by substantial enclosures fitted with gates, so designed as to prevent any person from falling down the hoistway or coming into contact with any moving part of the hoist. *FA: 22(4)*

Hoistways in buildings constructed after July 1st, 1938, must either have a vent at the top or else be covered at the top by some material easily broken by fire. All other parts of such hoistways, including doors giving access to the hoist or lift, must be constructed of fire-resisting materials. *FA: 48(4)*

Every hoist and hoistway must be so constructed as to ensure that the persons or goods carried are not trapped between the hoist and any fixed structure, or between the counterweight and any other part of the hoist. (This does not apply to hoists which are not connected to mechanical power and are not used for carrying persons.) *FA: 22(7) and HEO: Schedule (7)*

Gates of hoistways must have interlocking devices or other effective means of ensuring that they cannot be opened unless the cage or platform is at the landing, and that the cage or platform cannot move unless the gates are closed. *FA: 22(5)*

If persons are liable to travel in a hoist, either with goods or otherwise, the cage as well as the hoistway must have gates with interlocking or similar devices. (This requirement does not apply to hoists in which the doors of the hoistway are of solid construction and in which both hoistway interior and doors are completely flush and smooth so that there is no danger of trapping.) *FA: 23(1)(b) and HEO: Schedule (11)*

Exceptions and Exemptions—Continuous hoists are not subject to the requirements respecting gates or enclosures, and need not be marked with the safe working load. *FA: 25(2)*

Hoists not connected to mechanical power need not have interlocking devices so long as steps are taken to ensure that the gates are kept closed and fastened when the cage or platform is not at rest at the landing. *FA: 25(3)*

If it is not reasonably practicable to fit interlocking devices to a hoist or hoistway constructed or reconstructed before July, 1937, it is sufficient if the best alternative measures available are taken and the gates are kept closed and fastened when the cage or lift is not at rest at the landing. *FA: 22(6) and 23(2)*

Hoists of the special types shown in the table overleaf are subject to modified requirements as regards enclosures and gates.

Hoists and Hoistways exempt from certain Requirements (see item 78)

TYPE	NATURE AND CONDITIONS OF EXEMPTION
Hoists and hoistways with lattice gates.	The gates will be accepted as satisfying the regulations if, when shut, they extend to the full height and width of the entrance and if (in gates installed since April 1962) the meshes of the lattice do not exceed 2½ inches in width. Measures must be taken to prevent the access of feet through the cage gate or landing gate into the hoistway, and to prevent the access of fingers through the landing gate to reach the interlocking mechanism and control devices.
Hoists into or from which goods or materials are loaded or unloaded automatically, and to the cage of which there is no access for persons.	Gates need not be provided for the opening in the enclosure at which the automatic loading or unloading is done. At the loading and unloading openings, means must be provided to prevent, so far as reasonably practicable, the falls of persons down the hoistway and any contact with a moving part of the hoist.
Hoistways used only for goods and from which goods are loaded or unloaded with the top layer of goods level with the landing.	The enclosure gates need not have the normal type of interlock if the hoistway has a fixed enclosure, not less than 2ft. 9in. in height, below the bottom of the gate and reaching down to the level of the floor or ground. The gate must be such that it can only be opened, or remain open, when the floor of the cage or platform is at the landing level or not more than 5 feet below that level. When the gate is open the cage or platform must not be capable of being moved more than 12 inches at a time and at a speed of not more than 25 feet per minute. Provision must be made to prevent any person being trapped by the top of the cage. The arrangements must be such that when the gate is open the platform or cage cannot be in motion unless the button or other controlling device is being held or pressed by a person close to the gate.
Hoists used only for goods which are loaded or unloaded at a height of 2ft. 9in. above the level of the floor or ground.	The enclosure gates need not have the normal type of interlock if there is a fixed enclosure, not less than 2ft. 9in. in height, below the bottom of the gate and reaching to the level of the floor or ground. Every gate so exempted must be fitted with an efficient device to secure that the cage or platform cannot be raised or lowered unless the gate is closed and will come to rest when the gate is opened. (If such a device is not reasonably practicable the gate must be kept closed and fastened except when the cage or platform is at rest at the opening).
Mobile hoists used in various positions for the stacking of goods, or for loading or unloading directly onto vehicles, and with no fixed landings above the lowest landing.	Enclosures not necessary if the hoist is so constructed that it is stable and if its stability is maintained in all circumstances. If persons are carried and the height of the platform can exceed 6ft. 6in. above ground or floor, the edges of the platform on which persons stand must be protected to a height of at least 3 feet by suitable guard rails, lower rails, and toe-boards, or by other equally effective means. Any gate provided must, unless other and equally effective means are provided, open inwards only towards the platform and must be so arranged that it automatically returns to the closed and fastened position. The control button or other operating device must be so designed that the hoist cannot operate unless the device is being held or pressed by someone on the platform. If such a hoist has a platform raised by ropes or chains, it will be exempt from the requirement to provide duplicate ropes or chains (unless the maximum height of the platform is more than 6ft. 6in. above the ground or floor).
Fixed hoists used for stacking goods or for loading and unloading directly onto vehicles, with no fixed landing above the lowest landing and with a maximum platform height of 6ft. 6in. or less above the ground or floor.	Enclosure and gates need not extend for more than 7 feet above the floor or ground. A cage must be provided if persons are carried.
Hoists used solely for lifting material directly into a machine.	Enclosures and gates not required. Duplicate ropes or chains not required even if persons travel on the hoist.
Platform hoists which are fixed in position and which have a maximum platform height of 6ft. 6in. or less above the ground or floor.	Normal enclosures and gates not required if means are provided (by gates or otherwise) to prevent any person being endangered by the underside of the platform or by any fitting attached to it. Duplicate ropes or chains not required even if persons travel on the platform.
Pavement hoists which are in such a position that the provision of an enclosure at the top landing would obstruct a street, public place, yard, or other open space where persons (including factory workers) are required to pass.	No enclosure need be provided at the top landing but the top of the hoistway must be kept covered or fenced except when access is required for persons or materials. If there is only one landing place other than the top landing the gates at the lower landing need not have interlocks but they must be kept closed and fastened except when the platform or cage is at the landing.
Hoists used mainly for raising materials for charging lime kilns or for charging blast furnaces in which the process of smelting iron ore is carried on.	No gates required at bottom landing, and no interlocks required on any gate. Exemption is also granted from the normal requirement that trapping between fixed and moving parts, etc., must be prevented.
Hoists used for raising, lowering, or tipping standard-gauge or broader gauge railway rolling-stock.	Gates not required for the openings through which rolling stock passes, and no interlocks required on any gates. So far as is reasonably practicable, means must be provided at all entrances to the enclosure to prevent any person from falling down the hoistway or from being struck by any moving part of the hoist.
Drop-pit hoists used for raising or lowering wheels or bogies detached from standard-gauge or broader gauge railway rolling stock.	No enclosure needed. No safe working load need be marked up or observed. Precautions against trapping are not necessary. Over-running devices and duplicate ropes or chains not required.

All the above exemptions are made under the Hoists Exemption Order 1962 (SI 1962 No. 715) as amended by the Hoists Exemption (Amendment) Order 1967 (SI 1967 No. 759).

79 – Cranes and Lifting Machines other than Hoists

The following requirements apply to all cranes, crabs, winches, teagles, pulley blocks, gin wheels, transporters or runways, used in factories.

GENERAL REQUIREMENTS—All parts and working gear, both fixed and movable, must be of good construction, sound material, and free from patent defect. They must be properly maintained and must be examined by a competent person at least once every 14 months. (This requirement includes the anchoring and fixing appliances of the crane or other lifting machine.) *FA: 27(1) and (2)*

If the examination shows that the lifting machine cannot be used with safety unless certain repairs are carried out, the person making the examination must send a report to the factory inspector within 28 days. *FA: 27(2)*

A register must be kept in which the examinations of lifting machines are recorded. This register must show the name and address of the factory occupier; the distinguishing number or mark (if any) of the lifting machine and a description sufficient to identify it; the date of the examination; the name of the examiner; and particulars of any defect which would affect the safety of the appliance, and the repairs needed either immediately or within a specified time. *FA: 27(2) and Lifting Machines (Particulars of Examination) Order 1963*

All dangerous parts of a crane or other lifting machines must be guarded unless safe by position or construction. See item 48.

The safe working load must be plainly marked, and no lifting machine must be loaded beyond the safe working load except when being tested by a competent person. *FA: 27(4)*

Jib cranes must either have an automatic safe load indicator or else have a table attached to them showing the safe working load at various angles and radii. *FA: 27(4)*

Chains, ropes and lifting tackle used with cranes must comply with the requirements quoted in item 81.

TESTS—Before any lifting machine is taken into use for the first time in that particular factory, it must be tested and thoroughly examined by a competent person. A certificate of test, signed by the person making the examination, must be kept available for inspection and must show the safe working load or loads. No method of test is prescribed in the Act but the second schedule to the Shipbuilding and Ship repairing Regulations 1960 (item 244) gives detailed requirements which should be acceptable for lifting machines and tackle in factories. *FA: 27(6)*

ACCESS—So far as is reasonably practicable, safe means of access must be provided to the driver's cabin of any crane or lifting machine, and to such parts of the machine as must be reached for purposes of lubrication, etc. *FA: 29(1)*

TRACKS FOR TRAVELLING CRANES AND TRANSPORTERS—The rails on which a travelling crane moves must be of proper size and adequate strength and must have an even running surface. The same applies to the tracks of a transporter or runway. Rails and tracks must be properly laid, adequately supported or suspended, and properly maintained. *FA: 27(3)*

If any person has to work on or near the track of an overhead crane, and is thus liable to be struck by the crane, effective measures must be taken to prevent the crane approaching within 20 ft. of where the person is working. The means taken may consist of mechanical devices such as stop-blocks, or of a warning system whereby the crane-driver is informed when people are at work on or near the track. It must be said, however, that warning systems often break down owing to the negligence or forgetfulness of some of the employees concerned and, in such circumstances, the Courts will probably hold that the occupier has not taken effective measures. It should also be noted that the occupier's responsibility extends to any contractor's employees who may be working on or near the track; it is not limited to his own employees. *FA: 27(7)*

If any person has to work in any place above floor level, where he is liable to be struck by an overhead travelling crane or its load, effective measures must be taken to warn him of the approach of the crane—unless his work is so connected with the movements of the crane as to make such a warning unnecessary. *FA: 27(8)*

LIFTING MACHINES USED FOR SPECIAL PURPOSES—Cranes used on building sites, or for works of engineering construction, or for the loading and unloading of ships and barges, are subject to special requirements. See items 143 and 165.

When construction operations are carried out in a factory, and the normal factory lifting machinery is used, such machinery is subject to the normal requirements quoted above, with the addition of certain extra requirements set out in item 165.

Lifting appliances used in shipyards are subject to the Shipbuilding and Ship-repairing Regulations 1960. See item 244.

REPORTING OF ACCIDENTS—Under the Dangerous Occurrences (Notification) Regulations 1947 the overturning, failure or collapse of a lifting appliance must be reported to the factory inspector even if no one is injured. See item 296.

80 – Teagles

The following requirements apply to all teagles, whether operated by power or not.

Teagle openings and similar doorways must be securely fenced and provided with a secure hand-hold at each side of the opening. The fencing must be properly maintained and must be kept in position except when the hoisting or lowering of goods is actually being carried on. *FA: 24*

All teagles are classed as lifting machines and must comply with the requirements quoted in item 79. Slings and other lifting tackle must comply with the requirements quoted in item 81.

81 – Chains, Ropes and Lifting Tackle

The following requirements apply to all chains, ropes, chain slings, rope slings, rings, hooks, shackles and swivels, used for the purpose of raising or lowering goods or materials or persons

GENERAL REQUIREMENTS—All chains, ropes and lifting tackle must be of good construction, sound material, adequate strength and free from patent defect. *FA: 26(1)(a)*

Before being used for the first time, all wire ropes, all chains, and all lifting tackle except fibre rope slings, must be tested and thoroughly examined by a competent person. A certificate signed by the person making the test must be kept available for inspection and must specify the safe working load of the equipment in question. *FA: 26(1)(e)*

All chains, ropes and lifting tackle in use must be examined thoroughly by a competent person every 6 months or oftener. *FA: 26(1)(d)*

The safe working load of every chain, rope, and piece of lifting tackle must either be marked plainly upon it or else shown on a table posted up at the store where it is kept and at other prominent positions on the premises. For multiple slings, the safe working load at different angles of the legs must be shown. *FA: 26(1)(b) and 26(2)*

No chain, rope or piece of lifting tackle must be used for any load exceeding the safe working load. *FA: 26(1)(c)*

A register must be kept showing all items of rope, chain, and lifting tackle except fibre rope slings. This register must give the following particulars: name and address of factory occupier; distinguishing mark or number of each item, with a description sufficient for it to be identified by; date taken into use for the first time (if after June, 1938) and the dates of each examination since then; name of person making each examination; particulars of any defects found, if liable to affect the safe working load, and of any steps taken to remedy such defects; dates and numbers of certificates relating to tests and examinations, with the names and addresses of those issuing the certificates; and the dates of annealing or other heat treatment, where applicable. *FA: 23(1)(g) and Chains, Ropes and Lifting Tackle (Register) Order 1938*

ANNEALING—Chains and lifting tackle other than rope slings must be annealed at prescribed intervals, unless covered by one of the exemptions mentioned below.

The prescribed intervals are as follows: For chains and chain slings of ½ in. bar or smaller the interval is 6 months. For chains used in connexion with molten metal, regardless of size, the interval is also 6 months. For all other chains, and for all lifting tackle, the interval is 14 months. Chains and lifting tackle not in regular use, however, need be annealed only as often as is necessary. *FA: 26(1)(b)*

The following types of chain and lifting tackle are exempt from the requirement just quoted, and need not be annealed: plate link chains; chains made of malleable cast iron; pitched chains working on sprocket or pocketed wheels; chains, rings, hooks, shackles and swivels made of steel or of any non-ferrous metal; bordeaux connexions; socket shackles secured to wire ropes by white metal capping; rings, hooks, shackles and swivels permanently attached to pitched chains, pulley blocks or weighing machines; hooks and swivels having screw-threaded parts or ball-bearings or other case-hardened parts; and chains and lifting tackle which has been subjected to normalising instead of annealing. (*Certificate of Exemption No. 1, dated 4.8.38.*)

As mentioned above under General Requirements, the details of annealing and other heat treatment must be entered in the register of lifting tackle.

CHAINS, ETC., USED ELSEWHERE THAN IN FACTORIES—Chains, ropes and lifting tackle used on docks, wharves and quays are dealt with in item 144. Those used on construction sites are dealt with in item 169. Those used in shipyards are subject to the Shipbuilding and Ship-repairing Regulations 1960. See item 244.

Chapter VIII

Other Plant (Design, Construction and Maintenance)

This chapter deals mainly with items of plant, other than machinery, which are normally installed after the actual factory building has been erected. However it is difficult to make a clear division on all occasions between the structure of the factory and the plant installed therein. This chapter should therefore be read in conjunction with Chapter II.

82 – Furnaces and Chimneys

Furnaces installed after December 31st, 1956, must, so far as practicable, be capable of being operated continuously without emitting smoke when burning fuel of a type for which the furnace was designed. Notice that a furnace is to be installed must be given to the borough or district council. *CAA 56: 2*

Furnaces installed between June 1st, 1958 and October 1st, 1969 must be fitted with plant for arresting grit and dust if they are used to burn pulverised fuel or to burn other solid fuel at a rate of 1 ton per hour or more. *CAA 56: 6(1)*

Furnaces installed after October 1st, 1969 must be fitted with plant for arresting grit and dust if they are used to burn pulverised fuel, or to burn any other solid fuel at a rate of 100 lb. per hour or more, or to burn liquid or gaseous fuel at a rate equivalent to 1,250,000 Btu/hr. or more. *CAA 68: 3(1)*

Plant for arresting grit and dust must be approved by the local council or be installed in accordance with plans and specifications approved by the council. *CAA 56: 3 and CAA 68: 6*

When a new furnace chimney is to be built, or the combustion space of an existing furnace is to be increased by enlargement or replacement, application for approval of the chimney height must be made to the local authority. The form of application is given in the Clean Air (Height of Chimneys) (Prescribed Form) Regulations 1969. *CAA 68: 6*

In works subject to the Alkali Works Regulation Act (see item 247) the best practicable means must be used to prevent the escape of noxious or offensive gases by the exit flue of any apparatus. *AWRA: 2*

Cement works and smelting works may be required by the appropriate Ministry to adopt reasonable means for preventing the discharge of any noxious or offensive gases from furnaces or chimneys. *AWRA: 8*

For the operation of furnaces see item 119.

83 – Tanks, Chambers, Flues and other Confined Spaces

The following requirements apply to any chamber, tank, vat, pit, pipe, flue or similar confined space in which persons may have to work and in which dangerous fumes are liable to be present to such an extent as to involve risk.

Unless there is other means of escape, the confined space must be provided with a manhole. On tank wagons and other mobile plant, circular manholes must be at least 16 in. in diameter and other manholes must be at least 16 in. long and 14 in. wide. On non-mobile plant, circular manholes must be at least 18 in. in diameter and others must be at least 18 in. long and 16 in. wide. *FA: 30*

No person must enter such confined spaces unless the specified precautions are taken. See items 119 and 120.

84 – Steam Boilers

The term Steam Boiler includes any closed vessel in which, for any purpose, steam is generated under pressure greater than atmospheric pressure. It also includes any economiser used to heat water that is being fed to such a closed vessel, and any superheater used for heating steam. *FA: 38*

All steam boilers used in factories, building operations, works of engineering construction and in the loading or unloading of ships are subject to the requirements set out below, with the exception of those belonging to H.M. the Queen or used exclusively in Her Majesty's service, those belonging to ships or to locomotives on public railways, those belonging to the United Kingdom Atomic Energy Authority, and those used by the armed forces of other countries while stationed in Great Britain. *FA: 37*

CONSTRUCTION AND MAINTENANCE—Every steam boiler, and all its fittings, must be of good construction, sound material, adequate strength, and free from patent defect and must be properly maintained. *FA: 32(5) and 33(1)*

SAFETY VALVES—Every steam boiler, whether separate or one of a range, must have a suitable safety valve, separate from any stop-valve. The safety valve must be so adjusted as to prevent the boiler being worked at more than the maximum permissible working pressure. The safety valve must be fitted directly to the boiler or as close to it as is practicable. *FA: 32(2)*

A lever valve is not considered to be a suitable safety valve unless the weight is secured on the lever in the correct position. *FA: 32(4)*

There is no need to fit a safety valve to dental vulcanisers complying with the conditions of Certificate of Exemption No. 9 nor to economisers of the steaming type complying with the conditions of Certificate of Exemption No. 21 nor to certain German closed circuit steam generators using distilled water and complying with Certificate of Exemption No. 28; Zimmer KM 300 plastics-coating machines complying with Certificate of Exemption No. 33; Viscomat closed circuit steam generators complying with Certificate of Exemption No. 34; Stott self-generating jacketed boiling pans, complying with Certificate of Exemption No. 39 and the Willert Patent Vapour Cooling System complying with Certificate of Exemption No. 40 are also exempt.

STOP-VALVES—Every steam boiler, except an economiser, must have a suitable stop-valve connecting the boiler to the steam pipe. Independent cast iron sectional boilers used for steam heating by closed pipe systems will be exempt from this requirement if they fulfil the conditions of Certificate of Exemption No. 16: Viscomat closed circuit steam generators will be exempt if they comply with Certificate of Exemption No. 34. *FA: 32(2)*

PRESSURE GAUGES—Every boiler, except an economiser or superheater, must have a correct steam pressure gauge connected to the steam space and easily visible by the boiler attendant. It must indicate the pressure of steam in the boiler in lbs./sq. in. and must have marked on it, in a distinctive colour, the maximum permissible working pressure. *FA: 32(2)*

Every boiler except an economiser or superheater must also have means for attaching a test pressure gauge. *FA: 32(1)*

Pressure gauges are not required on inter-connected steam-water drum and steam generators of the evaporative cooling type complying with Certificate of Exemption No. 32; on Zimmer KM 300 plastics-coating machines complying with Certificate of Exemption No. 33; or on Viscomat closed circuit steam generators complying with Certificate of Exemption No. 34.

WATER GAUGES—Every boiler except an economiser or superheater and the special types referred to below must have at least one water gauge. This must be of transparent material except on externally fired egg-ended boilers, for which a float type gauge may be used. (The Chief Inspector of Factories has power to authorise any other type of gauge if he thinks fit.) *FA: 32(2) and Certificate of Approval No. 1*

If the water gauge is of the tubular glass type, and the pressure of the boiler normally exceeds 40 lbs./sq. in., the gauge must be fitted with an efficient guard. This guard must be so designed that it does not obstruct the reading of the gauge. *FA 37: 29(1)(a)(iv)*

Autoclaves, dental vulcanisers, and some vulcanisers used for repairing tyres need not have a water gauge if they satisfy the conditions laid down in Certificate of Exemption No. 9. This exemption also applies to coil type steam generators covered by Certificate of Exemption No. 27; certain German closed circuit steam generators using distilled water and complying with Certificate of Exemption No. 28; steam-water drum and steam generators of the evaporative cooling type complying with Certificate of Exemption No. 32; electrode boilers, calorifier type boilers, and electrical immersion-heated boilers covered by Certificate of Exemption No. 35; Gilbert steam generators used for baking and complying with Certificate of Exemption No. 30; Zimmer KM 300 plastics-coating machine complying with Certificate of Exemption No. 33; Viscomat closed circuit steam generators complying with Certificate of Exemption No. 34; forced flow once-through steam boilers complying with Certificate of Exemption No. 29; Stott self-generating jacketed boiling pans complying with Certificate of Exemption No. 39; the Willert Patent Cooling System complying with Certificate of Exemption No. 40; and and Benham gas-heated steam jacketed boiling pans complying with Certificate of Exemption No. 44.

FUSIBLE PLUGS—A suitable fusible plug or an efficient low water alarm must be fitted to all boilers except those of the following types: economisers; superheaters; externally fired boilers; cast iron sectional boilers used for steam heating and complying with Certificate of Exemption No. 16; vertical water tube boilers used solely in conjunction with fire engines; cylindrical multi-tubular boilers not exceeding 3 ft. in diameter and fired by town gas or oil and in which the steam and water are contained solely in the space between the tube plates; any steam boiler in which steam is generated solely by means of steam or hot water under pressure passing through a pipe or coil contained in the boiler; boilers heated by electrodes or electric immersion heaters; calorifier type boilers; and Viscomat closed circuit steam generators. *FA: 32(1) and Certificates of Exemption Nos. 10, 16, 18, 26, 34 and 35*

EXAMINATION OF BOILERS—Before a new boiler is taken into use the occupier must obtain a certificate from the maker or from a boiler insurance company or association. This certificate must specify the maximum permitted working pressure of the boiler and must state the nature of the tests to which the boiler and its fittings have been submitted. *FA: 33(5)*

A stationary boiler which has been installed in one factory after previously being used in another must be examined before it is used again. (This does not apply to boilers used in connexion with building operations or works of engineering construction.) *ESB: 4(a)*

Any boiler which has been repaired because of a defect which, in the opinion of a competent person, could have affected its safe working must be examined before being taken back into use. The examination must be carried out by a competent person, who must assure himself that the repairs have been properly carried out. *ESB: 6*

Boilers must be re-examined at the following intervals:

Water-tube boilers of which the drums and any headers are of fusion welded or solid forged construction and which have an evaporative capacity of not less than 50,000 pounds of steam per hour	26 months.
Any boiler in a group of water-tube boilers of the kind described above, where each boiler has an evaporative capacity of not less than 25,000 pounds of steam per hour and the total capacity of the complete group is not less than 100,000 pounds per hour	26 months.
A waste heat boiler or heat exchanger with fusion welded longitudinal and circumferential seams, or a superheater of fusion welded construction, which is an integral part of a continuous flow installation in a chemical or oil refinery processing plant	26 months.
Any boiler other than those described above	14 months.

Certain exemption orders made before June 27th, 1964, under which the re-examination of some boilers could be deferred beyond the periods quoted above, ceased to have effect in June 1967. The above requirements therefore apply in spite of these former exemption orders.

Certain steam boilers in which steam is generated by means of a coolant gas in a system associated with a nuclear reactor are subject to special requirements as to examination; these are set out in Certificate of Exemption No. 48.

REPORTS OF EXAMINATIONS—Reports of examinations must be attached to the general register within 28 days. The report must include the particulars laid down in the Examinations of Steam Boilers Report (No. 1) Order (SI 1964 No. 1070); these include the maximum permitted working pressure and the repairs required (if any). Forms for the purpose of making the reports are available from H.M. Stationery Office; they are Form F 55 (boilers when cold), Form F 55A (boilers under pressure), Form 56 (economisers) and Form 57 (superheaters). *FA: 33(4)*

When the report of an examination shows that the maximum permissible working pressure has been reduced, or that repairs are necessary to ensure the safe working of the boiler, the person making the report must send a copy to the district inspector of factories. *FA: 33(7)*

If the person employed to examine a boiler fails to make a thorough examination, or if he makes a false or deficient report, he will be liable to prosecution. *FA: 33(8)*

If the person making the examination is employed by a boiler-inspection company or association, the chief engineer of the company or association is responsible for sending any necessary report to the factory inspector. The chief engineer will be liable to prosecution if he permits a false or deficient report to be made. *FA: 33(7) and (8)*

IDENTIFICATION OF BOILERS—Every boiler in respect of which a certificate of test has been issued by the makers or insurance company must be so marked that it can be identified as the boiler referred to in the certificate. *FA: 33(5)*

If there is more than one boiler in a factory, each must have a plate bearing a distinguishing number. *FA: 32(2)*

ENTRY INTO BOILERS—When any person has to enter a boiler which is one of a range, special precautions must be taken for his safety. See item 119.

MACHINERY CONNECTED TO BOILERS—Automatic stokers, and any other machinery used in connexion with boilers, must be guarded as described in item 48.

BOILERS USED ON DOCKS—As mentioned at the beginning of this item, boilers used on docks, wharves and quays are included in the scope of the requirements quoted. It should be noted, however, that in these circumstances the responsibility for complying with the law rests with the owner of the boiler and not the occupier of the dock. *FA: 125(2)*

85 – Steam-Tube Ovens and Hotplates

By Certificate of Exemption No. 52 this type of steam boiler used in bakeries is exempted from the provisions of *FA: 32(1)* and *(2)* and *33(2)* and *(3)* which required a pressure gauge, safety valve, etc., but the conditions of the Certificate must be complied with in all respects.

86 – Platen Heating Apparatus

Certain apparatus made to the designs of the Gas Light and Coke Company (now the North Thames Gas Board) to generate steam for heating cast steel platens is exempt from the statutory requirements for steam boilers and steam receivers. Instead it must comply with the detailed conditions of Certificate of Exemption No. 24.

87 – Steam Containers

Every steam container must be so maintained as to secure that the outlet is at all times kept open and free from obstruction. For the purposes of this requirement, a steam container means any vessel (other than a steam pipe or steam coil) constructed with a permanent outlet into the atmosphere or into a space where the pressure does not exceed atmospheric pressure, and through which steam is passed at atmospheric pressure, or at approximately that pressure, for the purpose of heating, boiling, drying, evaporating, or other similar purposes. *FA: 35(7) and (8)*

Requirements for Steam Receivers (see item 88)

TYPE OF RECEIVER	REQUIREMENTS
All except those listed below.	Every part of the receiver must be of good construction, sound material, adequate strength and free from patent defect. If the receiver is not so constructed as to withstand the maximum working pressure of the boiler (or the maximum pressure obtainable in the receiver supply pipe) the following fittings must be provided: (*a*) a suitable stop valve, (*b*) suitable reducing valve or other automatic device to prevent the safe working pressure being exceeded, (*c*) a correct steam pressure gauge indicating the pressure in lbs./sq. in., (*d*) a plate bearing a distinctive number, easily visible, except when only one receiver is in use, (*e*) a suitable safety valve adjusted so that the steam escapes as soon as the safe working pressure is exceeded (or, alternatively, a device which automatically cuts off the steam as soon as the pressure is exceeded). The safety valve and pressure gauge must be on the receiver side of any reducing valve or similar device. A set of receivers supplied from a single pipe may be fitted with a single reducing valve, safety valve, and pressure gauge, so long as the reducing valve is in the single supply pipe. If a set of receivers forms part of a single machine a single stop valve is also sufficient. Receivers and their fittings must be properly maintained and must be examined by a competent person, so far as their construction permits, every 26 months or oftener. A report of every examination, giving the particulars required by Form 58, must be entered in or attached to the general register.
Receivers having a safe working pressure not less than nine-tenths of the maximum permissible pressure of the boiler to which they are connected.	As above, but a reducing valve need not be fitted if the receiver complies with the special conditions of Certificate of Exemption No. 13.
Receivers used in the preheating, pasteurising, and sterilising of milk.	As above, but a reducing valve need not be fitted if additional safety valves or automatic cut-offs are provided as laid down in Certificate of Exemption No. 20.
Dampfer or Indanthrene steamers and "steaming cottages" used in the textile industry.	As above, but reducing valve need not be fitted if the additional safety valves and cut-off prescribed in Certificate of Exemption No. 7 are fitted instead.
Steam heated rolls, the body of which is formed from a single piece of cast iron, steel, or semi-steel, with a thickness of metal equal to at least 1-5th of the bore at the same point.	As above, but identification plate need not be fitted and periodical examinations are not necessary. *CE* 12.
Steam heated tools and dies, heads, moulds, beds or platens of presses, and steam heated dies of extruding machines —but only if the steam passages are drilled. Certain receivers used in the woolcombing industry and listed in Certificate of Exemption No. 25. Steam heated forms or shapes for finishing individual garments or parts of garments in laundries, job dyeing, dry cleaning, and the manufacture, repair, cleaning or renovating of wearing apparel other than hats or caps.	Every part of the receiver must be of good construction, sound material, adequate strength, and free from patent defect. *CE* 25. Every receiver and its fittings must be properly maintained. *CE* 25. No periodical examination is required by law but voluntary examination at regular intervals will be necessary to ensure that the receiver is being properly maintained. *CE* 25.
Steam heated tools and dies, heads, moulds, beds or platens of presses, and steam heated dies of extruding machines (except where the steam passages are drilled or a pressing operation is effected by means of a hand-operated screw). Air heaters used in conjunction with a fan, tubular driers with headers, and radiators (including columnar radiators). Steam heated press jackets. Stretchers or conformers used in making or renovating hats and caps. Steam chambers of Rows patent glue heaters made by Royle's, Ltd. Steam heated portable hand irons used in making, repairing or renovating clothing, in laundries, job dyeing and dry cleaning. Steam heated heads and beds of garment pressing machines used in laundries, job dyeing, dry cleaning, and the making, repair or renovation of wearing apparel (except machines which have a roll or cylinder, or in which the pressing operation is effected by a hand-operated screw).	Every part of the receiver must be of good construction, sound material, adequate strength and free from patent defect. *CE* 25. Every receiver and its fittings must be properly maintained. *CE* 25. If the maximum pressure obtainable in the supply pipe exceeds the safe working pressure of the receiver the latter must have reducing valve, safety valve, pressure gauge, stop valve, and identification plate as described above. These fittings must be examined every 26 months by a competent person. *CE* 25. No other examination is required by law but voluntary examination at regular intervals will be necessary to ensure that the receiver is being properly maintained. *CE* 25.
Steam traps, steam separators, or driers, steam strainers, steam de-superheaters and oil separators covered by Certificate of Exemption No. 17.	Receivers must be properly maintained. Every part of the receiver and its fittings must be of good construction, sound material, adequate strength, and free from patent defect. If not constructed to withstand the maximum pressure that can be obtained, the receiver must have a suitable safety valve adjusted to permit the steam to escape as soon as the safe working pressure is exceeded. This valve may be either on the receiver or in the supply pipe.

88 – Steam Receivers

A steam receiver is defined as any vessel or apparatus used for containing steam under pressure greater than atmospheric pressure—with the exception of steam pipes and coils, steam boilers, steam containers, and parts of prime movers. *FA 37: 35(8)*

Most steam receivers, as defined, are subject to all the requirements set out in Section 35 of the Factories Act 1961, but various special types of receiver have been exempted from some or all of the requirements. The effect of this is shown in the table given on page 45.

89 – Air Receivers

The requirements in this item apply to the following types of plant, all of which are classed as air receivers.

(*a*) any vessel (other than a pipe or coil, or an accessory, fitting or part of a compressor) for containing compressed air and connected with an air compressing plant.

(*b*) any fixed vessel for containing compressed air or compressed exhaust gases and used for the purpose of starting an internal combustion engine.

(*c*) any fixed or portable vessel (except part of a spraying pistol) used for spraying paint, varnish, lacquer or similar material by means of compressed air.

(*d*) any vessel in which oil is stored and from which it is forced by compressed air.

Air pressure tanks used in conjunction with a fire sprinkler installation are exempt from all these requirements. *FA: 36(6) and Certificate of Exemption No. 22*

CONSTRUCTION AND MAINTENANCE—Every air receiver and its fittings must be of sound construction and must be properly maintained. *FA: 36(3)*

If the receiver is connected with an air compressing plant it must either be so constructed as to withstand with safety the maximum pressure of the compressor or else must be fitted with a suitable reducing valve or other device to prevent excess pressure. *FA: 36(1)(b)*

IDENTIFICATION MARKS—If more than one air receiver is in use, each must bear an identification mark. *FA: 36(1)(g)*

SAFETY VALVE AND PRESSURE GAUGE—Every receiver must have a correct pressure gauge, indicating the pressure in lbs./sq. in., and a safety valve so adjusted as to permit the air to escape when safe working pressure is exceeded. *FA: 36(1)(c) and (d)*

Where a set of receivers is supplied through a single pipe, one safety valve and one pressure gauge is sufficient for the whole set, so long as any reducing valve or similar device is fitted to the supply pipe supplying the whole set. *FA: 36(2)*

DRAINING, CLEANING AND EXAMINATION — Every air receiver, except those for oil storage and paint spraying and certain types made by Charles S. Madan and Company, must have a suitable draining appliance. *FA: 36(1) and (6) and Certificate of Exemption No. 31*

Every receiver must have a manhole, handhole, or other means whereby the interior may be cleaned. *FA: 36(1)(f)*

Every air receiver, except certain types used with Monotype machines and covered by Certificate of Exemption No. 23, must be thoroughly cleaned and examined every 26 months or oftener. The examination of solid drawn receivers may be deferred for a longer period if the person making the previous examination has so directed, but the cleaning must still be done after 26 months. If solid drawn receivers are so constructed that the interior cannot be properly examined a hydraulic test must be substituted. *FA: 36(4)*

Oil storage tanks for multiple-head oil fountains are subject to special requirements as regards tests and examinations; these are set out in Certificate of Exemption No. 8.

Air receivers used for "air of exceptional purity" as defined in Certificate of Exemption No. 46 (Form F 2308) are subject to concessions as regards cleaning and examination.

A report of every examination, containing the particulars asked for by Form 59, must be entered in or attached to the general register. *FA: 36(5)*

ACCIDENTS—Under the Dangerous Occurrences (Notification) Regulations 1947, any explosion of an air receiver must be reported even if no one is injured. See item 296.

90 – X-Ray Apparatus and Similar Equipment

Apparatus used for testing materials by X-ray examination, and any other apparatus liable to involve exposure to radioactivity is subject to special requirements. See items 250 to 257.

91 – Fixed Vessels, Sumps, etc.

Fixed vessels, sumps and pits containing scalding, corrosive or poisonous liquids must be securely fenced or covered unless the edge is at least 3 ft. above the ground or platform. See item 18.

The filling of petrol storage tanks is subject to special requirements. See item 102.

92 – Plant containing Explosive Dusts

If any grinding, sieving or other process gives rise to dust which is liable to explode on ignition, all practicable steps must be taken to prevent such explosions by enclosing the plant used and by preventing or removing any accumulation of dust. If practicable, possible sources of ignition must be excluded or enclosed. *FA: 31(1)*

If the plant is not so constructed as to withstand the pressure likely to be produced by an explosion of the dust therein, all practicable steps must be taken to restrict the spread of any such explosion. These means must consist of chokes, baffles and vents, or other equally effective appliances. *FA: 31(2)*

Explosions or fires resulting from the ignition of dust may have to be reported to the factory inspector even if no one is injured. See item 296.

93 – Blasting Enclosures

Every blasting enclosure must have effective exhaust ventilation to remove and dispose of the dust produced and to prevent its escape into any workroom. Every bag used for filtering the dust, and every other filtering or settling device situated in a workroom, must be completely separated from the general air of that room by means of an enclosure ventilated to the open air. *BCR: 9*

Blasting enclosures must be maintained in good condition and all practicable means must be taken to prevent dust escaping from the enclosures and any apparatus connected therewith. *BCR: 7*

In connexion with every blasting enclosure there must be apparatus for separating, so far as practicable, the abrasives used from any other dust or particles of material. Abrasives must not be re-used in the apparatus until it has been separated in this way. (Enclosures constructed before November, 1949, are exempt from this requirement if it is not necessary for anyone to enter them and if it is not reasonably practicable to install separating apparatus.) *BCR: 8*

Every blasting enclosure must be inspected weekly (except during a week in which it has not been used). It must be given a thorough examination and test every month, the purpose of the test being to ensure that the ventilating plant is in order. All such inspections, examinations and tests must be made by a competent person and it should be remembered that a person competent to do a general inspection weekly is not necessarily competent to do the more thorough monthly examination and test. *BCR: 11(1)*

Particulars of every inspection, examination and test must be entered in a register which must be available for inspection by any workman employed in connexion with blasting. *BCR: 11(2)*

Any defect found in the course of any inspection, etc., must be reported to the occupier or other responsible and appropriate person and must be remedied without avoidable delay. *BCR: 11(2)*

Work done in a blasting enclosure must be done in accordance with regulations. See item 133.

94 – Chromium Plating Tanks

Every bath must be equipped with efficient exhaust draught ventilation mechanically operated. This must operate on the vapour or spray as near as possible to its point of origin and must prevent it entering any workroom. The provision of exhaust ventilation does not apply if the liquids in the baths have been treated with a material for the suppression of spray and the temperature of the liquids, and the densities of the current used, are so controlled that there is no emission of spray from the liquids in the bath. *CP: 1*

A test of the efficiency of the measures taken must be done by an approved method once every 14 days. The test must be done by a responsible person whose appointment must be entered in a register kept for particulars of the tests. See Chromium Plating Regulations 1973 and *TDN: 40.*

The floor of every room in which there is a bath must be rendered even and impervious to water. It must be maintained in a sound condition and washed down daily. *CP: 2*

Special washing facilities must be provided in connexion with chromium tanks. See item 35.

Work done at a chromium bath must be done in accordance with regulations. See item 131.

95 – Cabinets and Workrooms - Highly Flammable Liquids

A cabinet or enclosure provided for a process or operation where a dangerous concentration of flammable vapour may reasonably be expected should be provided with mechanical exhaust and be a fire-resisting structure.

When similar work and conditions apply to a workroom it should be a fire-resisting structure and be provided with mechanical ventilation. *HFL* and *LPG: 10*

These requirements now replace those in the revoked Cellulose Solutions Regulations 1934.

All ducts, trunks or casings used in connexion with the means of ventilation must be made of fire-resisting materials. *HFL* and *LPG: 10* and item 130.

Any electrical apparatus used in connexion with cabinets, enclosures and workrooms must be so constructed or protected as to prevent danger through the ignition of vapour. *ER: 27*

Fans used for ventilating must have dangerous parts guarded unless safe by position or construction. See item 48. It should not be forgotten that the blades of a fan are dangerous and must be adequately guarded unless they are completely inaccessible.

Metal containers must be provided for the deposit of cotton waste, cleaning rags, and other materials liable to spontaneous combustion or contaminated with any highly flammable liquid unless these are removed to a safe place immediately.

96 – Plant for Manufacture of Lead Compounds

The following requirements apply to plant used in the manufacture of lead carbonates, lead sulphates, lead nitrates, or lead acetates.

Every lead melting pot must have a proper enclosure fitted with effective exhaust ventilation to prevent dust or fume containing lead from escaping into the air of any workroom. The enclosure must have hinged or sliding doors to cover all openings. *LCR: 9*

Every furnace must be fitted with effective exhaust ventilation to prevent dust or fumes containing lead from escaping into the air of any workroom. *LCR: 9*

Every stove which is entered for the purpose of emptying must have a window, or windows, with a total area of not less than 8 sq. ft., unless the Chief Inspector of Factories has, in writing, approved some other means of ventilation. The windows must be made to open and must be so placed as to admit an effectual through ventilation. In such stoves, racks for bowls must not be more than 10 ft. above the floor. *LCR: 5*

The floor surrounding rollers and open vats, and of any place where dry lead compounds are packed or handled, must be of smooth impervious material and must be kept constantly damp. The same applies to places in which old casks are coopered after having contained lead compounds. *LCR: 4*

97 – Factory Plant for other Special Processes

Machinery and apparatus used for asbestos processes must be kept clean and free from asbestos waste and dust. Such machinery, etc., must have exhaust equipment to prevent asbestos dust entering the air of any workplace (item 228).

Kiers used for boiling textiles in print works, bleaching and dyeing works, and works where cotton and cotton waste is bleached, must be designed and constructed in accordance with the Kiers Regulations 1938. See item 242.

Special requirements apply to the plant used for certain processes in the manufacture of indiarubber (item 200), the manufacture and repair of accumulators (item 205), the manufacture of patent fuel (item 226), the processing of refractory materials (item 227), spinning and weaving (item 239), and the use of radioactive materials (items 254 and 262).

98 – Water-sealed Gasholders

The following requirements apply to all water-sealed gasholders with a storage capacity of 5,000 cu. ft. or more.

Every gasholder must be of sound construction and must be properly maintained. *FA: 39(1)*

If there is more than one gasholder in the factory, each one must be marked in a conspicuous manner with a distinguishing letter or number. *FA: 39(5)*

Every gasholder must be thoroughly examined by a competent person at least once in every 2 years and a record must be entered in, or attached to, the general register. The particulars which must be recorded are specified in the Gasholders (Record of Examinations) Order, 1938. *FA: 39(2)*

If any gasholder has a lift which has been in use for more than 20 years, the internal state of the sheeting must be examined by a competent person at least once in every period of 10 years. The examination must be made by cutting samples from the crown and sides of the holder, or by other sufficient means. Samples, and a report signed by the person making the examination, must be kept available for inspection. *FA: 39(3)*

A record must be kept showing the date of construction of the oldest lift of every gasholder, so far as this can be ascertained. The record must be signed by the occupier or by a responsible person authorised for the purpose, and must be kept available for inspection. *FA: 39(4)*

If any gasholder has to be repaired or demolished, the work must be done under the direct supervision of an experienced person. See item 123.

Chapter IX

Petrol, Explosives, etc. (Storage and Use)

The requirements in this chapter are in addition to the general requirements affecting flammable or explosive substances, mentioned under items 117, 122 and 130.

Petroleum-spirit is subject to the Petroleum (Consolidation) Act 1928, where it is defined as such petroleum as gives off a flammable vapour at less than 73°F. when tested as prescribed by the Act.

Other substances—notably calcium carbide and various compressed gases—are also within the scope of the Petroleum Act. Under the Petroleum (Inflammable Liquids) Order 1971, SI 1971 No. 1040, certain provisions of the Petroleum (Consolidation) Act 1928 are applied to a number of substances other than petroleum spirit. Details are given below.

Explosives are subject to the various Explosives Acts and the orders made under them. Most of the requirements apply to the manufacture of scheduled explosives; the only requirements affecting users are those mentioned in item 111 below.

99 – Petrol used for Vehicles

Petroleum-spirit used solely for motor vehicles may be kept without a licence so long as the requirements quoted in this item are complied with. (The same applies to petrol for motor boats, motor lawn-mowers and rollers, and certain domestic and agricultural plant.) *PMVR: 1(1)*

Not more than 60 galls. must be kept in any one storage place. This amount includes any petrol in the fuel tanks of vehicles which may be in the storage space, and two storage places within 20 ft. of each other must be reckoned as one. *PMVR: 6*

Petrol must not be kept in vessels containing more than 2 galls. each (except fuel tanks of vehicles, etc.) unless the storage place is more than 20 ft. from the nearest building, highway or public footpath and unless provision has been made to prevent the petrol from flowing out in case of fire. *PMVR: 7*

If it is proposed to use containers holding more than 2 galls. the Local Authority must be notified annually. *PMVR: 7*

All containers must be of metal and must be so constructed as to be reasonably secure against breakage and to prevent the leakage of any liquid or vapour. *PMVR: 2*

Any container other than the fuel tank of a vehicle, etc., must have the words "petroleum-spirit" and "highly inflammable" marked indelibly in conspicuous letters. If marking is impracticable, a metal label must be attached bearing the same words. *PMVR: 4*

Unless the storage place is in the open air it must be effectively ventilated to the open air and must be entered direct from the open air. *PMVR: 5(a) and (b)*

Suitable fire-extinguishing apparatus must be kept in the storage place or as near to it as is reasonably practicable. (As an alternative to an extinguisher, a supply of sand or other effective extinguishant may be used.) *PMVR: 5(c)*

The storage place must not form part of, or be attached to, any building used as a dwelling or assembly place unless it is separated therefrom by a substantial floor or partition which is constructed of material not readily flammable and which has no opening in it. (This prohibition of an opening may be relaxed if not more than two 2-gall. containers are kept.) *PMVR: 5(d)*

The storage place must not be under any staircase or other means of exit likely to be required in case of fire, unless it is separated therefrom by a floor or partition as described in the previous paragraph. *PMVR: 5(e)*

If the storage place is within 20 ft. of any building, stack of timber, or other flammable substance the amount of petrol (other than that in fuel tanks of vehicles, etc.) must not exceed two 2-gall. containers unless notice is given annually to the Local Authority. *PMVR: 8*

In all storage places, all reasonable precautions must be taken to prevent any fire, or artificial light liable to cause ignition, from being brought dangerously near to any container. *PMVR: 9*

No operation involving the use of petroleum-spirit must be carried out in the neighbourhood of any fire or any artificial light which is liable to cause ignition. *PMVR: 10*

No petroleum-spirit must be used in any storage place except (*a*) in quantities not exceeding one gill at a time, as a cleaner or solvent or (*b*) as fuel for any lamp or other apparatus used for lighting or heating and so constructed and maintained as to be incapable of igniting any vapour other than the actual fuel of the apparatus. *PMVR: 11*

Vessels which have contained petroleum-spirit must not be repaired until all reasonable precautions have been taken to ensure that the vessel has been rendered free from vapour. *PMVR: 3*

No one must wilfully or negligently allow petroleum-spirit to enter any sewer, or any drain communicating with a sewer. *PMVR: 12*

Special regulations apply when petroleum-spirit is kept by the roadside in connexion with road-making and road repairs. *PMVR: 13*

Petrol kept without a licence may not in any circumstances be offered for sale.

Petrol kept for use in motor vehicles, etc., may be kept under licence from the Local Authority, if desired, instead of under the conditions quoted in this item. See item 100 below.

100 – Petrol for other Purposes (including re-sale)

Except when petroleum-spirit is kept for use in motor vehicles, etc., a licence must be obtained from the Local Authority (unless the total amount is 3 galls. or less and is kept in glass, earthenware or metal containers, securely stoppered and containing not more than 1 pint each.) *PCA: 1(1)*

If the Local Authority refuses to grant a licence, or grants it on conditions which do not satisfy the applicant, an appeal to the Home Secretary may be made. *PCA: 3*

A notice setting out the conditions on which the licence is issued must be displayed on the premises, where it can be read by employees. It must not be removed or defaced. The conditions laid down must be observed at all times. *PCA: 2*

A label conspicuously marked with the words "petroleum-spirit" and "highly inflammable" must be attached to every container or—if this is impracticable—must be displayed near it. The label must also show the name and address of the consignee or owner of the spirit. *PCA: 5*

The conveyance of petrol by road, and the filling of storage tanks from tank wagons are dealt with in item 102.

Precautions against the ignition of petrol during the testing of aircraft engines and accessories are laid down in the Factories (Testing of Aircraft Engines and Accessories) Special Regulations 1952. See item 191.

If loss of life or personal injury is caused by explosion or fire involving petrol stored under licence, a notification must be sent to H.M. Chief Inspector of Explosives, Home Office. *PCA: 13 and 14*

101 – Inspection of Petrol Stores

Inspectors have the right to enter and inspect premises licensed for the storage of petroleum-spirit and any other premises on which they suspect that petroleum-spirit is being kept in contravention of the law. The occupier and his employees must give the inspector necessary facilities. *PCA: 16*

Officers of the Local Authority may take samples of petroleum for the purpose of applying the prescribed test and discovering whether it is petroleum-spirit within the meaning of the Act. *PCA: 17 and 20*

A court of summary jurisdiction may grant a search warrant in respect of premises on which it is believed that petroleum-spirit is illegally kept. *PCA: 18*

102 – Conveyance of Petrol by Road

The conveyance of petrol by road is governed by the Petroleum Spirit (Conveyance by Road) Regulations 1957 as amended by the Petroleum Spirit (Conveyance by Road) Regulations 1958 and amplified by the Inflammable Substances (Conveyance by Road) (Labelling) Regulations, 1971.

CONVEYANCE OF SMALL QUANTITIES—The regulations do not apply to the following:—

(*a*) The conveyance of a quantity of petrol not exceeding 50 gallons and contained in a securely closed steel barrel;

(*b*) The conveyance of a quantity of petrol not exceeding 32 gallons and contained in securely closed metal cans or drums not exceeding 10 gallons in capacity, or in securely closed non-metal containers not exceeding 2 gallons in capacity and so packed or secured as to protect them against breakage;

(*c*) The conveyance of petrol for use only in the vehicle on which it is carried.

CONVEYANCE OF LARGER QUANTITIES—The conveyance of petrol in larger quantities than those mentioned above must (unless conveyance is by tank wagon or trailer) meet the following requirements:—

The vehicle on which the drums, tins, etc., of petrol are conveyed must be strongly constructed, with back and sides of adequate height. If the vehicle is mechanically propelled the engine must be of the internal combustion type and the fuel feed must have a clearly marked quick-action cut-off valve in an easily accessible position, except when certain types of non-gravity feed are used. The engine, fuel tank and electric batteries must be screened from the body of the vehicle by a fire-resisting shield carried down to within twelve inches of the ground and upwards to the level of the top of the cab. If windows are fitted to this shield they must be in fire-resisting framing with wired glass or other approved material and must not be capable of being opened. The exhaust system must be wholly in front of the shield (in certain circumstances the fuel tank may be behind the shield). The lighting system must be under 24 volts and must comply with the requirements laid down in the schedule to the regulations. *PCR: 22(1)*

If a vehicle conveying petrol breaks down, and no other vehicle complying with the regulations is available, a vehicle which does not comply may be used to take the petrol to its destination. *PCR: 22(2)*

The containers must be strong and of metal, in good condition and securely closed. No vessel other than the fuel tank of the vehicle must be filled or emptied on the vehicle. Empty petrol containers, if carried, must be securely closed. *PCR: 22(2) and (3)*

The load must be protected from sparks, lighted matches, etc., by a fire-resisting cover which may be either fixed or loose. *PCR: 24(1)*

No part of the load must project beyond the sides or back of the vehicle nor above the level of the top of the fire shield. *PCR: 24(2)*

A suitable and effective fire extinguisher must be carried on the vehicle. *PCR: 6*

Persons engaged in the conveyance, loading or unloading of petroleum must observe all precautions necessary to prevent fire and explosion and must ensure, as far as reasonably practicable, that no petroleum spirit is allowed to escape into a sewer or drain. *PCR: 2 and 3*

CONVEYANCE IN TANK WAGGONS OR TRAILERS—No trailer other than a tank trailer must be attached to a tank wagon and even a tank trailer must not be attached to a tank wagon of more than 1,500 gallons capacity. *PCR: 18*

The filling pipe of a tank wagon or tank trailer must be kept closed except during filling. Unless the filling pipe has a liquid seal or a device forming an approved flame-trap, the cover of the pipe must be kept locked and the keys carried elsewhere than on the wagon or trailer. *PCR: 12(1)*

The dipping pipe of a tank wagon or trailer must be kept securely closed except during filling or emptying. *PCR: 14*

During filling and emptying, the tank wagon or trailer must be constantly attended by the driver or other competent person of 18 or over. Mechanically propelled wagons must have the engine stopped until the process is over and the tank securely closed. *PCR: 15*

Sound metal piping or sound hose must be used to run petroleum-spirit into or out of tank wagons and trailers. Adequate provision must be taken against the accumulation of static electricity by earthing of the vehicle and the loading arm. *PCR: 15*

Before beginning to fill a tank wagon or trailer, the person in charge of the vehicle must ensure that the tank will receive the quantity it is proposed to run in. *PCR: 16*

No equipment or other articles must be placed in the safety space between the tank and the fire-shield of a tank wagon. No drum, can or other vessel containing petroleum-spirit must be carried on a tank wagon or trailer unless the vehicle is designed for the carriage of containers. *PCR: 17 and 18*

The fuel tank of the vehicle must not be filled direct from a tank wagon or trailer. *PCR: 9*

The cover of the fuel tank of the vehicle must be kept securely closed except during filling. *PRO: 10*

The box containing draw-off taps must be kept closed and locked. *PCR: 13*

Tractors used to draw petroleum-spirit trailers must have a fire-resisting shield similar to those required for vehicles and their electric lighting circuit must comply with the schedule to the regulations. *PCR: 8*

Trailers conveying petroleum-spirit must not be attached to any vehicle other than one intended to carry petroleum and complying with the requirements for such vehicles. *PCR: 12*

The total quantity of petroleum and petroleum-spirit conveyed by a vehicle and trailer combined must not exceed 2,500 galls. *PCR: 8*

Filling of Storage Tanks—Storage tanks must have a distinguishing number. Dip sticks, unless permanently fixed to a storage tank, must also have a number. *PCR: 16*

Where the filling point for a tank is not immediately adjacent to the tank itself it must be marked with the distinguishing number of the tank it serves. *PCR: 16(4)*

A competent person (other than the driver of the vehicle delivering the petrol) must be in charge of the storage tank during delivery. He must ensure that all pipes are securely connected to each other and to the tank, and are otherwise in good order. *PCR: 16(5) and (6)*

The person in charge of the tank, as well as the person in charge of the vehicle, must observe all precautions necessary to prevent fire and explosion. This includes the obligation to ensure, as far as reasonably practicable, that no petrol is allowed to run into a sewer or drain. *PCR: 2 and 3*

The person in charge of the storage tank must fill in and sign two copies of the form prescribed in the schedule to the regulations; this form has spaces for the tank number, the quantity and grade of petrol delivered, and the signature of the person in charge of the tank. One copy of the form must be given to the person in charge of the vehicle; the other must be kept on the premises for 6 months. *PCR: 16(7)*

During the filling of the storage tank, the person in charge of the tank and the person in charge of the vehicle must both keep constant watch on the operation. *PCR: 16(8)*

Other Requirements—The owner of a vehicle used for the conveyance of petroleum-spirit must ensure that every person employed in connexion with it is familiar with the requirements of the Regulations and carries them out. In particular, he must provide every such person with a copy of the Regulations, or, alternatively, display a copy in some place where it can conveniently be read by them. *PCR: 26*

Fires or explosions arising out of the conveyance of petrol must be reported to H.M. Chief Inspector of Explosives, Home Office, if they cause death or injury. The obligation to do this rests with the owner of the vehicle. *PCA: 13*

103 – Loading Petrol in Harbours and Canals

Harbour authorities are required to make byelaws regulating the loading, conveyance and landing of petroleum spirit. *PCA: 7, 8 and 9*

Fires or explosions arising out of the loading or unloading of petrol into ships must be reported to H.M. Chief Inspector of Explosives if they cause death or injury. The obligation to do this rests with the master of the vessel. *PCA: 13*

104 – Petroleum Mixtures

The requirements for petroleum-spirit quoted above apply also to petroleum mixture, i.e., to all mixtures, whether liquids, viscous or solid, which contain petroleum and which, when tested in the prescribed manner, give off flammable vapour at less than 73°F. *PMO: 1 and Schedule*

Instead of being labelled " Petroleum-spirit " and " Highly flammable ", petroleum mixtures must be labelled " Petroleum mixture giving off an inflammable heavy vapour ". *PMO: 3*

If a petroleum-mixture cannot be measured by liquid measure the quantities that can be kept without a licence (see item 100) should be read as 30 lb. in hermetically sealed package or vessels containing not more than 1 lb. in each. All other quantities mentioned should be interpreted as if 1 gall. were equivalent to 10 lb. and 1 pint to 1¼ lb. *PMO: 2 and 4*

105 – Highly Flammable Liquids Regulations

Petroleum spirit and petroleum mixtures with flash-point below 73°F, authorised to be kept by a licence in force under the Petroleum Consolidation Act, 1928, will not be subject to the storage requirements of HFL and LPG (item 130). This is the only exemption for petroleum spirit and mixtures from the HFL and LPG Regulations. *HFL and LPG: 5(4)*

106 – Calcium Carbide

A quantity of calcium carbide not exceeding 5 lb. may be kept without a licence if it is in hermetically closed metal tins with not more than 1 lb. in each. *PCCO: 2(1)*

A quantity not exceeding 28 lb. may be kept without a licence so long as notice is given to the Local Authority and the following conditions observed: the containers must be of metal, hermetically closed, and kept in a dry and well-ventilated place; precautions must be taken to prevent unauthorised persons having access to the carbide; and if a fixed generator is kept on the premises full instructions for its care and maintenance must be displayed where the generator attendant can refer to them. *PCCO: 2(ii)*

Quantities over 28 lb. must not be kept except under licence. *PCCO: 1*

The requirements quoted in item 100 regarding licences, labelling of containers, and reporting of accidents applies to calcium carbide as well as to petroleum-spirit, with the difference that the labels, instead of being marked " petroleum spirit" and "highly flammable" must read "Calcium carbide. Dangerous if not kept dry. The contents of this package are liable if brought into contact with moisture to give off flammable gas." *PCCO: 1 and 3*

107 – Carbon Disulphide

Under the Carbon Disulphide (Conveyance by Road) Regulations 1958 (SI 1958 No. 313) as amended by the Carbon Disulphide (Conveyance by Road) Regulations 1962 (SI 1962

No. 2527), the regulations covering the conveyance of petroleum by road apply also to carbon disulphide if the quantity carried exceeds 28 lb. or if the quantity in any one non-metallic container exceeds 7 lb.

Under the Petroleum (Carbon Disulphide) Order 1958 as amended by the Petroleum (Carbon Disulphide) Order 1968, containers in use or store must be labelled "Carbon Disulphide: highly inflammable" and must be labelled with the name and address of the owner or consignee. When conveyed by road, containers and vehicles must be labelled and marked as required by the Inflammable Substances (Conveyance by Road) (Labelling) Regulations 1971.

108 – Acetylene

Compressed acetylene must be kept in cylinders complying with the Acetylene Regulations 1919, and such cylinders must not be charged except on premises approved by H.M. Inspector of Explosives. All cylinders must be marked with the name of the manufacturer. *AR: 8 and 11*

Mixtures of acetylene with air or oxygen must not be kept or used except in apparatus approved by the Home Secretary or in apparatus where the acetylene/air or acetylene/oxygen mixture takes place only at a burner. *AR: 37*

Liquid acetylene, and acetylene gas at pressures exceeding 9 lb. per sq. in. are prohibited except in such cylinders or apparatus as have been mentioned. *AR: 37*

The conveyance of compressed acetylene by road is subject to the general requirements for the conveyance of compressed gases given in item 109 below.

109 – Other Compressed Gases

Compressed air, argon, carbon monoxide, coal gas, hydrogen, methane, neon, nitrogen, and oxygen, when contained in metal cylinders, must have such cylinders labelled with the name of the gas and the name and address of the firm by whom it was compressed. *PCGO: 1*

Compressed gases used on a vehicle for the purpose of propelling that vehicle are subject to the requirements of the Compressed Gas Cylinders (Fuel for Motor Vehicles) Regulation 1940 (SI 1940 No. 2009).

Any compressed gases conveyed by road are subject to the Gas Cylinders (Conveyance) Regulations 1931 (SI 1931 No. 679) as amended by the Gas Cylinders (Conveyance) Regulations 1947 (SI 1947 No. 1594) and the Gas Cylinders (Conveyance) Regulations 1959 (SI 1959 No. 1919). An exception is made of cylinders whose capacity is equal to not more than 12 lb. of water, and of air receivers used for starting internal combustion engines or compression plant.

Cylinders conveyed by road must comply with the regulations quoted as to their construction, and must be properly maintained. Valves must be securely closed and the cylinders must not project beyond the end of the vehicle. The working or internal pressure of the cylinders must not exceed 1,980 lb. per sq. inch (or 3,000 lb. per sq. inch if the cylinders are of the special type described in the schedule to the 1959 regulations). The contents of the cylinders must be indicated by the prescribed colour code.

Cylinders containing carbon monoxide, coal gas, hydrogen or methane must be specially protected against damage and their valves must have left-handed threads for their pipe connexions.

The obligation to report certain fires and explosions arising out of the conveyance of petrol by road or water (see items 102 and 103) apply also to the loading and unloading of cylinders containing these gases.

The powers of inspection, entry, and granting of search warrants mentioned in item 101 apply to places where these compressed gases are believed to be kept. *PCGO: 1*

110 – Other Substances under the Petroleum Acts

The Petroleum (Inflammable Liquids and Other Dangerous Substances) Order 1947 and the Petroleum (Inflammable Liquids) Order 1971 extend some sections of the Petroleum Act to many other inflammable and explosive substances but the only sections affecting those using or storing such substances is the duty, mentioned in item 100, of reporting fires or explosions causing death or injury.

The conveyance of these substances by road is subject to the Inflammable Liquids (Conveyance by Road) Regulations 1971 and the Inflammable Substances (Conveyance by Road) (Labelling) Regulations, 1971.

Corrosive Substances—Certain corrosive substances come within the PCA so that precautions have to be taken and notices displayed when these substances are conveyed by road—see the Petroleum (Corrosive Substances) Order, 1970 and the Corrosive Substances (Conveyance by Road) Regulations, 1971. (SI 1971 No. 618)

111 – Explosives

For the purpose of the Explosives Acts, the term "explosive" includes gunpowder, nitro-glycerine, dynamite, gun-cotton, blasting powders, fulminate of mercury or other metals, coloured fires, or other substances used or intended to produce a practical effect by explosion or a pyrotechnic effect. The term also includes fog-signals, fireworks, fuses, percussion caps, detonators, cartridges, and ammunition. Picric acid, picrates, and mixtures of picric acid with other substances (when in process of manufacture) are also included unless mixed with not less than half their own weight of water or in quantities below 1 lb. complying with *SRO 1926: 823*

Certificates must be obtained from the police for the storage of any explosive other than gunpowder, cartridges made from gunpowder, and safety fuse. If the total amount exceeds 10 lb. a licence must be obtained from the Local Authority (in addition to the Police certificate) unless the premises are registered under Section 21 of the Explosives Act. *EA 5 and 39 and OC: 6a, 12 and 16*

Licensed explosives stores, and registered premises, must be designed in accordance with the provisions of the Explosives Act.

Explosives used during construction operations must be handled only by a competent person. See item 183.

The use or storage of explosives in offices, or in premises situated immediately below offices, may effect the position in regard to fire certificates. See item 274.

112 – Celluloid and Cinema Film

Factories in which celluloid (or articles made wholly or partly from it) is manufactured, manipulated or stored are subject to the Celluloid Regulations, 1921. See item 192.

Factories in which cinema film is made, repaired, manipulated, used or stored are subject to the Cinematograph Film Regulations 1928. See item 193.

Chapter X

Operations to which Additional Requirements apply

The operations dealt with in this chapter are those which are liable to be carried out in many different types of industry. Operations which are found only in a few highly specialised industries have been omitted, but are listed in Chapter XIII (items 189 to 247).

The requirements quoted in this chapter are additional to the general requirements quoted in the earlier chapters as being applicable to all operations.

113 – Work done Sitting

If persons employed have, in the course of their employment, reasonable opportunities for sitting without detriment to their work, sitting facilities must be provided. These facilities must be suitable and sufficient for advantage to be taken of all opportunities for sitting. *FA: 60(1)*

If a substantial portion of the work can properly be done sitting, each person employed at such work must be provided with a seat. The design, construction and dimensions of the seat must be suitable for the user and the work he is doing. If the user cannot readily and comfortably support his feet without a foot-rest, a foot-rest must be provided. The seat itself must be properly and adequately supported while in use. *FA: 60(2)*

When the seat provided in accordance with the above paragraph is an adjustable one, it must be kept so adjusted that the dimensions are suitable for the particular person using it at that time. *FA: 60(3)*

The Act does not lay down any precise definition of a suitable seat. Some guidance is provided by the Factory Department Booklet No. 45 *Seats for Workers in Factories, Shops and Offices* (H.M.S.O.)

All seats provided under the Act must be maintained. *FA: 60(1)*

When a substantial part of the work in any room is done sitting and does not involve serious physical effort, a temperature of at least 60°F. must be maintained after the first hour and at least one thermometer must be provided and maintained in a suitable position in the workroom. *FA: 3(2)*

Requirements regarding seats for workers in offices and shops are dealt with in item 270.

114 – Lifting of Materials and Goods

No person must be allowed to lift, carry or move any load which is so heavy as to be liable to cause injury. *FA: 72(1)*

Maximum weights for workers of both sexes and various ages are prescribed for potteries (item 203), finishing and dyeing of wool textiles (item 240), and jute spinning (item 239).

If hernia or other injury results through an employee having to lift too heavy a load, this fact may be made the basis of a Common Law action, irrespective of any breach of statutory duty under the Factories Acts. See item 280.

Guidance on lifting and carrying is given in Health and Safety Booklet No. 3 (H.M.S.O.)

The lifting of heavy loads by office workers and shop workers is restricted by the Offices, Shops and Railway Premises Act; see item 270. Similar requirements apply to workers on building sites; see item 182.

115 - Stacking of Materials

If stacks are more than 6 ft. 6 in., precautions must be taken to prevent employees falling from them, so far as is reasonably practicable. *FA: 29(2)*

While there is no specific requirement in the Factory Act regarding the stacking of goods and materials (though for special regulations see the following paragraphs), failure to stack goods securely might, in the event of an accident, entitle the injured employee to damages at Common Law. See item 280.

Furthermore *FA: 29(1)* requires safe access and a safe place of work. See Health and Safety Booklet No. 47 (H.M.S.O.).

Goods and materials must not be stacked so close to any woodworking machinery as to obstruct the working space and cause unnecessary risk. *WWM: 3*

Goods and materials placed within 3 feet of a railway line must be so arranged as not to endanger people passing between the stacks and the track, and must have adequate recesses every 20 yards or oftener. *LR: 9*

Goods and materials must not be stacked in the space immediately around any capstan operated by power and used for hauling wagons. *LR: 20*

The regulations for the smelting of materials containing lead and the manufacture of certain lead compounds (item 199) restrict the extent to which lead and lead compounds may be allowed to remain in workrooms.

Goods stacked on docks, wharves and quays must be so placed as to leave safe access. See item 140.

The regulations for iron and steel foundries lay down requirements for the proper storage of various materials. See item 132.

116 – Processes endangering Eyesight

Under Section 65 of the Factories Act 1961 and the Protection of Eyes Regulations 1938 (SI 1938 No. 654) effective eye protection, consisting of either screens or goggles must be provided for employees engaged in any of the following processes:—

(*a*) the dry grinding of metals or articles of metal applied by hand to a revolving wheel or disc driven by mechanical power;

(*b*) the turning, whether internal or external, of non-ferrous metals, or of cast iron, or of articles of such metals or such iron, where the work is done dry. (This does not include precision turning, if the use of goggles or a screen would seriously interfere with the work. Nor does it include turning by means of hand tools);

(*c*) the welding or cutting of metals by means of an electrical, oxy-acetylene or similar process;

(*d*) the fettling of metal castings involving the removal of metal, when carried out with hand or other portable tools;

(*e*) the chipping or scaling of boilers or ships' plates, when carried out with hand or other portable tools;

(*f*) the breaking or dressing of stone, concrete or slag, when carried out with hand or other portable tools;

(*g*) the cutting out or cutting off of cold rivets or bolts from boilers or other plant, or from ships, when carried out by means of hand or other portable tools. (This does not include the drilling or punching back of such rivets or bolts.)

Eye protection must also be provided for certain work done in the course of building operations and works of engineering construction. See item 180.

Eye protection is also required for certain processes in cement works (item 229), chemical works (item 247), shipyards (item 244), foundries (item 132), and patent fuel manufacture (item 226).

The failure to provide effective eye protection for any of the processes mentioned constitutes a breach of the Factories Act. It does not follow, however, that a process not mentioned above may necessarily be performed without eye protection. If there is danger to the eyes the occupier has a Common Law duty to provide protection even if the particular operation is not mentioned in the statutory regulations. See item 280.

When goggles are provided to meet the requirements of the Factories Act they must be kept in a place where they come easily and obviously to the hand of the workman or, at least, the workman must have been given clear directions as to where he can get them. See *Finch v. Telegraph Company, 1949*

PROPOSED EXTENSION OF REQUIREMENTS—Under proposed new regulations now in draft it is probable that the list of processes for which eye protection is required by law will be extended. Among the processes likely to be added are the breaking of scrap metal, the manufacture of forgings by drop hammer, the routing of metal, the trimming or dressing of abrasive wheels or cylinders, the use of abrasive cutting-off wheels or discs to cut metal or stone, and the handling in open vessels of strong acids or dangerous corrosive liquids or materials.

The proposed new regulations also make more stringent requirements for the use of goggles, eye shields or other personal protective equipment for the eyes. Where such personal equipment is used, each worker exposed to the hazard will have to be supplied with his own goggles, etc. The factory occupier will be required to maintain a stock of spare eye protection in order to replace immediately any that becomes defective and users of such protection will have a statutory duty to report the defects.

117 – Processes producing Harmful or Explosive Dusts

EXPLOSIVE DUSTS—If any process gives rise to dust of such a character and to such an extent as to be liable to explode on ignition, precautions against explosion must be taken by the enclosure of the plant, the exclusion or enclosure of possible sources of ignition, and the removal (or prevention of accumulation) of any dust that escapes in spite of the enclosure. *FA: 31(1)*

Plant in which explosive dusts are present must either be constructed to withstand the pressure likely to be produced by an explosion or else must be provided with baffles, vents and other appliances for restricting the spread of the explosion. *FA: 31(2)*. See Health and Safety Booklet No. 22 (H.M.S.O.).

Electrical apparatus or conductors used in explosive atmospheres must be so constructed or protected as to prevent danger. (Details of electrical apparatus officially approved for certain specified atmospheres may be obtained from H.M. Factory Inspectorate. *ER: 27*

Certain fires and explosions resulting from the ignition of dust may have to be reported even if nobody is injured. See item 297.

OTHER DUSTS—If a process gives off any dust, fume or other impurity which is of such a character and in such quantity as is likely to be injurious or offensive to persons employed, all practicable measures must be taken to protect employees against inhaling the dust, etc., and to prevent its accumulation in the workroom. Where practicable, exhaust appliances must be provided and maintained for this purpose. A factory occupier is expected to keep up to date in his knowledge of the hazards of industrial processes, so that he knows whether or not any particular type of dust, etc., is likely to be harmful. (*See Graham v. C.W.S. Ltd., 1957.*) It should be noted that a particular dust may be harmful because it can cause dermatitis or injure the eyes; the need for precautions is not confined to dusts which are harmful only if inhaled, although this is the principal danger envisaged. *FA: 63(1)*

If a process produces any kind of dust in substantial quantities, whether injurious or not, the precautions mentioned in the last paragraph must be taken. *FA: 63(1)*

DUST FROM PARTICULAR PROCESSES—If lead, arsenic, or any other poisonous substances are so used as to give rise to dust or fume, no person may eat or drink in the workroom nor remain there during meal or rest intervals. Provision must be made for such persons to take their meals elsewhere in the factory. *FA: 64(1) and (3)*

Precautions against harmful dusts are also required by the regulations for the grinding of magnesium (item 128) the grinding of other metals (item 129), foundries (item 132), the blasting of castings (item 133), vitreous enamelling (item 134), building operations and works of engineering construction (item 183) and some of the special operations mentioned in Chapter XIII.

If a process gives rise to siliceous or asbestos dust, the Minister of Labour has power to make regulations preventing persons from remaining in the workrooms during meal intervals, but no such regulations have so far been made. *FA: 64(2)*

NUISANCE TO NEIGHBOURS—If the dust produced in a manufacturing process or other business is prejudicial to the health of the inhabitants of the neighbourhood it becomes a statutory nuisance within the meaning of the Public Health Acts and either the local authority or the aggrieved neighbours can take action.

118 – Work involving Risk of Falls

If a person has to work at a place from which he will be liable to fall more than 6 ft. 6 in. there must either be secure foothold (and secure handhold, if necessary) or else some other means must be provided, so far as is reasonably practicable, to ensure safety. This may consist of fencing.

All ladders used in a factory must be soundly constructed and properly maintained. *FA: 28(5)*

Additional precautions against falls are required when building operations or works of engineering construction are being carried out (items 156 to 164), shipbuilding and repairing (item 244) and docks (items 140 to 142).

119 – Operation of Boilers and Furnaces

EMISSION OF SMOKE—The Clean Air Act 1956 and the Dark Smoke (Permitted Periods) Regulations 1958 prohibit the emission of dark smoke and black smoke from any chimney except during certain periods permitted under the Regulations. (Dark smoke is any smoke which is as dark as, or darker than, Shade 2 on the Ringelmann Chart; black smoke is any which is as dark as, or darker than, Shade 4.)

The periods for which the emission of dark smoke and black smoke is permitted are as follows:—

	Number of furnaces served by chimney*			
	1	2	3	4 or more
Aggregate period of emission of dark smoke during any period of 8 hours within which soot-blowing is carried out	14 mins.	25 mins.	34 mins.	41 mins.
Aggregate period of emission of dark smoke during any period of 8 hours within which soot-blowing is *not* carried out	10 mins.	18 mins.	24 mins.	29 mins.
Maximum continuous period of emission of dark smoke (except during soot-blowing)	4 mins.	4 mins.	4 mins.	4 mins.
Aggregate period of emission of black smoke in any period of 30 minutes	2 mins.	2 mins.	2 mins.	2 mins.

* When a single boiler or unit contains two or more furnaces (as in a Lancashire boiler) the unit counts as one furnace only.

In legal proceedings for a breach of these regulations the occupier can escape conviction if he satisfies the Court that the illegal emission of smoke was solely due to the lighting up of the furnace from cold, or the unavailability of suitable fuel, or some failure of the furnace or plant. *CAA 56: 1*

WORK INSIDE BOILERS AND FLUES—No person may enter a boiler which is one of a range unless precautions are taken to prevent his being scalded by steam or water from another part of the range. The precautions must consist either of disconnecting all inlets through which steam or water could enter or else of closing and locking all valves or taps controlling such inlets. (If the boiler has a blow-off pipe in common with other boilers or delivering into a common blow-off vessel or sump, the blow-off valve or tap on each boiler must be so constructed that it opens with a key which cannot be removed until the valve or tap is closed and is the only key in use for that set of valves or taps.) *FA: 34*

No work must be done in any boiler furnace or boiler flue until it has been sufficiently cooled by ventilation or other means to make the work safe. *FA: 30(10)*

Work done in boiler flues is also subject to the general requirements for all work done in confined spaces where fumes are liable to be present. See item 120 below.

When chipping or scaling of boilers is done with hand tools or other portable tools, adequate eye protection must be provided. The same applies when cold rivets or bolts are cut off or cut out by means of hand or other portable tools. See item 116.

120 – Work in Confined Spaces

PRECAUTIONS AGAINST FUMES—The following requirements apply whenever work has to be done in any chamber, tank, vat, pit, pipe, flue or similar confined space in which dangerous fumes are liable to be present to such an extent as to involve risk of persons being overcome.

Unless the confined space has been certified by a responsible person as being safe for entry, all persons entering it must wear a suitable breathing apparatus and, where practicable, must also wear a belt attached to a rope, the rope being held by someone outside the confined space. No one must enter the confined space unless authorised. *FA: 30(3) and (4)*

A confined space must not be certified as safe for entry unless effective steps have been taken to prevent any ingress of dangerous fumes and unless the space has been ventilated and tested and has an adequate supply of air for ventilation. In addition, any sludge or other deposit liable to give off dangerous fumes must have been removed, and the space must contain no material liable to give off dangerous fumes except where such fumes will only be given off in insignificant quantities. *FA: 30(5)*

If any person enters a confined space without breathing apparatus, because it has been certified as safe, he must be warned of the period for which it will continue to be safe. *FA: 30(4)*

Breathing apparatus, belts and ropes, reviving apparatus, and oxygen must be kept readily available, the breathing apparatus being of a type approved by the Chief Inspector. This equipment must be examined at least once a month by a competent person, and a report of the examination must be kept available for inspection. See the Breathing Apparatus (Examination) Order 1961 (SI 1961 No. 1345). A sufficient number of persons employed must be trained and practised in the use of this equipment and in a method for restoring respiration. *FA: 30(6) and (7)*

For precautions to be taken in other industries before entry into confined spaces, see regulations for shipbuilding and repairing (item 244), chemical works (item 247), and construction (item 152).

The confined space must have a manhole or other means of egress. See item 83.

PRECAUTIONS AGAINST LACK OF OXYGEN—If the amount of oxygen in a confined space is liable to have been substantially reduced, no person not wearing a breathing apparatus must enter it unless it has been ventilated, and remains ventilated, and has been tested and certified by a responsible person as being safe for entry without breathing apparatus. *FA: 30(9)*

ADDITIONAL REQUIREMENTS IN CERTAIN INDUSTRIES—Additional requirements apply to kiers used for boiling textiles (item 242).

Work in excavations, tunnels, shafts, etc., is subject to the Construction (General Provisions) Regulations; see item 177. Work in cofferdams and caissons is subject to the same code of regulations; see item 175.

121 – Opening of Plant containing Inflammable Vapours

If part of a plant contains any explosive or flammable gas or vapour under pressure, no fastening of any joint, pipe or cover must be loosened until the flow of gas or vapour into that part of the plant has been effectively stopped (by stop-valve or otherwise) and all practicable steps have been taken to reduce the pressure of the gas or vapour to atmospheric pressure. *FA: 31(3)*

Once the fastening of any joint, pipe or cover has been removed or loosened, no explosive or flammable gas or vapour must be allowed to enter that part of the plant until the fastening has again been secured. *FA: 31(3)*

The requirements given in this item do not apply to plant which is installed in the open air.

122 – Welding, Cutting, etc.

Acetylene and oxygen cylinders used in oxy-acetylene welding or cutting must comply with the regulations for compressed gases. See items 108 and 109. Under the HFL and LPG Regulations (item 130) cylinders for containing liquefied petroleum gas must be in accordance with Certificate of Approval No. 2 (Form 2437); see also Certificate of Exemption No. 1 (Form 2438), item 130.

Equipment used for electric welding must comply with the Electricity Regulations (see items 69 to 77). Recommendations for the safe use of arc welding equipment are given in the Health and Safety Booklet No. 38 (H.M.S.O.).

Eye protection must be provided for all employees engaged in cutting or welding metals by electricity, oxy-acetylene apparatus, or similar processes. See item 116.

Vessels which have contained petrol must not be repaired until all reasonable precautions have been taken to render them free of vapours. *PMVR: 10*

No plant, vessel, or tank which contains, or has contained, any explosive or flammable substance must be subjected to any welding, brazing, soldering or cutting operation involving the application of heat until all practicable steps have been taken to remove the substance and any fumes arising therefrom, or to render them harmless. For the purpose of this requirement, cutting includes the taking apart of a tank or vessel and its removal from a vehicle, etc. *FA: 31(4)*

After a tank, vessel or other container has been subjected to any process involving the application of heat it must be allowed to cool before being used for any explosive or flammable substance. *FA: 31(4)*

Certain processes are exempt from the requirements regarding plant containing flammable substances, but only if the conditions laid down in the appropriate certificates of exemption are complied with. These processes are welding operations on water-sealed gasholders (CE No. 38); welding operations on steel or wrought iron gas mains and services (CE Nos. 3 and 5) and welding operations on the oil tanks of ships (CE No. 36).

Welding and cutting operations in shipyards are subject to the Shipbuilding and Ship-repairing Regulations 1960. See item 244.

The demolition of tanks, etc., which have contained flammable substances is subject to the Construction Regulations (item 178).

123 – Repair and Demolition of Gasholders

No water-sealed gasholder with a capacity of 5,000 cubic feet or more must be repaired or demolished except under the direct supervision of a person who, by his training and experience and his knowledge of the necessary precautions, is competent to supervise such work. This supervisor must know not only the precautions to be taken against explosion but also the precautions to be taken against gassing. *FA: 39(6)*

During the repair of gasholders, welding operations may be carried on if the conditions of item 122 are complied with or, alternatively, if electric welding only is employed and the gasholder contains only the following gases at more than atmospheric pressure—town gas, coke oven gas, producer gas, blast-furnace gas, and gases, other than air, used in their manufacture. For this alternative to be permissible, the work must be done by experienced operatives under proper supervision. *FA: 31(4) and (5) and Certificate of Exemption No. 38*

124 – Hot or Wet Processes

Hot or wet processes prescribed by the Minister of Labour must not be carried out in an underground room without the written consent of the District Inspector of Factories. So far, none has been so prescribed. *FA: 69(3)*

Processes carried out in a humid atmosphere are subject to special requirements under Section 68 of the Factories Act 1961 and the regulations for the textile industry. See item 239.

Steps must be taken to carry away the steam from the wash-houses in laundries. *FA: 71*

If any process makes the floor wet to such an extent that the wet can be removed by drainage, arrangements for such drainage must be made. *FA: 6*

Work near spouts delivering hot molten metal in foundries is restricted by regulations. See item 132.

125 – Making of Wooden Articles

All woodworking machinery must be guarded as described in items 49 to 51, and operated as described in item 126.

When 500 persons or more are employed in making articles of wood, or in a saw-mill, an ambulance room must be provided. *SMO: 5 and 9*

The ambulance room, when provided under these regulations, must be arranged and equipped as prescribed in the Ambulance and First Aid in Saw-mills Order, 1918 (SRO 1918: No. 1489).

The regulations no longer require an ambulance to be kept on such premises but there must always be available, during working hours, some responsible person or persons whose duty it is to summon an ambulance if needed. Notices indicating who such persons are must be prominently displayed. See the Blast Furnaces and Saw Mills Ambulance (Amendment) Regulations 1961 (SI 1961 No. 2434).

126 – Operation of Woodworking Machinery

All woodworking machinery must be guarded as described in items 49 to 51.

Every person while being trained to work a woodworking machine must be fully and carefully instructed as to the dangers arising in connexion with the machine and the precautions to be observed. *WWM: 9(a)*

No person may be employed at a woodworking machine unless he has been sufficiently trained to work that class of machine or unless he works under the adequate supervision of a person who has a thorough knowledge of the working of the machine. *WWM: 9(b)*

The guards and other appliances must be maintained in an efficient state and must be constantly kept in position while the machinery is in motion, except when, owing to the nature of the work being done, the use of the guards or appliances is rendered impracticable. The guards must be so adjusted as to enable the work to be carried on without unnecessary risk. (This duty is imposed on the occupier and is in addition to the operator's own duty quoted below.) *WWM: 21*

No planing machine which is not mechanically fed must be used for overhand planing unless it is fitted with a cylindrical cutter block. *WWM: 13*

PUSH-STICKS, ETC—A suitable push-stick must be kept available at the bench of every circular saw which is fed by hand. *WWM: 11*

A suitable "spike" or push-stick must be kept available for use at the bench of every vertical spindle moulding machine. *WWM: 19*

For such work as cannot be performed with an efficient guard for the cutter, the wood being moulded at a vertical spindle moulding machine must, if practicable, be held in a jig or holder of such construction as to reduce as far as possible the risk of accident to the worker. *WWM: 18*

ENVIRONMENTAL CONDITIONS—No woodworking machine may be used in any underground room which is certified by the Chief Inspector of Factories to be unsuitable for the purpose as regards construction, light, ventilation or on any other respect. (This regulation has virtually been superseded by Section 69 of the Factories Act 1961 which, as explained in item 15, restricts all work in underground rooms.) *WWM: 7*

The temperature of any part of a room in which a woodworking machine is being worked must not at any time fall below 50°F except where, and in so far as, the construction of the room and the necessities of the business carried on make it impracticable to maintain this temperature. *WWM: 8*

Where the natural light at a woodworking machine is inadequate and can be improved by the provision of additional or better windows not involving serious structural alteration, or by whitening the walls or tops of the factory, or by any other reasonable means, the occupier must take such steps to improve the natural light at the machine concerned. *WWM: 5*

The means of artificial lighting for every woodworking machine must be adequate, and must be so placed or shaded as to prevent direct rays of light from impinging on the eyes of the operator while he is operating his machine. *WWM: 6*

Sufficient clear and unobstructed space must be maintained at every woodworking machine while in motion, to enable the work to be carried on without unnecessary risk. *WWM: 3*

The floor surrounding every woodworking machine must be maintained in good and level condition and, as far as practicable, free from chips or other loose material. It must not be allowed to become slippery. *WWM: 4*

OTHER REQUIREMENTS—Every person employed on a woodworking machine must use and maintain in proper adjustment the guards provided, and must use the spikes, push-sticks or jigs or holders as may be necessary to reduce the danger of injury. (This does not apply when the nature of the work makes it impracticable to use a particular guard or appliance.) *WWM: 23*

The prescribed abstract of the Woodworking Machinery Regulations must be displayed. *FA: 139*

PROPOSED EXTENSION OF REGULATIONS—At present the regulations quoted apply only to circular saws, plain band saws, planing machines, vertical spindle moulding machines and chain mortising machines operating on wood. Proposed new regulations will widen the scope so as to include any such machines when used on any wood products, fibre-board, or cork. These proposed regulations will also include boring machines, chain saws, grooving machines, tenoning machines, trenching machines and lathes (automatic and semi-automatic) in addition to the machines already covered by the regulations.

A proposed new regulation regarding circular saws would provide that, if the saw can be operated at only one speed, the diameter of the smallest blade used must not be less than six-tenths of the largest diameter for which the saw-bench is designed. On multi-speed saws the diameter of the smallest blade would have to be not less than six-tenths that of the largest blade which can properly be used at the fastest working speed.

The new regulations would prohibit the use of a circular saw for cutting a rebate or a tenon unless the part of the blade above the table was efficiently guarded. They would also prohibit the use of a circular saw for cross-cutting material for firewood, unless the wood is firmly held by a gripping device securely fixed to a travelling table.

Another proposed new requirement is that, when a person other than the operator is employed to remove cut material from behind the saw blade, the bench table must be so constructed or extended that the distance between the near edge of the table (or extension) and the back of the blade is at least 1200 millimetres.

PROPOSED REQUIREMENTS FOR PLANING MACHINES—The proposed regulations mentioned above also contain some additional requirements for planing machines. One is that if the wider surface of squared stock is being planed, the underside of the bridge-guard must not be more than 10 millimetres above the upper surface of the material.

It must be made clear that the above requirements are only in draft form at the time of going to press and may not become law in the form quoted here. An inquiry into the draft regulations has been held and the final terms of the regulations will depend on the report of the inquiry.

127 – Operation of Horizontal Milling Machines

Horizontal milling machines must be guarded as described in item 54.

The guards or other appliances required by regulations must be maintained in an efficient state and must be constantly kept in position while the milling cutter is in motion, except when the tool setter is setting up the machine. *HMM: 6*

Every person employed on a horizontal milling machine must use and maintain in proper adjustment the guards or appliances provided in accordance with the regulations. *HMM: 7*

Effective measures must be taken for securing and maintaining sufficient and suitable lighting at the machines, and where artificial lighting is provided the lighting points must be so placed or shaded as to prevent direct rays of light from impinging on the eyes of the operator while he is operating the machine. *HMM: 2*

The floor immediately surrounding every horizontal milling machine must be maintained in good and even condition and kept clear of loose material, and effective measures must be taken to prevent it becoming slippery through the splashing of suds or otherwise. *HMM: 1*

When suds or other cutting lubricants are used on a horizontal milling machine, suitable arrangements must be made to enable the operator to apply the suds or lubricant or to adjust the supply pipe, and suitable means must be provided for removing the swarf. *HMM: 5*

128 – Grinding of Magnesium

The following requirements apply to the grinding or polishing of castings or other articles consisting wholly or mainly of magnesium or of alloys containing more than 20 per cent of magnesium (except during the manufacture of magnesium powder). These processes are also subject to the more general requirements for the grinding of metals quoted in item 129.

Dangerous parts of the machinery used must be guarded as described in item 48.

The occupier must provide and maintain in efficient working order and in good repair all plant and apparatus necessary for compliance with the regulations. *MAG: 4*

None of the processes must be carried out by means of any grinding or polishing device which has been used for abrading iron or other ferrous material, nor must any racing, with a tool capable of causing sparks, be done at any plant used in the processes. *MAG: 5*

Eye protection must be provided for persons occupied in the dry grinding of metals. See item 116.

PRECAUTIONS AGAINST DUST—None of the processes must be carried out without the use of adequate appliances for the interception of the dust as near as possible to the point of origin thereof, and for its safe removal. *MAG: 6*

These appliances must include an adequate extractor fan and duct, and a hood so placed as to intercept substantially all the dust thrown off. There must also be a scrubber in which the dust-laden air is effectively drenched by the time it has travelled a horizontal distance of ten feet from the hood. No scrubber may serve more than one grinding machine, and each scrubber must have an explosion relief. *MAG: 7*

Portable grinders and polishers need not have a hood if the work is done in an enclosure from which dust is removed by exhaust ventilation of the kind described above. *MAG: 7*

There must be an automatic arrangement to ensure that no grinding or polishing device can be started up until the fan and scrubber are in operation. *MAG: 8*

None of the processes must be actually begun on any grinding or polishing device unless the appliances serving that device have been in operation for the immediately preceding five minutes. *MAG: 9*

All dust, sludge and scale deposited in any scrubber used in connexion with the processes must be removed from the scrubber at least once a week, and no tool containing iron or ferrous material must be used for that purpose. *MAG: 10(1)*

Measures must be taken to prevent any dust of magnesium which may remain outside the appliances for the interception and safe removal of the dust from accumulating in work rooms in quantities likely to prove dangerous. Dust removed for this reason must, so far as reasonably practicable, be collected and placed in metal containers with closely fitting metal covers and these containers must be kept in a dry place. *MAG: 10(2)*

Dust, sludge or scale removed from any scrubber used in connexion with the processes must be disposed of without avoidable delay, either by being spread on the surface of the ground in the open air and burned at least 100 feet from any building in which persons are regularly present, or by removal from the factory. (If the material is so wet as to prevent it burning when spread on the ground, it may be burned in an open incinerator at least 100 feet from any such building.) *MAG: 11(1)*

Dust of magnesium, other than dust from scrubbers, must, after collection, be removed from the factory at intervals of not more than one week or be disposed of by burning in accordance with the regulations quoted, or, in so far as it is not so removed or disposed of within a week, be kept in metal containers with closely fitting metal covers in a dry room constructed of fire-resisting material and used only for storage. *MAG: 11(2)*

OVERALLS—The occupier must provide and maintain in good condition, for all persons engaged in the processes or in any other work involving substantial exposure to dust of magnesium, sufficient and suitable overalls of fire-resisting material of smooth surface and close texture and leather aprons with leather bibs. Every such overall and apron must be capable of being instantly taken off by the wearer. It must, when used, be brushed at the end of every shift during which it has been used, and at intervals during the shift if substantial quantities of dust accumulate upon it. If the fire-resisting properties are secured by means of proofing, the overall must be reproofed after every washing. *MAG: 12*

SMOKING AND NAKED LIGHTS—No smoking, open light, fire or other agency capable of igniting dust of magnesium must be permitted at any place less than 20 feet from any of the following: a grinding or polishing device used in the processes; any hood or casing or scrubber used in connexion with the processes; any part of a duct between such hood or casing and scrubber; any outlet for a duct between the scrubber and the open air; or any container in which magnesium dust is kept. (This does not apply if the place is effectively separated from the plant by substantial fire-resisting walls or partitions, nor to any room used for keeping dust of magnesium.) *MAG: 13*

No person must be permitted to smoke when handling dust of magnesium or magnesium sludge or scale. *MAG: 14*

DUTIES OF EMPLOYEES—No person employed in a factory to which these regulations apply may wilfully do anything which is prohibited by the regulations, nor use a tool containing iron or ferrous material for the removal of scale from scrubbers. He must not smoke or use an open light, fire, or other means of ignition within 20 feet of the plant named above, nor must he smoke when handling dust of magnesium or magnesium sludge or scale. *MAG: 15*

Every person engaged in any of the processes must, without delay, report to the occupier or some other responsible person any defect which he may find in any appliance or facility provided under the regulations. *MAG: 16*

129 – Grinding of Metals (General)

The following requirements apply, with certain exceptions, to the grinding or glazing of any metals other than gold, platinum or iridium. They also apply to processes incidental to grinding, and to the cleaning of castings.

EXCEPTIONS—These regulations do not apply to the sharpening of tools or other implements used in the factory so long as no one person is employed wholly or mainly in such work and so long as the sharpening is either carried out in the open air or in a room where such work is not carried out for a total of more than 12 hours in the day periods of any week and 12 hours in the night periods of any week. Such sharpening operations, however, are still subject to the provisions of the main Factories Act, including the obligation to provide protection against harmful dusts quoted in item 117.

These particular regulations do not apply to the manufacture of cutlery, edge tools, swords, bayonets, etc., but these operations are the subject of similar regulations quoted in item 189.

Factories in which only repairs are carried out are exempt from these regulations so far as they effect grinding, glazing, racing, hacking and rodding, so long as no one is employed wholly or mainly in such work and so long as it is done either in the open air or in a room where such work is not carried on for more than 12 hours in any week. As with the sharpening of tools, however, such operations are still subject to the requirements of the main Acts.

BUFFING—Portable grinding machines, portable glazing machines, and portable buffing machines are exempt under Certificate of Exemption No. 5.

PROTECTION OF WORKERS—Dangerous parts of all machinery used in grinding must be guarded as described in item 48.

Effective eye protection, in the form of a screen or goggles, must be provided for dry grinding or any other process endangering the eyesight of the operator or his assistants. See item 116.

ORGANISATION OF WORK—Not more than one person must at any time be allowed to perform the actual operation of grinding or glazing upon any grindstone, abrasive wheel, or glazing appliance. This regulation does not prevent the employment of other persons to assist in the manipulation of heavy or bulky articles. *GM: 3*

SPEED OF WHEELS AND SPINDLES—See item 53 and ABW: 6 and 7.

WET GRINDING—Wet grinding upon a grindstone must not be done in any room in which the height, measured from any part of the floor to the lowest part of the ceiling, is less than 10 ft., nor in which the total window area is less than one-sixth of the floor area; nor unless all the windows are properly glazed and the glass or other material of such windows is maintained whole and kept clean. *GM: 5*

Glazing or other processes, except processes incidental to wet grinding upon a grindstone, must not be carried on in any room in which wet grinding upon a grindstone is done. *GM: 4*

In every room in which wet grinding upon a grindstone is carried on there must be provided and maintained, while work is in progress, either adequate exhaust and inlet ventilation or else a supply of clean water conveyed by pipes and deposited upon the surface of the grindstone, together with suitable arrangements to ensure the drainage of the waste water from the grindstone trough. For the purposes of this regulation the ventilation will not be considered adequate unless (i) it ensures that the air of the room is renewed not less than 12 times per hour; (ii) it is arranged in such a manner as to secure a continuous movement of the air in a direction from the grinder towards the grindstone; and (iii) the fresh air inlets are so arranged and are of such dimensions that no worker is exposed to a direct draught from them. *GM: 2*

PRECAUTIONS AGAINST DUST—Hacking or rodding must not be done unless, during the process, either (*a*) an adequate supply of water is laid on at the upper surface of the grindstone or (*b*) the grindstone is adequately wetted by other means, so as to ensure as far as practicable the suppression of dust, or (*c*) adequate appliances for the interception of the dust are provided. *GM: 6*

Dry grinding, racing and glazing which ordinarily causes dust must not be carried on without the use of adequate appliances for intercepting the dust as near as possible to its point of origin: the appliances must also remove and dispose of the dust in such a way that it does not enter any occupied room. The appliances must include an adequate hood, duct and fan unless some alternative appliances are used which are as effective as a hood, duct and fan. Hoods, where used, must be so designed and arranged as to intercept substantially all the dust thrown off. Ducts must be of adequate size, air-tight, free from obstruction, and provided with a proper means of access for inspection and cleaning; where possible they must also have a connexion at the end remote from the fan to enable a factory inspector to attach a testing instrument. Fans must be capable of producing a draught sufficient to extract the dust. *GM: 1*

Rumbling must not be done unless (*a*) the rumbling appliance is provided with efficient exhaust draught, arranged and maintained so that any dust evolved is prevented from entering any occupied room, or (*b*) such other arrangements are made as will prove to be at least as effective in preventing the dust from entering any occupied room. *GM: 12*

In every room in which racing or grinding upon a grindstone is done the floor, walls, ceiling or top, and all other parts of the room and fixtures must be properly swept or otherwise cleaned at least once in every three months. (This regulation does not apply to any part of the room or fixtures exceeding 14 ft. in height from the floor.) *GM: 7*

In every room or part of a room in which cleaning of castings is done, the walls, ceiling or top, and all other parts of the room (except the floor) and fixtures must be properly swept or otherwise cleaned at least once in every three months. (This requirement does not apply to any part of the room or fixtures exceeding 14 ft. in height from the floor, nor to any room in which no work other than rumbling is normally done.) All accessible parts of the floor must be properly swept or otherwise cleaned at least once every day and for this purpose the floor must be maintained in a smooth and firm condition so as to permit of proper sweeping or cleaning. (This regulation does not apply to cleaning of castings done upon the foundry floor at or near the place where the metal for the castings is poured; or any room wherein the only castings dealt with are those which have been freed from sand elsewhere.) *GM: 10*

A register containing the dates and particulars of all sweeping or cleaning done in pursuance of the regulations and the name and the address of the person performing or supervising the sweeping or cleaning must be kept in a form approved by the Chief Inspector (Form F 89). This register must be available for inspection by any workman employed in any room in respect of which the register is required to be kept. *GM: 11*

All ventilating plant used for the purpose of extracting or suppressing dust must, at least once in every 6 months, be examined and tested by a competent person. Any defect disclosed by such examination and test must be rectified as soon as practicable. *GM: 17(a)*

A register containing particulars of examinations and tests must be kept in a form approved by the Chief Inspector (Form F 89). It must be available for inspection by any workman employed in any room in respect of which the ventilating plant is provided. *GM: 17(b)*

Duties of Employees—Every person who is employed or engaged in any work to which the regulations apply must make full and proper use of all appliances, facilities or accommodation provided for any of the purposes of the regulations. He must report forthwith to the owner, occupier, manager or other responsible person any defect in these appliances. *GM: 18*

No person employed at grinding, glazing, or processes incidental thereto may spit upon the floor, walls or any part of any room in which grinding, glazing or processes incidental thereto are carried on, nor into or upon any apparatus, plant or fixtures in any such rooms. *GM: 8*

Other Requirements—If any grinding, sieving or other process gives off a dust liable to explode on ignition, all practicable steps must be taken to prevent an explosion. The steps include the enclosure of the plant, the removal of dust or the prevention of its accumulation, and the exclusion or enclosure of any means of ignition. *FA: 31(1)*

Unless the plant used in such processes is strong enough to withstand any possible explosion, it must be fitted with chokes, baffles, vents or other effective appliances for restricting the spread of any explosion. *FA: 31(2)*

Eye protection must be provided for those doing dry grinding. See item 116.

Electrical apparatus used in proximity to explosive dusts must be so constructed or protected as to prevent danger of ignition. *ER: 27*

130 - Highly Flammable Liquids and Liquefied Petroleum Gases

The above regulations came into force in 1973 (HFL and LPG, SI 1972 No. 917). This is the first time that special regulations have applied to all the substances as defined and to all industries and processes subject to the FA: 61. The Cellulose Solutions Regulations 1934, and the Felt Hat Regulations 1902 are revoked. The regulations do not apply to premises (or parts of premises) holding a licence under the Explosives Act 1875, and the storage requirements do not apply to certain petroleum substances (see item 105). Furthermore these regulations do not displace the provisions of the Factories (Testing of Aircraft Engines) Regulations 1952. In other respects the regulations are in addition to the requirements of the FA: 61 (see for example item 122).

Other matters to note are: (i) the liquefied petroleum gases (butane and propane) are subject only to Regulation 7 (storage and marking) and Regulation 18 (duties of persons employed); and (ii) the requirements for means of escape in case of fire and fire exits apply to warehouses, docks and construction work (item 7) but not to factories defined in FA: 175 because somewhat similar provisions have applied to factories for many years (see items 1, 2 and 26).

Interpretation—Highly Flammable Liquid (HFL) is any liquid, liquid solution, etc. with a flash-point below 32°C (89.6°F) when tested in accordance with the Schedules to the regulations.

Liquefied Petroleum Gas (LPG) is commercial butane, commercial propane and any mixture of these substances.

Dangerous Concentration of Vapours is a concentration greater than the lower flammable limit of the vapours.

Fire Resisting Structure is a building, cabinet, enclosure, etc. constructed to conform with the Chief Inspector's specification. See Certificate of Approval No. 1 (Form 2434). *HFL and LPG: 2(2)*

Duties—The occupier of the premises is responsible for complying with the regulations. But when the occupier of the premises neither owns the HFL (or LPG) nor employs (or directs) the person using it, the person using it or his employer is responsible and deemed to be the occupier. *HFL and LPG: 3(3)*

Persons employed have duties and must report any defects in plant, etc. *HFL and LPG: 18*

Exemption Certificates—The Chief Inspector of Factories may by certificate grant exemption from any requirement. *HFL and LPG: 4*

Highly Flammable Liquids—HFL must be stored in: (i) fixed storage tanks in safe positions; (ii) suitable closed vessels in a safe position in the open air; and (iii) in a storeroom in a safe position or a storeroom which is a fire-resistant structure. But HFL may be stored in a workroom in closed vessels in a fire-resistant cupboard or bin if the quantity is less than 50 litres (11 gals.). This storage requirement does not apply to: (a) liquids with a storage licence under the Petroleum Act 1928; (b) HFL in tanks of vehicles or engines; (c) suitable small closed vessels containing not more than 500 c.c. of HFL. *HFL and LPG: 5*

Storerooms, cupboards, bins, tanks and vessels used for storing HFL must be marked " Highly Flammable " or " Flash-point below 32°C" or " Flash-point in the range 22°C to 32°C," or with appropriate indication of flammability. This requirement does not apply to small closed vessels containing no more than 500 c.c., to HFL in tanks of vehicles and engines, etc., and to certain aerosol dispensers. *HFL and LPG: 6*

When reasonably practicable HFL must be conveyed within the premises in a closed pipe system. When this is not reasonably practicable the HFL must be conveyed in vessels designed and constructed to avoid spillage. The quantity of HFL in a workplace to be as small as reasonably practicable.

Tanks and vessels must be kept closed except during manipulation of the HFL. Portable emptied tanks and vessels must be removed at once to a safe place, e.g. open air, fire resistant storeroom, etc. *HFL and LPG: 8*

No means of ignition should be present where a dangerous concentration of vapour is expected. Cotton waste or material (cleaning rags) contaminated with HFL must be placed in a metal container or in a safe place. *HFL and LPG: 9*

So far as is reasonably practicable the vapours of HFL should not be allowed to escape into the general atmosphere of any workplace. Where a dangerous concentration of vapour may reasonably be expected to be evolved, a fire-resistant cabinet or enclosure with mechanical ventilation, or a fire-resistant workroom with mechanical ventilation should be used to prevent escape of vapour into any workroom. This latter requirement does not apply if the only work with HFL is work to the room, e.g. decoration. *HFL and LPG: 10*

Steps must be taken to prevent the deposition of solid waste residues from HFL and, if such deposits occur, they should be removed and put in a safe place. An iron or steel implement must not be used to remove residues containing cellulose nitrate. *HFL and LPG: 13*

No one should smoke if there is a risk of fire. Notices prohibiting smoking should be displayed where HFL is present or notices displayed at the entrance to the premises. *HFL and LPG: 14*

Suitable plant is required for igniting HFL whether waste HFL or otherwise. But HFL may be disposed of as waste or burnt for training in fire fighting by a competent person in a safe manner and safe place. *HFL and LPG: 15*

From any room in which HFL is present there should be adequate and safe means of escape in case of fire and appropriate means for fighting fire should be readily available in premises to which this regulation applies. It should be noted that safe means of escape and fire fighting appliances are required under these regulations only for warehouses, docks and construction work (item 7) but similar requirements are required for factories (items 1 and 2) by virtue of FA: 45(d) and 51. *HFL and LPG: 12 and 17*

LIQUEFIED PETROLEUM GASES—As stated above only HFL and LPG: 7 and 18 apply to Liquefied Petroleum Gases.

LPG should be stored in: (i) underground reservoirs or fixed storage tanks or fixed storage vessels either in open air or below ground; (ii) suitable moveable tanks or moveable vessels in safe positions in the open air; or (iii) suitable cylinders in safe positions in the open air or, where this is not reasonably practicable, in a non-combustible storeroom which is either in a safe position or is fire-resistant. A storeroom should not be used other than for storage of LPG and acetylene cylinders.

LPG should not be present in a workplace except in cylinders or pipelines and the number of cylinders and pipelines should be as small as is reasonably practicable.

Every tank, vessel, reservoir, cylinder and storeroom used for storing LPG should be marked " Highly Flammable—LPG " or otherwise to the like effect. If this is impracticable " Highly Flammable—LPG " should be displayed near to it.

This regulation does not apply to LPG in: (i) the fuel tanks of vehicles and engines; (ii) small closed vessels containing not more than 500 c.c.; and (iii) aerosol dispensers where the LPG does not exceed 45 per cent by weight of total contents or 250 grammes by weight.

In this regulation " cylinder " means a cylinder approved by the Chief Inspector of Factories. *Certificate of Approval No. 2 (Form 2437), Certificate of Exemption No. 1 (Form 2438) and HFL and LPG: 7*

DUTIES OF PERSONS EMPLOYED—Every person employed has a duty to co-operate in carrying out the regulations and if he discovers any defect in the plant, etc., to report it without delay. *HFL and LPG: 18*

This regulation applies to HFL and LPG.

131 – Chromium Plating

The following requirements apply whenever any electrolytic chromium process is carried on. This is defined as the electrolytic plating or oxidation of metal articles by the use of an electrolyte containing chromic acid or other chromium compounds.

Chromium baths and the rooms in which they are situated, must comply with the requirements given in item 94. Washing facilities for chromium workers must comply with the requirements given in item 35.

No young person below the age of 18 may be employed at a chromium bath. *CP: 9*

The occupier must provide aprons with bibs for the use of all persons employed and, for the use of those working at a bath, loose-fitting rubber gloves of suitable length, and rubber boots or other waterproof footwear. The aprons and bibs must be of sufficient length and suitable material (for persons working at a bath they must be of rubber, leather or some other impermeable material). All this clothing must be maintained in good condition. *CP: 3*

The occupier must provide and maintain, for the use of all persons employed, suitable accommodation for the storage of the protective clothing, with adequate arrangements for drying it. *CP: 4*

Every person employed must wear the protective clothing provided and must deposit the protective clothing when not being worn in the place provided. *CP: 12*

Hands and forearms must be examined twice a week by a responsible person and a record kept in a register. *CP: 10*

No person employed must misuse any appliance provided under the regulations, nor must he interfere with it in any way except with concurrence of the occupier or a responsible person in charge. *CP: 11*

A supply of drinking water, complying with the requirements set out in item 32, must be maintained at suitable points, conveniently accessible at all times to all persons employed. Each supply must be clearly marked " Drinking water ". *CP: 6*

The floors of every room containing a bath must be rendered even and impervious to water, and must be maintained in a sound condition. They must be washed down daily. *CP: 2*

The official Factory Department placard must be displayed warning employees of the danger of chrome ulceration. *CP: 10*

In addition to the usual First Aid requisites shown in item 39, all First Aid boxes must contain a sufficient supply of waterproof adhesive plaster and of assorted sizes of waterproof adhesive wound dressings. *FA(MI)O: 1960*

Chrome ulceration is one of the industrial diseases which must be notified to the employment medical adviser (see item 296). *TDN 40*

132 – Foundries

These requirements apply to factories and parts of factories where iron and steel castings are produced by casting in moulds or by shell moulding or by centrifugal casting in metal moulds, but not to die-casting or to the production of pig-iron or steel ingots.

The design and layout of the foundry must comply with the requirements quoted in item 24.

Stacking and Arrangement of Equipment — Moulding boxes, loam plates, ladles, patterns, pattern plates, frames, boards, box weights, and other heavy articles kept inside the foundry must be so arranged and placed as to enable work to be carried on without unnecessary risk. *ISF: 4(a)*

Other gear and tools must be kept in racks, bins or other receptacles. *ISF: 4(b)*

Sand, fuel, metal scrap and other materials or residues stored in bulk must be kept in bins, bunkers or other receptacles. *ISF: 4(c)*

Main gangways and pouring aisles must, so far as is reasonably practicable, be kept free from obstruction. *ISF: 6(1)(b) and (2)(b)*

Location of Work — No person may carry out any work within 12 feet of a vertical line passing through the delivery end of any spout of a cupola or furnace used for delivering molten metal, nor within 8 feet of a vertical line passing through the nearest part of any ladle in position at the end of such a spout. (This prohibition does not apply when it is necessary, for the proper maintenance or use of the cupola or furnace, that work should be done within the distances named. Nor does it apply when work is being done at such a time and under such conditions that there is no danger of the person doing the work being splashed by the molten metal.) *ISF: 5*

All knock-out operations must be carried out either (*a*) in a separate room or part of the foundry, equipped so far as reasonably practicable with effective exhaust ventilation and a high standard of general ventilation or else (*b*) in an area of the foundry which has effective exhaust ventilations or, if such ventilation is not reasonably practicable, with a high standard of general ventilation. *ISF: 7(5)*

All dressing and fettling operations must be carried out in a separate room or separate part of the foundry suitably partitioned off or in an area of the foundry set apart for that purpose. In any event, there must, where reasonably practicable, be effective exhaust ventilation or other equally effective means of suppressing dust, operating as near as possible to the point of origin of the dust. *ISF: 7(6)*

Prohibition on certain Types of Fire — Open coal, coke or wood fires of a portable nature must not be used for heating workrooms. *ISF: 7(1)*

Open coal, coke or wood fires must not be used for heating or drying ladles inside a workroom unless adequate measures are taken to prevent, so far as practicable, fumes or other impurities from entering into or remaining in the atmosphere of the room. *ISF: 7(2)*

Open coal, coke or wood fires must not be used for drying moulds except in circumstances in which the use of such fires is unavoidable. *ISF: 7(3)*

Mould and Core Stoves—Mould and core stoves must be so maintained and worked as to prevent, so far as practicable, offensive or injurious fumes from entering any part of a workroom while people are working therein. This also applies to annealing furnaces. *ISF: 7(4)*

Protective Clothing and Equipment—Goggles or other eye protection must be provided for workers engaged in working at the spout of a cupola or furnace, or in attending a cupola or furnace, if there is risk to the eyes from molten metal. They must also be provided for those pouring molten metal or engaged in work which involves risk to the eyes from hot sand being thrown off. *ISF: 8(1)*

Gloves or other hand protection must be provided for those handling hot material likely to cause burns, scalds or sears, and those handling pig iron, rough castings, and other articles likely to cause cuts or abrasions. *ISF: 8(1)*

Respirators of a type approved by the Chief Inspector of Factories must be provided for workers carrying out operations creating a heavy dust concentration, if this concentration cannot be dispelled quickly and effectively by existing ventilation arrangements. Respirators must be marked to show who it is to be used by and no person must wear another person's respirator unless it has been disinfected. *ISF: 8*

See the Foundries (Protective Footwear and Gaiters) Regulations 1971 in Appendix III.

Effective screens or suitable goggles must be provided for the protection of those engaged in the fettling of metal castings involving the removal of metal. See item 116.

Parting Powders—No material may be used as a parting material if it contains compounds of silicon calculated as silica to the extent of more than 3 per cent weight of the dry material. (This prohibition does not apply to the following materials if any one of them is used without the admixture of other silica: natural sand, calcined aluminous fireclay, calcined china clay, calcined or fused alumina, olivine, sillimanite, and zirconium silicate.) *FPM: 4(1)*

Dust or other matter deposited from a fettling or blasting process must not be used as a parting material, nor as a constituent of a parting material. *FPM: 4(2)*

These requirements cover the application of a material to the surface, or parts of the surface, of a pattern or mould to facilitate the separation of the pattern from the mould, or the separation of parts of the mould. *FPM: 2(3)*

Blasting of Castings—The cleaning, smoothing, roughening, etc., of castings is subject to the detailed requirements set out in item 133.

Ambulance Rooms—Foundries in which more than 500 people are employed must have an ambulance room and arrangements for summoning an ambulance carriage. See item 41.

Other Requirements—Requirements concerning the width and surfacing of gangways, and the provision of baths, changing rooms and lockers, are given in item 24.

Persons employed must make full and proper use of all equipment provided under the regulations and must report any defect or loss. *ISF: 8(3)*

Non-Ferrous Metals—The regulations quoted in this item apply only to iron and steel foundries. The melting and founding of brass and other non-ferrous metals is covered by the regulations mentioned in item 224.

133 – Blasting of Castings

The following requirements apply to the cleaning, smoothing, roughening, or removing part of the surface of, any article by means of an abrasive jet of sand, metal shot, grit, or other material propelled by compressed air, steam or a wheel. For this purpose the cleaning of castings means the freeing of the castings from adherent sand or other substance, and includes the removal of cores and the general smoothing of the castings where such freeing is done; it does not include the freeing of castings from scale formed during annealing or heat treatment.

PROTECTION AGAINST HARMFUL DUST, ETC.—No sand or substance containing free silica must be introduced as an abrasive into any blasting apparatus. *BCR: 5*

Blasting must not be done except in a blasting enclosure, and no work must be performed in a blasting enclosure except blasting and work immediately incidental thereto, and the cleaning and repairing of the enclosure and of plant and appliances situated therein. Every door of a blasting enclosure must be kept closed while blasting is being done. *BCR: 6*

The blasting enclosure must comply with the requirements given in item 93.

PROTECTIVE CLOTHING—There must be provided and maintained for the use of all persons who are employed in a blast ing chamber (whether in blasting or in any work connected therewith or in cleaning inside such a chamber) protective helmets of a type approved by certificate of the Chief Inspector. Every such person must wear the helmet provided for his use while he is in the chamber and must not remove it until he is outside the chamber. *BCR: 12(1)*

Each protective helmet must carry a distinguishing mark indicating the person by whom it is intended to be used, and no person must wear, or be allowed or required to wear, a helmet not carrying his mark or a helmet which has been worn by another person and has not since been thoroughly disinfected. Each protective helmet when in use must be supplied with clean and not unreasonably cold air, at a rate of not less than six cubic feet per minute. *BCR: 12(2) and (3)*

Suitable gauntlets and overalls must be provided for the use of all persons while performing blasting or assisting at blasting, and every such person must, while so engaged, wear the gauntlets and overalls provided. *BCR: 12(4)*

Adequate and suitable storage accommodation for the helmets, gauntlets and overalls must be provided outside, and conveniently near to, every blasting enclosure and such accommodation must be kept clean. Helmets, gauntlets and overalls, when not in actual use, must be kept in this accommodation. *BCR: 14*

All helmets, gauntlets, overalls and other protective devices or clothing provided and worn for the purposes of the regulations must be kept in good condition and, so far as is reasonably practicable, must be freed from dust on every week-day on which they are used. Where dust arising from the cleaning of such protective clothing or devices is likely to be inhaled, all practicable measures must be taken to prevent such inhalation. Vacuum cleaners must, wherever practicable, be used for removing dust from such clothing and compressed air must not be used for removing dust from any clothing. *BCR: 15*

The question of making the wearing of protective footwear compulsory for those handling castings is being considered and protective footwear code is now in draft.

RESTRICTIONS ON EMPLOYMENT OF YOUNG PERSONS—No person under 18 years of age may be employed in blasting or assisting in blasting, or in any blasting chamber, or in the cleaning of any blasting apparatus or any blasting enclosure or apparatus or ventilating plant connected therewith, or be employed on maintenance or repair work on such apparatus, enclosure or plant.

No person under 18 years of age may be employed to work regularly within 20 feet of any blasting enclosure in which blasting is done by means of compressed air or steam, unless the enclosure is in a room and he is outside that room and is effectively separated from any dust coming from the enclosure. *BCR: 17*

MISCELLANEOUS REQUIREMENTS—Vacuum cleaning plant used for the purposes of the regulations must be properly maintained. *BCR: 16*

The ventilating plant provided for the purposes of the regulations must be kept in continuous operation whenever the blasting enclosure is in use, whether or not blasting is actually taking place therein. Ventilating plant in a blasting chamber must be in operation when any person is inside the chamber for the purpose of cleaning or repair work. *BCR: 10*

If any person engaged in blasting, cleaning or other work connected with the observance of these regulations finds any defect in any enclosure apparatus, plant, clothing or accommodation provided for the purposes of the regulations, he must, without delay, report the defect to the occupier, manager, or other appropriate person. *BCR: 18*

If any person, while cleaning plant or doing any other work connected with blasting, is liable to inhale dust which has arisen from blasting, all practicable measures must be taken to prevent such inhalation. *BCR: 13*

In cleaning the plant, and the removal of dust from filters and settling devices, all practical measures must be taken to dispose of the dust in such a manner that it does not enter the air of any room. Vacuum cleaners must be provided and used wherever practicable for such cleaning operations. *BCR: 13*

Blasting enclosures must be constantly maintained in good condition, and all practicable measures must be taken to prevent dust escaping from such enclosures, and from any apparatus connected therewith, into the air of any room. *BCR: 7*

134 – Vitreous Enamelling

The requirements quoted in this item apply to all vitreous enamelling of metal or glass except the enamelling of jewellery and watches, the manufacture of stained glass, or enamelling by means of glazes or colours containing less than 1 per cent of lead.

ENAMELLING ROOMS—Rooms in which enamelling processes are carried on must have at least 500 cubic feet of air space for each person employed. In calculating the amount of space, no height above 14 feet may be taken into account. *VER: 1(a)*

Enamelling rooms must be efficiently lighted. For this purpose there must be efficient means of lighting both by natural and by artificial light. *VER: 1(b)*

Floors of enamelling rooms must be well and closely laid and must be maintained in good condition. *VER: 2(a)*

Floors and benches must be cleaned daily and kept free of collections of dust. *VER: 2(b)*

PRECAUTIONS AGAINST DUST AND SPRAY—Enamelling processes which give rise to dust or spray must be done under conditions which secure the absence of dust or spray or else with an efficient exhaust so arranged as to intercept the dust or spray and prevent it from diffusing into the air of the room. *VER: 3*

Dusting or laying on, and brushing or woolling off, must be done over a grid, with a receptacle placed beneath it to intercept the dust falling through. (This requirement does not apply where glaze is applied to a heated metallic surface.) *VER: 4*

FURNACES—If firing is done in a room not specially set apart for that purpose, no person must be employed in other processes within 20 feet of the furnace. *VER: 5*

Effective arrangements must be made to prevent the gases generated in the muffle furnaces from entering the workrooms. *VER: 6*

PROTECTIVE CLOTHING—Suitable overalls and head-coverings must be provided for all persons employed in vitreous enamelling. These must be collected at the end of each day's work and must be cleaned or renewed at least once a week. *VER: 11(a)*

A suitable place, separate from the cloakroom and meal-room, must be provided for the storage of overalls and head-coverings. *VER: 11(b)*

All persons employed in vitreous enamelling must wear the overalls and head-coverings provided, and must so arrange their hair that it is effectively protected from dust by the head-covering. On removing these overalls and head-coverings they must deposit them in the storage place provided. *VER: 14*

CLOAKROOMS AND MESSROOMS—A suitable cloakroom must be provided, separate from the place used for storing overalls and head-coverings, for clothing put off during working hours. *VER: 11(c)*

Unless the works are closed during meal hours, a suitable mealroom must be provided, separate from any room in which enamelling is carried on. *VER: 11(d)*

Persons employed must deposit in the cloakroom all clothing put off during working hours. *VER: 14(b)*

Persons employed must not partake of food, drink, or tobacco in any room in which enamelling is done, nor must they bring food, drink or tobacco into such rooms even if they intend to partake of it elsewhere. *VER: 15(b)*

WASHING FACILITIES—Persons employed must carefully clean their hands before leaving the premises and before partaking of any food. *VER: 14(c)*

Washing facilities must be provided, under cover, and must include a sufficient supply of clean towels (renewed daily), soap and nail brushes. There must either be a washbasin for every 5 persons employed in vitreous enamelling or a trough of sufficient length as to allow at least 2 feet for every 5 persons. *VER: 12*

If washbasins are used they must either have a waste pipe and plug or must be placed in a trough which has a waste pipe. They must have a constant supply of clean running hot and cold water, or warm water. *VER: 12(b) and FA: 35; and Washing Facilities (Miscellaneous Industries) Regulations 1960.*

If troughs are used they must have a smooth impervious surface and must be fitted with a waste pipe without plug. They must have a constant supply of warm water from taps or jets placed above the trough at intervals of not more than 2 feet. *VER: 12(a)*

Washing facilities must be kept in a clean and orderly state and in good repair. *VER: 12 and FA: 35*

MEDICAL INSPECTION—Every person employed in vitreous enamelling must be examined by the employment medical adviser at least once in every 3 months. Due notice of such examinations must be given and persons employed must present themselves for examination at the appointed time. *VER: 9 and 14(a)*

A health register showing the names of all persons employed in vitreous enamelling must be kept. An official form (No. F 605) is published for this purpose. *VER: 8*

The examining doctor has the power to suspend any person from working in any enamelling process. Once suspended, a person must not again work in such a process until written permission from the doctor is entered in the health register. If a suspended person works in an enamelling process without this permission he, as well as the employers, is guilty of an offence. *VER: 10 and 15(a)*

Medical examinations must include a haemoglobin estimation as prescribed by the Lead Processes (Medical Examinations) Order 1964 (SI 1964 No. 1728) and Certificate of Approval F 2199. Copies of the appropriate entry in the health register must be sent to the district inspector within 7 days.

EMPLOYMENT OF YOUNG PERSONS—Young persons between 16 and 18 may be employed, subject to the same regulations as apply to adults working in enamelling processes and subject also to the general conditions applying to all young persons working in factories, as set out in items 257 and 261. *VER: 7*

TAKING OF SAMPLES—A factory inspector may take a sample of any enamelling material in use, or mixed ready for use. No analysis of such a sample may be published without the consent of the occupier, except when necessary in the course of legal proceedings. *VER: 13*

DUTIES OF PERSONS EMPLOYED—Persons employed in enamelling have a legal obligation to use the overalls and head-coverings provided; to clean their hands before taking food and before leaving the works; to present themselves for medical examination at the appointed times; and to abstain from bringing food, drink or tobacco into rooms where enamelling is done. *VER: 14 and 15*

If suspended from working in an enamelling process by the doctor, a person must not resume such work until written authority from the doctor has been entered in the health register. *VER: 15(a)*

It is an offence for an employed person to interfere with the means and appliances provided for the removal of dust or fumes, or to interfere with the carrying out of any of the regulations. No offence is committed, however, if the person employed acts with the concurrence of the manager or occupier. *VER: 15(c)*

135 – Use of Locomotives and Wagons

The following requirements apply to operations carried out on any line of rails which is used for the purposes of a factory and is not part of a public railway system, with the exception of lines less than 3 ft. in gauge and certain other exceptions mentioned in item 20. (Separate requirements may apply when locomotives are used on building sites or in works of engineering construction.) See item 179.

All lines of rails subject to these regulations must be laid out as described in item 20.

RESTRICTIONS ON EMPLOYMENT OF YOUNG PERSONS—No young person under the age of 18 may be employed as a locomotive driver. *LR: 21*

No young person under the age of 18 must work a capstan operated by power and used for the traction of wagons. *LR: 20(c)*

PROVISION AND USE OF POLES AND OTHER APPLIANCES—Coupling poles or other suitable mechanical appliances for coupling and uncoupling must be provided where required. *LR: 5*

Proper sprags and scotches, where required, must be provided for, and used by, persons in charge of the movement of wagons. *LR: 6 and 12*

Wherever it is reasonably practicable without structural alterations, locomotives and wagons must be coupled and uncoupled only by means of a coupling pole or other suitable appliance. (This does not apply if the construction of the locomotives or wagons is such that the coupling and uncoupling can be safely performed without any part of the person's body being between the buffers or ends of one locomotive or wagon and another.) *LR: 11*

MOVEMENT OF LOCOMOTIVES AND WAGONS—Wagons must not be moved on a line of rails by means of a prop or pole when other reasonably practicable means can be adopted. In no case may props be used unless made of iron or steel, or of strong timber hooped with iron to prevent splitting. (This prohibition does not apply to the movement of ladles on furnace rails.) *LR: 13*

Wagons must not be moved by means of a rope or chain attached to a locomotive or wagon moving on an adjacent line of rails, unless no other reasonably practicable means can be adopted. *LR: 13*

When locomotives or wagons are in motion no person must ride on the buffer unless there is secure handhold, and no person must stand on the buffer unless there is both handhold and secure foothold. *LR: 15*

In no circumstances may any person ride on a locomotive or wagon by means of a coupling pole or similar appliance. *LR: 15*

No locomotive or wagon must be moved on a line of rails until the person in charge has given warning to persons whose safety is likely to be endangered. (This does not apply to a self-moving crane inside a building, nor to a charging machine or other vehicle used in or about an actual process of manufacture.) *LR: 16*

When a locomotive pushes more than one wagon and risk of injury may thereby be caused to persons employed, a man must accompany or precede the front wagon if it is safe and reasonably practicable to do so, or else some other efficient means must be taken to obviate risk. (This does not apply to fly-shunting, nor to the movement of wagons used for conveyance of hot material or other dangerous substances.) *LR: 14*

The driver in charge of a locomotive, or a man preceding it on foot, must give an efficient sound signal on approaching any level crossing regularly used by persons employed, or any curve where sight is intercepted, or any other point where there could be danger to persons employed. *LR: 18*

USE OF CAPSTANS—The mechanism of a capstan worked by mechanical power and used for the purpose of traction of wagons on a line of rails must be maintained in an efficient condition. If it is treadle-operated it must be tested daily before use. *LR: 8*

Capstans must not be set in motion until signals have been exchanged between the man in charge of the capstan and the man working the rope or chain attached to it. *LR: 20(b)*

The space immediately around capstans used for traction must be kept clear of obstruction. *LR: 20(a)*

LIGHTING—At places where persons employed have to work or pass on foot, no locomotive or wagon must be moved during the hours of darkness or during foggy weather unless the approaching end, wherever it is safe and reasonably practicable, is distinguished by a suitable light or accompanied by a man with a lamp, or unless the whole area is efficiently illuminated by stationary lights. (The hours of darkness, for this purpose, are from one hour after sunset to one hour before sunrise.) *LR: 17*

Where shunting or other operations likely to cause danger are frequently carried on during the hours of darkness or in foggy weather, efficient lighting must be provided either by hand lamps or stationary lights as the case may require, at all points where such lighting is necessary for safety. *LR: 7*

SMOKE ABATEMENT—The owner of a locomotive must use any practicable means there may be for minimising the emission of smoke from the chimney of the engine. *CAA 56: 19(2)*

The restrictions on the emission of dark smoke and black smoke from furnaces (see item 119) apply also to the emission of smoke from locomotives. *CAA 56: 1 and 19(1)*

MISCELLANEOUS PRECAUTIONS—Lines of rails must be examined periodically and kept in efficient order, having regard to the nature of the traffic. *LR: 3*

No person must cross the line by crawling or passing underneath a train or wagon, if there is a risk of danger from traffic. *LR: 10*

If a wagon or a train of wagons is undergoing repair and persons employed thereat are liable to be endangered by the approach of other wagons or locomotives, a danger signal must be exhibited at or near to the ends of the wagon or train. *LR: 19*

If goods are stacked within 3 feet of a line, and persons employed have to pass over them, or between them and the line, such material must be so placed as to prevent danger as far as practicable and adequate recesses must be left every 20 yards or oftener. *LR: 9*

If a line crosses a road or any other place used by the general public the occupier has a duty at Common Law to take all necessary precautions for the safety of the public. See item 286.

136 – Handling of Food

The requirements summarised in this item apply to every food business. This term includes all manufacturing processes in which persons handle food, and it also includes canteens and shops. *FHR: 2 and 3*

CONDITIONS OF PREMISES—No food business must be carried on in or at any insanitary premises, nor in any premises which, because of their situation, construction or condition, expose food to the risk of contamination. *FHR: 6*

The falls, floors, doors, windows, ceiling, woodwork, and all other parts of the structure of any room in which food is handled must be kept clean and in such a condition as to enable it to be effectively cleaned and to prevent, so far as is reasonably practicable, any risk of infestation by rats, mice, and insects. *FHR: 25*

No room in which food is handled may be used as a sleeping place, and no room which connects directly with a sleeping place may be used for the handling of food which is not in a closed container. *FHR: 24*

All rooms in which food is handled must be suitably and sufficiently lighted and, unless they are humidity-controlled or temperature-controlled, must have sufficient and suitable ventilation. *FHR: 22 and 23*

Accommodation for Clothing—Unless adequate provision is made elsewhere, all rooms in which food is handled must have suitable and sufficient cupboards or lockers for clothing and footwear not worn during working hours by those handling food. *FHR: 20*

Water Supply—A sufficient supply of clean and wholesome water must be provided. The supply must be constant in all premises where such a supply is practicable and is in accordance with good practice in businesses of a similar class or type. *FHR: 17*

Washing Facilities—Sufficient and suitable washbasins must be provided, in a conveniently accessible position, for all persons engaged in handling food. Adequate supplies of soap or other detergent, nail brushes, and clean towels or other suitable drying facilities, must be provided for each basin. *FHR: 18*

In addition to the washbasins for personal cleanliness mentioned in the previous paragraph, there must be sufficient sinks or other facilities for washing food and equipment (except in premises where no open food is handled). *FHR: 21*

Both the washbasins for personal cleanliness and the facilities for washing food and equipment must have an adequate supply of hot and cold water, or of hot water only at a controlled temperature. Hot water need not, however, be provided for apparatus used only for washing drinking vessels with a suitable bacterial agent, nor to sinks or other facilities used only for washing fruit, vegetables, or fish.

If there is no open food handled, the washbasins for personal cleanliness need not have hot water so far as the Food Hygiene Regulations are concerned but on factory premises some basins with hot water will be required to meet the requirements of the Factories Acts, as explained in item 34. *FHR: 18 and 21*

All washbasins, sinks and other washing facilities, including all traps and connexions for washbasins, must be kept clean and in efficient working order. *FHR: 18 and 21*

Drainage and Sanitary Conveniences—A fresh-air intake of a ventilation pipe included in the soil-drainage system of food premises must not be situated in a room in which food is handled. Inlets to such soil-drainage systems, if situated in any food room, must be trapped. *FHR: 14*

Sanitary conveniences situated in, or regularly used in connexion with, a food business must be kept clean and in efficient order and must be so placed that no offensive odours from them can penetrate any room in which food is handled. If the cistern supplying a sanitary convenience also supplies a food room, a flushing apparatus must be used to ensure that the water supply is not contaminated. *FHR: 15 and 16*

A room or other place which contains a sanitary convenience must be suitably and sufficiently lighted and ventilated and must be kept clean. No food may be handled in such rooms. *FHR: 16(2) and (3)*

If a room in which food is handled communicates directly with a room or place containing a sanitary convenience, it must not be used for the handling of uncovered food or for the cleaning of equipment used for food. *FHR: 16(4)*

A clearly legible notice requesting users to wash their hands must be displayed in a prominent position near every sanitary convenience regularly used by persons handling food. *FHR: 16(5)*

Prevention of Contamination—Equipment with which food is liable to come into contact must be of such construction, material and condition as will enable it to be thoroughly cleaned and will prevent, as far as is reasonably practicable, the contamination of the food and the absorption of any matter by the equipment. All such equipment must be kept clean. *FHR: 7(1)*

All food containers, except non-returnable containers, must be protected and kept free from contamination, so far as is reasonably practicable. This applies even if the food does not come into direct contact with the container. *FHR: 7(2)*

Paper and other wrapping material used for wrapping food must be clean and must not be of such a nature as to involve the risk of contamination. No printed paper or other printed material must be allowed to come into contact with food (other than uncooked vegetables) unless it is printed material designed exclusively for wrapping food. *FHR: 12(b)*

Food must not be carried in any container on vehicles which also contain any article liable to contaminate it, or which contain any animals or live poultry, unless all practicable steps are taken to avoid contamination. *FHR: 12(a)*

Food must not be placed anywhere where it will be in danger of contamination. In forecourts, yards, etc., it must not be placed less than 18 inches from the ground unless it is adequately protected from risk of contamination. *FHR: 9*

When meat is carried, otherwise than in a closed container, persons carrying it must wear overalls and, if necessary, head-coverings. (See below under "Duties of Persons Employed".)

No refuse or filth, either solid or liquid, must be allowed to accumulate in any food room, except so far as may be unavoidable for the proper carrying on of the trade or business. *FHR: 26(2)*

Duties of Persons Employed—Persons handling food must keep themselves and their clothing as clean as is reasonably practicable, and must cover with a suitable waterproof dressing any open cut or abrasion on any exposed part of their bodies. *FHR: 10*

Persons handling food must not spit and, while near uncovered food, must refrain from using snuff, tobacco, or any other smoking mixture. It has been held in Court that a man with an unlit cigarette in his mouth was "using" tobacco; the same would presumably apply to an unlit pipe. *FHR: 10*

Persons handling food must take all reasonably necessary steps to protect it from risk of contamination. *FHR: 9*

If a person handling food discovers he is suffering from or carrying any of the diseases mentioned below under "Infectious Diseases" he must notify his employer, who must in turn notify the medical officer of health. *FHR: 13*

FIRST AID—In addition to the First Aid requisites provided under the Factories Acts (see items 38 and 39), waterproof dressings and antiseptic must be readily available for all persons handling food. *FHR: 19*

INFECTIOUS DISEASE—The medical officer of health must be notified if any person handling food is known to be suffering from, or is a carrier of, typhoid fever, paratyphoid fever or any other salmonella infection or dysentery or any staphylococcal infection likely to cause food poisoning. *FHR: 13*

TEMPERATURE OF FOOD IN CATERING ESTABLISHMENTS—In premises used for a catering business (including a canteen) the foods mentioned below must, as soon as possible after being brought on to the premises, be brought to a temperature which is either above 145°F. or below 50°F. When such foods have been cooked or partly cooked on the premises they must, unless immediately required, either be left at or above 145°F. or else be cooled as quickly as possible to below 50°F. and must be kept at one or other of such temperatures until they are either required for service or further cooked or prepared. *FHR: 27*

Generally speaking, the foods to which these requirements apply are meat, fish, gravy, imitation cream, foods made from or containing any of those substances, and food containing or made from milk or eggs in any form. The following, however, are *not* subject to the requirements, even though they may be within the general definition just quoted:

(*a*) bread, biscuits, cake or pastry in which the only use made of the substances mentioned above has been in the form of egg or milk introduced prior to baking;

(*b*) chocolate or sugar confectionery;

(*c*) ice-cream covered by the provisions of the Ice Cream Regulations;

(*d*) food which is bottled, canned or otherwise preserved in an effectively closed container of impermeable material;

(*e*) butter, margarine, lard, shortening, cooking fats, or beef suet;

(*f*) cheese, uncooked bacon, uncooked ham, dry pasta, dry pudding mixes, dry soup mixes and dry mixtures for the preparation of beverages;

(*g*) unskinned rabbits or hares and unplucked game or poultry;

(*h*) any food which is exposed for sale, or is necessarily being kept available to replenish food exposed for sale, or which has been brought to the premises before they are open for business and is to be exposed for sale within 4 hours. *FHR: 27*

137 – Other Processes

The loading and unloading of ships and barges, including the coaling of ships, is dealt with in items 138 to 151. Building operations and works of engineering construction, including the repair and maintenance of buildings and other structures, are dealt with in items 152 to 188.

RADIOACTIVE SUBSTANCES—Operations involving the use of radioactive substances and the exposure of workers to radiation are dealt with in items 248 to 263, and item 204.

WORK IN OFFICES AND SHOPS—Requirements for offices and shops are dealt with in items 264 to 279.

HIGHLY SPECIALISED PROCESSES—Many highly specialised processes, unlikely to be found outside a few special industries, have been omitted from this chapter but the requirements affecting them have been briefly summarised in Chapter XIII, items 189 to 247.

Chapter XI

Loading and Unloading of Ships and Barges

The requirements in this chapter apply not only to docks but to all loading and unloading operations at docks, wharves and quays. They therefore affect any factory which has its own wharf on a canal, river, estuary, etc. Revision of these regulations (Docks Regulations 1934) has been under discussion with industry for some years. A preliminary draft of new regulations was issued in 1967 but the matter seems to have been postponed indefinitely.

138 – Operations Affected

The regulations quoted apply to the loading, unloading, moving and handling of goods in, on, or at any dock, wharf or quay, and to the loading or unloading of ships in docks, harbours and canals. They also apply to the coaling of ships.

Except for items 140 and 144 these regulations do not apply to the unloading of fish from fishing-boats.

139 – Responsibility

The responsibility for the approaches to the dock, wharf or quay, the fencing of dangerous places, and the provision of First Aid and Ambulance facilities, rests with the person or persons who have control of that dock, wharf or quay.

The responsibility for providing safe access from ship to shore, from ship to ship, and from deck to hold, and for matters relating to hatch coverings, rests with the owner or master of the vessel. (Where the vessel is the property of the factory occupier, the responsibility naturally remains with him.) If the owner or master fails to take these precautions, the employer of any persons endangered thereby must take them. *DR: 50*

The responsibility for matters connected with the construction and maintenance of lifting machinery and other plant lies with the owners but where the plant is on a ship which is not registered in the United Kingdom the master of the ship is also responsible. If any plant does not comply with the regulations an employer must not allow his men to use it. *DR: 49*

If the master or owner of a vessel fails to provide the required safe access from shore to ship or from one ship to another (see item 140) the employer of the persons needing the access must provide it. *DR: 50*

140 – Safe Access and Safe Place of Work (General)

Every regular approach over a dock, wharf or quay which persons employed have to use for going to or from a working place, and every such working place on shore, must be maintained with due regard to the safety of the persons employed. *DR: 1*

In particular, the following parts must, as far as is practicable having regard to the traffic and working, be securely fenced so that the height of the fence is in no place less than 2 ft. 6 in. and the fencing is maintained in good condition ready for use: (*a*) All breaks, dangerous corners and other dangerous parts or edges of a dock, wharf, or quay; (*b*) both sides of such footways over bridges, caissons, and dock gates as are in general use by persons employed, and each side of the entrance at each end of such footway for a sufficient distance not exceeding five yards. *DR: 1*

The fencing must not be removed except to the extent, and for the period, reasonably necessary for carrying on the work of the dock or ship, or for repairing any fencing. If removed it must be restored forthwith at the end of that period by the persons engaged in the work that necessitated its removal. *DR: 46*

All places in which persons are employed, and any dangerous parts of the regular road or way forming the approach to any such place from the nearest highway, must be efficiently lighted. The towing-path of a canal or canalised river is not deemed to be "an approach" for the purpose of this Regulation. *DR: 3*

Where goods are placed on a wharf or quay, other than a wharf or quay on a shallow canal, a clear passage leading to the means of access to the ship must be maintained on the wharf or quay and if any space is left along the edge of the wharf or quay, it must be at least 3 feet wide and clear of all obstructions other than fixed structures, plant and appliances in use. *DR: 35*

Provision for the rescue from drowning of persons employed must be made and maintained, and must include a supply of life-saving appliances, kept in readiness on the wharf or quay and reasonably adequate having regard to all the circumstances. It must also include means situated at or near the surface of the water, at reasonable intervals, for enabling a person immersed to support himself or escape from the water. *DR: 2*

141 – Safe Access to Vessels

If a vessel (other than a barge or lighter) is lying at a wharf or quay for the purpose of loading or unloading or coaling, there must be safe means of access for the use of persons employed at such times as they have to pass from the ship to the shore or from the shore to ship. Where reasonably practicable this must consist of the ship's accommodation ladder or a gangway or a similar construction not less than 22 inches wide, properly secured and fenced throughout on each side to a clear height of 2 ft. 9 in. by means of upper and lower rails, taut ropes or chains or by other equally safe means (except that in the case of the ship's accommodation ladder such fencing shall be necessary on one side only provided that the other side is properly protected by the ship's side). Where an accommodation ladder, etc., is not available, the means of access must be a ladder of sound material and adequate length which must be properly secured to prevent slipping. These requirements do not apply to cargo stages or cargo gangways if other proper means of access is provided. As regards any sailing vessel not exceeding 250 tons net and any steam vessel not exceeding 150 tons gross, the requirements do not apply if and while the conditions are such that it is possible, without undue risk, to pass to and from the ship without the aid of any special appliances. *DR: 9*

If a ship when being loaded or unloaded is alongside any other ship, vessel, or boat, and persons employed have to pass from one to the other, safe means of access must be provided for their use unless the conditions are such that it is possible to pass from one to the other without undue risk without the aid of any special appliance. If one of such ships, vessels or boats is a sailing barge, flat, keel, lighter or other similar vessel of relatively low freeboard, the means of access must be provided by the ship which has the higher freeboard. *DR: 10*

When any person employed has to proceed to or from a ship by water, proper measures must be taken to provide for his safe transport. Vessels used for this purpose must be in charge of a competent person, must not be over-crowded and must be properly equipped for safe navigation and maintained in good condition. *DR: 44*

142 – Precautions to be taken on board

Precautions must be taken to facilitate the escape of the workers when employed in a hold or on 'tween decks in dealing with coal or other bulk cargo. *DR: 32*

When work is proceeding on any skeleton deck, adequate staging must be provided unless the space beneath the deck is filled with cargo to within a distance of two feet of such deck. *DR: 40*

Where stacking, unstacking, stowing or unstowing of cargo, or any handling in connexion therewith, cannot be safely carried out unaided, reasonable measures to guard against accident must be taken, by shoring or otherwise. *DR: 41*

No deck-stage or cargo-stage must be used unless it is substantially and firmly constructed, adequately supported, and where necessary, securely fastened. *DR: 36(a)*

No truck must be used for carrying cargo between ship and shore on a stage so steep as to be unsafe. *DR: 36(b)*

Any stage which is slippery must be made safe by the use of sand or otherwise. *DR: 36(c)*

Safe Access to Holds—If the depth from the level of the deck to the bottom of the hold (on any vessel except a barge or lighter) exceeds 5 feet, safe means of access from the deck to the hold must be maintained while work is going on. Such access must be afforded by ladder, and by ladder cleats or cups on the coamings. *DR: 11(1) and (2)*

Ladders between the lower decks must be in the same line as the ladder from the top deck, if this is practicable having regard to the position of the lower hatch or hatches. Ladders must provide firm handhold and a foothold of a depth (including any space behind the ladder) of not less than 4½ inches for a width of 10 inches. *DR: 11(2)(a) and (b)*

Cleats or cups provided on coamings must provide a firm handhold and a foothold of a depth (including any space behind the cleats or cups) of not less than 4½ inches for a width of 10 inches. They must be so constructed as to prevent a man's foot slipping off the side and must be placed vertically one above the other and in the same line as the ladders to which they give access. *DR: 11(2)(c)*

Cargo must be stowed sufficiently far from the ladder to leave, at each rung of the ladder, foothold of a depth (including any space behind the ladder) of not less than 4½ inches for a width of 10 inches as well as a firm handhold. *DR: 11(2)(d)*

There must be room to pass between any winch or other obstruction and the coamings, at the place where the ladder leaves the deck. *DR: 11(2)(e)*

Ladders must not be recessed under the deck more than is reasonably necessary to keep the ladder clear of the hatchway. *DR: 11(2)(f)*

Where the provision of a ladder on a bulkhead or in a trunk hatchway can be shown to be reasonably impracticable, access may be provided by cleats or cups complying with the requirements quoted above. *DR: 11(2)(i)*

Access may be provided by ladders or steps, separate from any hatchway or sloping from deck to deck, if such ladders or steps comply with the requirements quoted. *DR: 11(2)(ii)*

Shaft tunnels must be equipped with adequate handhold and foothold on each side. *DR: 11(3)*

All places in the hold and on the decks where work is being carried on, and the means of access provided, and all other parts where persons are employed must be efficiently lighted. *DR: 12*

Hatch Covers—All fore and aft beams, and thwartship beams used for hatch covering, and all hatch coverings themselves must be maintained in good condition. *DR: 15*

Except on barges and lighters, all fore and aft beams and thwartship beams used for hatch covering must have suitable gear for lifting them on and off, and it must not be necessary for any person to go on the beams to adjust such gear. *DR: 13*

Except on barges and lighters all hatch coverings including beams must be kept plainly marked to indicate the deck and hatch to which they belong, unless all the hatch coverings of the ship are interchangeable. They must also be marked to show their position in relation to other parts of the same hatch covering unless all the coverings of that hatch are interchangeable. *DR: 14*

Except on barges and lighters, adequate hand grips must be provided on all hatch coverings, having regard to their size and weight, unless the construction of the hatch or the hatch coverings is of a character rendering the provision of handgrips unnecessary. *DR: 16*

Where the working space around a hatch (except on a barge or lighter) is less than 2 ft. wide, such provision must be made as will enable persons employed to remove and replace in safety all fore and aft beams and thwartship beams used for hatch covering, and all hatch coverings. *DR: 17*

If any hatch of a hold accessible to any person employed and exceeding 5 ft. in depth is not in use for the passage of goods, coal or other material, or for trimming, and if the coamings are less than 2 ft. 6 ins. in height, such hatch must either be fenced to a height of 3 ft. or else be securely covered. (This requirement does not apply to vessels not exceeding 200 tons net registered tonnage which have only one hatchway, nor to any vessel during meal times or other short interruptions of work during the period of employment. Nor does it apply to barges and lighters.) *DR: 37(a)*

Hatch coverings must not be used in the construction of deck or cargo stages, or for any other purpose which may expose them to damage. *DR: 37(b)*

Hatch coverings must be replaced on the hatches in the positions indicated by the markings made thereon. *DR: 37(c)*

The beams of any hatch in use for the process must, if not removed, be adequately secured to prevent their displacement. *DR: 42*

143 - Lifting Machinery (Construction)

The following requirements affect all lifting machinery used in loading, unloading and handling of goods at docks, wharves and quays, whether the machinery is on the dock or on the vessel. (Lifting machinery means cranes, winches, hoists, derrick booms, derrick and mast bands, goose necks, eyebolts, and all other permanent attachments to the derricks, masts and decks, used in hoisting or lowering.)

General Requirements—Every crane and derrick must have the safe working load plainly marked upon it. Every shore crane, if so constructed that the safe working load may be varied by the raising or lowering of the jib or otherwise, must have attached to it an automatic indicator of safe working loads. (Where the jib may be raised or lowered, provision on the crane of a table showing the safe working loads at the corresponding inclinations or radii of the jib is considered sufficient.) *DR: 29*

Cranes and winches must be provided with such means as will reduce to a minimum the risk of the accidental descent of a load while being raised or lowered; in particular, the lever controlling the link motion reversing gear of a crane or winch must be provided with a suitable spring or other locking arrangement. *DR: 27*

Appropriate measures must be taken to prevent the foot of a derrick being accidentally lifted out of its socket or support. *DR: 31*

The driver's platform on every crane or tip driven by mechanical power must be securely fenced and must be provided with safe means of access. Where access is by ladder, the sides of the ladder must extend to a reasonable distance beyond the platform or else some other suitable handhold must be provided, the landing place on the platform must be maintained free from obstruction, and (in cases where the ladder is vertical and exceeds 30 ft. in height) a resting place must be provided approximately midway between the platform and the foot of the ladder. *DR: 28*

Adequate measures must be taken to prevent exhaust steam from any crane or winch obscuring any part of the decks, gangways, stages, wharf or quay where any person is employed. So far as practicable, the same applies to live steam supplied to a crane. *DR: 30*

Examinations and Tests—All derricks and permanent attachments (including bridle chains) to the derrick, mast and deck, used in hoisting or lowering must be inspected once in every 12 months and be thoroughly examined once at least in every 4 years. All other lifting machinery must be thoroughly examined once at least every 12 months. For the purpose of this regulation, thorough examination means a visual examination, supplemented if necessary by other means such as a hammer test, carried out as carefully as the conditions permit, in order to arrive at a reliable conclusion as to the safety of the parts examined. If necessary for the purpose, parts of the machines and gear must be dismantled. *DR: 18*

Before being taken into use for the first time, every crane and other hoisting machine, together with its accessory gear, must have been tested with a proof load calculated according to the following table:—

Safety working load	Proof load
Up to 20 tons	25 per cent in excess
20-50 tons	5 tons in excess
Over 50 tons	10 per cent in excess

The proof load must be hoisted and swung as far as possible in both directions. In the case of a jib-crane, if the jib has a variable radius, it must be tested with a proof load as defined above at the maximum and minimum radii of the jib. In the case of hydraulic cranes or hoists, where, owing to the limitation of pressure, it is impossible to hoist a load 25 per cent in excess of the safe working load, it is sufficient to hoist the greatest possible load. *DR: 18 and Schedule*

Before being taken into use for the first time, every winch and the whole of the gear accessory thereto (including derricks, goose necks, eye-plates, eye-bolts or other attachments) must be tested with a proof load calculated according to the table above. The proof load must be applied either by hoisting movable weights or by means of a spring or hydraulic balance or similar appliance, with the derrick at an angle to the horizontal which must be stated in the certificate of the test. In the former case, after the movable weights have been hoisted, the derrick must be swung as far as possible in both directions. In the latter case, the proof load must be applied with the derrick swung as far as practicable first in one direction and then in the other. *DR: 18 and Schedule*

After being tested, all lifting machines, with the whole of the gear accessory thereto and all loose gear, must be examined, the sheaves and the pins of the pulley blocks being removed for the purpose to see that no part is injured or permanently deformed by test. *DR: 18 and Schedule*

Certificates in the prescribed forms and containing the prescribed particulars with regard to the tests, examinations and inspection must be entered in or attached to the prescribed register before the machinery, or other gear to which the certificate refers, is taken into use. The prescribed forms for certificates of test are F 1945 for cranes and hoists and F 1944 for winches and derricks; the prescribed form for keeping a register of lifting machines is F 99. *DR: 22 and 51*

Machinery in use before 1934 — Lifting machinery in use before 1st June, 1934, when the present regulations came into operation, may not have been tested in the manner prescribed. This does not matter so long as the machinery was tested as required by the Docks Regulations 1925 (SRO 1925: No. 231).

144 - Chains, Ropes and Lifting Gear

General Requirements—No rope must be used in hoisting or lowering unless it is of suitable quality and free from patent defect. Wire ropes must have had a sample tested to destruction and the safe working load calculated as one-fifth of the breaking load of sample. *DR: 20(a) and Schedule*

No wire rope must be used in hoisting or lowering if in any length of 8 diameters the total number of visible broken wires exceeds 10 per cent of the total number of wires, or if the rope shows signs of excessive wear, corrosion or other defect which, in the opinion of the person who inspects it, renders it unfit for use. *DR: 20(c)*

A thimble or loop splice made in any wire rope must have at least 3 tucks with a whole strand of the rope and 2 tucks with one half of the wires cut out of each strand. The strands in all cases must be tucked against the lay of the rope. (This Regulation does not prevent the use of another form of splice which can be shown to be as efficient as that laid down.) *DR: 20(d)*

Means must be provided to enable any person using a chain or wire rope sling to ascertain the safe working load for such chain or sling under such conditions as it may be used. As regards chain slings, such means must consist of marking the safe working load in plain figures or letters upon the sling or upon a tablet or ring of durable material attached securely thereto. As regards wire rope slings, such means must consist of as those just mentioned or a notice or notices, so exhibited as to be easily read by any person concerned, stating the safe working loads for the various sizes of wire rope slings used. *DR: 24*

No pulley block must be used in hoisting or lowering unless the safe working load is clearly stamped upon it. For the purpose of this requirement, a pulley block means pulley, block, gin and similar gear, other than a crane block specially constructed to use with a crane to which it is permanently attached. *DR: 23*

ANNEALING—All chains, other than bridle chains attached to derricks or masts, and all rings, hooks, shackles and swivels used in hoisting or lowering must, unless they have been subjected to such other treatment as may be prescribed, be effectually annealed under the supervision of a competent person and at intervals of not more than 6 months for ½-inch and smaller chains, rings, hooks, shackles and swivels in general use; and not more than 12 months for all other chains, rings, hooks, shackles and swivels in general use. (In the case of such gear used solely on cranes and other hoisting appliances worked by hand, the maximum intervals are increased to 12 months and 2 years respectively.)

Where the Chief Inspector of Factories is of opinion that, owing to the size, design, material or infrequency of use of any such gear or class of such gear, the requirements as to annealing are not necessary for the protection of persons employed, he may by certificate in writing (which he may in his discretion revoke) exempt such gear or class of gear from such requirement, subject to such conditions as may be specified in such certificate. The following have been exempted from annealing in accordance with this provision—chains made of malleable cast iron; plate link chains; pitched chains; chains, rings, hooks, shackles and swivels made of steel; bordeaux connexions; hooks and swivels having screw-threaded parts or ball bearings or other case-hardened parts; and rings, hooks, shackles and swivels permanently attached to pitched chains, pulley blocks, or weighing machines. This exemption is subject to the condition that gear is given a thorough examination by a competent person at least once a year; the nature of the examination is laid down in Certificate of Exemption (Docks) No. 1. *DR: 19(b)*

Certificates giving the required particulars of routine annealing must be made out on form F 99; details of examinations carried out in lieu of annealing (when permissible under the certificate of exemption) must be entered on form F 1952. All forms must be attached to the prescribed register of lifting machines and lifting tackle kept in form F 99. *DR: 22*

INSPECTIONS AND TESTS—All chains, other than bridle chains attached to derricks or masts, and all rings, hooks, shackles, swivels and pulley blocks must be inspected by a competent person immediately before each occasion on which they are used in hoisting or lowering, unless they have been inspected within the preceding three months. *DR: 19(c)*

Every wire rope in general use for hoisting or lowering must be inspected by a competent person once at least in every three months. After any wire has broken in such a rope it must be inspected once at least in every month. *DR: 20(b)*

Before being taken into use for the first time, every piece of lifting gear (whether it is accessory to a machine or not) must be tested with a proof load at least equal to that shown in the following table:—

Article of Gear	Proof Load
Chain; Ring; Hook; Shackle; Swivel	Twice the safe working load
Pitched chains and hand-operated pulley blocks used with each other, and rings, hooks, shackles or swivels attached permanently thereto	One and a half times the safe working load
Pulley Blocks:	
Single Sheave Block	Four times the safe working load
Multiple Sheave Block with safe working load up to and including 20 tons	Twice the safe working load
Multiple Sheave Block with safe working load over 20 tons up to and including 40 tons	20 tons in excess of the safe working load
Multiple Sheave Block with safe working load over 40 tons	One and a half times the safe working load

Where the Chief Inspector of Factories is of opinion that, owing to the size, design, construction, material or use of any such loose gear or class of such gear, any of the requirements as to testing is not necessary for the protection of persons employed, he may by certificate in writing (which he may at his discretion revoke) exempt such gear or class of gear from such requirement, subject to such conditions as may be stated in the certificate. *DR: 19 and Schedule and Certificate of Exemption (Docks) No. 2*

All chains, rings, hooks, shackles or swivels used in hoisting or lowering which have been lengthened, altered or repaired by welding must, before being again taken into use, be adequately tested and re-examined. *DR: 19(d)*

After testing, all chains, ropes and lifting gear must be examined to ensure that no part has been injured or permanently deformed by the test. This examination must include the removal and inspection of the sheaves and pins of pulley blocks. *DR: Schedule*

The result of all tests and examinations must be entered in, or attached to, the register of lifting machinery and lifting gear kept in form F 99. The official forms for making out certificates of test are F 86 for pulley blocks, F 87 for wire rope, and F 97 for chains, chain slings, wire rope slings, and lifting tackle. *DR: 22*

Draft regulations covering the testing and examination of wire ropes by the makers were published in 1967 but have been withdrawn for the time being. See item 81.

CHAINS AND LIFTING GEAR USED BEFORE 1934—Chains and lifting gear originally used before June 1st, 1934, and therefore not tested in the prescribed manner, may still be used if they have been tested as required by the Docks Regulations 1925 (S.R. & O. 1925: No. 231).

145 – Lifting Machinery and Gear (Use)

No lifting machinery, chains or other lifting appliance must be loaded beyond the safe working load, except that a crane may be loaded beyond the safe working load in exceptional cases to such extent and subject to such conditions as may be approved by the engineer in charge or other competent person, if on each occasion the written permission of the owner or his responsible agent has been obtained and a record of the overload is kept. *DR: 33(a)*

Where the load upon a single sheave pulley block is attached to the pulley block instead of to the chain or rope passing round the sheave, the load on the pulley block may be deemed to be half the actual load. *DR: 33(a)*

No load must be left suspended from a crane, winch, or other machine unless there is a competent person actually in charge of the machine while the load is so left. *DR: 33(b)*

No person under 16 years of age, and no person who is not sufficiently competent and reliable, must be employed as driver of a crane or winch, whether driven by mechanical power or otherwise, or to give signals to a driver or to attend to cargo falls on winch-ends or winch-bodies. *DR: 34*

Chains must not be shortened by tying knots in them; and suitable packing must be provided to prevent the links coming into contact with sharp edges of loads of hard material. *DR: 25*

No cargo must be loaded or unloaded by a fall or sling at any intermediate deck unless either the hatch at that deck is securely covered or a secure landing platform of a width not less than that of one section of hatch coverings has been placed across it. This regulation does not apply when the whole process of unloading will be completed within a period of half an hour. *DR: 38*

When the working space in a hold is confined to the square of the hatch, hooks must not be made fast in the bands or fastenings of bales of cotton, wool, cork, gunny bags or other similar goods, nor must can hooks be used for raising or lowering a barrel when, owing to the construction or condition of the barrel or of the hooks, their use is likely to be unsafe. (Nothing in this requirement applies to breaking out or making up slings.) *DR: 39*

When cargo is being loaded or unloaded by a fall at a hatchway, a signaller must be employed, and where more than one fall is being worked at a hatchway, a separate signaller must be employed to attend to each fall. (This does not apply where a barge, lighter or other similar vessel is being loaded or unloaded if the driver of the crane or winch working the fall has a clear and unrestricted view of those parts of the hold where work is being carried on. Moreover, where the Chief Inspector is of opinion that, owing to the nature of the crane or winch or other appliance in use, or by reason of any special arrangements, the requirements of this Regulation are not necessary for the safety of persons employed he may by certificate in writing, which he may in his discretion revoke, suspend such requirements subject to such conditions as may be specified in such certificate.) *DR: 43*

146 – Other Machinery and Plant

All motors, cog-wheels, chain and friction gearing, shafting, live electric conductors and steam pipes must (unless it can be shown that by their position and construction they are equally safe to every person employed as they would be if securely fenced) be securely fenced so far as is practicable without impeding the safe working of the ship and without infringing any requirement of the Board of Trade. *DR: 26*

147 – Steam Boilers

All steam boilers used in connexion with the loading and unloading of ships are subject to the provisions of Section 32 to 34 of the main Act (see item 84). If they do not belong to the occupier of the premises the actual owner is responsible for carrying out the legal requirements. *FA: 125*

148 – Warehouses on Docks, Wharves and Quays

A warehouse belonging to the owners, trustees or conservators of a dock, wharf or quay is subject to certain provisions of the main Factories Act even if it is not part of a factory. The provisions in question are those relating to the posting of abstracts and notices and the keeping of registers, etc. (see items 297 and 298) and those relating to the safeguarding of machinery (items 43 to 62), hoists, cranes and lifting appliances generally (items 78 to 81), and the safety of floors, passages and stairs (items 12 to 14). *FA: 125*

149 – First Aid and Ambulance

A sufficient number of first-aid boxes or cupboards must be provided at every working place, and, if more than one is provided, at reasonable distances from each other. Each first-aid box or cupboard must be marked plainly with the words FIRST AID and must have the contents shown in item 40. *DR: 4 and Docks (First Aid Boxes) Order 1959*

Nothing except appliances or requisites for first aid must be kept in a first-aid box or cupboard. A first-aid box or cupboard must be kept stocked and in good order and must be placed under the charge of a responsible person who must always be readily available during working hours. Such person must, except at docks, wharves or quays at which the total number of persons employed at any time does not exceed 50, be a person trained in First Aid. The standard of training is similar to that for factories (see item 40) except that the approved training organisations do not include Leeds University, Birmingham University, or Newcastle upon Tyne University. *DR: 5 and 6*

There must be provided for use at every dock, wharf or quay at which the total number of persons employed at any time exceeds 50, a suitably constructed ambulance carriage maintained in good condition, for the purpose of the removal of serious cases of accident or sickness, unless arrangements have been made for obtaining such a carriage when required from a hospital or other place situate not more than 2 miles from the dock, wharf or quay, and in telephonic communication therewith. *DR: 7*

Notices must be exhibited in prominent positions at every dock, wharf or quay stating the position of each first-aid box and the place where the person in charge thereof can be found; the position of stretchers or other appliances; and the position of the ambulance carriage or, where such is not provided, the position of the nearest telephone and the name and telephone number of the hospital or other place from which such carriage may be obtained. *DR: 8*

150 – Duties of Persons Employed

Every person employed must use the means of access provided in accordance with regulations and no person may authorise or order another to use means of access other than those provided in accordance therewith. *DR: 47*

No person must go upon the fore and aft beams or thwartship beams for the purpose of adjusting the gear for lifting them on and off nor must any person authorise or order another to do so. (This does not apply to a barge or lighter.) *DR: 48*

No person must, unless duly authorised or in case of necessity, remove or interfere with any fencing, gangway, gear, ladder, hatch covering, life-saving means or appliances, lights, marks, stages or other things whatsoever required by the regulations. If necessarily removed, such things must be restored at the end of the period during which their removal was necessary by the persons last engaged in the work that necessitated such removal. *DR: 45*

151 – Other matters

A copy of the prescribed abstract of the Docks Regulations must be displayed. If the dock, wharf or quay is not part of factory premises (which should already be displaying an abstract of the main Act) the prescribed abstract of the Factories Act must also be displayed. See item 298.

REGISTER—The prescribed register, with the certificates required to be attached to it, must be kept on the premises (unless some other place has been approved in writing by the Chief Inspector) and must, on the application of any of H.M. Inspectors of Factories, be produced by the person in charge thereof. If it relates to the lifting machinery and other gear of a ship and is kept on the ship, it must be produced, together with the certificate of the ship's register, by the person for the time being in charge of the ship. *DR: 22 and 51*

The form of register to be used is prescribed by SI 1966 No. 1588.

COMPETENT PERSONS FOR PURPOSES OF TESTS—In connexion with the carrying out of tests, examinations and inspections by a competent person, the Chief Inspector of Factories may give notice in writing that a particular person is not considered technically competent. Such a person may appeal to the Minister of Labour against this decision. *DR: 21*

REPAIRS—Repairs carried out to a ship which is in dock (unless carried out only by the master or crew) will be subject to the Shipbuilding and Ship-repairing Regulations 1960. See item 244.

DIVING—Any diving operations carried out in connexion with a dock, wharf or quay are subject to the Diving Operations Special Regulations. See item 245.

OFFICES—Offices on docks, wharves and quays are subject to the Offices, Shops and Railways Premises Act. See items 264 to 279.

WELFARE AMENITIES—Under the Docks and Harbours Act 1966, welfare amenities (sanitary conveniences, washing facilities, cloakrooms and canteens) have to be provided for ports specified in Schedule 1 to the Act.

FREIGHT CONTAINERS—The voluntary scheme for type-testing and certification for safe construction, customs and infestation operated by H.M. Chief Inspector of Factories commenced in August 1972. In addition the International Convention on Freight Containers was signed by Great Britain in 1972 but at the time of going to press the Convention had not been ratified

ASBESTOS REGULATIONS 1971—The regulations call for cleanliness and dust suppression in factories and warehouses and so importing procedures are important. Lined sacks, containers, etc., have replaced hessian sacks and methods of handling at the docks and wharves should be arranged to eliminate dust.

Chapter XII

Special Requirements for Construction Operations

The requirements quoted in this chapter apply to all building operations and works of engineering construction, as defined in item 152, whether they are carried out on factory premises or not. It will be noted that repair and maintenance of buildings are included under the heading of building operations, so that every factory will at some time or another be affected.

When building operations and works of engineering construction are being conducted in factory premises, the Factories Act 1961 will continue to apply; so will the provisions applied to building operations and works of engineering construction by FA: 127, including the regulations quoted in this chapter. See FA: 127(8).

In the main the requirements referred to in this chapter are to be found in four codes of regulations which apply to construction work, namely the General Provisions, Lifting Operations, Working Places and Health and Welfare Regulations. For definitions of the terms used (scaffold, hoist, lifting appliance, sloping roof, etc.) see the relevant code of regulations. Other codes of regulations which apply are dealt with in other chapters e.g. abrasive wheels (item 53), asbestos (item 228), woodworking machinery (item 126), electricity (item 69), compressed air (item 246), diving (item 245) and use of radioactive substances (item 249).

The regulations are in Imperial measurements. For metric equivalents see Technical Data Note No. 22 obtainable free from H.M. Factory Inspectorate.

152 – Operations affected

All the requirements in this chapter apply to building operations, and works of engineering construction. The meaning of these two terms is as shown below.

Building Operations—This term covers all or any of the following operations, if carried on by way of trade or business or for the purpose of any industrial or commercial undertaking or by or on behalf of the Crown or any municipal or other public authority, and to plant and machinery used in such operations:—

(*a*) Construction or structural alteration of any building;
(*b*) Repair or maintenance of a building (including any re-pointing, re-decorating and external cleaning);
(*c*) Demolition of any building or part of a building;
(*d*) Preparation for an intended building;
(*e*) Laying the foundations of any building.

Normal window cleaning is not "external cleaning" of a building within the meaning of the Regulations and is therefore not a building operation; this was laid down in the case of *Lavender v. Diamints* (*1949*). Window cleaning on factory premises is subject to the relevant portions of the main Factories Act, e.g., ladders, safe access, etc., and this applies whether the window cleaner is an employee of the occupier or of an outside contractor.

Works of Engineering Construction—This term covers the construction of any railway line or siding (otherwise than on an existing railway) and the construction, structural alteration, repair (including re-pointing and re-painting), or demolition of any dock, harbour, inland navigation, tunnel, bridge, viaduct, waterworks, reservoir, pipeline, aqueduct, sewer, sewage works or gasholder, except where carried on upon a railway or tramway. It also covers the following operations except when they are carried out in a factory, electricity station, railway or tramway: the construction, structural alteration, repair, re-pointing, re-painting or demolition of any steel or reinforced concrete structure other than a building, any road, airfield, sea defence works, or river works, and any other civil or constructional engineering works of a similar nature. *FA: 176*(*1*)*; the Engineering Construction* (*Extension of Definition*) *Regulations 1960; and the Engineering Construction* (*Extension of Definition*) *Regulations 1968*

153 – Responsibility

When building operations or works of engineering construction are carried out on factory premises and the work is done by the factory occupier's own men, the full responsibility naturally falls on the occupier.

When a contractor's employees go into a factory to carry out operations covered by the Construction Regulations, the contractor is responsible for seeing that the regulations themselves are complied with, but the factory occupier is responsible for carrying out any relevant requirements of the main Act, e.g., by seeing that all machinery near which the contractor's men have to work is securely fenced. In some circumstances the responsibility of occupier and contractor may overlap; for example, under the regulations the contractor must provide safe means of access for his men (see item 156), while under the Factories Act the occupier must provide safe means of access for every person employed or working on the premises, and this includes all contractor's men. If, in such circumstances, safe access is not provided proceedings may be taken against either the occupier or contractor, or both.

If several contractors or sub-contractors are working on the same premises (regardless of whether it is a factory or a construction site elsewhere than in a factory) at the same time the position is more complicated. In general, each contractor or sub-contractor is responsible for the safety of his own men whether or not the hazard to be guarded against has been created by him. For example, if a contractor's men have to work near an opening in the floor or near an excavation, that contractor is responsible for seeing that they do not work there unless the opening or excavation is fenced as required by the Regulations. This is regardless of the fact that the opening or excavation may have been made by some other contractor.

In some operations a contractor (or employer of workmen) may be responsible when he endangers workers employed by another contractor as well as his own men, e.g., in the use of explosives (CGP: 19) or the overloading of a crane (CLO: 31).

Under Regulation 3 of the Construction (Health and Welfare) Regulations, two or more contractors may arrange to share welfare facilities but details of such arrangements must be entered in the prescribed register (Factory Form F 2202) and must be kept available on the site.

In view of the complications which may arise when one or more contractors have to carry out building operations or works of engineering construction on the same premises, it is recommended that a conference be held before such operations begin so that the occupier and the contractors can discuss what precautions are necessary and who is responsible for taking them. (When demolition operations are to be carried out by two or more different contractors such consultations are compulsory. See item 178.)

154 – Notification of Operations, Accidents, etc.

When any new building operation or work of engineering construction is begun, notice must be given to the district inspector of factories within 7 days, unless the operations are not expected to last for more than 6 weeks. The form to be used for this purpose is Factory Form No. 10. *FA: 127(6) and (7)*

The notice must be in writing and must give the name, trade, and business address of the firm or person undertaking the operations; the place and nature of the operations, with the telephone number (if any) of the site; the number of workers expected to be employed by the firm or person on that particular site; the approximate date on which the operations are expected to begin; the expected duration of the work; the name of the district council in whose area the site is located; whether mechanical power is to be used and, if so, its nature; and whether the person or firm is a main contractor or a sub-contractor. *FA: 127(6) and (7) and the Construction (Notice of Operations and Works) Order 1965*

If operations are already in progress on a construction site, and due notice has been given, a firm or person beginning further operations on the same site need not give notice to the factory inspector if the notice originally given included all the information required. *FA: 127(7)*

The obligation to notify the factory inspector of any accident or specified dangerous occurrence, and to notify the employment medical adviser of cases of industrial disease (see item 296) applies to building operations and works of engineering construction whether or not these are being carried out on factory premises. *FA: 80, 81, 82 and 127*

If a canteen is provided and any person handling food in the canteen is found to be suffering from an infectious disease, the medical officer of health must be informed. See item 136.

155 – Supervision

An employer who normally has more than 20 persons working on building operations or works of engineering construction must appoint a qualified person or persons to advise on safety requirements and supervise the safe conduct of the work. This applies whether the men are employed on one site or on several different sites. *CGP: 5(1)*

The appointment of such persons must be made in writing and the name of the person responsible on each site must be posted up on the copy of the Construction Regulations displayed there. See item 188. *CGP: 5(2)*

Persons appointed as safety supervisors must not be given such other work as will interfere with the proper performance of their duties under the Regulations. *CGP: 6(1)*

It is permissible for two or more employers to appoint a joint safety supervisor, either for one site or for several sites. *CGP: 6(2)*

When demolition work is carried out it must be under the supervision of a competent person experienced in demolition operations, and the name of such person must be posted up in a prominent position on the site. See item 178.

Explosives must only be handled or used under the supervision of a competent person with a knowledge of the dangers involved. See item 181.

156 – Safe Access and Safe Place of Work (General)

The requirements quoted in this item are of general application to all building operations and works of engineering construction. More detailed requirements for particular types of plant and equipment, and for particular circumstances, are quoted in items 157 to 164.

So far as is reasonably practicable, sufficient safe means of access and egress must be provided to and from every place at which any person works. In addition to this general requirement, special mention is made of safe access for persons inspecting cranes (see items 165, 167 and 168) and of the precautions to be taken if access to any workplace is rendered unsafe by the proximity of rail tracks (see item 179). *CWP: 6(1)*

So far as is reasonably practicable, every working place must be made safe and kept safe for any person working there. Special mention is made of the need to protect workmen against being struck by falling materials. *CWP: 6(2) and 46(1)*

Any side of a working place from which a person may fall more than 6ft. 6in. is subject to the requirements for guard-rails and toe-boards set out in item 160. This includes working places which are part of a permanent building or other structure as well as temporary working platforms. *CWP: 28*

When work cannot safely be done on or from the ground, or from part of a building or other permanent structure, either scaffolds, ladders, or some other appropriate means of support must be provided. Such scaffolds, ladders, etc. must be suitable and sufficient for the particular conditions under which they are to be used. Scaffolds must comply with the detailed requirements set out in items 158 to 164; ladders and folding step-ladders must comply with those set out in item 158. *CWP: 7*

All gangways, stairs and runs used as a means of access or egress must satisfy the requirements set out in item 159.

All means of access and egress, and all scaffolds, must be properly maintained and scaffolds must be inspected at the intervals shown in item 164. *CWP: 6 and 7*

No part of a building or other structure may be used to support a scaffold, ladder, step-ladder or crawling-board unless it is of sound material and sufficiently strong to provide safe support. Gutters must not be used as supports unless they and their fixings are of adequate strength; overhanging eaves gutters must not be so used unless designed as walkways. *CWP: 18*

The prevention of danger from temporary or insecure structures is dealt with in item 183.

When a scaffold is used by the employees of two or more employers, each employer is responsible for seeing that it complies with the requirements at the time when his men are using it, even though it may have been erected by another employer. *CWP: 23*

SAFETY NETS AND SAFETY BELTS—If the nature of the work makes it impracticable to comply with all or any of the requirements for preventing falls of persons, these requirements must be complied with as far as possible and suitable and sufficient safety nets or safety sheets must be installed to safeguard workers not protected against falls by normal means. *CWP: 38(1)*

Safety belts or similar equipment may be used as an alternative to nets or sheets if it is practicable for workmen using a belt to keep it continuously attached to a suitable and safe anchorage.

Belts may also be used when it is not practicable to provide all the nets or sheets necessary to satisfy the regulations or where, because of the nature of short duration of the work, the use of nets is not reasonably practicable or would be unreasonable. *CWP: 38(3)*

Safety nets and sheets must be so designed, constructed and installed as to prevent injury to those falling onto or into them, so far as this is practicable. They must be kept in position at all times when work is in progress, except when temporarily removed for the access of persons, movement of materials, or other necessary purposes of the work. *CWP: 38(1)*

Safety belts and similar equipment must have suitable fittings and must be so designed and constructed as to prevent serious injury in the event of the wearer falling. *CWP: 38(3)*

All safety nets, safety sheets, safety belts and other equipment provided to meet the above requirements must be properly maintained. *CWP: 38(4)*

See B.S. 3913—Industrial Safety Nets.

157 – Specially Hazardous Location

The requirements quoted in this item apply when persons have to work or pass on or near fragile surfaces, openings, sloping roofs and certain other specially hazardous locations. They are additional to the general requirements already quoted in item 156.

FRAGILE SURFACES—If any person has to work on or from, or pass across, material which is liable to fracture beneath his weight and cause him to fall more than 6ft. 6in., suitable and sufficient ladders, crawling-ladders, crawling-boards, or duck-boards must be provided; they must be securely supported and must be secured, where necessary, to prevent slipping. *CWP: 36(1)*

If any person has to work or pass near to fragile materials through which he might fall more than 6ft. 6in., guard-rails, coverings or other suitable means must be provided to prevent such falls, so far as is reasonably practicable. *CWP: 36(2)*

Prominent warning notices must be fixed at the approaches to all such fragile surfaces as are mentioned above, unless the material consists wholly of glass and is therefore obviously fragile. *CWP: 36(3)*

All ladders, crawling-boards, guard-rails, etc., provided to meet the above requirements must be of good construction, suitable and sound material, adequate strength for the purpose, and free from patent defect, and must be properly maintained. *CWP: 36(5)*

In considering whether any material is liable to fracture under a person's weight, regard must be had not only to his own weight but to the weight of any tools materials, etc., which he may be carrying. *CWP: 36(4)*

OPEN JOISTING—If work is done on or immediately above any open joisting through which persons are liable to fall more than 6ft. 6in., the joisting must be securely covered by boards or other temporary covering, to a sufficient extent to ensure safe access to, or foothold for, the work being done, unless other effective measures are taken to prevent such falls. *CWP: 33(4)*

Coverings over open joisting may be temporarily removed for the passage of persons or materials, or for other necessary purposes of the work, but they must be replaced as soon as this purpose is accomplished. They may also be removed when this is necessary for the purpose of covering the joisting permanently. *CWP: 34(1)*

OPENINGS, CORNERS, EDGES, ETC.—Any opening, corner, break or edge in any floor, roof, platform, gangway, run or wall must, if persons are liable to fall through or from it to a distance of more than 6ft. 6in., be provided with a covering or else be protected by suitable guard-rails to a height of between 3ft. and 3ft. 9in. and toe-boards at least 6 inches high, with a space between the toe-board and the lowest guard rail-of not more than 30 inches. *CWP: 33(2)*

When the covering provided for an opening, etc., is not securely fixed in position it must be clearly and boldly marked to show its purpose. *CWP: 33(2)*

Openings, corners, breaks and edges through or from which persons are not liable to fall more than 6ft. 6in. must also be covered, or provided with toe-boards, if there is a danger that materials or articles may fall through or from them so as to endanger persons below. *CWP: 33(3)*

Coverings, guard-rails, toe-boards, etc. may be temporarily removed for the passage of persons or materials, or for other necessary purposes of the work, but must be replaced as soon as this purpose is accomplished. They may also be removed to permit the final and permanent covering, filling in or enclosure of the opening, etc. *CWP: 34(1)*

The above requirements do not apply to any opening, corner, break or edge created in the course of the demolition of a building or structure, or any substantial part therefore; such demolition is subject to the requirements set out in item 178. When the demolition does not involve a substantial part of the building or structure (so that the requirements quoted in item 178 do not apply) the guarding of openings corners, breaks and edges must be carried out as described above unless they are never left unattended. *CWP: 34(2)*

SLOPING ROOFS—The following requirements apply to any roof or part of a roof which has a slope of more than 10 degrees and which is either in course of construction, maintenance repair or demolition or which is used as a means of access or egress to or from some part of the roof where construction operations are being carried on. *CWP: 35(1)*

When work is done on or from a sloping roof, sufficient and suitable crawling-ladders or crawling-boards must be provided unless the battens or similar structural members offer adequate handhold and foothold. If persons are liable to fall more than 6ft. 6in. from the eaves of the roof there must also be an adequate barrier at the lower edge of the roof, unless all the work is done from a securely supported working platform which is at least 17 inches wide and which satisfies the requirements set out in item 160. *CWP: 35(4), (6) and (7)*

When a sloping roof is used as a means of access to or egress from a place where construction work is being done, sufficient and suitable crawling-boards or crawling ladders must be provided, unless the battens or other structural members provide adequate handhold and foothold. *CWP: 35(3) and (6)*

Crawling-boards and crawling-ladders must be of good construction, suitable and sound material, adequate strength for their purposes, and free from patent defect, and must be properly maintained. *CWP: 35(5)*

Crawling-boards and crawling-ladders, when in use, must be properly supported and must be securely fixed or anchored to the sloping surface or over the roof ridge, unless they are secured in some other effective way. No part of a building or other structure must be used to support a crawling-board or crawling-ladder unless it is stable and of sufficient strength; gutters must not be used as supports unless they are of adequate strength and overhanging eaves gutters must never be used unless they have been designed as walkways. *CWP: 35(5) and 18*

When work is done on or near a roof with a pitch of over 30 degrees it must be done only by workmen who are suitable for such work. The same applies to roofs with lower pitches if the nature or condition of the surface, or the state of the weather, is such that workmen are liable to slip or fall in such a way that they may fall from the edge of the roof. *CWP: 35(2)*

Suitable and sufficient means must be provided to prevent articles and materials from falling from the roof. *CWP: 35(8)*

If a sloping roof consists, in whole or in part, of fragile materials, the requirements quoted earlier in this item apply.

Any openings, breaks, corners or edges through or from which a person may fall more than 6ft. 6in. must be guarded in the way described earlier in this item.

158 – Ladders (including Step-Ladders)

The following requirements apply to all ladders and folding step-ladders used as working places or as a means of access or egress, with the exception of crawling-ladders used on sloping roofs and so subject to the requirements set out in item 157.

CONSTRUCTION—All ladders and folding step-ladders must be of good construction, suitable and sound material, and adequate strength, and must be properly maintained. *CWP: 31(1)*

Every rung of a ladder must be properly fixed to the side or stiles. Rungs must not be supported solely by nails, spikes or other similar fixings. *CWP: 31(3)*

If the tenon joints on a wooden ladder are not secured by wedges, reinforcing ties must be used. Wooden stiles or sides, and wooden rungs, must have the grain running lengthwise. *CWP: 31(3)*

Wooden ladders and folding step-ladders must not be so painted or treated that defects cannot easily be seen. *CWP: 9(4)*

USE OF LADDERS AND STEP-LADDERS—A ladder must not be used if any rung is missing or is defective. *CWP: 31(2)*

No part of a building must be used to support a ladder or folding step-ladder unless it is stable and of sufficient strength. Gutters must not be used as supports unless they are of adequate strength; overhanging eaves gutters must never be so used unless they have been designed as walkways. *CWP: 18*

Every folding step-ladder, when in use, must have a firm and level footing. It must not stand on loose bricks or other loose packing. *CWP: 32(7)*

Every ladder must, where practicable, extend for at least 3ft. 6in. above the landing place, or above the highest rung reached by the feet of persons using it, unless there is other adequate handhold. If it is impracticable for the ladder to extend to the full distance of 3ft. 6in. it must extend as far as practicable. *CWP: 32(5)*

At each rung the space between the ladder and the face of the building must be sufficient to provide adequate foothold. *CWP: 32(5)*

Except for certain ladders not more than 10 feet in length (referred to in the next paragraph) every ladder standing on a base must, where practicable, be securely fixed near to its upper resting place or, if vertical, near to the upper end; if such fixing is impracticable the ladder must be fixed securely at or near to its lower end and if even this is impracticable a person must be stationed at the base to prevent the ladder from slipping. Every such ladder must be equally and properly supported on each stile or side, must be secured where necessary to prevent undue swaying or sagging, and must have a firm and level footing; it must not stand on loose bricks or other loose packing. *CWP: 32(2) and (3)*

A ladder which is not more than 10 feet long, and which is not used as a means of communication, need not comply with the requirements quoted in the previous paragraph so long as it is securely placed so as to prevent it from slipping or falling. *CWP: 32(4)*

A ladder which does not stand on a base must be securely suspended and secured where necessary to prevent swaying or swinging. It must be equally and properly suspended by each stile or side. *CWP: 32(6)*

So far as practicable, a run of ladders rising a vertical distance of 30 feet or more must have intermediate landing places at intervals of not more than 30 feet. Every landing place must be of adequate dimensions and the opening through which the ladder passes must be as small as is reasonably practicable. If persons are liable to fall more than 6ft. 6in. from a landing place there must, if reasonably practicable, be guard-rails to a height of between 3 feet and 3ft. 9in. and toe-boards to a height of at least 6 inches the distance between the toe-board and the lowest guard-rail not being more than 30 inches. *CWP: 32(8)*

159 – Stairs, Gangways and Runs

All stairs used during building operations must have handrails or other efficient means of preventing falls; these must continue beyond the ends of stairs if this is necessary to prevent danger. The handrails must be kept in position except when temporary removal is necessary for the passage of materials or persons. *CWP: 29(1)*

If persons are liable to fall more than 6ft. 6in. from any stair, gangway or run, guard-rails must be provided to a height of between 3ft. and 3ft. 9in. and gangways and runways must also have toe-boards or other barriers, to a height of at least 6 inches, the distance between the toe-board and the lowest guard-rail being not more than 30 inches. (These requirements do not apply to temporary gangways used by workmen erecting the framework of a building or other permanent structure, if the work is of such short duration as to make the use of guard-rails and toe-boards unreasonable. *CWP: 29(2)*

If persons are liable to fall more than 6ft. 6in. from any part of a gangway or run it must be at least 17 inches wide if used only for the passage of persons and at least 25 inches if used for the passage of materials, a greater width being provided if the nature of the materials makes a wider gangway and run necessary in the interests of safety. (If limitations of space make it impracticable to provide a gangway or run of the required width, the width must be as great as is reasonably practicable.) *CWP: 27(2)*

If the gangway or run from which persons are liable to fall more than 6ft. 6in. consists of open metalwork, the interstices must not exceed 6 sq. in. in area; if it consists of boards, planks or plates with spaces between them, the spaces must not exceed 1 inch in width and the boards, planks or plates must be fixed to prevent movement. Neither type of gangway or run must be used if there is a risk of materials or articles falling through and striking persons below. *CWP: 24(1)*

If a gangway or run from which persons are liable to fall more than 6ft. 6in. does not satisfy the requirements outlined in the previous paragraph it must be closely boarded or planked. *CWP: 24(1)*

Boards and planks used to form gangways and runs must be of such thickness as will give adequate security, having regard to the distance between the supports. Boards of a thickness of 2 inches or less must be at least 8 inches wide; boards over 2 inches thick must be at least 6 inches wide. *CWP: 25(1)*

Every board or plank forming part of a gangway or run must rest on at least three supports unless, taking into account the distance between the supports and the thickness of the board, sagging can be prevented without a third support. Each board or plank must rest securely and evenly on its supports. *CWP: 25(4)*

No board or plank which forms part of a gangway or run must project beyond its end support to a distance exceeding 4 times its thickness, unless it is adequately supported to prevent tipping. In no circumstances may it project to a distance which, having regard to its thickness and strength, renders the projecting part unsafe for any weight liable to be placed on it. *CWP: 25(1)*

No gangway or run must have a slope exceeding one vertical to one and a half horizontal, and no slope of more than 1 vertical to 4 horizontal must be used unless stepping laths have been placed at suitable intervals. More gradual slopes must also have laths if circumstances make additional foothold necessary. All stepping laths must extend the full width of the plank except for a gap of not more than 4 inches which may be left for barrow wheels. *CWP: 24(2)*

If the boards forming part of a gangway or run overlap, or are not of a reasonably uniform thickness, the risk of tripping must be reduced to a minimum by the provision of adequate bevel pieces or by some other suitable means. Similar precautions must be taken if for any other reason (e.g., warping) the boards do not provide an even surface. (This requirement does not apply to a gangway or run if one side of it is contiguous to a curved surface of any cylindrical or spherical structure forming part of a work of engineering construction.) *CWP: 25(3)*

Stairs, gangways and runs must be kept free of unnecessary obstructions and materials, and from rubbish and projecting nails. If they become slippery they must be sanded, cleaned or otherwise treated as soon as reasonably practicable. *CWP: 30*

Openings, breaks, corners and edges in gangways and runs are subject to the requirements set out in item 157.

160 – Working Platforms

The requirements quoted in this item apply to permanent working platforms as well as to those specially erected for the purpose of the building operations or works of engineering construction for which they are being used.

General Requirements—If a working platform from which persons are liable to fall more than 6ft. 6in. consists of open metalwork, the interstices must not exceed 6 sq. in. in area; if it consists of boards, planks or plates with spaces between them, the spaces must not exceed 1 inch in width and the boards, planks or plates must be fixed to prevent movement. Neither type of working platform must be used if there is a risk of materials or articles falling through and striking persons below. *CWP: 24(1)*

If a working platform from which persons are liable to fall more than 6ft. 6in. does not satisfy the requirements outlined in the previous paragraph it must be closely boarded, planked or plated (except insofar as provision has to be made for draining the platform of a suspended scaffold). *CWP: 24(1) and 19(13)*

Boards and planks used to form platforms must be of such thickness as will give adequate security, having regard to the distance between the supports. Boards of a thickness of 2 inches or less must be at least 8 inches wide; boards over 2 inches thick must be at least 6 inches wide. *CWP: 25(1)*

Every board or plank forming part of a working platform must rest on at least three supports unless, taking into account the distance between the supports and the thickness of the board, sagging can be prevented without a third support. Each board or plank must rest securely and evenly on its supports. *CWP: 25(4)*

No board or plank which forms part of a working platform must project beyond its end support to a distance exceeding 4 times its thickness, unless it is adequately supported to prevent tipping. In no circumstances may it project to a distance which, having regard to its thickness and strength, renders the projecting part unsafe for any weight liable to be placed on it. *CWP: 25(1)*

If the boards or planks forming a working platform overlap, or are not of a reasonably uniform thickness, the risk of tripping must be reduced to a minimum by the provision of adequate bevel pieces or by some other suitable means. Similar precautions must be taken if for any other reason (e.g., warping) the boards do not provide an even surface. (This requirement does not apply to a gangway or run if one side of it is contiguous to a curved surface of any cylindrical or spherical structure forming part of a work of engineering construction.) *CWP: 25(3)*

The space between the face of a building or other structure and a working platform must be as small as practicable. Where workmen sit on the edge of a platform it is permissible to leave a gap of not more than 12 inches between the building and the platform. *CWP: 26(3)*

Where work has to be done at the end of a wall, the working platform must, wherever practicable, extend at least 24 inches beyond the end of the wall. *CWP: 25(2)*

No working platform must be used for the passage of materials unless it affords a clear passage which is adequate in width without the removal of guard-rails and toe-boards and which, in any event, is 25 inches wide. *CWP: 26(1)*

A clear passage at least 17 inches wide must be left between the side of the platform and any deposited material. *CWP: 26(1)*

Working platforms must be kept free of unnecessary obstructions and materials, and from rubbish and projecting nails. If they become slippery they must be sanded, cleaned or otherwise treated as soon as reasonably practicable. *CWP: 30*

Openings, breaks, corners and edges in working platforms are subject to the requirements set out in item 157.

Widths of Working Platforms—Working platforms from which persons are liable to fall more than 6ft. 6in. must (except in the special circumstances mentioned below) be of the following minimum widths:

If used only for footings	25 in.
If used for footings and also for the deposit of material ..	34 in.
If used to support a higher platform	42 in.
If used for the dressing or rough shaping of stone	51 in.
If used both for the support of a higher platform and for the dressing or rough shaping of stone	59 in.

The special types of scaffold on which narrower working platforms may be used are as follows:—

Platforms on the outside of sloping roofs	17 in.
Platforms of ladder scaffolds	17 in.
Platforms supported directly by folding trestles or folding step-ladders	17 in.
Platforms under a roof, used for work on or in the vicinity of the roof, and supported by or suspended from the roof or roof members, where the work is light and if short duration in any one position and can be done with safety from a platform narrower than the standard minimum widths ..	17 in.
Platforms used for work in connection with cylindrical or spherical metal structures	17 in.

Where limitations of space make it impracticable to provde a platform of the minimum width prescribed, it is permissible to use a narrower platform so long as it is as wide as is practicable. *CWP: 26*

The above figures are the minimum widths prescribed under the Construction Regulations but there is also a general requirement that every working platform must be wide enough to afford adequate working space at every part. This means that platforms wider than the legal minimum may have to be provided; in particular, attention is drawn to the requirement, quoted earlier in this item, that spaces of a prescribed minimum width must be allowed for the passage of materials and between stacked materials and the edge of the platform. *CWP: 19(13) and 26(1)*

Guard-rails and Toe-boards—Except in the special circumstances mentioned below, all platforms and other workplaces from which persons may fall more than 6ft. 6in. must have guard-rails to a height of between 3ft. and 3ft. 9in. and toe-boards or other barriers to a height of at least 6in., the gap between the toe-board and the lowest guard-rail being not more than 30 inches. Toe-boards or barriers of greater height than 6 inches must be provided if this is necessary to prevent the fall of persons articles or materials from the platform. *CWP: 28(1) and (3)*

Unless guard-rails and toe-boards or other barriers are so designed and used that outward movement is impossible, such movement must be prevented by placing the rails and boards on the inside of the uprights or by other equally effective means. So far as practicable, all guard-rails, toe-boards and barriers must be so secured or placed in position as to prevent accidental displacement. *CWP: 11 and 28(2)*

Guard-rails, toe-boards and other barriers must be maintained in position whenever the platform is in use, except when temporary removal is necessary for the passage of persons or materials, or for other purposes of the work. All guard-rails, toe-boards and barriers temporarily removed for this reason must be replaced as soon as practicable. *CWP: 28(4)*

Exemptions Regarding Guard-rails and Toe-boards—Suspended scaffolds on the edge of which workers sit need not have guard-rails or toe-boards on that side of the platform but ropes or chains must be provided to give safe handhold. Other suspended scaffolds must have guard-rails and toe-boards on all sides, but the rails on the side next to the wall or working face need not rise to a height of more than 27 inches if work would be impracticable with the rails at a greater height. *CWP: 28(5)*

The following types of working are exempt from the requirements regarding hand-rails and toe-boards or barriers:

(*a*) The platforms of ladder scaffolds on which secure handhold is provided to the full length of the platform;

(*b*) The platforms of trestle scaffolds when supported on folding trestles, split-heads or similar devices, or folding stepladders;

(*c*) Platforms used only in the course of erecting the framework or prefabricated units of a building or structure, where the work consists of jointing, bolting-up, riveting or welding work and the period for which the platform is used is so short as to make the provision of guard-rails and toe-boards or other barriers unreasonable. (If advantage is taken of this exemption the platform must be at least 34 inches wide, adequate handhold must be provided, and any materials or articles deposited on the platform must be in boxes or other receptacles which will prevent them falling;

(*d*) Platforms of a temporary nature passing between two adjacent glazing bars of a roof with a sloping surface, so long as the bars or the roof framework afford secure handhold along the full length of the platform and so long as toe-boards or similar barriers are provided whenever the nature of the work makes this practicable;

(*e*) Any platform used beneath a roof and supported by, or suspended from, the roof members or the roof itself and used only for work on or in the vicinity of the roof—provided that the work is of a light nature and of such short duration as to make the provision of guard-rails and toe-boards unreasonable and provided also that there is adequate handhold at every working position and that the material required for the work is such that a platform without guard-rails or toe-boards can be used with safety;

(*f*) Any working platform or working place which has one of its sides contiguous to the concave surface of a cylindrical or spherical structure, so long as reasonably practicable steps are taken to prevent persons falling a distance of more than 6ft. 6in. *CWP: 28(6)*

161 – Construction of Scaffolds*

The following requirements apply to the construction of all scaffolds. Additional requirements for certain special types of scaffold are given in items 162 and 163.

Materials—Sufficient materials must be provided and used. All materials must be suitable and sound. *CWP: 9(1) and (2)*

Timber used for scaffolds must be of suitable quality and in good condition, and must have the bark completely stripped off. It must not be so painted or treated that defects cannot easily be seen. *CWP: 9(3) and (4)*

No timber or other material may be used if it has projecting nails. *CGP: 48(1)*

Metal parts of scaffolds must be in good condition, of suitable quality, and free from corrosion or other patent defects likely to affect their strength materially. *CWP: 9(5)*

No defective materials or defective parts may be used in the construction of scaffolds. (Special mention is made of ropes or bonds which may have become defective through contact with acid or other corrosive substance or through some other means.) *CWP: 10(1) and (2)*

Materials and parts not in use must be kept under good conditions, separate from materials and parts unsuitable for scaffolds. *CWP: 10(3)*

---

* For exemptions in regard to scaffolds used in the alteration, repair or maintenance of steeples, towers and chimney stacks, see Certificate of Exemption No. 1 (External Scaffolds on Steeples), Form 2284, 18th August 1967.

ERECTION—A competent person must inspect materials before each occasion on which they are to be used. *CWP: 8*

The erection, alteration, substantial additions and dismantling must be done under the immediate supervision of a competent person and, so far as practicable, by competent and experienced workmen. *CWP: 8*

Every part of a scaffold must be of good construction, of suitable and sound material, and of adequate strength for the purpose for which it is used. Every part must be so fixed, secured or placed in position as to prevent accidental displacement so far as is practicable. *CWP: 9(1) and 11*

Every scaffold must be securely supported or suspended and must, where necessary, be properly strutted or braced to prevent collapse. *CWP: 15(1)*

Scaffolds must be rigidly connected to the building or other structure unless designed and constructed to ensure stability without such connection. *CWP: 15(1)*

No part of a building or other structure may be used to support a scaffold unless it is of sound material and sufficiently strong to provide safe support. Gutters must not be used as supports unless they and their fittings are of adequate strength; overhanging eaves gutters must not be so used unless designed as walkways. *CWP: 18*

Loose bricks, drain pipes, chimney pots and other unsuitable materials must never be used for the construction or support of scaffolds (except that a platform only 2 feet or less above the ground or floor may be supported by bricks or small blocks if these provide a firm support. *CWP: 15(4)*

After erection, all scaffolds must be properly maintained and must be inspected at the intervals given in item 164.

Partly erected or partly dismantled scaffolds must not be used unless they comply with the regulations even in their incomplete condition. See item 164.

SUPPORTS—Structures and appliances used to support scaffolds must be of sound construction and, where necessary, must be sufficiently strutted and braced to ensure stability. They must have a firm footing or else must be firmly supported. *CWP: 15(2)*

STANDARDS, UPRIGHTS AND LEDGERS—Standards or uprights must be vertical or slightly inclined towards the building or other structure where this is practicable and must be fixed sufficiently close together to secure stability. *CWP: 13(1)*

The foot or base of any standard or upright must be placed on an adequate base-plate to prevent slipping or sinking, unless displacement is prevented in some other sufficient way. *CWP: 13(2)*

Ladders used as the uprights of scaffolds must be of adequate strength, secured to prevent slipping, and so placed that the two stiles or sides of each ladder are evenly supported or suspended. *CWP: 14(1)*

Ledgers must be horizontal, as nearly as possible, and must be securely fastened to the standards or uprights by efficient means. *CWP: 13(4)*

PUTLOGS—Putlogs or other supports on which a platform rests must be securely fastened to ledgers, standards or uprights, unless movement is prevented by other efficient means. *CWP: 13(4)*

Putlogs supported at one end by a wall must extend into it or onto it for a sufficient distance to provide an adequate supporting area. *CWP: 13(4)*

Distances between any two consecutive putlogs or other supports must be fixed with due regard to the nature of the platform and the load it will bear. As a general rule the distance must not exceed 3ft. 3in. for a 1¼-inch plank, 5 feet for a 1½-inch plank, and 8ft. 6in. for a 2-inch plank but these distances must be reduced if the anticipated load, or the nature of the platform, makes a shorter distance necessary to ensure safety. *CWP: 13(5)*

162 – Slung and Suspended Scaffolds

The following requirements are additional to those affecting all types of scaffold and quoted in item 161.

SLUNG SCAFFOLDS—A slung scaffold is defined as one which is suspended by means of lifting gear, ropes, chains or rigid members and which is not provided with means of raising or lowering. *CWP: 4*

All chains, ropes, lifting gear, metal tubes or other means of suspension must be suitable and of adequate strength for the purpose for which they are used. *CWP: 16(1)*

All chains, ropes and lifting gear used as a means of suspension must comply with the requirements of the Construction (Lifting Operations) Regulations as set out in item 169. *CWP: 16(1)*

Means of suspension must be properly and securely fastened to safe anchorage points and to the scaffold ledgers or other main supporting members. They must be so placed as to ensure stability and must be as nearly vertical as is reasonably practicable. *CWP: 16(1)*

Ropes and chains used for suspension must be kept taut and steps must be taken to prevent them coming into contact with edges, where this would cause danger. *CWP: 16*

No ropes except wire ropes may be used and no wire rope may be used if it has become defective through contact with acid or corrosive substances or through other means. *CWP: 10(2) and 16(2)*

Every slung scaffold must be secured to prevent undue horizontal movement while it is in use. *CWP: 16(4)*

The platform of a slung scaffold must comply with the general requirements for working platforms set out in item 160.

SUSPENDED SCAFFOLDS OPERATED BY POWER—The raising, lowering or carrying of persons by the use of suspended scaffolds raised and lowered by power-operated lifting appliances is permissible only when the Chief Inspector of Factories has given special approval. See item 170.

SUSPENDED SCAFFOLDS NOT OPERATED BY POWER—The following requirements apply to scaffolds which are suspended by ropes or chains and can be raised or lowered but which are not operated by a power-driven appliance. *CWP: 4(2) and 19(1)*

Every part of a suspended scaffold, and all plant and equipment used in connexion with it, must be of good construction, suitable, and of adequate strength for its purpose, and must be properly maintained. *CWP: 19(11)*

Metal parts must be free of any corrosion or other patent defect likely to affect their strength materially. *CWP: 19(11)*

Suspended scaffolds must be suspended from suitable outriggers, joists, runways, rail tracks or other equally safe anchorages and must be provided with adequate and suitable chains or ropes and with adequate and suitable winches or other appliances for raising and lowering. *CWP: 19(3)*

Every runway, joist or rail track supporting a suspended scaffold must be of suitable and sound material, free from patent defect, and of adequate strength for its purpose. It must have adequate stops at each end and must be properly secured to the building or other structure or to the outriggers, if any. *CWP: 19(8)*

Winches or other lifting appliances used to raise and lower suspended scaffolds must comply with the Construction (Lifting Operations) Regulations as summarised in items 167 and 168. In addition, they must have brakes or similar devices which automatically come into operation when the operating handle or lever is released, and must be adequately protected against the effects of weather, dust or materials likely to cause damage. Winches must be marked to show the length of the rope used. *CWP: 19(1), (4) and (10)*

Outriggers must be of adequate length and strength, properly installed and supported, and properly spaced having regard to the construction of the scaffold and its supports. Except when used with lightweight scaffolds (see below) outriggers must be horizontal and must have adequate stops at the outer ends. *CWP: 19(5)*

If counterweights are used with outriggers they must be securely attached and must weigh not less than three times the weight which would counterbalance the weight suspended from the outriggers (including the weight of any runway, joist or rail track and the weight of the scaffold and its load. *CWP: 19(6)*

The points of suspension of a suspended scaffold must be an adequate horizontal distance from the face of the building or other structure. If workmen are to sit on the edge of the platform, the space between the platform and the building must not be more than 12 inches and, if necessary, devices must be used to keep the platform a sufficient distance from the wall. When workmen do not sit on the edge of the platform, the distance between the platform and the building must be as small as is reasonably practicable. *CWP: 19(7) and (13)*

Ropes, chains and lifting gear used to support suspended scaffolds must comply with the requirements of the Construction (Lifting Operations) Regulations as set out in item 169. No ropes other than wire ropes may be used, except for the suspension of lightweight scaffolds (see below). No rope must be used which has been rendered defective through contact with acid or other corrosive substance or from any other cause. *CWP: 10(2) and 19(1) and (2)*

Suspension ropes or chains must be kept in tension and must be securely attached to the outriggers or other supports, and to the platform framework or any lifting devices attached thereto. *CWP: 19(9)*

Suspension ropes used with winches must be long enough to leave at least two turns on each winch drum when the scaffold is at its lowest position. The length of the rope must be clearly marked on its winch. *CWP: 19(10)*

Adequate arrangements must be made to prevent undue tipping, tilting or swinging of a suspended scaffold and to prevent undue horizontal movement while it is in use. *CWP: 9(11)*

Platforms of suspended scaffolds must comply with the general requirements for working platforms set out in item 160.

CRADLES AND OTHER LIGHTWEIGHT SCAFFOLDS—Cradles and other lightweight suspended scaffolds may be used where the nature of the work, and the materials to be carried, enable such a scaffold to be used with safety. *CWP: 19(15)*

Unlike other suspended scaffolds, cradles and other lightweight scaffolds may be suspended by fibre ropes. The ropes must operate on pulley blocks spaced at intervals of not more than 10ft. 6in. *CWP: 19(14)*

The platform of a cradle or other lightweight scaffold must be at least 17 inches wide. *CWP: 19(15)*

In all other respects, cradles and other lightweight scaffolds are subject to the same requirements as other suspended scaffolds, except that outriggers need not be horizontal and need not have end-stops. *CWP: 19(15)*

BOATSWAINS' CHAIRS—Boatswains' chairs and similar appliances are not classed as suspended scaffolds for the purposes of the regulations but are subject to special requirements set out in item 163. *CWP: 4*

PERMANENT CRADLES, ETC.—Suspended platforms and cradles which are part of the permanent equipment of a building are treated as suspended scaffolds for the purposes of the regulations and are subject to the requirements quoted above. *CWP: 19(1)*

163 – Other Special Types of Scaffold

The following requirements are additional to the general requirements for all scaffolds set out in item 161.

TRESTLE SCAFFOLDS—Trestles and supports used for a trestle scaffold must be of good construction, suitable and sound materials, adequate strength for their purpose, and free from patent defect. *CWP: 21(1)*

Timber used for trestles must not be so painted or otherwise treated that defects cannot readily be seen. *CWP: 9(4)*

Trestles scaffolds with folding supports must consist of one tier only. *CWP: 21(2)*

No trestle scaffold may be used if it is so situated that a person might fall more than 15 feet from the working platform. *CWP: 21(2)*

If a trestle scaffold is erected on a scaffold platform the latter must be wide enough to allow sufficient clear space for the transport of materials along the platform and the trestles or other supports must be firmly attached to the scaffold platform and adequately placed to prevent displacement. *CWP: 21(2)*

The platform of a trestle scaffold must comply with the general requirements for working platforms set out in item 160.

LADDER SCAFFOLDS—Ladder scaffolds must be used only for work of light nature and for such materials as enable them to be used with safety. *CWP: 14(2)*

Ladders must be of adequate strength and secured to prevent slipping. They must be so placed that the two stiles or sides of each ladder are evenly supported or suspended. *CWP: 14(1)*

The platform of a ladder scaffold must comply with the general requirements for working platforms set out in item 160.

CANTILEVER OR JIB SCAFFOLDS—Cantilever or jib scaffolds must be adequately supported, fixed and anchored. Outriggers must be of adequate length and strength. *CWP: 17(1)*

The scaffold must be strutted or braced where this is necessary to ensure rigidity and stability. *CWP: 17(1)*

The platform of a cantilever or jib scaffold must comply with the general requirements for working platforms set out in item 160.

SCAFFOLDS MOUNTED ON WHEELS OR SKIDS—Scaffolds mounted on wheels or skids must be constructed with due regard to stability and, where necessary, must be adequately weighted at the base. They must be used only on a firm and even surface which is not sloping sufficiently to cause instability. They must be secured to prevent movement when any person is working on them, or on any ladder or other plant supported by them. *CWP: 15(3)*

Such scaffolds must be moved only by the application of force at or near the base. *CWP: 15(3)*

The platform of all such scaffolds must comply with the

general requirements for working platforms set out in item 160.

FIGURE OR BRACKET SCAFFOLDS—Figure or bracket scaffolds supported or held by dogs, spikes or other fixings liable to pull out of the stonework or brickwork must never be used. *CWP: 17(2)*

BOATSWAINS' CHAIRS, ETC.—Boatswains' chairs, cages, skips and similar equipment, when raised or lowered by power-driven lifting appliances, are subject to the Construction (Lifting Operations) Regulations, as summarised in items 165 to 170. If not raised or lowered by power-driven lifting appliances they are subject to the Construction (Working Places) Regulations and must comply with the following requirements.

Boatswains' chairs, etc., must not be used as working places in circumstances in which the use of a suspended scaffold is reasonably practicable, unless the work is of such short duration as to make the use of a suspended scaffold unreasonable. *CWP: 20(2)*

Every boatswain's chair, etc., must be installed and used under the supervision of a competent person. It must be of good construction, suitable and sound material, adequate strength and free from patent defect, and must be properly maintained. *CWP: 20(1)*

Outriggers or other supports must be of adequate strength and must be properly installed and supported. Chains, ropes, lifting gear or other means of suspension must be securely attached and must satisfy the requirements of the Construction (Lifting Operations) Regulations as set out in item 169. *CWP: 20(1)*

Suitable measures must be taken to prevent any occupant of a boatswain's chair, etc., from falling out; in particular, skips or other receptacles must be at least 3 feet deep. Measures must also be taken to prevent spinning or tipping in a manner dangerous to the occupant. *CWP: 20(1)*

Boatswains' chairs, cages, skips, etc., when occupied by any person, must be free of materials or articles liable to interfere with the occupant's handhold or foothold or otherwise to endanger his safety. *CWP: 20(1)*

Boatswains' chairs, cages, skips, etc., used as working places must be inspected at the same intervals as other scaffolds. See item 164.

164 – Inspection, Care and Maintenance of Scaffolds

All scaffolds must be properly maintained and every part must be so fixed, secured, or placed in position as to prevent accidental displacement as far as is reasonably practicable. *CWP: 11*

All scaffolds used must have been inspected by a competent person within the preceding 7 days, unless no part has been erected for over 7 days. *CWP: 22(1)*

Scaffolds must also be inspected after being exposed to weather conditions likely to affect strength or stability or likely to have displaced any part. *CWP: 22(1)*

Results of inspections must be entered in, or attached to, Factory Form 91 (except for ladder scaffolds, trestle scaffolds, and scaffolds from which persons cannot fall more than 6ft. 6in.). *CWP: 22(1)*

Each employer whose men use a scaffold must satisfy himself that it complies with the regulations, whether or not his own men have built it. *CWP: 23*

Platforms, gangways, runs and stairs must be kept clear of unnecessary obstructions, material or rubbish and from projecting nails. *CWP: 30(2)*

Slippery platforms, gangways, runs and stairs must be sanded, cleaned or otherwise remedied as soon as practicable. *CWP: 30(1)*

Materials must not be kept on scaffolds unless needed within a reasonable time. Scaffolds must not be overloaded and, as far as practicable, loads on scaffolds must be evenly distributed. *CWP: 37*

Movement of materials on or on to scaffolds must be done without causing any violent shock. *CWP: 37*

Partly erected or partly dismantled scaffolds must not be used unless, in spite of their state, they still comply with the regulations. Use of such scaffolds must be prevented either by blocking the approaches to them, so far as this is reasonably practicable, or by posting warning notices at every point from which the scaffold is likely to be approached. *CWP: 12*

165 – Cranes

Cranes used wholly or mainly on building operations or works of engineering construction are subject to the requirements quoted in this item.

Cranes which are installed in a factory as part of its normal equipment also become subject to the following requirements if they are used for building operations or works of engineering construction—except for the special exceptions mentioned in the appropriate places.

MATERIALS AND CONSTRUCTION—All cranes, including all working gear and all anchorages and fixing devices, must be of good mechanical construction, sound material, adequate strength, and free from patent defect, and must be properly maintained. *CLO: 10(1)*

Cranes must be adequately and securely supported, and every part of a stage, framework or other structure supporting a crane must be of good construction, sound material, and adequate strength. (This requirement includes any mast, beam, pole or other article of plant supporting a crane.) *CLO: 11(1) and (2)*

Any anchoring or fixing arrangements provided in connexion with a crane must be adequate and secure. *CLO: 12(4)*

Timber must not be used for structural members of cranes. Timber used for parts other than structural members must not have protruding nails if these would be a source of danger. *CLO: 24 and CGP: 48(1)*

Drums and pulleys must be of suitable diameter and construction for the chain or rope used. Chains or ropes must be properly secured to drums and at least two turns of chain or rope must remain on the drum in every operating position. *CLO: 15*

Cranes must have efficient brakes or other safety devices to prevent the fall of the load and to control the lowering of the load. *CLO: 16(1)*

Every dangerous mechanical part of a crane must be securely fenced, unless it is in such a position or of such construction as to be as safe to every person working on the site as it would be if securely fenced. *CGP: 42*

CONTROL LEVERS, SWITCHES, ETC.—Every lever, handle, switch or other device which is provided for controlling the operation of a crane, and which could cause danger if accidentally moved or displaced, must either be so placed to prevent the possibility of such accidental movement or else must have a suitable spring or locking device. *CLO: 16(2)*

Every such lever, switch, etc., must have on it, or near it, a clear indication of its purpose and mode of operation.

(This does not apply to rotating handles used for raising or lowering on winches, nor to non-derricking jib cranes which are not operated by mechanical power.) *CLO: 16(3)*

These requirements regarding control levers, etc., do not apply to cranes which are part of the permanent equipment of a factory and which are only occasionally used for building operations or works of engineering construction. *CLO: 6 and Schedule*

A temporary exemption from some of these requirements was formerly granted to cranes used in works of engineering construction, but these exemptions ceased to have effect in March 1964. *CLO: 16(2)*

MARKING OF SAFE WORKING LOAD, ETC.—Every crane must be marked plainly with the safe working load and means of identification. If designed to be used at various radii it must be marked to show the safe working load at different radii and must be fitted with an accurate indicator, visible to the driver or operator, which shows the radius of the jib, trolley or crab, and the safe working load for that radius. (If a crane is part of the permanent equipment of a factory and is used only occasionally for building operations or works of engineering construction a safe working load indicator is not necessary if there is a table showing safe working loads at different radii as provided for by Section 27 of the Factories Act, summarised in item 79.) *CLO: 29(1) and (2) and Schedule.*

If, as a result of tests made after re-erection, a lower safe working load is prescribed for the crane as then erected, a loading diagram indicating the modified safe working load must be affixed where it can readily be seen by the crane driver. *CLO: 19(5)*

If a crane is occasionally dismantled, wholly or partially, and re-erected, any jib or boom which is seperated from the crane by dismantling must be clearly marked to show which it is part of. *CLO: 11(6)*

Crawler-tracked excavators and crawler-tracked dragline excavators which have been temporarily adapted for use as cranes by the attachment of lifting gear to the shovel or bucket are, while so used, exempt from the above requirements but are subject to the special requirements of Certificate of Exemption No. 2 (General) issued under the Construction (Lifting Operations) Regulations 1961; this certificate is published as Factory Form 2209.

ACCESS—Safe access must, so far as is reasonably practicable, be provided for persons examining, repairing or lubricating the crane, if such persons are liable to fall more than 6ft. 6in. This includes the provision of handholds and footholds if necessary. *CLO: 17*

PLATFORMS AND CABINS—Any platform provided for the operation of a crane must be of sufficient size for those using it, must be closely boarded or planked, and must have safe means of access. On any side of the platform from which a a person might fall more than 6ft. 6in. there must be suitable guard-rails to a height of at least 3 feet and toe-boards to a height of 8 inches or such greater height as is necessary to prevent the fall of persons, tools or materials. The distance between the top of the toe-board and the lowest guard-rail must not be greater than 27 inches and both guard-rails and toe-boards must be kept in position except when necessarily removed for the passage of persons or materials. (When a crane is part of the permanent equipment of a factory, and is only occasionally used for building operations or works of engineering construction, the only requirement for platforms is that they should be of sufficient area and should have safe means of access.) *CLO: 13*

Except in the special circumstances mentioned in the next paragraph, the driver of a power-driven lifting appliance must be provided with a suitable cabin affording adequate protection from the weather; in cold weather the cabin must be adequately heated by suitable means, if this is reasonably practicable. The design and construction of the cabin must be such that the driver has a sufficiently clear and unrestricted view to operate the crane safely and has ready access to such parts of the crane as are within the cabin and need periodic inspection or maintenance. *CLO: 14(1) and (3)*

These requirements for cabins do not apply in the following circumstances:—

(*a*) Where the driver is indoors or is otherwise adequately protected from the weather.

(*b*) When the crane is a mobile one and has a safe working load of one ton or less.

(*c*) When the crane is to be used only occasionally, or for only a short period at any one time.

(*d*) When it has not been reasonably practicable to erect the cabin completely before the crane was taken into general use. This exemption operates only if other adequate protection from the weather has been provided pending the erection of the cabin.

(*e*) When the crane forms part of the permanent equipment of a factory and is only occasionally used for building operations or works of engineering construction. *CLO: 14 and Schedule*

RAIL-MOUNTED CRANES—Cranes mounted on rails must have effective brakes unless sprags, scotches or chocks are available. *CLO: 20(2)*

Rails on which cranes move must be of adequate section, with an even-running surface, and must be sufficiently and adequately supported on a surface sufficiently firm to prevent undue movement of the rails. *CLO: 20(2)*

Rails must be jointed by fish plates or double chairs and must be securely fastened to sleepers or bearers, unless other adequate steps are taken to ensure the proper junction of the rails and to prevent any material variation in their gauge. (This requirement does not apply to overhead cranes on bridge rails.) *CLO: 20(1)*

Rails must be laid in straight lines or in curves of such radii that the crane can be moved freely and without danger of derailment. There must be adequate stops or buffers on each rail at each end of the track, except when the crane is part of the permanent equipment of a factory and is only occasionally used for building operations or works of engineering construction. *CLO: 20(1) and Schedule*

All rails and other equipment used in connexion with rail-mounted cranes must be properly maintained. *CLO: 20(1)*

Every bogie, trolley or wheeled carriage on which a crane is mounted must be of good construction, sound material, and adequate strength and must be suitable to support the crane having regard to the purposes for which it is being used. It must be properly maintained. *CLO: 21*

Travelling cranes running on rails must be provided with guards to remove from the rails any loose materials likely to cause danger. (This does not apply to cranes which form part of the permanent equipment of a factory and which are used only occasionally for building operations or works of engineering construction.) *CLO: 20(4) and Schedule*

When a scotch derrick crane is mounted on more than one bogie, trolley or wheeled carriage, the crane sleepers or land ties, or else the bogies, trolleys or wheeled carriages, must be rigidly braced and properly connected together. The rails on which each bogie, etc., moves must be level and the crane must be moved only in a manner not liable to cause instability, racking or distortion either of the crane or of the supporting framework or track. *CLO: 20(3)*

ERECTION OF CRANES—All cranes must be erected under the supervision of a competent person. *CLO: 25*

Cranes must be securely anchored or adequately weighted by suitable ballast, properly placed and secured against accidental displacement. If stability is obtained by removable weights, a diagram or notice showing the position and number of such weights must be fixed to the crane in a position where it can easily be seen. *CLO: 19(2) and (6)*

All the appliances for the anchorage or ballasting of a crane must be examined by a competent person on each occasion before the crane is erected. *CLO: 19(3)*

Temporary attachments or connexions used in the erection or dismantling of cranes must be adequate and secure. (This does not apply to cranes which are part of the permanent equipment of a factory and are only occasionally used for building operations or works of engineering construction. *CLO*: 11(5)

No part of any rails on which a crane is mounted, or the sleepers supporting such rails, must be used as an anchorage for a crane. *CLO: 19(2)*

A crane must not be erected under weather conditions likely to endanger its stability. After exposure to weather conditions likely to affect stability its anchorage and ballast must be examined by a competent person and any necessary steps taken to assure stability before it is used again. *CLO: 19(7)*

When a crane is used on a soft or uneven surface, or on a slope, appropriate precautions must be taken to ensure stability. *CLO: 19(1)*

TESTS FOR THE STABILITY OF CRANES—After a crane has been erected or re-erected its stability must be tested by a competent person before it is taken into use. The test must consist either of the imposition (at the position where there is the maximum pull on each anchorage) of a load 25 per cent above the maximum load to be lifted by the crane as there erected, or else the imposition of a lighter load so arranged as to provide an equivalent test of the anchorage or ballasting arrangements. *CLO: 19(4)*

Similar tests of stability must be made after any removal or adjustment which involves changes in the arrangements for anchoring or ballasting a crane. *CLO: 19(4)*

The person making one of the above tests must forthwith make a written report on Factory Form 91, Section D. *CLO: 19(4)*

If the person making the test decides that the maximum load which can safely be lifted by the crane as erected is less than its normal or previous safe working load he must specify this modified safe working load in his report. A loading diagram appropiate to the stability of the crane as at the time of the test, and showing the modified safe working load, must be affixed in a position where it is clearly visible to the crane driver, and if the crane is a mobile one the loading diagram must take into account the conditions of the track at the time. *CLO: 19(4) and (5)*

A crane which is part of the permanent equipment of a factory, and which is used only occasionally for building operations or works of engineering construction, need not undergo these stability tests except when it is specially erected for use in connexion with such operations. *CLO: 6 and Schedule*

OTHER TESTS, EXAMINATIONS, ETC.—No crane must be used unless it has been thoroughly examined within the previous 14 months and unless it has been given a test (followed by a thorough examination) within the previous 4 years. Reports of such tests and examinations must be made on Factory Form 96 (for tests followed by examinations) and Factory Form 91, Section G (for examinations only); these reports must be made within 28 days and those referring to tests must show the safe working load and, where appropiate, the maximum safe working radius of the jib and the safe working loads for various radii. *CLO: 28*

After any substantial alteration or repair a crane must be given a further thorough examination and a further report must be made. If the alterations or repairs were such as might have affected the strength or stability the crane must be tested as well as being examined. *CLO: 28(2) and (3)*

As far as its construction permits, every crane must be inspected once a week by its driver (if he is competent for the purpose) or by some other competent person. A report of the examination must be made on Factory Form 91, Section C as soon as the inspection has been carried out and must be signed by the person who carried it out— except that, when the building operations or works of engineering construction in question are not expected to last for more than 6 weeks, the person making the inspection can give his employer an informal written report and the employer himself can make the entry on Form 91C. *CLO: 10(1) and (2)*

If any test or examination shows that the crane cannot be used with safety unless certain repairs are carried out (either immediately or within a specified time) the person making the test or examination must, within 28 days, send a copy of his report to the district inspector of factories. *CLO: 28(7)*

The above requirements respecting the testing, examination and inspection of cranes do not apply to any crane which, is part of the permanent equipment of a factory and which is used only occasionally for building operations or works of engineering construction. (Such cranes will, of course, be subject to testing and examination under the Factories Act as explained in item 79.) *CLO: 6 and Schedule*

Crawler-tracked excavators and crawler-tracked dragline excavators which have been temporarily adapted for use as cranes by the attachment of lifting gear to the shovel or bucket are, while so used, subject to special requirements set out in Certificate of Exemption No. 2 (General) issued under the Construction (Lifting Operations) Regulations 1961; this certificate is published as Factory Form F 2209.

OTHER REQUIREMENTS—Additional requirements for jib cranes are given in the next item. Chains, ropes and lifting tackle are dealt with in item 169. The operation of cranes is dealt with in item 170.

166 – Special Requirements for Jib Cranes

The following requirements for jib cranes used in building

operations are in addition to the general requirements for cranes quoted in the previous item. They apply to any crane with a fixed or derricking jib, except as stated below under "Exceptions".

SAFE LOAD INDICATORS—An automatic safe load indicator, of a type approved by the Chief Inspector of Factories, must be fitted and properly maintained. *CLO: 30(1) and (2)*

On cranes other than mobile cranes the indicator must be tested (by a competent person other than the driver or operator) each time the crane is installed or erected On mobile cranes the indicator must be tested by a competent person before the crane is taken back into use after being wholly or partially dismantled and after each re-erection, alteration or removal likely to have affected the indicator. *CLO: 30(1) and (2)*

All automatic safe load indicators must be inspected weekly by the person carrying out the weekly inspection referred to in item 165. *CLO: 30(1) and (2)*

A report of every test and every weekly inspection of an automatic safe load indicator must be made on the prescribed form (Factory Form 91E for tests and Factory Form 91C for weekly inspections). *CLO: 30*

Crawler-tracked excavators and crawler-tracked dragline excavators which have been temporarily adapted for use as cranes by the attachment of lifting gear to the shovel or bucket need not have a safe-load indicator but are subject to special requirements as to maximum loads. These are set out in Certificate of Exemption No. 2 (General) made under the Construction (Lifting Operations) Regulations 1961; this certificate is published as Factory Form F 2209.

INTERLOCKS—When a crane has a derricking jib operated through a clutch there must be a properly maintained and effective interlocking arrangement between the derricking clutch and the pawl sustaining the derricking drum, to ensure that the clutch cannot be disengaged unless the pawl is in effective engagement with the derricking drum and the pawl cannot be disengaged unless the clutch is in effective engagement with the derricking drum. *CLO: 22*

This does not apply to any crane on which the derricking drum is driven by self-locking mechanism or on which the hoisting and derricking drums are independently driven. *CLO: 22*

OTHER REQUIREMENTS—The jib of a Scotch derrick must not be erected between the back stays. *CLO: 22*

Appropriate measures must be taken to prevent the foot of the king post of any Scotch derrick crane from being lifted out of its socket or support while in use. *CLO: 33(3)*

If the guys of a guy derrick crane cannot be fixed at approximately equal inclinations to the mast and in such a way that the angles between adjacent pairs of guys are equal, other effective measures must be taken to ensure the stability of the crane. *CLO: 33(4)*

Scotch derrick cranes mounted on more than one bogie, etc., are subject to the special requirements mentioned in the previous item in connexion with mounted cranes.

EXCEPTIONS—The requirements regarding interlocking devices for derricking clutches and drums do not apply to cranes which form part of the permanent equipment of a factory and are used only occasionally for building operations or works of engineering construction. *CLO: 6 and Schedule*

The requirements regarding the approved type of safe load indicators do not apply to the following:—

(*a*) Cranes with a safe working load of under one ton.

(*b*) Hand cranes used solely for erecting or dismantling other cranes.

(*c*) A guy derrick crane the mast of which is held upright solely by means of ropes with the necessary fitting and tightening screws.

(*d*) A crane which forms part of the permanent equipment of a factory and is used only occasionally for building operations and works of engineering construction and which complies with Section 27(4) of the Factories Act 1961 by having either a safe load indicator or a table showing the safe working loads at various radii. *CLO: 30(4) and Schedule*

167 – Crabs and Winches

All crabs and winches must be of good mechanical construction, sound material, adequate strength and substance and free from patent defect and must be properly maintained. *CLO: 10(1)*

Any anchoring or fixing arrangements provided in connexion with a crab or winch must be adequate and secure. *CLO: 11(4)*

Every part of the framework of a crab or winch other than a jack-roll, including the bearers, must be of metal. *CLO: 11(3)*

The safe working load of every crab or winch and a means of identification must be plainly marked on it. *CLO: 29(1)*

Every crab and winch must be adequately and securely supported and every part of a stage, framework or other structure and every mast, beam, pole or other article of plant supporting any part of a crab or winch must be of good construction, sound material and adequate strength having regard to the nature of the lifting appliance, its lifting and reaching capacity, and the circumstances of its use. *CLO: 1(1) and (2)*

Every drum or pulley round which the chain or wire rope of any crab or winch is carried must be of suitable diameter and construction for the chain or rope used. Every chain or rope which terminates at the winding drum must be properly secured thereto and at least two turns of such chain or rope must remain on the drum in every operating position of the appliance. *CLO: 15*

Every crab and winch other than a jack-roll must be provided with an efficient brake or brakes or other safety device which will prevent the fall of the load when suspended, and by which the load can be effectively controlled while being lowered. *CLO: 16(1)*

ACCESS—Safe access must, so far as is reasonably practicable, be provided for persons examining, repairing or lubricating crabs and winches, if such persons are liable to fall more than 6 ft. 6 in. This includes the provision of handholds and footholds where necessary. *CLO: 16(1)*

On every stage, gantry or other place where a crab or other lifting machine with a travelling motion is in use, an unobstructed passageway at least 2 feet wide must be maintained between any such moving part of the appliance and any guard-rail, fencing, or other nearby fixture; if at any time it is not practicable to maintain this passageway at any point, access to that point must be prevented during the time in question. (This requirement as to passageways does not apply to lifting appliances which are part of the permanent equipment of a factory and are only occasionally used for building operations or works of engineering construction.) *CLO: 12 and Schedule*

ERECTION—Every temporary attachment or connexion of a rope, chain or other plant or gear used in the erection or dismantling of a crab or winch must be adequate and secure. (This does not apply to a crab or winch which is part of the permanent equipment of a factory and is only occasionally used for building operations or works of engineering construction.) *CLO: 11(5)*

INSPECTIONS, EXAMINATIONS AND TESTS—The weekly inspections and the periodic examinations and tests prescribed for cranes apply also to crabs and winches. The prescribed forms to be used for reports are Factory Form 91, Section C (for weekly inspection), Factory Form 91, Section G (for examinations) and Factory Form 80 (for tests followed by examination). *CLO: 10 and 28*

OTHER REQUIREMENTS—Chains, ropes and lifting gear used with crabs and winches are covered by the requirements quoted in item 169. The operation of crabs and winches is dealt with in item 170.

The requirements regarding control levers and switches, quoted in item 165, apply to crabs and winches as well as to cranes (except that the rotating handle of a winch need not be marked to show its purpose and mode of operation).

The requirements for drivers' cabins, quoted in item 165, apply to the operators of power driven crabs and winches as they do to crane drivers.

Every dangerous mechanical part of a crab or winch must be securely fenced, unless it is in such a position or of such construction as to be as safe to every person working on the site as it would be if securely fenced. *CGP: 42*

168 – Other Lifting Appliances (except Hoists)

The requirements quoted in this item apply to any pulley block or gin wheel used for lowering and to any sheer legs, excavator, dragline, piling frame, aerial cableway, aerial ropeway, or overhead runway.

GENERAL REQUIREMENTS—All the lifting appliances mentioned must be adequately and securely supported and any anchoring or fixing arrangements provided in connexion with them must be adequate and secure. *CLO: 11(1) and (4)*

Every part of such lifting appliances, including the anchoring and fixing devices, must be of good mechanical construction, sound material, adequate strength, and free from patent defect and must be properly maintained. *CLO: 10(1)*

Every part of a stage, scaffold, framework or other structure, and every mast, beam, pole or other article of plant or equipment supporting any of these lifting appliances, must be of good construction and adequate strength. *CLO: 11(2)*

Drums and pulleys must be of suitable diameter and construction for the chain or rope used. Chains and ropes must be properly secured to drums, and at least two turns of chain or rope must remain on the drum in every operating position. *CLO: 15*

Every dangerous mechanical part of a lifting appliance must be securely fenced, unless it is in such a position or of such construction as to be as safe to every person working on the site as it would be if securely fenced. *CGP: 42*

The requirements respecting control levers and switches, quoted in item 165, apply to the lifting appliances mentioned in this item just as they apply to cranes.

The safe working load and a means of identification must be plainly marked on every aerial cableway, derrick pole, and derrick mast used to raise or lower loads of 1 ton or more. *CLO: 29(1)(a)*

The safe working load or loads must also be marked on every crawler-tracked excavator and crawler-tracked dragline excavator which has been temporarily adapted for use as a crane by the attachment of lifting gear to the shovel or bucket. *CE No. 2 General) under the Construction (Lifting Operations) Regulations (Factory Form F 2209)*

ERECTION—Every temporary attachment or connexion of a rope, chain or other plant or equipment used in the erection or dismantling of any of the above lifting appliances must be adequate and secure. (This does not apply to lifting appliances which are part of the permanent equipment of a factory and are only occasionally used for building operations and works of engineering construction.) *CLO: 11(5) and Schedule*

When a lifting appliance is used on a soft or uneven surface, or on a slope, appropriate precautions must be taken to ensure stability. *CLO: 19(1)*

ACCESS, PLATFORMS AND CABINS—Safe access must, so far as is reasonably practicable, be provided for persons examining, repairing or lubricating lifting appliances, if such persons are liable to fall more than 6 ft. 6 in. This includes the provision of handholds and footholds where necessary. *CLO: 17*

On every stage, gantry or other place where a lifting machine which has a travelling or slewing motion is in use, an unobstructed passageway at least 2 feet wide must be maintained between any such moving part of the appliance and any guard-rail, fencing, or other nearby fixture; if at any time it is not practicable to maintain this passageway at any point, access to that point must be prevented during the time in question. (This requirement as to passageways does not apply to lifting appliances which are part of the permanent equipment of a factory and are only occasionally used for building operations or works of engineering construction.) *CLO: 12 and Schedule*

The requirements for drivers' cabins, quoted in item 165, apply to the drivers and operators of all power driven lifting appliances, just as they do to cranes.

TESTS, EXAMINATIONS AND INSPECTIONS—No pulley wheel, gin wheel or sheer legs must be used unless it has been examined by a competent person within the previous 14 months, and such lifting appliances must not be used to lift or lower a load of one ton or more unless (in addition to having been examined within the previous 14 months) they have also been tested by a competent person. *CLO: 28(1) and (3)*

A pulley block, gin wheel or sheer legs which has undergone any substantial alteration or repair must be thoroughly examined by a competent person before it is used again and must not be used to lift or lower a load of 1 ton or more unless it has been tested as well as examined. *CLO: 28(1) and (3)*

An excavator, dragline, piling frame, aerial cableway, aerial ropeway, or overhead runway must not be used unless it has been thoroughly examined by a competent person within the previous 14 months. It must also be thoroughly examined before being taken back into use after any substantial alteration or repair. *CLO: 28(3)*

All lifting appliances must be inspected once a week, so far as their construction permits. The inspection may be carried out by the driver or operator of the appliance if he is competent to do so; if not some other competent person must make the inspection. *CLO: 10(1)*

Reports of tests, examinations and inspections must be made on the prescribed forms—Factory Form 80 for tests, followed be examinations, Factory Form 91, Section G, for examinations only, and Factory Form 91, Section C for weekly inspections. Reports of tests and examinations must be made within 28 days; reports of weekly inspections must be made forthwith but if the building operations or works of engineering construction in question are not expected to last for more than 6 weeks it is permissible for the person making the inspection to make an informal written report to his employer and for the employer himself to make the entry on Form 91C. *CLO: 10 and 28*

If any test or examination shows that the appliance in question cannot safely be used unless certain repairs are carried out (either immediately or within a specified time) the person making the test or examination must send a copy of his report to the distict inspector of factories. *CLO: 28(7)*

These requirements for tests, examinations and inspections do not apply to lifting appliances which are part of the permanent equipment of a factory and which are used only occasionally for building operations or works of engineering construction. (Such appliances will, of course, be subject to the appropriate tests and examinations under the Factories Act as explained in item 79.) *CLO: 6 and Schedule*

ADDITIONAL REQUIREMENTS APPLICABLE ONLY TO PULLEY BLOCKS AND GIN WHEELS—The safe working load must be marked on any pulley block or gin wheel used to raise or lower a load of one ton or more. *CLO: 29(1)(b)*

No pulley block or gin wheel suspended from or supported by a pole or beam must be used for raising or lowering materials unless it is effectively secured to the pole or beam. The pole or beam must be of adequate strength for the purpose for which it is being used; and must be adequately and properly secured so as to support the load with safety and so as to prevent undue movement of the pole or beam. *CLO: 18*

PULLEYS—Pulleys must be of suitable diameter and construction for the chain or rope used. *CLO: 15*

169 – Chains, Ropes and Lifting Gear

All chains, ropes and lifting gear used in building operations or works of engineering construction are subject to the following requirements. (Except where otherwise stated, the requirements apply to chains, ropes and gear which form part of the normal equipment of a factory as well as to those used specifically for building operations and works of engineering construction.)

For the purpose of these requirements, the term lifting gear means any chain sling, rope sling, plate clamp, ring, link, hook, shackle, swivel or eyebolt. It will be noted that this is a wider definition than that of Lifting Tackle given in Section 26 of the main Act (see item 81). One result of this is that an eyebolt or plate clamp which is part of the normal equipment of a factory may not be subject to any statutory requirements until it comes to be used for building operations. *CLO: 4*

CONSTRUCTION AND CONDITION—All chains, ropes, and lifting gear used in raising or lowering, or as a means of suspension, must be of good construction, sound material, adequate strength, suitable quality, and free from patent defect. *CLO: 34(1)*

No wire rope must be used for raising or lowering or as a means of suspension if, in any length of 10 diameters, the total number of visible broken strands exceeds 5 per cent of the total number. *CLO: 34(3)*

Every sling must be securely attached to the lifting appliance with which it is being used. The method of attachment must be one which does not damage any part of the sling or of any lifting gear supporting it. *CLO: 37(1)*

Double or multiple slings must have their legs connected by a shackle, ring or link of adequate strength. *CLO: 37(2)*

All lifting gear (except fibre rope slings), all chains, and all wire ropes first taken into use after March 1st, 1962, must have been tested and examined by a competent person and a certificate of test must be kept either on the site or at the office of the owner. The prescribed forms are F 87 (wire ropes) and F 97 (chains and lifting gear). The latter must be used in the new version introduced by the Construction (Lifting Operations) Certificates (Amendment) Order 1964.

Regulations published in draft in 1967 provided that no new wire rope should be taken into use as a means of suspension, raising or lowering unless a sample had been tested to destruction and a certificate given in a prescribed form. The same regulations would have made it compulsory for the safe working load to be specified by someone aware of the purpose for which the rope was to be used. However, the draft regulations were withdrawn without being put into effect and the matter is now being reconsidered.

All chains, ropes and lifting gear must have been examined by a competent person within the previous 6 months. (This does not apply to chains, ropes and gear which are used only occasionally; these need only be examined when necessary.) *CLO: 40*

Except when the chain, rope or lifting gear examined is part of the permanent equipment of a factory, and is only occasionally used for building operations and works of engineering construction, the persons making the 6-monthly examination must make a written report on the prescribed form (Factory Form 91, Section J). *CLO: 40*

MARKING OF CHAINS, ROPES AND GEAR—All chains, ropes and lifting gear must be marked with some means of identification. *CLO: 34(1)*

Fibre ropes and fibre rope slings must be marked with the safe working load unless this can be obtained either from the register or from a table displayed on the site of the operations. *CLO: 34(1) and (2)*

Wire ropes and wire rope slings must be marked with safe working load unless this can be obtained from the register. (If a wire rope was first used before March 1st, 1962, the safe working load may be shown on a table posted on the site instead of in the register.) *CLO: 34(1) and (2)*

All chains and lifting gear must be marked with the safe working load unless they are part of the normal equipment of the factory and are only occasionally used for building operations or works of engineering construction, in which case it is sufficient if means of ascertaining the safe working load are available to any person using the chain or lifting gear concerned. *CLO: 31(1) and Schedule*

ALTERATIONS AND REPAIRS—Load-bearing chains and ropes must not be knotted in any part which is under direct tension and no chain must be shortened, or joined to another, by means of bolts and nuts. *CLO: 39*

If a chain, ring, link, hook, plate clamp, shackle, swivel or eyebolt is lengthened, altered or repaired by welding it must not be used again for raising, lowering or as a means of suspension until it has been tested and thoroughly examined by a competent person and a certificate of test has been given in the form (Factory Form 97) prescribed by regulations. If a chain is attached to the bucket of a dragline or excavator it need only be given a thorough examination; it need not be given a test. *CLO: 35*

HOOKS—Hooks used for raising and lowering, or as a means of suspension, must either have an efficient device to prevent the displacement of the sling or load, or else must be of a shape that renders such a device unnecessary. This does not apply to hooks which are part of the normal equipment of a factory and are only occasionally used for building operations or works of engineering construction. *CLO: 36 and Schedule*

* RECEPTACLES—Every receptacle used for raising or lowering stone, bricks, tiles, slates or other objects must be so enclosed, constructed or designed as to prevent the accidental fall of such objects. This does not apply to grabs, shovels or similar excavating receptacles, if effective steps are taken to prevent any person being endangered by a fall of objects therefrom. *CLO: 49(3)*

ANNEALING—All chains, and all lifting gear other than rope slings, must be annealed or subjected to some other approved form of heat treatment at the intervals prescribed, unless of one of the types mentioned below as being exempt. The prescribed interval is 6 months for chains and slings of half-inch bar or smaller material and 14 months for all other chains and lifting gear. *CLO: 41*

Chains and lifting gear not in regular use, or used solely on lifting appliances worked by hand, need not be annealed or subjected to other heat treatment except at such intervals as are necessary even if these intervals are longer than those prescribed above. *CLO: 41*

The following chains and lifting gear are completely exempt from the annealing requirements: plate link chains; chains made of malleable cast iron; pitched chains working on sprocket or pocketed wheels; chains, rings, links, hooks, plate clamps, shackles, swivels and eyebolts made of steel or of a non-ferrous metal; socket shackles secured to wire ropes by white metal capping; bordeaux connexions; hooks, eyebolts and swivels which have screw-threaded parts or ball-bearings or other case-hardened parts; and rings, links, hooks, shackles and swivels permanently attached to pitched chains, pulley blocks, or weighing machines. *CLO: 41 and Schedule*

The annealing or other treatment must be carried out under the supervision of a competent person and (except when the chain or lifting gear is part of the permanent equipment of a factory and is only used occasionally for building operations or works of engineering construction) a written report must be made on Factory Form 91, Section K. *CLO: 40*

* These receptacles are not " lifting gear " within the meaning of the regulations and are therefore not subject to the other requirements quoted in this item.

170 – Operation of Cranes and other Lifting Appliances

The following requirements apply whenever a crane or other lifting appliance is being used in connexion with building operations or works of engineering construction.

PERSONNEL—Only trained and competent persons may operate a lifting appliance except when persons are being trained under direct supervision of a competent person. *CLO: 26(2)*

No person under 18 may operate any lifting appliance driven by mechanical power or give signals to the driver of a power-operated lifting appliance except when being trained under competent supervision. *CLO: 26(2)*

SAFE WORKING LOADS AND RADII—No part of any crane, crab, winch, pulley block, gin wheel, sheer legs, derrick pole, derrick mast, chain, rope or lifting gear, must be loaded beyond its safe working load, except when it is being tested by a competent person, duly appointed for the purpose, and then it must only be overloaded to such an extent as the appointed person may authorise. *CLO: 31 and 34(4)*

It must be remembered that a crane which has been dismantled and re-erected may have a lower safe working load than it did when previously erected. See item 167 under "Tests for Stability".

If the load on a crane, crab, sheer legs or aerial cableway, or on a winch other than a piling winch, is equal to the safe working load (or only slightly less than the safe working load) the lifting must be temporarily halted after the load has been lifted for a short distance, unless the load is already sustained wholly by the appliance before the lift begins. *CLO: 32(1)*

When a double or multiple sling is used, care must be taken to ensure that the safe working load is not exceeded by reason of the excessive angle between the legs. *CLO: 37(2)*

When a crane with a derricking jib is used, the radius of the load must not exceed the maximum working radius for the jib. *CLO: 23(2)*

SLINGING AND SUSPENSION—Every part of the load must be securely suspended and supported, and must be secured to prevent displacement. *CLO: 49(1)*

Slings must be attached securely to the appliance and in a way not likely to damage slings or lifting gear. *CLO: 37(1)*

Knots must not be tied in those parts of chains or wire ropes which are to be used under direct tension. *CLO: 39(1)*

No chains may be shortened or joined by means of nuts and bolts. *CLO: 39(2)*

Packing or other means must be used to prevent edges of loads causing damage to slings, chains, ropes, etc., and so providing a source of danger. *CLO: 38*

RAISING AND LOWERING—Cranes must be used only for raising and lowering vertically unless they can be used otherwise without endangering stability and without imposing undue strain on any part of the crane structure or mechanism. If used otherwise than for vertical raising and lowering, the operation must be supervised by a competent person. *CLO: 23(1)*

Scotch derricks must not be used to lift loads lying in the angle between back stays. *CLO: 33(2)*

All reasonably practicable measures must be taken to prevent a load coming into contact with, and displacing any other object. *CLO: 49(2)*

Loads being lowered on to scaffolds must be deposited without causing any violent shock to the scaffold. *BR: 33*

SIGNALS — When aerial cableways and aerial ropeways are used there must be efficient signalling arrangements between the driver or operator and those at the loading and unloading points. *CLO: 26(5)*

When a hoist is used, signals are required in the circumstances outlined in item 171.

When other types of lifting appliance are used, signals are not needed if the operator has an unrestricted view of the load or point of suspension at every position necessary for safety. *CLO: 26(3)*

If the driver or operator has not an unrestricted view of the load or point of suspension at every point necessary for safety, the following arrangements must be made:—

(*a*) If the lifting appliance can raise or lower the load in a vertical direction only, and safe operation can be ensured if the operator knows the position of the load when it is in the vicinity of certain points only, arrangements must be made, by means of position indicators, signalling systems, or otherwise, for giving the operator the necessary information;

(*b*) If the lifting appliance can move loads by a horizontal or slewing motion, one or more competent signallers must be stationed where they can give all necessary signals. If this is not practicable, steps must be taken to inform the operator when the load is near any loading or unloading points and any other point where danger may reasonably be expected, or else the safe movement of the load must be ensured by other means. *CLO: 26(3)*

Signals must be of distinctive character, easily seen or heard by the persons to whom they are given. *CLO: 27(1)*

No person under 18 may give signals to operators of power-driven lifting appliances except when being trained under competent supervision. *CLO: 26(2)*

Devices or apparatus used for giving sound, colour or light signals must be properly maintained and the means of communication must be adequately protected from accidental interference. *CLO: 27(2)*

Platforms provided for signallers must comply with the same requirements as platforms for crane drivers. See item 165.

CARRIAGE OF PERSONS ON LIFTING APPLIANCES—Persons must not be raised, lowered or carried by a power driven lifting appliance except in one or other of the following ways:—

(*a*) On the driver's platform of a crane.

(*b*) On a hoist satisfying the requirements set out in item 171.

(*c*) On a type of suspended scaffold approved by the Chief Inspector of Factories.

(*d*) In a suitable chair, cage, skip or other receptacle used in circumstances where the use of a hoist or approved suspended scaffold is not reasonably practicable.

(*e*) In a suitable chair, cage, skip or other receptacle carried by an aerial cableway or aerial ropeway, the winches of which (if any) comply with the requirements quoted in item 167.

All skips and other receptacles used for raising or lowering persons must be at least 3 feet deep. *CLO: 47*

All chairs, cages, skips and other receptacles must be of good construction, sound material and adequate strength, and must be properly maintained. They must have suitable means to prevent persons falling out, and must not contain any materials or tools liable to interfere with the handhold or foothold of the occupant, or otherwise endanger him. They must also be prevented, by some suitable means, from spinning or tipping in a manner dangerous to any occupant. *CLO: 47*

OTHER PRECAUTIONS—No load must be left suspended unless a competent person is actually in charge of the lifting appliance. *CLO: 49(7)*

Lifting appliances must not be used on soft or uneven surfaces, or on slopes, unless precautions are taken against instability, *CLO: 19(1)*

Where more than one appliance has to be used for a load, work must be so arranged that no appliance is overloaded or rendered unstable and the operation must be supervised by a competent person. *CLO: 32(2)*

No crane must be used in weather conditions likely to endanger its stability and after being exposed to such weather it must not be used until it has been examined by a competent person and any necessary steps taken to ensure stability. *CLO: 19(7)*

When any overhead electrical cable or other live electrical apparatus is liable to be a source of danger to persons engaged in any lifting operation, precautions must be taken to prevent danger, by the erection of barriers or otherwise. *CGP: 44*

If a truck or vehicle is being loaded with loose material from a grab or excavator, no person may remain in that truck or vehicle if this would expose him to danger. *CGP: 36*

Scotch derrick cranes mounted on more than one bogie, trolley of wheeled carriage must be moved on the track only in such a way as will avoid the risk of instability, racking or distortion of the crane or track. *CLO: 20(3)*

On every stage, gantry or other place where a lifting machine which has a travelling or slewing motion is in use, an unobstructive passageway at least 2 feet wide must be maintained between any such moving part of the appliance and any guard-rail, fencing or other nearby fixture; if at any time it is not practicable to maintain this passageway at any point, access to that point must be prevented during the time in question. (This requirement as to passageways does not apply to lifting appliances which are part of the permanent equipment of a factory and are only occasionally used for building operations or works of engineering construction.) *CLO: 12 and Schedule*

171 – Hoists*

Every hoist, and every part thereof, including all working gear, must be of good mechanical construction, sound material, adequate strength, and free from patent defect, and must be properly maintained. *CLO: 10(1)*

Every hoist and hoistway must be adequately and securely supported and every part of a stage, scaffold, framework or other structure supporting a hoist must be of good construction, adequate strength, sound material, and free from patent defect. *CLO: 11(1) and (2)*

Any anchoring or fixing arrangement used in connexion with a hoist must be adequate and secure. *CLO: 11(4)*

Every temporary attachment or connexion of a rope, chain

* For exemptions for hoists used in chimneys of less than 120 sq. ft. cross sectional area, see Certificate of Exemption No. 1 (Hoists in Certain Chimneys) Form 2006, 9th July 1962.

or other plant or equipment used in the erection or dismantling of a hoist must be adequate and secure. *CLO: 11(5)*

MECHANICAL DETAILS—Ropes, chains and lifting gear used to raise or lower the cage or platform of a hoist must satisfy the requirements outlined in item 169.

Every dangerous mechanical part of a hoist must be securely fenced unless it is in such a position, or of such construction, as to be as safe to every person working on the site as it would be if securely fenced. *CGP: 42*

*† Any winch used to operate a hoist must be so constructed that the brake is applied when the control lever, handle or switch is not held in the operating position. Such a winch must not be fitted with a pawl or ratchet gear on which the pawl has to be disengaged before the platform or cage can be lowered. *CLO: 44*

* The construction and installation arrangements must, where practicable, be such that the hoist can be operated from only one position at any one time. *CLO: 43(1)*

* A hoist must not be operated from within the cage unless both the cage and the hoistway comply with the requirements for passenger hoists quoted below. *CLO: 43(1)*

* Every hoist must have an efficient automatic device to ensure that the platform or cage does not over-run the highest point to which it is, for the time being, constructed to travel. *CLO: 42(3)*

*† Where practicable, every hoist must have devices which will support the platform or cage, together with its full safe working load, in the event of failure of the hoist ropes or of any part of the hoisting gear. *CLO: 42(2)*

*† When a hoist is used for carrying persons it must have suitable automatic devices to ensure that the cage comes to rest at a point above the lowest point to which it can travel. *CLO: 48(3)*

* The drum round which the chains or ropes supporting the hoist platform or cage are wound must be of suitable diameter and construction for the chains or ropes used. Chains and ropes must be properly secured to the drum and at least two turns of a chain or rope must remain on the drum in every operating position. *CLO: 15*

CONTROL LEVERS, ETC.—Any lever, handle, switch, etc., which is used for operating a hoist and which could cause danger if accidentally moved or displaced, must where practicable be provided with a suitable spring or other locking device or else be so placed or constructed as to prevent accidental movement or displacement. *CLO: 16(1)*

Every lever, handle, switch or other device used for operating a hoist must have clear markings, on it or adjacent to it, to show its purpose and mode of operation. *CLO: 16(1)*

These requirements regarding levers, handles, switches, etc., do not apply to a hoist which is part of the permanent equipment of a factory and is only occasionally used for building operations and works of engineering construction. *CLO: 6 and Schedule.*

* MARKING OF SAFE WORKING LOAD, ETC.—The safe working load must be clearly marked on the cage or platform of the hoist. *CLO: 45*

Where a hoist is to be used for the carriage of persons, the maximum number of persons that may be carried must be plainly marked on the cage, in addition to the safe working load. *CLO: 45*

If a hoist is not suitable for the carriage or persons, a readily legible notice prohibiting its use for this purpose must be affixed to the platform or cage. *CLO: 45*

* HOISTWAYS—At every point at which there is access to a hoistway, or at which persons are liable to be struck by a moving part of the hoist, a substantial enclosure must be provided. The height of the enclosure must be at least 6 ft. 6 in. except where a lesser height is sufficient to prevent persons from falling down the hoistway and where there is no danger of persons coming into contact with a moving part; even in the latter circumstances the enclosure must be at least 3 feet high. *CLO: 42(1)*

Where access to the hoistway is needed, gates must be provided and must be kept closed except when the cage or platform is at rest at the landing place concerned and the gates are necessarily opened for the passage of goods, plant, material or persons. The gates must be of the minimum heights laid down for the rest of the enclosure. *CLO: 42(1)*

The contractor or employer is legally responsible for seeing that the gates are kept shut except when necessarily opened but, in addition to this, every person who actually uses the gateway of a hoist has a legal obligation to close it after him unless it is necessary to leave it open for the use of another person. *CLO: 42(1)*

If a hoist is used for carrying persons the hoistway gates must have an efficient interlock or other device to ensure that the gates cannot be opened unless the cage is at the landing place and that the cage cannot be moved until the gates are closed. *CLO: 48(2)*

*† CAGES FOR PASSENGER HOISTS — No person may be carried by a hoist unless it has a cage which is so constructed that, when the gates are shut, no one in the cage can fall out, be struck by articles falling down the hoistway, or be trapped between the cage and any fixed or moving part of the hoist. *CLO: 48(1)(a)*

Cages in which persons travel must have gates on all sides on which there is access to landings. So far as is reasonably practicable, cage gates must have interlocking devices or other means of ensuring that the gates cannot be opened except at a landing stage and that the cage cannot be moved unless the gates are shut. (A more stringent requirement, respecting the

* Hoists forming part of the permanent equipment of any structure or underground shaft, and regularly used for the carriage of persons or goods, are exempt from these requirements provided that, when used in connexion with building operations or works of engineering construction, they satisfy the following conditions:

(*a*) A maximum number of persons to be carried must have been specified by the manufacturer, insurer, or lift engineers, and this number must not be exceeded.

(*b*) No materials, tools, or other articles (other than light articles carried by someone riding in the hoist) must be carried unless a safe working load has been specified by the manufacturer, insurer, or lift engineers, and this safe working load must not be exceeded.

(*c*) Hoistway gates must not be left open except when this is necessary for some immediate purpose. *CLO: 8*

† If a hoist was manufactured before March 1st, 1962, and it is not reasonably practicable to comply fully with these requirements, it is sufficient if the hoist has been brought as near as is reasonably practicable to the standard called for and a certificate to this effect, signed by a competent person, has been obtained either under the current Construction (Lifting Operations) Regulations or under the former Building (Safety, Health and Welfare) Regulations. *CLO: 9*

gates of the hoistway, is mentioned above.) *CLO: 48(1)(b)*

The maximum number of persons which may be carried by the hoist must be marked plainly in the cage. *CLO: 45*

* TESTS, EXAMINATIONS AND INSPECTIONS—A hoist which has been manufactured, or substantially altered or repaired, since March 1st, 1962, must not be used unless (since such manufacture, alteration or repair) it has been tested and thoroughly examined by a competent person and a certificate of test provided. *CLO: 46(1)*

A hoist used for carrying persons must not be used unless it has been tested and thoroughly examined since it was last erected. It must be given a further test and thorough examination if, after erection, the height of travel of the cage has been altered. *CLO: 46(1)*

No hoist must be used unless it has been thoroughly examined within the previous six months. *CLO: 46(1)*

So far as its construction permits, every hoist must be inspected at least once a week by the operator (if he is competent to do so) or other competent person. *CLO: 10(1)(c)*

Written reports of tests, examinations and inspections must be made in the prescribed forms. These are Factory Form 75 for the first test and examination of a hoist; Factory Form 91, Section F, for test and examination of passenger hoists after re-erection or alteration to the height of travel; Factory Form 91, Section H, for the periodic examination of any hoist; and Factory Form 91, Section C, for weekly inspections. (If operations on the site are expected to last for 6 weeks or less, the person making the weekly examination of a hoist not worked by mechanical power may make an informal written report to his employer and the latter may make the official entry on Form 91C.) *CLO: 46(3) and 10(2)*

If any test or examination shows that a hoist cannot safely be used unless certain repairs are carried out (either immediately or within a specified time) the person making the test or examination must send a copy of his report to the district inspector of factories within 28 days. *CLO: 46 (3)*

OPERATION—Only a trained and competent person who has reached the age of 18 may operate a power-driven hoist, except when a person under 18 is being trained under the direct supervision of a competent person. *CLO: 26(1) and (2)*

Only hoists which comply with the additional requirements laid down for hoists carrying persons (see above) may be operated from within the cage. *CLO: 43(1)*

The safe working load of a hoist must not be exceeded except for the purpose of being tested under the directions of a competent person. In no circumstances may a hoist used for the carriage of persons be allowed to carry more than the permitted number. *CLO: 45*

SIGNALS—If the operator of a hoist does not have a clear and unrestricted view of the cage or platform (except at points where such a view is not necessary for safety) effective arrangements must be made for signals to be given from each landing place. *CLO: 26(3)*

Every signal given for the movement or stopping of a hoist must be distinctive in character, and of such a nature that the person to whom it is given can see or hear it easily. *CLO: 27(1)*

Devices or apparatus used for giving signals must be properly maintained, and the means of communication must be protected from accidental interference. *CLO. 27(2)*

No person under 18 must give signals to the operator of a hoist operated by mechanical power, except when receiving instruction under the direct supervision of a competent person. *CLO: 26(2)*

OTHER MATTERS—Safe access must, so far as is reasonably practicable, be provided for persons examining, repairing or lubricating a hoist, if such persons are liable to fall more than 6 ft. 6 in. The means provided must include the provision of handholds and foothold if necessary. *CLO: 17*

The requirements respecting cabins for crane operators, mentioned in item 165, apply also to hoists operated from one position alongside the winch. They do not apply to other hoists. *CLO: 14(4)(b)*

If a hoist is erected on a soft or uneven surface, appropiate precautions must be taken to ensure stability. *CLO: 19(1)*

Certain hoists erected inside chimneys are exempt from some of the regulations if they comply with the terms of Certificate of Exemption No. 1 (Form F 2006)

172 – Machinery (General)

All machinery used in building operations, or works of engineering construction, on factory premises must comply with the requirements made by the Factories Act as regards guarding, etc. Machinery used in building operations or works of engineering construction elsewhere than on factory premises is subject to similar requirements contained in Regulations 42 and 43 of the Construction (General Provisions) Regulations 1961; these two Regulations actually apply to machines used on factory premises also but in practice they merely duplicate, in different terms, the requirements to which all factory machinery is subject under the main Act.

Excavators, draglines, piling frames, aerial cableways, and overhead runways used in building operations or works of engineering construction are also subject to the requirements for lifting appliances set out in items 168 and 170.

Woodworking machinery used in building operations and works of engineering construction must comply with the requirements outlined in items 49 to 51.

173 – Electrical Equipment and Cables

All electrical equipment used in connexion with building operations or works of engineering construction, whether it is permanent or temporary, is subject to the requirements of the Electricity Regulations 1908. See items 69 to 77.

If building operations or works of engineering construction are being carried on in a building which is not subject to the Factories Act, fixed electrical apparatus which is part of the permanent equipment of that building may be used for purposes connected with the operations even though it does not comply with the Electricity Regulations. However, if an accident occurs through the use of unsafe apparatus of this kind there might be a claim for damages at Common Law. See item 284.

If any overhead cable or other live apparatus is liable to be a source of danger to persons working on the site whether from the operation of a lifting appliance or otherwise, all practicable precautions must be taken to prevent such danger, either by erecting barriers or by some other means. *CGP: 44*

Before any construction operations begin, all practicable steps must be taken to safeguard persons employed from danger through contact with live cables or apparatus, and such precautions must be continued throughout the whole period of the operations. The steps taken may consist either of making the cables or apparatus electrically dead or of some other effective means. *CGP: 44*

174 – Boilers and Steam Receivers

Under Section 127 of the Factories Act 1961, the legal requirements for boilers and steam receivers (see items 84 and 88) are extended to include those used in connexion with building operations and works of engineering construction, whether on factory premises or elsewhere.

175 – Cofferdams and Caissons

Every part of a cofferdam or caisson must be of good construction, suitable and sound material, free from patent defect, and of adequate strength. *CGP: 15*

Materials used for the construction or fixing of a cofferdam or caisson must be inspected by a competent person before each occasion on which they are used. *CGP: 17(2)*

The construction, positioning and dismantling of a cofferdam or caisson must be supervised by a competent person. Any additions or alterations must likewise be supervised. *CGP: 17(1)*

As far as possible, only experienced workers are to be employed in the erection, positioning, dismantling, and alterations or additions to a cofferdam or caisson. *CGP: 17(1)*

Cofferdams and caissons must be properly maintained. *CGP: 15*

Inspections and Examinations—No cofferdam or caisson must be used unless it has been inspected by a competent person either on the same day or previous day. *CGP: 16(1)*

A cofferdam or caisson which has been in position in the same place for more than 7 days must not be used unless it has been examined by a competent person within the preceding 7 days. *CGP: 18(1)(c)*

After a cofferdam or caisson has been substantially damaged, no person must be allowed to work in it until it has been thoroughly examined by a competent person. *CGP: 18(1)*

Such an examination by a competent person must also be made after explosives have been used in or near a cofferdam or caisson in a manner likely to affect its strength, and no persons must work inside it until the examination has been made. *CGP: 18(1)*

Reports of examinations must be made, on the day of examination, on the form (Factory Form 91, Section B) prescribed. *CGP: 18(1)*

The restrictions on persons entering cofferdams or caissons until they have been inspected or examined do not apply to persons entering during the actual erection, placing, repairing, alteration, examination, or inspection, so long as appropriate precautions are taken to ensure their safety so far as possible. *CGP: 18(2)*

Other Matters—So far as is reasonably practicable, cofferdams and caissons must have adequate means for persons to reach safety in the event of an inrush of water. *CGP: 16*

An atmosphere fit for respiration must be maintained in all cofferdams or caissons, and dangerous or injurious fumes must be rendered harmless as far as is reasonably practicable. If there is reason to suppose that the atmosphere is poisonous or asphyxiating, no one must enter until it has been tested by, or under the supervision of, a competent person who has satisfied himself that there is no danger. *CGP: 21*

176 – Painting

The following requirements apply to the re-painting of existing buildings as well as to the painting of new ones.

For the purpose of these requirements, lead paint is any paint, spray, stopping, filling, or other material used in painting which contains a specified percentage of lead. The technical definition is laid down in Section 132 of the Factories Act and in an order dated December 24th, 1926 (SRO 1926 No. 1621)

Restrictions on Use of Lead Paint—Lead paint must not be procured or used except in the form of a paste or paint ready for use. (Except when red lead is used in a raw or dry state for preparing stopping or filling material.) *LPR: (1)(a)*

All receptacles containing lead paint must be legibly marked to show that they contain lead. *LPR: (1)(b)*

Lead paint must not be sprayed in the interior of building *LPR: (2)*

Rubbing Down—No painted ironwork or steelwork must be rubbed down or scraped by a dry sand-paper process. No painted surface, other than ironwork or steelwork, must be rubbed down or scraped by any dry process. All debris produced by rubbing down or scraping of any painted surface must be removed before it becomes dry. (These precautions need not be taken if the employer is in a position to prove that the surface rubbed down does not contain lead paint.) *LPR: 3*

Persons employed in rubbing down or scraping have a statutory duty to observe these requirements. *LPR: 10*

Clothing—Overalls must be worn by all persons employed in, or in connexion with, the painting of buildings and liable to come into contact with lead paint. Overalls must be worn during the whole of the working period but not at mealtimes. (This requirement does not apply to those who are only occasionally employed in painting buildings, for an aggregate period not exceeding 26 working days a year.) *LPR: 9*

Clothing taken off during working hours must be placed where it cannot be soiled by lead paint. Facilities for storing such clothing must be provided, outside any apartment in which painting is carried on if practicable. This does not apply to those occasionally employed. *LPR: 5 and 11*

Washing Facilities—Adequate and suitable washing facilities, including nail brushes, soap and towels, must be provided for persons liable to come into contact with lead paint. At least one bucket or basin must be provided for every 5 such persons (not counting those who only occasionally are so employed). *LPR: 4 and BR: 83(1)*

Every person liable to come into contact with lead paint must wash his hands before eating food or leaving premises (except those who are only occasionally employed). *LPR: 12*

Women and Young Persons—A male young person under 18 may be employed in painting with lead paint if he is working under an indenture of apprenticeship or under an established custom of regular apprenticeship. The names and ages of such apprentices, with the dates on which they were first engaged, must be entered on a special list attached to the register of painters mentioned below under "Notices and Records". *SRO: 1927: 1094*

Women and young persons may be employed to use lead paint in the decorative painting of walls and ceilings, or similar work of a decorative nature. *SRO: 1927: 1904*

Except in the circumstances just mentioned, no woman or young person may be employed in painting buildings with lead paint. *FA: 131*

NOTICES AND RECORDS—Notice that persons are regularly employed in painting of buildings must be sent to the factory inspector and a register of persons so employed must be kept on Factory Form 92. *FA: 129 and LPR: (8)*

Each person so employed must be given a copy of the prescribed leaflet (Form 394). Further copies must be given to each person on the first pay day of each year. *LPR: 7(a)*

A copy of the regulations (Form 996) must be displayed in workshops and paint stores, in any apartment in which paint is mixed, and on any sites where more than 12 are employed in painting with lead paint. *LPR: 7(b)*

OCCASIONAL EMPLOYMENT AS PAINTERS—Where persons are only occasionally employed in painting buildings, the notice to the factory inspector need not be given, leaflets need not be issued, and a copy of the regulations need not be displayed, but a record of such occasional employment must be kept. *FA: 129(4)*

For this purpose, a person is considered to be occasionally employed if he is not engaged in painting with lead paint for more than 26 normal working days in any calendar year and is engaged in some other occupation on other days. *FA: 129(4)*

OTHER REQUIREMENTS—Persons employed in painting with lead paint must be medically examined periodically if the Chief Inspector of Factories so directs. In such circumstances persons employed have a legal obligation to attend for examination at the times appointed. Medical examinations must satisfy the requirements of the Lead Processes (Medical Examinations) Regulations 1964 (SI 1964: No. 1724) and must include the haemoglobin estimation approved by the Certificate of Approval made under those regulations and published as Factory Form F 2199. *LPR: 6 and 13.*

Scaffolds, working platforms, ladders, and other workplaces and means of access used by painters must comply with the general requirements quoted in items 156 to 164.

177 – Excavations, Shafts, Earthworks and Tunnels

The following requirements apply to all excavations, shafts, earthworks and tunnels made in the course of building operations or works of engineering construction.

BARRIERS—Barriers must be provided round any excavations, shafts, pits or other openings into which persons are liable to fall a vertical distance of more than 6ft. 6in. These barriers must be erected as soon as possible after excavation, etc., begins. *CGP:* 13

The barriers must be as close as practicable to the edge of the excavation or other opening, and must be maintained in position except when any part is necessarily removed for the passage of persons or material. *CGP: 13*

SUPPLY AND USE OF TIMBER—As soon as practicable in the course of the work, any necessary timber or other support must be provided and used to prevent, so far as is reasonably practicable, any danger from the fall or dislodgement of earth, rock or other material forming a side or roof of an excavation, shaft, tunnel or earthwork, or any earth, etc., adjacent to any of these. *CGP: 8(1)*

Timbering is not required if the nature and slope of the sides of the excavation, etc., and the other circumstances of the work, are such that no fall or other dislodgement of earth or material is likely to trap or bury any person or to strike any person from a height of more than 4 feet. (This exemption does *not* apply when there is danger of a fall of rock, whatever the distance involved.) *CGP: 8(1)*

Persons actually engaged in placing the timbering will obviously have to enter the excavation, etc., before the precautions against falls of earth, etc., are complete. The regulations allow for this, but only on the condition that all appropriate precautions are taken to ensure safety so far as the circumstances permit. *CGP: 8(1)*

Material used for timbering and other supports must be inspected by a competent person before it is taken into use. *CGP: 10(1)*

All timbering and other supports must be of good construction, sound material, free from patent defect, and of adequate strength for their purpose. *CGP: 10(2)*

No timber or other material with projecting nails must be used if this would provide a source of danger. *CGP: 48(1)*

Struts and braces must be properly and adequately secured to prevent accidental displacement or fall. *CGP: 10(3)*

The erection and dismantling of timbering and other supports, and any subsequent additions or alterations, must be directed by a competent person and, so far as possible, must be carried out by experienced workmen. *CGP: 10(1)*

INSPECTIONS AND EXAMINATIONS—The following requirements regarding the inspection and examination of excavations, shafts, and earthworks do not actually apply when the circumstances are such that no person is likely to be trapped or buried by a fall or dislodgement of earth or other material, and no person is liable to be struck by a fall of earth or material from a height of more than four feet.

The working end of every trench more than 6ft. 6in. deep must be inspected by a competent person before the beginning of every shift. *CGP: 9(1)*

The face of every tunnel, and the base or crown of every shaft, must also be inspected by a competent person before the beginning of every shift. *CGP: 9(1)*

Every part of every excavation, shaft, earthwork and tunnel must be inspected by a competent person at least once on every day on which persons are employed therein. *CGP: 9(1)*

If the timbering or other support of an excavation, shaft, earthwork, or tunnel has been in position for more than 7 days, no person must be allowed to work in the excavation, etc., unless the timbering or supports have been thoroughly examined by a competent person within the previous seven days. *CGP: 9(2)*

A thorough examination must also be made by a competent person after an unexpected fall of rock, earth or other material; or after substantial damage to timber or other supports; or after explosives have been used in or near the excavation, etc., in a manner likely to affect stability. On such occasions no persons must be allowed to resume work until the examination has been made. *CGP: 9(2)*

Reports of all thorough examinations must be made on the

prescribed form (Factory Form 91, Section B). Normally such report must be made on the day of the examination, and signed by the person making it, but if the employer on whose behalf the examination is made has good reason to believe that the operations will be completed in 6 weeks it is sufficient if the person making the examination provides an informal written report within 7 days and the employer himself makes the official report on the prescribed form. *CGP: 9(3)*

VENTILATION OF EXCAVATIONS, ETC.—Effective steps must be taken to secure and maintain adequate ventilation of working places in excavations, pits, holes, adits, tunnels, shafts, caissons or other confined spaces and to render harmless, so far as is reasonably practicable, all fumes, dust or other impurities which may be dangerous or injurious to health. *CGP: 21(1)*

If there is reason to believe that the atmosphere in any excavation, shaft, tunnel, etc., is poisonous or asphyxiating, no persons must be allowed to enter until the atmosphere has been tested by, or under the supervision of, a competent person and the latter has satisfied himself that there is no danger. *CGP: 21(2)*

Stationary internal combustion engines must not be used in any excavation, shaft, or other confined space unless specific provision is made for conducting the exhaust gases into the open air or some other effective method is used to keep the space free from such gases. *CGP: 22*

MOVEMENT OF MATERIALS—No materials must be placed near the edge of an excavation, shaft, etc., in such a manner as to endanger persons working below. *CGP: 14(1)*

No load may be moved or placed near the edge of an excavation, shaft, etc., if it is likely to cause the collapse of the sides and so endanger any person. *CGP: 14(2)*

When a vehicle is used to tip material into a pit or excavation, or over the edge of an embankment or earthwork, means must be used to prevent over-running of the vehicle. *CGP: 37*

When loose material is being loaded into a truck or vehicle by means of an excavator or grab, persons must not remain in the truck or vehicle if it would expose them to danger. *CGP: 36*

OTHER REQUIREMENTS—Before work begins on the making of any excavation, shaft, tunnel or earthwork, all practicable steps must be taken to protect persons employed from any live electrical cable or other apparatus; such steps may consist either of cutting off the current or of some effective means of preventing contact with any live cable or apparatus. *CGP: 44(1)*

All excavations, shafts, earthworks and tunnels, and the approaches to them, must be well lighted. *CGP: 47*

All electrical equipment must comply with the statutory requirements summarised in items 69 to 77.

If any excavation, etc., is likely to affect the security of another structure (whether permanent or temporary) all necessary steps must be taken to safeguard persons from danger through the possible collapse of that structure. *CGP: 12(1)*

If there is likely to be danger from rising water, or the eruption of water or material, persons employed must have means of reaching a place of safety, so far as this is reasonably practicable. *CGP: 11(1)*

Explosives must be handled and used only by a competent person, or under the control of a competent person, who observes the statutory requirements. See item 181.

All excavators and other lifting appliances must comply with the requirements summarised in items 165 to 170, and all machinery must be guarded as described in item 172.

178 - Demolition

The following requirements apply to the demolition of any building or structure, or any substantial part thereof, whether or not it is on factory premises.

SUPERVISION—The work must be placed under the supervision of a competent person experienced in demolition work. The names of competent persons must be posted up in a prominent position on the site. *CGP: 39(1)*

Where two or more contractors take part in work, each is responsible for appointing a competent person. (This does not prevent the joint appointment of one person by two or more contractors.) *CGP: 39(1)*

The following operations must be carried out only by workmen experienced in the particular kind of work concerned, and working under the direction of an equally experienced foreman or chargehand, unless the foreman or chargehand gives *immediate* supervision as distinct from direction only:—

(*a*) The actual demolition of any part of a building or structure in circumstances where there is a special risk of some part of the building or structure collapsing in such a way as to endanger persons employed;

(*b*) The cutting of reinforced concrete, steelwork or ironwork forming part of the building or structure which is being demolished;

(*c*) Any other actual demolition of a building or structure, or any part thereof, unless the circumstances are such that there is no foreseeable risk of the building or structure collapsing as a result of the demolition. *CGP: 41(2)*

CONSULTATIONS—When two or more contractors have appointed different persons to supervise their own particular sections of the work, no operations must be started until all the supervisors on the site have discussed the method and time of the operation. *CGP: 39(1)*

When part of the demolition work is to be done by an individual contractor (i.e., one who works himself and employs no one else) the latter must not begin any operation until he has consulted any other individual contractors and the persons supervising demolition work on behalf of contractors other than individual contractors. *CGP: 39(2)*

A contractor other than an individual contractor must not begin any operation until the person appointed by him to supervise the operation has had consultations with any individual contractors who may also be working on the site. *CGP: 39(3)*

PRECAUTIONS AGAINST COLLAPSE—Shoring or other steps must be taken to prevent the collapse of the building being demolished, unless circumstances make this precaution unnecessary. Similar precautions must be taken against collapse of any adjacent building, if this would involve danger. *CGP: 41(4)*

Persons erecting shoring or other safeguards must be protected from danger as far as practicable. *CGP: 41(4)*

No steelwork or ironwork must be cut or released unless all

practicable precautions are taken to avoid danger from sudden twist, spring, or collapse. *CGP: 41(2)*

No framing must be removed unless all practicable steps are taken to avoid danger from collapse of the structure. *CGP: 41(3)*

Other Requirements—Before demolition operations begin, all practicable steps must be taken to prevent persons employed from being endangered from any electrical cable or other apparatus; such steps may consist either of cutting off the current or of some effective means of preventing contact with live cables or apparatus. *CGP: 44(1)*

If persons carrying out demolition operations are liable to be endangered by live overhead electrical cables or apparatus, all practicable steps must be taken to safeguard them, either by erecting barriers or by some other means. *CGP: 44(2)*

Risk of fire or explosion caused by gas or vapour must be prevented by all practicable steps. Risk of flooding must also be guarded against. *CGP: 41(4)*

No floor, roof or other part of building must be overloaded with debris or materials. *CGP: 41(1)*

During demolition operations, adequate steps must be taken to protect persons employed from flying or falling debris. *CGP: 46(1)*

Where demolition operations are being carried out near any road or other public place, or near property occupied by someone other than those for whom the demolition is being done, there is an obligation at Common Law to safeguard members of the public and other third parties from being struck by falling materials, or otherwise injured. See item 286.

The legal requirements respecting safe access, lifting appliances, and all other requirements quoted in this chapter apply to demolition work as to other building operations or works of engineering construction.

179 – Vehicles, Locomotives, and other Site Transport

The following requirements apply when lorries, trucks, locomotives and other mechanically operated means of transport are used on sites where building operations or works of engineering construction are being carried on. They only apply when the vehicle, truck, etc., is actually on the site; when taken off the site on to the public highway they become subject to the Road Traffic Acts, like any other vehicle.

General Requirements for Site Transport — Drivers of vehicles, locomotives, power driven capstans, and haulage winches must be 18 or over and must be fully trained and competent—except when a person under the age of 18 is being trained under the direct supervision of a competent person. *CGP: 32**

No person must be allowed to remain on a vehicle, truck or wagon which is being loaded by means of a grab, excavator or similar appliance unless the circumstances are such that he can do this without endangering himself. *CGP: 36*

Persons must not ride on the running board of a vehicle, the buffer of a locomotive or wagon, or any other insecure position. *CGP: 35*

* As it stands, this regulation forbids the driving of a vehicle by *any* untrained person over 18, even for the purpose of training him under competent supervision. It is understood that this was due to an error in drafting and that the regulation will subsequently be amended so that persons of any age may be trained on the site.

When a vehicle is used for tipping material into an excavation or pit, or over the edge of any embankment or earthwork, all necessary measures must be taken to prevent the vehicle from over-running the edge of the excavation, etc. *CGP: 37*

No load, whether on a vehicle or otherwise, must be moved near to the edge of an excavation, shaft, pit or opening where it is likely to cause a dangerous collapse of the sides of the excavation, etc., and thereby endanger any person. *CGP: 37*

Special Requirements for Vehicles and Trailers—Mechanically operated vehicles and trailers used for conveying workmen, goods or materials while on the site, and owned, hired, used or controlled by an employer undertaking operations on the site must be maintained in an efficient state, effective working order, and good repair. *CGP: 34(1)*

Such vehicles and trailers must not be used in an improper manner and must not be loaded in such a manner, or to such an extent, as to interfere with their safe driving. *CGP: 34(1)*

The requirement regarding vehicles being in an efficient state, etc., does not prohibit the movement of a vehicle which has broken down or been damaged while on the site, so long as it is moved only for purpose of repair, disposal, removal of obstruction, or unloading of goods and materials which were being carried at the time of the breakdown or damage, and so long as no persons remain on the vehicle. Where a broken-down or damaged lorry is moved in such circumstances all precautions must be taken to safeguard persons employed and no goods or materials must be carried except to such an extent as is necessary to enable them to be unloaded after the breakdown or damage. *CGP: 34(1)*

Special Requirements for Locomotives, Wagons, etc.—Locomotives, trucks and wagons must be of good construction, sound material, adequate strength and free from patent defect, and must be properly maintained. *CGP: 26*

Trucks and wagons must have effective brakes unless used in circumstances which make brakes unnecessary for safety. *CGP: 29*

Sufficient sprags or scotches, in good condition, must be provided for all persons using trucks and wagons and must be used whenever necessary. *CGP: 29*

Locomotives must have effective whistles or other warning devices, which must be properly maintained. Persons in charge of the movement of locomotives, trucks or wagons must see that adequate warning is given to any person endangered by such movement. *CGP: 31*

A locomotive driver must be warned, by warning devices, warning notices, or other means, when he is approaching any point at which there is not adequate clearance beside the rail track to obviate the danger of persons being struck. *CGP: 27(3)*

Suitable equipment must be available for replacing any derailed locomotive, truck or wagon, and such replacement must be done with the aid of the equipment provided. *CGP: 30*

Emission of smoke from locomotives must be minimised by all practicable means and the emission of dark smoke must be confined to the periods permitted under the appropriate regulations. See item 82.

CAPSTANS AND WINCHES—Power-driven capstans and winches used for the movement of trucks or wagons must be of good construction, sound material, adequate strength, and free from patent defect, and must be properly maintained. *CGP: 26*

The space in the vicinity of a power-driven capstan or haulage winch must be sufficient for safe working and must be kept clear of all obstruction. *CGP: 33*

Power-driven capstans and haulage winches must not be set in motion for moving trucks or wagons until adequate warning has been given, by the person in charge, to anyone likely to be endangered. The warning must be given by sound signals or visual signals. *CGP: 33*

RAIL TRACKS AND GANTRIES—Rails on which locomotives, trucks or wagons move must have even running surfaces and must be of adequate section and adequately supported on a surface firm enough to prevent undue movement. *CGP: 25*

Rails must be laid in straight lines, or in curves of such radii that the locomotive, truck or wagon can be moved freely and without danger of derailment. They must be jointed by fish plates or double chairs and must be securely fastened to sleepers or bearers, unless other means are used to provide adequate junctions and to prevent variations of gauge. *CGP: 25*

Adequate stops or buffers must be provided at each end of the track. *CGP: 25*

All rails and the equipment associated with them must be properly maintained. *CGP: 25*

So far as is reasonably practicable, tracks must be so laid that there is adequate clearance to prevent persons being crushed or trapped by passing locomotives, trucks or wagons, or their loads. Where such clearance is not reasonably practicable over the whole length of the track, recesses or other suitable arrangements must be made (if practicable) so that lack of clearance does not extend for more than 20 yards at any one place. Effective warning arrangements must be made where persons are liable to be crushed through unavoidable lack of adequate clearance. *CGP: 27*

Headroom below low clearances or other obstructions must, where reasonably practicable, give at least 3 ft. 6 in. clearance above the driver's seat or, if the driver stands, 6 ft. 6 in. clearance above the footplate.

Gantries and other elevated tracks must have suitable and adequate footways in any places where persons have to pass on foot. If footways are on the outside of the gantry they must have guard-rails to a height of at least 3 feet if persons are liable to fall more than 6 ft. 6 in. *CGP: 28*

180 – Protective Equipment and Clothing

PROTECTION OF EYES—When any of the following operations are carried out in the course of building operations or works of engineering construction, goggles or screens must be provided for the protection of the workers' eyes. (For the legal meaning of "provided" in connexion with eye protection, see item 116.)

(*a*) Welding or cutting of metal by arc or flame;
(*b*) Breaking, cutting, dressing or carving stone, concrete, slag or similar materials by means of a hand tool (other than a trowel) or a portable tool driven by mechanical power;
(*c*) Chipping and scaling of painted or corroded metal surfaces;
(*d*) Wire brushing of painted or corroded metal surfaces by mechanical power;
(*e*) Dry grinding of surfaces of metal, stone, concrete or similar materials by means of a wheel or disc driven by mechanical power;
(*f*) Cutting out or cutting off of cold rivets or bolts.

CGP: 52 and Schedule

When building operations or works of engineering construction are carried out on factory premises the further requirements for the protection of eyes contained in the main Factories Acts will apply. See item 116.

In all building operations and works of engineering construction, wherever carried out, there is a Common Law obligation to provide eye protection, even for processes not specified in the Acts or Regulations. See item 284.

PROTECTION AGAINST WEATHER—New regulations in draft at the end of 1964 propose that when a contractor has more than 25 persons in his employment on any one site he shall be obliged to provide adequate and suitable protective clothing for any persons who, by reason of their work, are required to continue working in the open air during bad weather.

PROTECTION AGAINST DUST, FUMES, ETC.—Respirators must be provided if there is no alternative way of protecting employees against dangerous dust or fumes. See item 183.

181 – Petrol and Explosives

Explosives used in building operations or works of engineering construction must not be handled or used except by a competent person, with adequate knowledge of dangers, or by someone under his control. *CGP: 19*

All persons employed must be in positions of safety before any charge is fired. *CGP: 19*

Excavations, tunnels, shafts, earthworks and cofferdams must be examined after explosives have been used in or near them, to ensure that the explosion has not rendered them unsafe. See items 177 and 175.

The storage and use of petrol and explosives used during building operations and works of engineering construction is subject to the relevant Acts and Regulations. See items 99 to 111.

If petrol is kept by the roadside in connexion with the making or repairing of roads, special requirements apply under Regulation 13 of the Petroleum-Spirit (Motor Vehicles, etc.) Regulations 1929 (SI 1929 No. 952). One of these requirements is that notice must be sent to the district council informing them of the intention to keep petrol by the roadside.

The conveyance of petrol between the contractor's depot and the site is subject to the Petroleum Spirit (Conveyance by Road) Regulations. See item 102.

182 – Handling and Stacking of Materials on Sites

HANDLING OF MATERIALS—No person must be required to lift, carry or move any load which is so heavy as to be likely to cause injury to him. *CGP: 55*

The movement of materials on or on to scaffolds must be made without causing violent shock. *CWP: 37*

Materials, tools and other objects must not be thrown, tipped or shot from a height if liable to cause injury (unless proper lowering is impracticable, in which circumstances steps must be taken to protect persons from falling objects.) *CGP: 46(2)*

No ironwork or steelwork on which there is wet paint or wet cement wash (other than paint used for jointing) must be handled on the site, except during the actual painting or cement washing of such ironwork and steelwork. *CGP: 51*

Lead paint must be handled and stored only in receptacles marked to show that they contain lead. *LPR: (1)(b)*

Gangways and runs must not be used for the passage of materials unless, without removal of guard-rails or toe-boards, there is adequate passageway at least 25 in. wide. *CWP: 26(1)*

Materials must not be placed or moved near the edge of any excavation, shaft, pit, or opening if this is liable to cause collapse of the sides or otherwise endanger persons employed. *CGP: 37*

STACKING OF MATERIALS—Materials must not be stacked insecurely in places where they might cause danger. *CGP: 48(2)*

Platforms, gangways, runs and stairs must be kept free from unnecessary material and obstructions. *CWP: 30(2)*

Scaffolds must never be overloaded, and loads must be evenly distributed as far as is practicable. No materials must be kept on a scaffold unless needed within a reasonable time. *CWP: 37*

Clear passageway at least 17 in. wide must be left between one side of a working platform and any material placed on it. *CWP: 26(1)*

Materials must not be stored in places provided for meals or for storage of clothing. *CHW: 11*

183 – Miscellaneous Requirements affecting Safety

LIGHTING—Adequate and suitable lighting must be provided for all working places, approaches, dangerous openings and places where lifting or lowering is going on. *CGP: 47*

All electric lighting fittings and connexions, whether permanent or temporary, must comply with the Electricity Regulations. See items 69 to 77.

PROTECTION AGAINST FALLS OF MATERIAL—At all places on the site where persons are habitually employed, steps must be taken to prevent any person being struck by falling material. *CGP: 46(1)*

PROJECTING NAILS—No material with projecting nails must be used or remain where they would be a source of danger. *CGP: 48(1)*

TEMPORARY AND INSECURE STRUCTURES—Temporarily unstable or weak structures must be supported by guys, stays, etc., where necessary to prevent danger. *CGP: 50(1)*

Temporary structures must be of good construction, sound material and adequate strength. *CGP: 49*

Shoring or other means of protection must be used if work is likely to reduce the stability of a building. *CGP: 50(2)*

Structures in course of demolition are the subject of special requirements. See item 178.

DUST, FUMES, SMOKE, ETC.—If grinding, cleaning, spraying or manipulation of any material gives off dangerous dust or fumes there must be adequate ventilation or other means of preventing inhalation (e.g. respirators). *CGP: 20*

If steam, smoke or vapour is generated on the site, all practicable steps must be taken to prevent it obscuring any working place. *CGP: 45*

Precautions must be taken against persons being injured by fumes, etc., when working in caissons, excavations, or other confined spaces. See items 175 and 177.

Stationary internal combustion engines must not be used in any confined or enclosed space unless specific provision is made for conducting the exhaust gases into the open air or some other effective method is used to keep the space free of such gases. *CGP: 22*

PILE DRIVING—Helmets and crowns used in connexion with pile driving must be of good construction, sound and suitable material, adequate strength, and free from patent defect. *CGP: 53*

RISK OF DROWNING—If any person, in the course of his employment, is liable to fall into any water on or near the site and thereby be in danger of drowning, suitable rescue equipment must be provided and kept readily available in an efficient state and arrangements must be in force for prompt rescue of any person so endangered. *GCP: 24*

If there is a special risk of persons falling into such water, from the edge of any adjacent land, structure or floating stage secure fencing must be provided to prevent such falls. This fencing must be maintained in position except when necessarily removed for the passage of persons or materials. *CGP: 24*

Precautions must be taken against persons being drowned through the flooding of excavations, tunnels, shafts, earthworks, or cofferdams, or through flooding which occurs in the course of demolition work. See items 177, 175 and 178.

When persons employed are taken to or from a working place by water, proper measures must be taken for their safe transport. Vessels used for the purpose must be of suitable construction, properly maintained and in charge of a responsible person, and must not be overloaded. *CGP: 23*

DIVING—All diving operations carried out during building operations or works of engineering construction are subject to special regulations. See item 245.

WORK IN COMPRESSED AIR—When works of engineering construction involve working in compressed air, special regulations apply. See item 246.

184 – Welfare Facilities

The following welfare facilities must be available to persons employed in building operations and works of engineering construction. When such operations are carried out in a factory it will usually be sufficient to arrange for the construction workers to have access to the facilities provided for factory workers, but care must be taken to ensure that the facilities are available whenever the construction operations are in progress and not only during normal factory hours. It will also be necessary to ensure that the facilities are adequate for the increased number of persons who are likely to use them.

The employer of persons engaged in construction operations is not obliged to provide the welfare facilities himself if he can make arrangements for his employees to use the facilities provided by others. He must, however, satisfy himself that the facilities so provided are readily available and comply with the legal requirements, and the arrangement must be recorded on Factory Form F 2202; the form is to be retained by the person providing the facilities and a copy is given to the employer of those using them. *CHW: 4(3)*

Drinking Water—An adequate supply of wholesome drinking water must be available, marked "Drinking Water" or patently intended for drinking. *CHW: 11(1)(d)*

Shelters and Accommodation for Clothing—Adequate and suitable accommodation must be available for shelter during wet weather. If more than 5 persons have to be provided for, the shelter must have adequate and suitable arrangements for them to warm themselves and to dry wet clothing. If 5 or fewer persons are being provided for, such arrangements for warming and drying must also be made if it is reasonably practicable to do so. *CHW: 11(1)(a)*

Accommodation must be provided for depositing clothing not worn during working hours; this can be provided in the shelters already mentioned. *CHW: 11(1)(a)*

Suitable and adequate accommodation must be provided for the deposit of protective clothing used for the work and kept, when not in use, at or near the site. There must be such arrangements for drying the clothing as are reasonably practicable *CHW: 11(1)(b)*

Weatherproof Clothing—Any employee who, because of the nature of his work, is required to continue working in the open air during rain, snow, sleet or hail, must be provided with adequate and suitable protective clothing. *CHW: 15*

Washing Facilities—If an employer has any employee or employees likely to spend more than 4 hours on a construction site at any one time, adequate and suitable washing facilities must be provided. *CHW: 12(1)*

If the employer has more than 20 workers engaged in the same construction operations, or if the operations are expected to last for 6 weeks or more, the facilities must include a sufficient supply of hot and cold (or warm) water and adequate means of cleaning and drying—either in the form of soap and towels or some other means, such as liquid soap dispensers and hot-air dryers. There must also be an adequate number of troughs, basins or buckets, all of which must have a smooth and impervious internal surface. *CHW: 12(2)*

When an employer has more than 100 persons engaged on the same construction operations, and the operations are expected to last for more than 12 months, wash-basins (not troughs or buckets) must be provided on a scale of 4 basins for the first 100 persons and one basin for every additional 35 persons or part thereof. *CHW: 12(3)*

When persons are engaged in painting with lead paint, or in any other process involving the use of lead compounds or other poisonous substances, the washing facilities provided for them must include nail-brushes and the number of basins, troughs or buckets must be on a scale of 1 for every 5 persons so employed. *CHW: 12(4)*

The washing facilities must be conveniently accessible from the accommodation provided for taking meals. *CHW: 12(4)*

Messrooms and Canteens—Adequate and suitable accommodation must be provided for taking meals; the accommodation must afford protection from the weather and must have facilities for boiling water, with a sufficient number of tables and benches or other seats. If an employer has more than 10 persons engaged on the same construction operations, the accommodation must include adequate facilities for heating food, unless heated food is otherwise available on the site. (In deciding whether the accommodation for taking meals is adequate, regard may be had to the number of persons likely to use such accommodation. *CHW: 11(1)(c)* and *(2)*

There is no legal compulsion to provide a canteen for construction workers, however many are employed, but if one is provided it must comply with the Food Hygiene Regulations summarised in item 137.

Sanitary Conveniences—If an employer has fewer than 100 men working on the same building operations or works of engineering construction, sanitary conveniences must be provided on a scale of 1 convenience for every 25 employees or part thereof. (No account must be taken of conveniences which can be used only as urinals.) *CHW: 13(1)*

If more than 100 are employed, the employer may choose between providing sanitary conveniences, other than urinals, on the same scale of 1 for every 25 or, alternatively, he can provide adequate urinals and reduce the scale of other conveniences to 4 for the first 100 employees and 1 for every 35, or part thereof, above 100. *CHW: 13(2)*

Every sanitary convenience, other than one used merely as a urinal, must be under cover. It must be partitioned off to secure privacy, with a proper door and fastening. *CHW: 14(2)*

Urinals must be so placed or screened as not to be visible from other places, either on or off the site. *CHW: 14(2)*

Every sanitary convenience must be adequately lit and sufficiently ventilated and must not communicate with any workroom or messroom except through the open air or an intervening ventilated space. *FA: 7 and CHW: 14(1)*

If it is intended to employ members of both sexes, separate sanitary conveniences must be provided for members of each sex. *FA: 7*

Accessibility of Welfare Facilities—All the welfare facilities required by the regulations quoted in this item must be in such places as to be conveniently accessible to all the persons for whom they are provided. In deciding whether any shelter, accommodation for meals, or storage for protective clothing is conveniently accessible, account may be taken of any transport provided at appropriate times to enable employees to reach these facilities easily. *CHW: 11, 12 and 14*

Washing facilities must be conveniently accessible from the place provided for taking meals. *CHW: 12(5)*

Safe means of access and egress to and from all welfare facilities must, so far as is reasonably practicable, be provided and maintained. *CHW: 16*

Maintenance of Welfare Facilities—All the welfare facilities provided by the regulations must be kept in a clean and orderly condition and, so far as is reasonably practicable, must be kept in a safe condition for those using them. *CHW: 11, 12, 14 and 16*

Accommodation provided for shelter, meals and the deposit of protective clothing and other clothing must not be used for the deposit or storage of materials or plant. *CWP: 11(4)*

185 – First Aid and Ambulance Facilities

The following requirements apply to all places where building operations or works of engineering construction are being carried on. When they are carried on in a factory it will usually be sufficient to arrange for the construction workers to use the

First Aid facilities provided for the factory workers, but care must be taken to ensure that the facilities are available whenever any construction workers are on the premises, and not only during normal factory hours. It is also necessary to ensure that the facilities provided are adequate for the increased number of persons likely to need them.

If a contractor arranges for his employees to use the First Aid facilities provided by the factory occupier, this arrangement must be registered on Factory Form F 2202; the register must be kept by the employer providing the facilities and he must give a copy to the employer of those using them. *CHW: 4(3)*

FIRST AID BOXES—When an employer has more than 5 persons working on the same building operations or works of engineering construction, sufficient First Aid boxes must be provided. (If the operations are taking place in a factory which has been authorised to have an ambulance room instead of First Aid boxes, arrangements may be made, by registration on Factory Form F 2202, for the construction workers to use the ambulance room instead of having boxes provided.) *CHW: 5(1) and (3)*

Where the number of employees does not exceed 25, the contents of the First Aid boxes must be the same as for a factory with between 1 and 10 persons (see item 40). When more than 25 employees have to be provided for, the contents of the boxes must be the same as for a factory with over 50 employees. *CHW: 6 and Schedule*

Every First Aid box must be in the charge of a responsible person who must be readily available when the persons for whom the box is provided are at work. When the box is provided by an employer who has more than 50 persons working on the construction operations in question, the person in charge of the box must either be a state-registered or state-enrolled nurse or else must have a certificate of training in First Aid issued within the previous 3 years by the St. John Ambulance Association, the St. Andrew's Ambulance Association, the British Red Cross Society, or some other approved organisation. (The organisations so far approved for this purpose are Birmingham University, Newcastle upon Tyne University, Harlow Industrial Health Service, Central Middlesex Health Service, Leeds University, the Inner London Education Authority, and the Greater London Council's full course of First Aid training for civil defence.) If an employer is prosecuted for failing to have an adequately trained person in charge of a First Aid box it will be a sufficient defence if he can show that he has used due diligence to endeavour to comply with the law in this respect. *CHW: 5(2) and 7 and Factory Form F 2277*

Every First Aid box must be clearly marked with the words FIRST AID and the name of the person responsible for it must be prominently displayed on or near the box. When the person in charge is required to have had the prescribed standard of training, as described above, the box must contain details of that training and an indication of the date on which evidence of his training was last inspected by the employer. *CHW: 5(2) and 7*

FIRST AID ROOMS—When the total number of persons employed on the same building operations or works of engineering construction exceeds 250, any employer who has more than 40 employees working there must provide, or arrange for the provision of, a First Aid room complying with Regulation 9 of the Construction (Health and Welfare) Regulations 1966. This requirement is not likely to affect factory occupiers, since construction operations on the scale described seldom take place on factory premises except in circumstances which place full responsibility on the contractor instead of the occupier.

AMBULANCES—The following requirements apply when an employer has more than 25 persons working on the same building operations or works of engineering construction.

The ambulance authority (or, in Scotland, the Common Services Agency for the Scottish Health Service) must be notified in writing, within 24 hours, of the location and address where the operations are being carried out, the nature of the operations, and the probable date of their completion. *CHW: 8(1)*

A suitable stretcher (or more than one, if necessary) must be provided and maintained. *CHW: 8(1)*

A responsible person or persons must be appointed who will be readily available to summon an ambulance or other means of transport in the event of accident or illness. *CHW: 8(1)*

Prominent notices in one or more places must show the name of the persons responsible for summoning an ambulance. The notices must also give instructions for making emergency telephone or radio calls. *CHW: 8(1)*

If telephonic or radio communications are not readily accessible, a motor vehicle suited for the conveyance of a person or persons on stretchers must be readily available during working hours. A card obtained from the ambulance authority and showing the address of the nearest accident hospital must be kept in a prominent place on the vehicle. *CHW: 8(2)*

FIRST AID FOR OFFICE WORKERS—Office workers engaged in connexion with building operations or works of engineering construction must be allowed for when First Aid facilities are being arranged, but in calculating the numbers employed only 1 office worker in 3 need be counted. *CHW: 10*

ACCESSIBILITY AND MAINTENANCE—First Aid boxes must be reasonably accessible from all positions where the persons for whom they are provided are working. *CHW: 5(1)*

Safe means of access to First Aid facilities must, so far is as reasonably practicable, be provided and maintained. *CHW: 16*

First Aid boxes must be kept clean and in good repair and must contain nothing but First Aid requisites. *CHW: 5 and 6*

186 – Site Offices

If office workers on a building or construction site are accommodated in movable structures in which they are not expected to work for more than 6 months, or in permanent structures in which they are not expected to work for more than 6 weeks, the requirements of the Offices, Shops and Railway Premises Act are not applicable, except as regards notification to the factory inspector that persons are employed in office work *OSRA: 86*

In other circumstances, site offices are subject to the requirements summarised in items 264 to 279, but with the following exceptions:—

The requirement that offices must be maintained at a reasonable temperature (with a minimum of 16°C. after the first hour) does not apply and is replaced by a requirement that office workers must have effective means of warming themselves. Such means need not be in the office itself but must be conveniently accessible, and office workers must be given reasonable opportunities of using them. The means of warming adopted must not be such as might allow any injurious or offensive fumes, gas or vapour to escape into any workroom or workplace. *OSRPA (Exemption) No. 1 Order*

The washing facilities provided for office workers need not include running water. They must, however, still include hot and cold (or warm) water. *OSRPA (Exemption) No. 1 Order*

Office workers need not have their own First Aid boxes but must be able to use those provided for other persons working on the site. In reckoning the number of persons employed, for the purposes of deciding on the First Aid requirements, office workers must be counted as well as others. *OSRA: 26(1) and Offices at Building Operations (First Aid) Regulations 1964*

What has been said in this item applies irrespective of whether the office used in connexion with the building operations or works of engineering construction is actually on the site or is on a separate but adjacent site.

187 – Duties of Employees

Persons employed in building operations and works of engineering construction have an obligation, under the various Construction Regulations to co-operate with their employers and fellow-workers in carrying out those regulations. They also have an obligation to observe the requirements of the regulations in so far as their own work is concerned.

Under the same codes of regulations, persons employed in building operations or works of engineering construction have a legal obligation to report to the occupier, foreman, or other authorised person, any defects they may discover in any scaffold, plant or appliance.

Persons employed in building operations and works of engineering construction must not, wilfully and without reasonable cause, do anything liable to endanger themselves or others. Nor must they interfere with, or misuse, anything provided under the Factories Acts for securing safety. *FA: 143*

Persons employed in building operations and works of engineering construction must make use of any appliance provided under the Factories Acts for securing their safety. (This does not apply to safety appliances supplied as a voluntary act by the employer, except in so far as the failure to use such a safety appliance is "liable to endanger" the employee or someone else, as mentioned in the previous paragraph.) *FA: 143*

Persons using woodworking machinery in the course of building operations or works of engineering construction must comply with the requirements of the Woodworking Machinery Regulations. See items 49 to 51.

Persons handling food in a canteen on a building site or during works of engineering construction must comply with the Food Hygiene Regulations. See item 136.

Persons using hoists must close the landing gates immediately after use. See item 171.

Persons using lead paint or rubbing down surfaces which may have been painted with lead paint must observe the legal requirements governing this work. See item 176.

An employee who fails in his legal obligations is liable to prosecution. This does not necessarily free the occupier or contractor from the liability to prosecution also. *FA: 155*

188 – Other Matters

Posting of Notices—Copies of the various codes of regulations applicable to building operations and works of engineering construction must be displayed either on the site or else at each office or yard at which persons employed in such operations attend. *FA: 127 and 139*

Abstracts of the Factories Act and, where applicable, the Electricity Regulations, the Woodworking Machinery Regulations, and other relevant regulations must be similarly displayed. *FA: 127*

Placards of the Lead Paint Regulations must be displayed if persons are employed in painting buildings. These placards must be displayed in the paint store or workshop and on any site where more than 12 painters are employed. *LPR: 7(b)*

If there is a canteen provided in connexion with building operations or works of engineering construction, any sanitary convenience regularly used by canteen workers must have a notice near it urging such workers to wash their hands after using the convenience. *FHR: 14*

Official placards containing the prescribed abstracts (where published) are obtainable through H.M. Stationery Office. The abstract of the Factories Act to be posted up in connexion with building operations or works of engineering construction is Factory Form 3 and differs slightly from the version used in factories.

Keeping of Registers—The requirements mentioned in item 297 regarding the keeping of a register and the recording of the results of examinations, etc., apply to building operations and works of engineering construction. The register must be kept at the office of the person or firm undertaking the operations. *FA: 127*

Where any welfare or First Aid facilities used by the employees of one employer are shared with those of another employer the register recording details of this sharing arrangement (Factory Form F 2202) must be kept either on the site of the operations or at the office of the contractor or other person who is actually providing the facilities. *CHW: 4(5)*

Medical Examinations and Fitness of Young Persons—The Employment Medical Service Act 1972 applies to medical examinations (item 42). See also EMASO for medical examinations in special processes, e.g. Compressed Air and Diving Regulations.

Chapter XIII

Safety and Welfare Requirements for Special Industries and Processes

The industries and processes dealt with in this chapter are so highly specialised that they are unlikely to be encountered in the majority of factories. The various codes of regulations applying to them have not, therefore, been given in full. From the brief summary given in each of the following items it is possible for a factory occupier to see whether or not a particular set of regulations applies to him. The actual text of the regulations can then be obtained and, to facilitate this, the official of each set of regulations is given. Copies can be ordered through any bookseller and generally cost only a few pence.

189 – Grinding Cutlery and Edge Tools

The Grinding of Cutlery and Edge Tools Regulations 1925 (SRO 1925: No. 1089) and the Grinding of Cutlery and Edge Tools (Amendment) Regulations 1950 (SI 1950: No. 270) apply to any grinding or glazing in connexion with the manufacture of cutlery, edge tools, swords, bayonets, files, saws, ploughs or other cutting or piercing implements of iron or steels.

The regulations are similar to those in force for the grinding of metals (see item 129) and deal with suppression and removal of harmful dusts (including the examination and testing of dust extraction plant, etc.); height and arrangement of workrooms; cleaning of workrooms; accommodation for clothing, and prohibition of spitting.

Abrasive wheels used for grinding or cutting were made the subject of special regulations and which lay down requirements regarding speeds, guards, and certain other matters affecting safety (item 53).

The grinding of cutlery, in so far as it involves the dry grinding of metals, is subject to the Protection of Eyes Regulations. See item 116.

190 – File Cutting by Hand

The File-Cutting Regulations (SRO 1903: No. 507) apply to all factories where the process of file-cutting by hand is carried on.

The regulations make provision for minimum air-space in workrooms; spacing of stocks; floors; ventilation; washing facilities; limewashing of walls; cleaning of workrooms and wearing of protective clothing.

191 – Testing of Aircraft Engines

The Factories (Testing of Aircraft Engines and Accessories) Regulations 1952 (SI 1952: No. 1689) apply to all factories in which aircraft engines, or carburetters or fuel pumps for aircraft are tested.

The order makes provisions for the construction of test rooms; separation from other processes; drainage of tanks and pipework; other drainage; ventilation; control valves for cutting off petrol; flame-proof electrical apparatus; earthing of magnetos, engines and other equipment; testing of electrical apparatus; prohibition of smoking and of naked flames; fire protection; use of petroleum in test rooms; and reporting of defects by employees.

Work inside aircraft under pressure test is not subject to the Work in Compressed Air Regulations unless the pressure is over 10 lb./sq. in. above atmospheric pressure. See item 246.

192 – Manufacture and Use of Celluloid

The Celluloid Regulations 1921 (SRO 1921: No. 1825) apply to all factories in which celluloid, or any articles made wholly or partly of celluloid, is manufactured, manipulated or stored, except when the only celluloid used is in solution and is not applied to fabrics of a readily flammable nature or when the premises are covered by the regulations for cinematograph films (see next item). The regulations make provision for special store-rooms; removal of celluloid waste and finished articles from workrooms; prohibition of smoking; precautions regarding naked lights and open fires; sawing of celluloid; packing of celluloid articles; fire precautions; and supervision by a competent person.

For the purpose of the regulations, the term celluloid does not include any material which does not contain nitrated-cellulose.

The Chief Inspector of Factories has power to grant exemption to a factory on the ground that only small quantities are used, or for any other good reason.

The keeping of raw celluloid is also covered by the Celluloid and Cinematograph Film Act 1922 which applies if more than one hundredweight is kept at any one time or if smaller quantities are kept otherwise than in a properly closed metal box or case. The Act prohibits the keeping of celluloid on certain types of premises and makes provision for the construction and use of storerooms. This Act also applies to cinematograph film.

193 – Film manufacture, etc.

The Manufacture of Cinematograph Film Regulations 1928 (SRO 1928: No. 82) applies to premises where cinematograph film is manufactured, repaired, manipulated, used or stored. For the purpose of the regulations the term Cinematograph Film applies only to film which contains nitro-cellulose or other nitrated product.

The regulations make provision for storage; removal of waste and scrap from workrooms; construction of workrooms; fire precautions; design and construction of storerooms; safely of electrical equipment; and supervision of work by a competent person.

The Cinematograph Film Stripping Regulations 1939 (SRO 1939: No. 571) apply to premises where the stripping or drying of cinematograph film is carried on. The regulations lay down detailed requirements respecting the way the work shall be carried out; the construction of workrooms; the removal of waste and scrap; design and construction of storerooms; prohibition of smoking and naked lights; design of electrical apparatus; and supervision of work.

Cinematograph film is also covered by the Celluloid and Cinematograph Film Act 1922, mentioned in item 192 above, if the quantity kept on the premises at any one time exceeds 12 reels in number or 80 lb. in weight, or if smaller quantities are kept otherwise than in separate and closed metal cases.

194 – Felt Hat Manufacture with Flammable Solvents

The Manufacture of Felt Hats Regulations 1902 (SRO 1902: No. 623) were revoked by the HFL and LPG Regulations, see item 130.

195 – Manufacture of Tin or Terne Plates

An order of October 5th, 1917 (SRO 1917: No. 1035) applies to all premises where the manufacture of tin or terne plate is carried on. Provision is made for the supply of waterproof aprons and clogs; accommodation for clothing; messrooms; and washing facilities.

196 – Hollow-ware Manufacture and Galvanising

The Hollow-ware and Galvanising Welfare Order 1921 (SRO 1921: No. 2032) applies to premises where hollow-ware is manufactured or where galvanising (other than the galvanising of wire) is carried on. The order requires the provision of finger stalls or gloves, acid-proof aprons, and clogs for all persons employed in wet processes.

197 – Tinning of Hollow-ware, etc.

The Tinning of Metal Hollow-ware Regulations 1909 (SRO 1909: No. 720) apply to premises where tinning is carried on in the manufacture of metal hollow-ware, iron drums and harness furniture. For the purpose of the regulations, Tinning means the dipping and wiping of any metal in the process of coating it with a mixture of tin and lead, or lead alone, where hydrochloric acid or a salt of hydrochloric acid is used. The regulations do not apply to silver plating, the use of soldering irons, or any other process that the Chief Inspector of Factories may exempt.

The regulations prohibit the employment of persons under 16 and make provisions for ventilation; collection of dust and refuse; the keeping of a health register and the medical examination of employees; the provision of cloakrooms and messrooms; the provision of protective clothing for women; and washing facilities. The medical examination must be carried out in accordance with the Lead Processes (Medical Examination) Regulations 1964 (SI 1964: No. 1728) and must include the haemoglobin estimation laid down in Factory Form F 2199.

198 – Bronzing in Letterpress Printing, etc.

The regulations for Bronzing with Dry Metallic Powders, 1912 (SRO 1912: No. 361) apply to the application of dry metallic powders to surfaces previously printed or otherwise prepared by letterpress printing, lithographic printing, or coating of metal sheets. They also apply to the dusting off of such powders from the surfaces.

The regulations require the suppression of dust; provision of exhaust ventilation; washing facilities; protective clothing; and accommodation for clothing. They also prohibit the taking of food, drink (except milk or tea) and tobacco in the workrooms.

199 – Processes involving Contact with Lead

The Regulations for the Manufacture of Lead Compounds (SRO 1921: No. 1443) apply to the manufacture of all carbonates, sulphates, nitrates and acetates of lead and all lead material used in the manufacture of such compounds. The regulations lay down detailed requirements regarding the way in which operations are to be carried out; design and layout of plant; medical examination of employees; protective equipment and clothing; messrooms and cloakrooms; and the provision and use of washing facilities. See also item 96.

The Regulations for the Smelting of Materials Containing Lead (SRO 1911: No. 752) apply to the smelting of materials containing lead, the manufacture of red or orange lead, and the manufacture of flaked litharge. They lay down detailed requirements regarding the way in which the operations are to be carried out; the provision of protective clothing; messrooms and cloakrooms; provision and use of washing facilities; medical examination of employees; and the prohibition of women and young persons under 16 from any employment in the process.

Section 74 of the Factories Act, 1961, prohibits the employment of women and young persons in the following processes: work at a furnace where the reduction or treatment of lead ores is carried on; the manipulation, treatment and reduction of ashes containing lead; the desilvering of lead; the melting of scrap lead; the manufacture of solder or alloys containing more than 10 per cent of lead; the manufacture of lead oxide, carbonate, sulphate, chromate, acetate, nitrate and silicate; the mixing or pasting in connexion with the manufacture or repair of electric accumulators; and the cleaning of workrooms where any of these processes have been carried on.

Section 75 of the Factories Act, 1961, requires special precautions to be taken if women and young persons are employed in any process involving the use of lead compounds if the process is one which produces dust or fume or if employees are liable to be splashed by the compound. The precautions include exhaust ventilation; medical examination; protective clothing; messrooms, cloakrooms and washing facilities; and the cleaning of workrooms. The requirements are amplified by Orders of November 8th, 1921 (SRO 1921: No. 1714, and 1715) and the meaning of the term Lead Compounds is defined in a further Order of the same date (SRO 1921: No. 1713).

Section 64 of the Factories Act, 1961, prohibits the taking of meals in workrooms where lead processes give rise to dust or fume, and also prohibits employees remaining in such rooms during meal or rest intervals.

Section 82 of the Factories Act, 1961, requires notice to be given to the District Inspector of Factories and to the employment medical adviser in charge of the area in which the factory is situate when any case of lead poisoning occurs. The appropriate form (Form 41) is prescribed by the Notice of Industrial Diseases Order 1964 (SI 1964: No. 369).

Danger from lead and lead compounds arises in various other processes covered by special regulations. These are accumulator repair and manufacture (item 205); vitreous enamelling (item 134); indiarubber manufacture (item 200); manufacture of paints and colours (item 201); painting of buildings (item 176); painting of vehicles (item 202); manufacture and decoration of pottery (item 203); tinning of hollow-ware (item 197); the heading of yarn (item 239) and construction work (item 183).

Medical examinations of persons employed in lead processes must be carried out in accordance with the Lead Processes (Medical Examination) Regulations 1964 (SI 1964; No. 1728) and must include the haemoglobin estimation laid down in Factory Form F 2199.

Lead poisoning is one of the industrial diseases which must be notified to the employment medical adviser for the area. See item 296 and the Code of Practice " Lead ", obtainable free from the Department of Employment.

200 – Manufacture of Indiarubber, etc.

The Indiarubber Regulations 1922 (SRO 1922: No. 329) apply to the manufacture of indiarubber and of any article made wholly or partly of indiarubber, including vulcanised waterproof cloth. They do not apply to the repair of any article, nor to any process in respect of which the Chief Inspector of Factories has granted a certificate of exemption.

The regulations prohibit the employment of males under 16 and females under 18 and restrict the employment of women generally; lay down detailed provisions regarding the method of carrying out the process; design of plant; protective clothing; medical examination of employees; messrooms and cloakrooms; the provision and use of washing facilities; the taking of samples by the factory inspector and the manner of ascertaining the percentage of a dry compound of lead present in a mixture.

Medical examinations of persons subject to the Indiarubber Regulations must be carried out in accordance with the Lead Processes (Medical Examination) Regulations 1964 (SI 1964: No. 1728) and must include the haemoglobin estimation laid down in Factory Form F 2199.

The Indiarubber Regulations 1955 (SI 1955: No. 1626) prohibit the use of carbon disulphide in the cold-cure process of vulcanising in the proofing of cloth with rubber.

The Carcinogenic Substances Regulations, 1967 (SI 1967 No. 879) prohibit the use in the indiarubber industry (and elsewhere) of benzidine, 4-aminodiphenyl, 4-nitrodiphenyl, and beta-naphthylamine. These regulations also control the use of alpha-naphthylamine, orthotolidine, auramine, magenta, etc.

201 – Manufacture of Paints and Colours

The Regulations for the Manufacture of Paints and Colours (SRO 1907: No. 17) apply to factories in which dry carbonate of lead or red lead is used in the manufacture of paints and colours or in which chromate of lead is produced by boiling. They do not, however, apply when paints and colour are manufactured solely for the use of the occupier nor to the manufacture of varnish paints or artists' colours.

The regulations restrict the employment of women and young persons and make provision for exhaust ventilation, protective clothing, cloakrooms, preparation and taking of food, provision and use of washing facilities, and medical examination of employees. The medical examinations must be carried out in accordance with the Lead Processes (Medical Examination) Regulations 1964 (SI 1964: No. 1728) and must include the haemoglobin estimation laid down in Factory Form F 2199.

Lead poisoning is one of the industrial diseases which must be notified to the employment medical adviser. See item 296.

202 – Painting of Vehicles

The Vehicle Painting Regulations (SRO 1926: No. 299) apply to factories in which lead paint is used in the painting of vehicles (including locomotives). They do not, however, apply to premises on which not more than 2 persons are employed in such painting, nor to the occasional painting of a vehicle used solely in the business of the factory.

The regulations make provision for the storing and use of lead paint, rubbing down, spraying of lead paint, preparation of stopping material, medical examination of employees, and the provision of mealrooms, accommodation for clothing, washing facilities, the taking of samples by factory inspectors and the method of treating lead paint to ascertain the percentage of dry compound of lead. The medical examinations must be carried out in accordance with the Lead Processes (Medical Examination) Regulations 1964 (SI 1964: No. 1728) and must include the haemoglobin estimation laid down in Factory Form 2199.

Lead poisoning is one of the industrial diseases which must be notified. See item 296.

Fixed and portable vessels (except parts of a spraying pistol) used for spraying paint are subject to the requirements laid down for air receivers. See item 89.

203 – Manufacture and Decoration of Pottery

The Pottery (Health and Welfare) Special Regulations 1950 (SI 1950: No. 65) apply to factories in which pottery is manufactured or decorated or in which lithographic transfers, frits and glazes are made, or flint or quartz is ground or powdered or mixed with other material, in connexion with the manufacture or decoration of pottery. They do not apply to the manufacture of potter's colours in factories where no pottery is made or decorated, nor to factories in which the only pottery made consists of glazed or unglazed bricks, architectural terracotta made from plastic clay and not glazed except with a leadless glaze, or unglazed and salt-glazed ware made from natural clay in the plastic state to which no form of free silica has been added.

The regulations restrict the employment of women and young persons in certain processes; provide for medical examination of employees; and lay down requirements for respirators and protective clothing, cloakroom accommodation, washing facilities, messrooms and food storage, ventilation, temperature, construction and maintenance of floors, design of work-benches, accommodation for moulds, preparation and storage of clay dust, design and spacing of tile presses, handling of raw lead compounds, glazing, colour blowing, use of hydrofluoric acid, lithographic transfer making, separation of processes, suppression of dust, surfacing and maintenance of works yards, and the appointment of competent persons to supervise the carrying out of the regulations.

The medical examination of pottery workers must be carried out in accordance with the Lead Processes (Medical Examination) Regulations 1964 (SI 1964: No. 1728) and must include the haemoglobin estimation laid down in Factory Form F 2199.

The Pottery (Health) Special Regulations 1947 (SRO 1947: No. 2161) restrict the use of certain glazes and of powdered flint or quartz.

204 – Ionising Radiations (Unsealed Radioactive Substances)

The former Luminising Regulations have been replaced by the Ionising Radiations (Unsealed Radioactive Substances) Regulations 1968, which apply not only to luminising but to any process in which unsealed radioactive substances are used unless the total activity is below a prescribed minimum.

These regulations provide for the giving of notice to the factory inspector when such substances are to be used; the appointment of competent persons to supervise the work; the restriction of exposure to radiation and the protection of workers against contamination; ingestion and inhalation; instructions to persons employed; the recording of radiation dosage; medical supervision; the marking of radiation areas and, where necessary, the provision of enclosures; the design of benches, tables and seats; the provision of special washing facilities; the provision of personal protective equipment; measures to account for all amounts of unsealed radioactive substances received in the factory; cleaning of active areas and precautions against accidental spillage or escape of radioactive substances; provision and use of monitoring instruments; prevention of bodily and other contamination; maximum permissible radiation doses; maximum permissible levels of contamination and methods of assessment; storage; and reporting of dangerous occurrences.

205 – Manufacture and Repair of Accumulators

The Electric Accumulator Regulations, 1925 (SRO 1925: 28) apply to all factories where accumulators or accumulator parts containing lead or lead compounds are manufactured or repaired (except for the repair of parts of a stationary battery used on the premises).

The regulations restrict the employment of young persons under 18 and of women and make detailed requirements regarding the carrying out of processes; design and maintenance of plant including floors and work-benches; general and local ventilation; spacing of workers; medical examination of workers; protective clothing; messrooms; cloakrooms and washing facilities. They also prohibit the taking of food, drink and tobacco in workrooms. The medical examinations must be carried out in accordance with the Lead Processes (Medical Examination) Regulations 1964 (SI 1964: No. 1728) and must include the haemoglobin estimation laid down in Factory Form F. 2199.

Section 74 of the Factories Act 1961 also prohibits the employment of women and young persons in mixing or pasting in connexion with the manufacture or repair of accumulators.

206 – Manufacture and Importation of Matches

White phosphorus must not be used in the manufacture of matches and no matches made with white phosphorus may be imported into the United Kingdom. For the purpose of these requirements the term "white phosphorus" means the substance usually known as white or yellow phosphorus. *FA: 67 and 77(1)*

207 – Tallow Melting

Permission of the Local Authority must be obtained before any building in England and Wales is used for tallow melting. Permission is also needed before a building already so used is enlarged. *PHA: 107*

208 – Blood Boiling and Drying and Bone Boiling

The requirements quoted in the preceding item apply also to buildings used for blood boiling, blood drying or bone boiling.

209 – Oil Cake Manufacture

The Oil Cake Welfare Order 1929 (SRO 1929: No. 534) applies to factories where the manufacture of oil cake, extracted meal, or compound cake is carried on—including the incidental operations of refining and grease manufacture.

The regulations make provision for protective clothing, accommodation for clothing, messrooms, washing facilities and ambulance rooms. Requirements for sitting facilities formerly included were revoked in 1951 as they are now covered by the Factories Act itself.

210 – Melting and Extraction of Fats and Boiling of Soap

Permission of the Local Authority must be obtained before any building in England and Wales is used for the melting and extraction of fats or for soap boiling. *PHA: 107*

211 – Glue and Size Making

The requirement quoted in the preceding item also applies to the making of glue and size.

212 – Food Manufacture

The manufacture of food is subject to the Food and Drugs Acts which make provisions for many matters which are outside the scope of this book, such as purity of food, adulteration, and so on. In addition, however, the Food Hygiene Regulations made under the Acts lay down requirements affecting the premises in which food is manufactured. The requirements are summarised in item 136.

For certain food manufacturing processes there are special safety and welfare requirements under the Factories Acts. These are summarised in items 213 to 221 below.

213 – Sale of Food

The sale of food by retail is subject to the Offices, Shops and Railway Premises Act (see items 264 to 279) as well as to the Food and Drugs Act and the Food Hygiene Regulations. See item 136.

214 – Baking and Biscuit Making

Section 70 of the Factories Act 1961 imposes special restrictions on the use of basement bakehouses and prohibits altogether the use of basements as bakehouses unless they were being so used on July 30th, 1937.

An order dated December 30th, 1903 (SRO 1903: No. 1157) increases the minimum amount of air space (see item 14) to 500 cubic feet per person in underground bakehouses.

The Bakehouse Welfare Order 1927 (SRO 1927: No. 191) applies to all premises where the baking of bread or flour confectionery is carried on. The order makes provision for washing, clothing accommodation, drinking water facilities, and the posting of statutory notices warning employees against dermatitis.

Section 21 of the Factories Act 1961, which restricts the employment of young persons on certain types of machinery, applies to dough mixers and dough brakes and to pie and tart making machines. See item 63.

The Biscuit Factories Welfare Order 1927 (SRO 1927: No. 872) applies to factories in which are carried out the processes of icing, creaming and filling biscuits and wafers, and the mixing of the ingredients therefor. The order makes provisions for washing facilities, accommodation for clothing, drinking water, medical inspection, and the display of statutory notices warning employees against dermatitis.

The First Aid requirements formerly included in some of the orders quoted here have now been repealed, as they are covered by First Aid requirements of the main Factories Act.

All bakehouses and biscuit factories are subject to the Food and Drugs Acts. See item 212.

215 – Sugar Refining and Manufacture

The Sugar Factories Welfare Order 1931 (SRO 1931: No. 684) applies to all factories where the making or refining of sugar is carried on. It provides for washing and bathing facilities, messrooms, accommodation for clothing, and the display of the statutory notice warning employees against the risk of dermatitis.

Sugar Factories are also subject to the Food and Drugs Acts. See item 212.

216 – Evaporating of Brine and Stoving of Salt

Female young persons below the age of 18 must not be employed in a part of the factory where the stoving of salt or the evaporation of brine in open pans is being carried on. *FA: 73*

Salt works in which the extraction of brine is carried on and in which muriatic acid is evolved are subject to certain requirements of the Alkali Works Regulation Act. See item 247.

217 – Gut Scraping, Gut Washing and Tripe Dressing

An order dated July 28th, 1920 (SRO: No. 1437) applies to gut-scraping and gut-washing and processes incidental thereto and to the preparation and dressing of tripe, except in factories where these processes are only occasionally carried on The order requires the provision of protective clothing, messrooms, washing facilities, and accommodation for clothing. The First Aid requirements formerly included in this order have now been repealed, as they are covered by the First Aid provisions of the main Factories Act.

Gut scraping and tripe boiling are listed as offensive trades under Section 107 of the Public Health Act 1936 and must not be carried out in any building in England or Wales without permission from the Local Authority. Permission must also be obtained before a building used for these purposes is extended.

The preparation of tripe is also subject to the Food and Drugs Acts. See item 212.

218 – Meat Mincing

Meat mincing machines driven by mechanical power must not be used by young persons unless the latter have been fully instructed in the dangers and have either been adequately trained or else are under adequate supervision of a person with a thorough knowledge of the machine. *FA: 21 and DMO*

Mincing machines used in shops are subject to special requirements under the Offices, Shops and Railway Premises Act. See item 276.

The mincing of meat in preparation for its sale in any form is subject to the Food and Drugs Acts. See item 212.

219 – Herring Curing

Herring gutting, salting and packing is subject to different codes of regulations according to the locality in which it is carried on. An order dated September 9th, 1920 (SRO 1920: No. 1662) applies to Norfolk and Suffolk. The Herring Curing Welfare Order 1927 (SRO 1927: No. 813) applies to the rest of England and Wales. The Herring Curing (Scotland) Welfare Order 1926 (SRO 1926: No. 535/S24) applies to Scotland.

The requirements of the three orders differ to some extent but their general purpose is to make provision for washing facilities, First Aid, messrooms, cloakrooms, and drinking water. Some of the First Aid requirements formerly included in these orders have now been repealed, as they are covered by the First Aid requirements of the main Factories Act but (except in Norfolk and Suffolk) there remains the obligation to make a properly equipped dressing station available.

The curing of herrings for sale is subject to the Food and Drugs Acts. See item 212.

220 – Fruit Preserving

The preservation of fruit, including peeling, sorting, preparing, boiling, bottling and canning, is subject to an order dated August 15th, 1919 (SRO 1919: No. 1136). This requires the provision of protective clothing, cloakrooms, messrooms and washing facilities. It also requires the display of a statutory notice warning employees against the effect of orange and lemon peel on the skin. The First Aid requirements of this order have now been repealed, as they are covered by the First Aid requirements of the main Factories Act.

Fruit preserving is subject to the Food and Drugs Acts. See item 212.

221 – Manufacture of Aerated Water

The Aerated Water Regulations 1921 (SRO 1921: No. 1932) apply to the manufacture of aerated water and processes incidental thereto. They lay down requirements affecting the construction of bottle-filling machines, the polishing of filled syphons and the provision of protective clothing.

The First Aid requirements formerly included in this order have now been repealed as they are covered by the requirements of the main Factories Act.

The Abstract of Special Regulations (Aerated Water) Order 1963 (SI 1963: No. 2058) prescribes the abstract of the regulations which is required to be posted up in all premises to which the regulations apply. This abstract (Factory Form 981) is obtainable from H.M. Stationery Office.

The manufacture of aerated water is subject to the Food and Drugs Acts. See item 212.

222 – Slaughterhouses

Slaughterhouses were first brought within the compass of the Factories Acts by Section 7 of the Slaughterhouses Act 1958. This is now replaced by Section 175(1)(d) of the Factories Act 1961. See item 1.

In addition, slaughterhouses are subject to the Slaughterhouses Acts and the various regulations made under them. These are concerned with the hygienic and other aspects of slaughtering animals and are therefore outside the scope of this book.

223 – Manufacture of Glass Bottles and Articles

An order dated May 15th, 1918 (SRO 1918: No. 558) applies to the making of glass bottles and of pressed glass articles. It requires the provision of cloakrooms, messrooms, and drinking water.

Girls under 18 must not be employed in such parts of a factory as are used for the melting of glass, the blowing of glass other than lamp blown glass, or the annealing of glass other than plate or sheet glass *FA: 73*

The Glass Bevelling Welfare Order 1921 (SRO 1921 No. 288) lays down regulations for the bevelling of glass and all processes incidental thereto. The order requires the provision of protective clothing (except when splash-guards are provided for all wheels), washing facilities including nail-brushes, cloakrooms or clothing lockers, and facilities for drying clothes.

224 – Casting of Non-Ferrous Metals

The Non-Ferrous Metals (Melting and Founding) Regulations 1962 (SI 1962: No. 1667) apply to the production of non-ferrous castings by casting metal in moulds made of sand, loam, metal, moulding composition or other material or mixture of materials, or by shell mouldings. They also apply to die-casting, centrifugal casting, or continuous casting, and to various incidental processes. Certain parts of the regulations also apply to the melting and casting of non-ferrous metal for the production of ingots, billets, slabs or other similar produsts, and to the stripping thereof.

The regulations lay down requirements for gangways and pouring aisles, the construction and cleanliness of floors, the temperature of workrooms, the carrying out of manual operations involving molten metal, protection against gases and fumes, the provision of washing facilities, the provision of facilities for taking meals and storing clothing, the provision of protective equipment, the carrying out of dressing operations in weatherproof buildings, the disposal of dross and skimmings, the disposal of waste generally, and the arrangement and storage of dies, patterns, moulding boxes, and other equipment and materials, both indoors and out of doors.

These regulations replace an early order, made in 1908, which applied only to the casting of brass.

A number of processes are exempt from the regulations. These are processes for the purposes of a printing works, smelting processes in which metal is obtained by a reducing operation, the manufacture of solder, the melting and casting of lead and lead-based alloys for the production of ingots, etc., and processes covered by the Electric Accumulator Regulations (see item 205) or the regulations for smelting materials containing lead (see item 199).

The Foundries (Protective Footwear and Gaiters) Regulations 1971 require the provision of suitable footwear and gaiters in ferrous and non-ferrous foundries.

225 – Blast Furnaces, Copper Mills, Foundries, etc.

An order dated October 12th, 1917 (SRO 1917: No. 1067) as amended by the Blast Furnaces and Saw Mills Ambulance (Amendment) Regulations 1961 (SI 1961: No. 2434) requires the provision of an ambulance room for all blast furnaces, copper mills, iron mills, foundries and metal works in which 500 or more persons are employed, The order prescribes the contents of the ambulance room and makes certain other requirements including the making of arrangements for summoning an ambulance. See item 41.

Iron-foundries and steel-foundries are subject to additional regulations. See item 24 and 132.

226 – Manufacture of Patent Fuel

The Patent Fuel Manufacture (Health and Welfare) Special Regulations 1946 (SRO 1946: No. 258) apply to the manufacture in factories of briquettes, ovoids or other blocks of fuel consisting of coal, coal dust, coke or slurry, with pitch as a binding substance. They make provisions affecting the design and maintenance of plant, dust suppression, washing facilities, accommodation for clothing, medical supervision and examination, provision of eye protection and barrier creams, and messrooms.

227 – Processing Refractory Materials

The Refractory Material Regulations 1931 (SRO 1931: No. 359) apply to all processes in the manufacture of silica bricks and to the handling, moving, breaking, crushing, grinding or sieving of any refractory material containing at least 80 per cent of total silica, for the purposes of the manufacture of crucibles, articles used in the construction of furnaces and flues, and materials used in the preparation of moulds for metal-casting. (For the purpose of the regulations, the term silica brick means any brick or article composed of refractory material and containing not less than 80 per cent total silica.)

The regulations prescribe the method of carrying out the work and make provisions for the enclosure of plant, provision of exhaust ventilation, and the cleaning of floors.

228 – Processing of Asbestos

The Asbestos Regulations 1969 (SI 1969 No. 690) apply to every process involving asbestos or any article composed wholly or partly of asbestos, except a process in connexion with which asbestos dust cannot be given off.

Asbestos is defined and the regulations apply to factories, warehouses, docks, construction work and shipbuilding. Before crocidolite is used 28 days notice should be given to the District Inspector of Factories. The regulations deal with exhaust ventilation equipment, respirators, protective clothing, cleanliness, construction of buildings where asbestos process is carried on, storage, distribution, cleaning of protective clothing and employment of young persons.

The parts of the regulations dealing with cleanliness and measures against dust are in substitution for the corresponding measures in the Factories Act, i.e. item 28—FA: 1(2) and item 117—FA: 63(1).

Asbestos dust can be very injurious and cause asbestosis, lung cancer and crocidolite (see above) is associated with mesothelioma. See Health and Safety Booklet No. 44 (H.M.S.O.) and TDN 35.

229 – Cement Manufacture

The Cement Works Welfare Order 1930 (SRO 1930: No. 94) applies to all factories where Portland Cement, or cement of a similar character, is manufactured. It lays down requirements for protective equipment and clothing, messrooms, accommodation for clothing, cleaning of sacks, and washing facilities.

Cement works are also subject to certain provisions of the Alkali, etc., Works Regulation Act (see item 247) which now incorporates some of the restrictions on the emission of smoke and grit made under the Clean Air Act.

230 – Clay, Brick and Tile Manufacture

The Clay Works (Welfare) Special Regulations 1948 (SI 1948: No. 1547) apply to factories in which clay, shale, sand, lime or similar materials are made into bricks, tiles, blocks, slabs, pipes, stilts and spurs, nozzles, or similar articles (except for any part of the factory which may be covered by the Pottery Regulations quoted in item 203).

The regulations lay down requirements respecting shelters for kiln workers, washing facilities, protective clothing, accommodation for clothing, rest rooms and ambulance rooms, canteens and messrooms, and the supervision of the cleaning of the facilities provided.

Brick and tile presses operated by mechanical power must not be used by young persons except under supervision or after proper training. See item 63.

231 – Manufacture of Gas

The repair of gasholders is subject to certain requirements under the main Factories Act and is also classed as a work of engineering construction. See items 123 and 152.

The Third Schedule to the Gas Act 1948 includes restrictions on the discharge of waste products into rivers, etc., and drains connected therewith. The Water Act 1945 gives water boards power to impose similar requirements in circumstances where water supplies are likely to be contaminated.

Certain processes ancillary to the production of gas may be subject to the Alkali, etc., Works Regulations Act 1906 and the Chemical Works Regulations. See item 247.

232 – Distillation of Tar and Turpentine

The distillation and heating of coal tar is one of the processes scheduled under the Alkali, etc., Works Regulations Act 1906 and the Chemical Works Regulations. See item 247.

Under Section 1 of the Fires Prevention Act 1785, which has never been fully repealed, the quantity of tar or turpentine which may be distilled or boiled within 75 feet of a building is restricted to 10 gallons, except in certain special circumstances. (This applies only in England.)

Epitheliomatous ulceration due to tar, pitch or bitumen is one of the industrial diseases which must be notified to the employment medical adviser. See item 296.

233 – Cleaning and Repairing Sacks

The Sacks (Cleaning and Repairing) Welfare Order 1927 (SRO 1927: No. 860) applies to factories where the cleaning and repairing of sacks is carried on, except when it is done only occasionally and is ancillary to another business. (If it is done *regularly* the regulations apply in any event.)

The order lays down requirements regarding protective clothing, messrooms, washing facilities and accommodation for clothing.

The cleaning and repairing of sacks in cement works is not covered by this order but by the Cement Works Welfare Order. See item 229.

The cleaning of sacks which have contained asbestos is subject to the Asbestos Industry Regulations (see item 228). The cleaning of bags which have contained wool or hair is covered by regulations quoted in item 238.

234 – Laundries

The Laundries Welfare Order 1920 (SRO 1920: No. 654) applies to all laundries, including parts of a factory where laundering is done ancillary to another business. The order makes requirements regarding protective clothing, messrooms, washing facilities, accommodation for clothing and drinking water The First Aid requirements formerly included in this order have now been repealed, as they are covered by the First Aid requirements of the main Factories Act.

Hydro-extractors, calenders, washing machines and garment presses used in laundries are subject to the Dangerous Machines (Training of Young Persons) Order. See item 63.

Special requirements for ironing rooms are laid down in Section 71 of the Factories Act 1961.

235 – Tanning and the Handling of Hides and Skins

The liming and tanning of raw hides and skins (including the re-tanning of tanned or partly tanned hides and skins) is subject to the Tanning Welfare Order 1930 (SRO 1930: No. 312). This lays down requirements respecting protective equipment, accommodation for clothing, messrooms, washing facilities, and the display of prescribed cautionary notices. The First Aid requirements formerly included in this order have now been repealed, as they are covered by the First Aid requirements of the main Factories Act.

The use of bichromate of potassium or sodium in tanning by the two-bath process was made the subject of an earlier order dated March 22nd, 1918 (SRO 1918: No. 368) but this order no longer applies to premises covered by the 1930 order quoted above. The requirements of both orders are similar but not identical.

The Hides and Skins Regulations 1921 (SRO 1921: No. 2076) apply to the handling of dry or drysalted hides and skins imported from Africa (including Madagascar) or Asia (including Japan and the Malay Archipelago). They lay down requirements respecting washing facilities, messrooms, accommodation for clothing, First Aid, the display of cautionary notices, the disposal of wrappers in which hides and skins have been packed, and the reporting by employees of any cuts or sores.

Fellmongering is an offensive trade within the meaning of the Public Health Acts 1936 and the permission of the Local Authority must be obtained before premises are used for this purpose, or before any premises already so used are enlarged. (This does not apply to Scotland.)

Anthrax and chrome ulceration are among the industrial diseases which must be notified. See item 296.

236 – Use of Horsehair

An order dated December 20th, 1907 (SRO 1907: No. 984) applies to all processes involving the use of horsehair from China, Siberia and Russia, including horsehair which has been wholly or partially prepared after leaving those countries.

The order restricts the employment of young persons under 18, and all persons suffering from sores or open cuts. It also lays down requirements respecting the sorting, storage and disinfecting of horsehair, collection and disposal of dust, cleaning of plant, protective clothing and equipment, messrooms, cloakrooms, washing facilities, and the display of cautionary notices.

An order dated March 11th, 1908, and made under the regulations quoted above, prescribes the particulars which must be kept in a register recording the receipt of Chinese, Siberian or Russian horsehair.

Anthrax is one of the industrial diseases which must be notified to the employment medical adviser. See item 296.

237 – Use of East Indian Wool

The use of East Indian Wool is subject to an order dated December 18th, 1908 (SRO 1908: No. 1287). This order makes provision for the design of dust-extracting plant and the provision of overalls and respirators and requires employees to report any defects found in the extracting plant.

238 – Wool Sorting, Washing, Combing, etc.

An order dated December 12th, 1905 (SRO 1905: No. 1293) applies to the sorting, willeying, washing, combing and carding of wool, goat hair and camel hair. The types of wool or hair covered by the order are alpaca, camel hair (Russian or Pekin), East Indian cashmere, mohair, pelitan, Persian and so-called Persian (including Karadi and Bagdad).

The order lays down the methods for carrying out certain processes, including the opening of bales, and makes requirements respecting storage; air-space and temperature; ventilation; cleaning and disinfecting of rooms; cleaning of bags which have contained wool or hair; washing facilities; protective clothing; messrooms; accommodation for clothing and food, the taking of samples by the factory inspector, and provision for treating scratches and slight wounds. It also restricts the opening of bales to skilled men and prohibits the employment, in certain processes, of persons suffering from sores or open cuts.

Carding machines and gill boxes used in wool textile trades, if operated by mechanical power, must not be used by young persons unless they are under adequate supervision or have been properly instructed. See item 63.

Anthrax Prevention Order 1971—This came into operation on 1st September, 1971 and provides that some imported goods (e.g. goat hair) should be disinfected by approved factories.

239 – Spinning and Weaving

The spinning and weaving of flax and tow, and the roughing, sorting, and hand-hackling of flax and tow, are subject to an order dated February 26th, 1906 (SRO 1906: No. 177). This lays down requirements affecting humidification, ventilation, temperature, wet-spinning troughs and frames, drainage of floors, suppression of dust and accommodation for clothing.

The spinning and weaving of hemp and jute and hemp and jute tow are subject to an order dated August 28th, 1907 (SRO 1907: No. 660). This lays down requirements affecting humidification, ventilation, temperature, dust suppression, and the provision of respirators for certain employees.

The spinning and weaving of jute and incidental processes, and the calendering and cropping of jute cloth, are subject to the Jute (Safety, Health and Welfare) Regulations 1948 (SI 1948: No. 1696). These lay down requirements affecting ventilation, dust control, removal of steam and vapour, temperature and heat insulation, humidification, maximum weights to be lifted by women and young persons, washing facilities, cloakroom and lockers, messrooms and canteens examination and maintenance of dust collection equipment, separation of engine rooms and boiler houses from workrooms, and the guarding of machinery.

Spinning by self-acting mules is subject to an order dated October 17th, 1905 (SRO 1905: No. 1103) which makes special provision for the fencing of certain specified parts and imposes on the minder certain obligations relating to the presence of other persons near the machine. These machines are also covered by Section 19 of the Factories Act 1961. See item 55.

The Mule Spinning (Health) Special Regulations 1953 (SI 1953: No. 1545) make provision for the medical examination of employees engaged in spinning with self-acting mules and define the types of oil which may be used for lubricating the spindles of mules.

Approved methods of testing the colour and viscosity of the oil for the purposes of these regulations are laid down in official form 1050, dated December 14th, 1953, and official form 1051, dated November 30th, 1954.

The weaving of cotton cloth is covered by the Cotton Cloth Factories Regulations 1929 (SRO 1929: No. 300). These make provisions respecting humidification, ventilation and temperature, design of weaving sheds, separation of boiler-houses and engine-houses from weaving sheds, whitewashing of roofs and roof windows, and the provision of cloakrooms. The Hygrometers Order, 1929, issued in conjunction with the regulations, makes requirements for the design and maintenance of the hygrometers used for checking humidity. The Cotton Cloth (Record of Humidity) Order 1964 (SI 1964: No. 558) prescribes the official form (Form 317) on which the hygrometer readings are to be entered.

The heading of yarn which has been dyed by means of a lead compound is covered by an order dated August 6th, 1907 (SRO 1907: No. 616). This prohibits the employment, for this purpose, of young persons under 16 and makes provision for exhaust ventilation, cloakrooms, messrooms, protective clothing, washing facilities, the taking of food or drink or tobacco in a workroom, the medical examination of employees, and the keeping of a health register. The medical examination must be carried out in accordance with the Lead Processes (Medical Examination) Regulations 1964 (SI 1964: No. 1728) and must include the haemoglobin estimation laid down in Factory Form F 2199.

Under the Factories (Cotton Shuttles) Regulations 1952 (SI 1952: No. 1495) shuttles other than non-suction shuttles must not be used, except in factories which have been granted a certificate of exemption by the Chief Inspector of Factories.

In the cold-cure process of vulcanising in the proofing of cloth with rubber, the use of carbon bisulphide is prohibited by the Indiarubber Regulations 1955 (SI 1955: No. 1626).

240 – Manufacture, Dyeing and Finishing of Wool Textiles

The Woollen and Worsted Textiles (Lifting of Heavy Weights) Regulations 1926 (SRO 1926: No. 1463) apply to factories in which the manufacture, dyeing or finishing of woollen or worsted textiles, or any process ancillary or incidental thereto, is carried on. These regulations specify the maximum weights which may be lifted by men, women and young persons employed in these processes.

241 – Dyeing with Chrome Solutions

An order dated March 22nd, 1918 (SRO 1918: No. 369) applies to factories in which bichromate of potassium or sodium is used in dyeing (other than job-dyeing). The order lays down requirements affecting protective clothing, cloakrooms and messrooms, washing facilities, and the display of cautionary notices. The First Aid requirements formerly included in this order have now been repealed as they are covered by the First Aid requirements of the main Factories Acts.

Chrome ulceration is one of the industrial diseases which

must be notified. See item 296.

242 - Boiling Textiles in Kiers

The Kiers Regulations 1938 (SRO 1938: No. 106) apply to kiers used for boiling textile materials in print works, bleaching and dyeing works, and works in which cotton or cotton waste is bleached. (They do not apply, however, to kiers in which the material is boiled in a container or wagon, or on a movable carriage, provided that the loading and unloading of such containers, etc., is carried on outside the kiers.)

The regulations lay down requirements affecting the admission of steam liquor and water to kiers, internal and external circulation pipes, precautions against accidental starting of pumps, discharge of liquor from kiers, position of valves and taps, kier covers, distinguishing marks on kiers, heights of kier edges and water and liquor levels, safe means of access, spacing of kiers, precautions before entering kiers, maintenance of taps and valves and safety appliances, and the appointment of a competent person to supervise the operation of kiers.

243 - Dry Cleaning

The Dry Cleaning Special Regulations 1949 (SI 1949: 2224) apply to factories in which dry cleaning is carried on otherwise than by spotting. An exception is made, however, of factories in which no articles of a textile character and no articles of wearing apparel are cleaned, and of the cleaning of textiles which are part of the equipment of a machine used in the factory. The regulations prohibit the use of cleaning liquids having a flash point below 90°F., except for cleaning by spotting. The Chief Inspector of Factories has power to issue certificates of exemption in special circumstances.

244 - Shipbuilding and Ship-repairing

The Shipbuilding and Ship-repairing Regulations 1960 (SI 1960: No. 1932) apply to work done in a shipyard, whether or not it forms part of a harbour or dry dock, and to work done in a harbour or wet dock (other than work done by the crew of a ship). The regulations replace the earlier Shipbuilding Regulations 1931.

The regulations provide for safe means of access, staging, ladders, precautions against falls, construction and use of lifting appliances, precautions against injurious or flammable gases, cutting and welding plant, precautions against fire, fencing of machinery, air receivers, lighting, protective clothing, precautions against dust, employment of young persons, use of lead paint, ambulances and ambulance rooms, and the appointment of safety supervisors.

A certificate of approval (Form F 2044) specifies the types of electric lamp which may be used in dangerous atmospheres. Two certificates of approval (Forms F 2051 and F 2053) specify the types of respirator and breathing apparatus which may be used.

Certain exemptions in respect of access stairs adjacent to chutes are given in a certificate of exemption (Form F 2080). Exemptions from some of the requirements for lifting gear are given in certificates of exemption for pulley blocks with calibrated load chains (Form F 2054), wrought iron chains and lifting gear (Form F 2048), and types of chain and lifting gear exempt from annealing (Form F 2057). Exemptions from some of the requirements for stages suspended by ropes are given in Factory Forms F 2193 and F 2194.

The prescribed particulars to be included in reports of the various examinations and tests are laid down in the following statutory instruments: 1961 No. 114; 1961 No. 115; 1961 No. 116; 1961 No. 117; 1961 No. 430; 1961 No. 431 as amended by 1964 No. 530; and 1961 No. 433.

Diving operations in connexion with shipbuilding or ship-repairing are subject to the regulations quoted in the next item.

The provisions in regulations 76 (a) (b) (c) and (d) and 77 (a) (b) (c) and (d) were revoked by the Asbestos Regulations AS: 1 (item 228).

245 - Diving Operations

The Diving Operations Special Regulations 1960 (SI 1960: No. 688) apply to all diving operations carried out on factory premises or in connexion with the loading and unloading of ships, shipbuilding and ship-repairing, building operations and works of engineering construction.

The regulations cover the provision of proper diving plant and equipment, the employment of properly trained divers, the presence of competent persons to assist the diver, the medical examination of divers, and the keeping of a fitness register.

246 - Work in Compressed Air

The Work in Compressed Air Special Regulations 1958 (SI 1958: No. 61) as amended by the Work in Compressed Air (Amendment) Regulations 1960 (SI 1960: No. 1307) apply to all work in compressed air carried out in factories, electrical stations, docks or shipyards, or in connexion with building operations or works of engineering construction.

The regulations provide for supervision by a competent person, construction and maintenance of bulkheads, air-locks, etc., the design of compressed air supply plant, the duties of lock attendants, rules for compression and decompression, means of egress from working chambers, temperature of working chambers, medical supervision and medical examinations, the keeping of registers, the issue of advisory leaflets, the provision of cloakrooms and washing facilities, and the supply of hot drinks. The advisory leaflet must be in the form prescribed by the Work in Compressed Air (Prescribed Leaflet) Order 1967 (SI 1967: No. 112).

Certificate of Exemption No. 1, dated October 9th, 1961, provides that the regulations shall not apply to work undertaken in aircraft under test pressures, so long as the pressure does not exceed 10 lb./sq. in. above atmospheric pressure.

Compressed air illness is one of the industrial diseases which must be notified to the employment medical adviser. See item 296.

247 - Chemical Works and Alkali Works

The Chemical Works Regulations 1922 (SRO 1922: No. 731) as amended by the Chemical Works Ambulance (Amendment) Regulations 1961: (SI 1961 No. 2435) apply to works in which certain scheduled processes are carried on. They lay down requirements respecting exhaust ventilation, smoking, precautions against dangerous gases and fumes and against falls into fixed vessels, protective equipment, ambulance rooms, drinking water, eyewash bottles, facilities for drenching people splashed with acid, and the reporting of defects noticed by employees. (The First Aid requirements formerly included in this order have now been repealed, as they are covered by the First Aid requirements of the main Factories Act.) The regulations also lay down detailed requirements for the carrying out of certain specific processes.

The Alkali, etc., Works Regulations Act 1906, and the Alkali, etc., Works Regulations (Scotland) Act 1951, as extended by statutory orders made under them, cover a large number of scheduled processes. They make provision for the control of gases, fumes and smoke, evolved in any processes, prohibit the discharge of certain liquids into drains and sewers, regulate the disposal of alkali waste, give occupiers powers to make and enforce special regulations, subject to the approval of the Minister, and require all works covered by the Act to be registered. Those sections which restrict the discharge of noxious and offensive fumes from cement works and smelting works must now be read in conjunction with the Clean Air Acts, which extend this restriction to include the discharge of smoke, grit and dust, and with the Alkali, etc., Works Order 1965 (SI 1965 No. 1143) and the Alkali, etc., Works (Scotland) Order 1965 (SI 1965: No. 478), which extend the list of noxious and offensive gases.

The types of works covered by the Chemical Works Regulations and the Alkali, etc., Works Regulation Acts are shown in Appendix VI.

Breathing apparatus approved for the purpose of the Chemical Works Regulations is listed in Form 893 obtainable from the Chief Inspector of Factories.

Chapter XIV

Atomic Energy and Radioactive Materials

The production of atomic energy, and the growing use in industry of X-rays and radiation from radioactive substances, has led within the last few years to new legislation, much of which is designed to give protection to factory workers against the effects of radiation. Most of the requirements quoted in this chapter apply to the use of radioactive materials in ordinary factories rather than to the special circumstances of nuclear installations. See the Health and Safety Booklet No. 13 (H.M.S.O.).

248 – Scope of Legislation

The keeping of radioactive materials on any premises, and the disposal of radioactive waste, is covered by the Radioactive Substances Acts 1948 and 1960. See items 259 to 261.

The use of ionising radiations from sealed sources, and of machines or apparatus which emit such radiations, is covered by the Ionising Radiations (Sealed Sources) Regulations 1969 (SI 1969 No. 808). See items 249 to 258.

Unsealed radioactive substances, including radioactive luminising compounds, are subject to the Ionising Radiations (Unsealed Radioactive Substances) Regulations 1968. (SI 1968 No. 780). See item 204.

The control of premises on which atomic energy and nuclear fuel is produced is dealt with by the Nuclear Installations Act 1965. See item 262.

249 – Regulations for Sealed Sources

The Ionising Radiations (Sealed Sources) Regulations 1969 apply to radioactive substances which are sealed in a container (otherwise than for the sole purpose of storage, transport or disposal) or which are bonded within material. For the purposes of the regulations, the immediate container or bonding of a sealed source is considered to be part of that sealed source. They also apply to certain machines and apparatus, as explained below. *IRR. 2(2)*

For the purposes of these particular regulations, a radioactive substance is a substance which consists of, or contains, radionuclides, whether natural or artificial, and of which the activity exceeds 0.002 of a microcurie per gramme of substance; in the case of a chain of radionuclides, consisting of a parent and daughters, the only nuclide to be taken into consideration is that having the highest activity of those present.

PREMISES AFFECTED—Except as mentioned later in this item, the regulations apply to the following premises:—

(*a*) Factories in which any sealed source is stored, manipulated, maintained, operated, used or installed.

(*b*) Factories in which machines or apparatus intended to produce ionising radiations are operated or used.

(*c*) Factories in which any machine or apparatus is operated or used which emits ionising radiations and in which charged particles are accelerated by a voltage of five kilovolts or more.

(*d*) Factories in which it is proposed to do any of the things just mentioned, even though they are not actually being done.

(*e*) Construction sites, electrical stations, warehouses using mechanical power, institutions subject to the Factories Act, and shipbuilding and ship-repairing subject to the Factories Act, if any of the operations just described are being done or are about to be done. *IRR 2 and 3*

EXCEPTIONS—The regulations do not apply to any apparatus exclusively used (in a room set aside for that purpose) for the prevention, diagnosis or treatment of illness or injury. *IRR: 3(4)*

The following are outside the scope of the regulations:—

(*a*) Any premises, plant or process exempt by certificate of the Chief Inspector of Factories, provided that a copy of the certificate, showing the conditions (if any) subject to which it has been granted is kept posted in the factory.

(*b*) Any sealed source at or near the surface of which the dose rate of ionising radiations does not exceed ten millirems in air per hour (except when several such sources are placed together so that their collective dose rate at or near the surface does exceed this figure even though the rate for individual sources does not).

(*c*) Ionising radiations which do not arise from a sealed source or from such machines as are referred to in the earlier part of this item.

(*d*) Apparatus used only for receiving visual images by television and operated at a voltage of not more than 20 kilovolts in the course of manufacture, repair, maintenance or testing and which in other circumstances has a dose rate at or near the surface which does not exceed 0.5 millirems per hour.

(*e*) Any plant or installation prescribed under Section 1(1)(b) of the Nuclear Installations Act 1965 (see item 262) and situated on a site in respect of which a nuclear site licence has been granted under that Act and is still in force.

RESPONSIBILITY FOR CARRYING OUT REGULATIONS—If a sealed source, or a machine subject to the regulations, is owned or hired by the occupier of the premises and is used by his employees he is responsible for carrying out the regulations.

If the sealed source or machine is owned or hired by someone other than the occupier, and someone other than the occupier employs those using it, the responsibility will rest with the person under whose direction it is used. *IRR: 3(2)*

If a sealed source or machine owned or hired by the occupier is used by classified workers employed by some other person, the occupier must make effective arrangements to ensure that that other person complies with his obligations as respects such classified workers. *IRR: 3(3)*

250 – Notification of Use of Sealed Sources

Before beginning to use, store, manipulate, operate, maintain or install any sealed source, or to use any machine of the types mentioned in item 249, the occupier must give notice to the District Inspector of Factories. At least one month's notice must be given except in an emergency or when the inspector agrees to accept shorter notice. *IRR: 5(1)*

When the use of premises for the purposes mentioned in this item has ceased, notice to that effect must be sent to the inspector within 7 days, unless the cessation is only a temporary one. Once such use has ceased, and notice to that effect has been given, the premises must not again be used for any operation covered by the regulations until further notice has been given. *IRR: 5(2)*

REGISTRATION OF SEALED SOURCES—An authorised person must keep a record showing the following particulars of all sealed sources under his control, except sealed sources which are in course of manufacture or which are being stored (without having been used) on the premises where they were manufactured or in which their manufacture was completed:—

(*a*) Distinguishing number or other identification mark of each sealed source.

(*b*) Date on which the sealed source was received into the factory.

(*c*) The nature of the radioactive substance in the sealed source at the date of its receipt.

(*d*) The activity, expressed in curies, of the radioactive substance in the sealed source at a date specified in the record.

(*e*) The whereabouts of the sealed source, kept up to date on each working day.

(*f*) The date and manner of disposal of the sealed source when it left the factory. *IRR 36(1) and 36(2)*

For the purpose of this register, a sealed source which has been reactivated, or has been received back into the occupier's control after reactivation, must be regarded as having been received into the occupier's control for the first time, and must be made the subject of a fresh entry in the register. *IRR: 36(1)*

251 - Classified Workers

The regulations for sealed sources, etc., make a distinction between classified workers and others. The term covers the following workers:—

Persons who are employed in radiation areas in work which involves the storage, manipulation, maintenance operation, use or installation of sealed sources, or in work which involves the operation or use of the types of machine mentioned in item 249. (This does not apply when workers operate under a scheme of work approved by the Chief Inspector of Factories because he is satisfied that the system of control and instruction is such that the radiation doses will not exceed three-tenths of those permitted, as given in item 254.) *IRR: 16(1) and 16(2)*

No person under 18 may be employed in work which would cause him to come under the designation of a classified worker. *IRR: 16(3)*

No person must be employed in work which would cause him to be designated as a classified worker unless he has undergone the prescribed medical examination (see item 257). Such a person must not continue in work of this kind without undergoing further examination at the prescribed intervals.

The names of all classified workers employed on the premises must be entered in the health register referred to in item 258.

EXEMPTION FROM CLASSIFICATION—Under various certificates of exemption certain workers are excluded from the designation of classified workers even though the nature of their work is within the terms of the definition given below. The types of worker concerned are shown below, with the factory form numbers by which the certificates of exemption can be identified.

(*a*) Workers whose only exposure to radiation is in the operation or use (otherwise than in the course of manufacture or repair) of a portable level indicator made by Panex Equipment Limited and incorporating a sealed source containing Caesium 137, so long as the apparatus is used under the conditions laid down in Factory Form F 2134.

(*b*) Workers (other than employees of Pye Unicam Limited) whose only exposure to radiation is in the operation or use of a chromatograph manufactured by W. G. Pye and Company Limited which contains a sealed source—including operations during which it is necessary to open the outside casing of such a chromatograph; this exemption is subject to the conditions set out in Factory Form F 2147.

(*c*) Workers whose only exposure to radiation is in the manipulation, operation or use (otherwise than in the course of manufacture or repair) of a portable level indicator made by Walter Kidde Limited and incorporating a sealed source containing Caesium 137, if used under the conditions laid down in Factory Form F 2147.

(*d*) Workers over 18 whose only exposure to radiation is in the operation or use (otherwise than in the course of manufacture or repair) of a portable gamma ray backscatter gauge manufactured by Ekco Electronics Limited and incorporating a sealed source containing either Cobalt 60 or Caesium 137, if used under the conditions laid down in Factory Form F 2159.

(*e*) Workers whose only exposure to radiation is in the operation or use (otherwise than in the course of manufacture or repair) of a portable beta particle backscatter gauge manufactured by Royston Burndept Research Limited and incorporating two sealed sources containing Strontium 90, subject to the conditions laid down in Factory Form 2183.

The certificates of exemption are listed under Ionising Radiations (Sealed Sources) Regulations 1969, in Sectional List 18 (H.M.S.O.)

252 - Supervision of Use of Sealed Sources

The occupier of premises to which the regulations apply must appoint one or more competent persons to exercise special supervision with regard to the regulations and to assist in enforcing the observance of them. *IRR: 7(1)*

The appointment of all such persons must be made in writing and their names must be posted up in the factory where they can be conveniently read by persons employed. If different competent persons are appointed for different parts of the factory, or for different processes, their names must be posted up in such a way that any person employed can readily identify the competent person appointed for his own part of the factory or process. *IRR: 7(2) and 7(3)*

The competent person appointed for the area or process concerned must be informed of the loss, suspected loss, or breakages of any sealed source and any leakage or suspected leakage of a radioactive substance beyond the approved extent (see item 255). On receiving any such report he must investigate the circumstances and give an account to the occupier, with recommendations as to the action which needs to be taken. *IRR: 8 and 9*

MEASUREMENT OF RADIATION—An appropriate and efficient radiation dosemeter or dose rate meter must be provided and maintained and must be used at such intervals as are necessary to ascertain the efficiency of the method used to restrict, or shield against, exposure to radiation. *IRR: 39(1)*

Each dosemeter and dose rate meter must be tested by a qualified person when first taken into use for the purpose of the regulations. It must be retested at least once in every 14 months and after any repair of a defect likely to have affected its accuracy. A register (Factory Form 2069A) must be maintained, recording the prescribed particulars of each test. *IRR: 39(3)*

Measurements required by the regulations must be made by the person appointed to supervise the observance of the regulations, or by some other person authorised by the occupier. *IRR: 39(4)*

A dosemeter or dose rate meter may be used in more than one factory.

253 – Construction and Maintenance of Sealed Sources

The immediate container or bonding of every sealed source must be of adequate mechanical strength and free from patent defect. *IRR: 34(1)*

A distinguishing number or other identifying mark must be attached to each sealed source. *IRR: 34(2)*

The immediate container or bonding of every sealed source must be protected, as far as practicable, from accidental damage. *IRR: 34(3)*

LEAKAGE TESTS OF SEALED SOURCES—Leakage tests must be made at least once in every period of 26 months. If the sealed source is permanently installed in a container not forming part of the sealed source itself, the test must be made on the container; in other circumstances the immediate container or bonding of the sealed source must be tested. *IRR: 34(4)*

Leakage tests must be made by a qualified person and in the manner laid down by the Ionisation Radiations (Sealed Sources) (Leakage Tests) Order 1969. A certificate of approval (Factory Form F 2184), issued under this order, specifies a type of sealed source which may be used for leakage testing and sets out a method of test.

Particulars of every leakage test must be entered in a register (Factory Form 2068), containing the prescribed particulars. *IRR: 34(5)*

The register, or an approved copy of it, must be kept available for inspection for a period of 3 years. *IRR: 10 and SI 1961 No. 1711*

Under a certificate of exemption (Form F 2136) leakage tests need not be made on a sealed source in which the only radioactive substance is krypton 85 of activity not exceeding 2 curies.

254 – Precautions against excessive Exposure

Persons employed must not be exposed to ionising radiations unless they have received appropriate and sufficient instruction regarding the hazards involved and the precautions to be observed. *IRR: 14*

Wherever it is reasonably practicable to do so, barriers must be used to mark the boundaries of radiation areas. Where this is not reasonably practicable, the boundaries must be marked by other suitable means. *IRR: 32(1)*

Suitable warning notices must be displayed at a sufficient number of places on or near the boundaries of all radiation areas. *IRR: 32(2)*

DIRECTION AND SIZE OF USEFUL BEAM—The useful beam must be limited, by appropriate means, to the minimum size reasonably necessary for the work. (In the case of X-rays, the useful beam is that part of the radiation from an X-ray tube that passes through the aperture, cone or other device for collimating the beam; in other cases the useful beam means any ionising radiation from a sealed source that can be employed for the purpose for which the sealed source is being used.) *IRR: 2(2) and 13(2)*

Wherever practicable, the useful beam must be directed away from adjacent occupied areas. *IRR: 13(1)*

Where appropriate, suitable measures must be taken to limit scattered radiation. *IRR: 13(3)*

SHIELDING AGAINST IONISING RADIATIONS—All sources of ionising radiation must be adequately shielded, where this is reasonably practicable. *IRR: 12*

For the purpose of these regulations, adequate shielding means the maintenance of a demarcation barrier or shielding outside which the radiation dose rate averaged over one minute does not exceed 0.75 millirems in air per hour (or, where only classified workers are affected, 2.5 millirems). *IRR: 2(2)*

RESTRICTIONS ON EXPOSURE—All that is reasonably practicable must be done to restrict the extent to which persons employed are exposed to ionising radiations.

Persons employed must not expose themselves to ionising radiations except to such an extent as is reasonably necessary for the purposes of their work.

In no circumstances may workers be exposed to more than the maximum dose specified below. *IRR: 11*

MAXIMUM PERMISSIBLE DOSES—The maximum dosage that a person employed may be allowed to receive in the course of his work is as follows:—

(*a*) To the hands, forearms, feet and ankles: 75 rems in any calendar year, of which not more than 40 rems must be received in any calendar quarter;

(*b*) To the lenses of the eyes: 15 rems in any calendar year, of which not more than 8 must be received in any calendar quarter;

(*c*) To other parts of the body: 30 rems in any calendar year, of which not more than 15 must be received in any calendar quarter. *IRR: Schedule.*

SPECIAL LIMITS FOR CERTAIN RADIATIONS—As well as the general limits quoted above there are stricter limits which apply to the dosage received, on parts of the body other than the eyes, hands, forearms, feet and ankles, from X-rays, gamma rays and neutrons.

The dosage received from these sources in any calendar quarter must not exceed 3 rems for men and 1.3 rems for women.

The cumulative dose from these sources must not exceed a figure calculated at the rate of 5 rems per year of the employee's age, counting from the calendar year in which he attained the age of 18.

For a woman whom the employer knows or believes to be pregnant, the dosage received on all parts of the body from X-rays, gamma rays and neutrons must not exceed 1 rem for the remaining period of the pregnancy. *IRR: Schedule.*

ADDITIONAL PRECAUTIONS—If the Chief Inspector of Factories has reason to believe that any employees have received, or are likely to receive, an annual or quarterly dosage greater than three-tenths of the permitted dose in the schedule to the regulations he may serve a notice on the occupier requiring other specified precautions to be taken. These may include the wearing of films or dosemeters, the monitoring of any part of the factory, the medical examination of any person employed and the suspension of any person from work in which he will be exposed to ionising radiations (or the imposing of special conditions on his continued employment in such work). *IRR: 15*

255 – Handling, Storage, etc., of Sealed Sources

No sealed source may be handled by direct contact with the bare hand. *IRR: 33*

STORAGE—Sealed sources, when not in use, must be kept securely in a suitable store reserved for the storage of radioactive substances. *IRR: 37(1)*

If reasonably practicable, the sealed sources must be kept in appropriate protective receptacles. *IRR: 37(1)*

A suitable warning notice must be prominently displayed outside every store which contains a sealed source. *IRR: 37(3)*

If a sealed source is liable to give off any radioactive gas, adequate and suitable arrangements must be made for ventilating the store to the open air by mechanical means. *IRR: 37(2)*

TRANSPORT OF SEALED SOURCES—Sealed sources transported within the factory must either be in a suitable container or else be transported by some other appropriate method. *IRR: 38*

The transport of a sealed source within the factory must be done by, or under the immediate supervision of, a person authorised by the occupier. *IRR: 38*

Every container containing any sealed source must be kept marked with a suitable warning notice to indicate that its contents are radioactive. *IRR: 38*

A sealed source must be transported and handed over in such a way that the person receiving it is made aware that he is receiving a sealed source. *IRR: 38*

BREAKAGE OF SEALED SOURCES—If the immediate container, or the bonding which forms part of a sealed source, should break, all practicable measures must at once be taken to safeguard persons employed. If necessary these measures must include the immediate vacation of all the areas likely to be affected. *IRR: 35(a)*

The immediate container or bonding must immediately be placed in a leakproof container and must not be brought into use until any necessary repairs have been effected. *IRR: 35(b)*

As soon as practicable after the breakage, effective steps must be taken to decontaminate areas affected by the radioactive substance. These steps must be taken by, or under the supervision of, a person authorised by the occupier and all persons taking part in such work must be properly equipped for the purpose. *IRR: 35(c)*

Notification of the breakage must immediately be given to the appointed supervisor referred to in item 252, as well as to the District Inspector of Factories. *IRR: 6 and 8*

LEAKAGE OF SEALED SOURCES—Where there are reasonable grounds for believing that any radioactive substance is leaking, or is likely to leak, beyond the approved extent, from the immediate container or from the bonding which forms part of the sealed source, the same action must be taken as if the sealed source were broken. *IRR: 35*

LOSS OF SEALED SOURCES—Any person who has reason to believe that a sealed source has been lost or mislaid must at once inform the competent person appointed, as described in item 252, to exercise special supervision. The competent person must take steps to locate the sealed source and if it is not accounted for within 24 hours the district inspector of factories must be notified. *IRR: 36(3)*

256 – Special Apparatus and Processes

Certain types of apparatus and processes involving the use of sealed sources are subject to the additional requirements given below.

MEASURING DEVICES AND STATIC ELIMINATORS—When sealed sources are used in thickness gauges, density gauges, package monitors, level gauges, static eliminators, analysers or other analytical, inspection or gauging equipment, every such sealed source must have an adequate and efficient cover plate, shutter or shield capable of being easily, securely and quickly placed or moved so as to attenuate the useful beam as far as is reasonably practicable. The cover plate, shutter or shield must be used whenever practicable to attenuate the useful beam and, whenever reasonably practicable, must be arranged to operate automatically. Means must be provided for indicating whether or not the cover plate, shutter or shield is in the closed position. *IRR: 46(2)*

The housing of every sealed source used for the purposes mentioned here must be legibly engraved, stamped or otherwise permanently marked to give warning that it contains radioactive material. *IRR: 46(3)*

Machines or apparatus producing ionising radiations and used in thickness gauges, density gauges, package monitors, level gauges, analysers or other analytical, inspection or gauging equipment must be adequately shielded. *IRR: 47(2)*

Separate light signals or audible signals (or both) must be arranged to operate automatically when the machine or apparatus is *about to be* energised, during the period when it *is* energised, when any shutter used to attenuate the beam is *about to be* opened, and when any such shutter *is* open. The four signals used for these purposes must be distinguishable from each other. *IRR: 47(3)*

When such machines or apparatus are in use, effective arrangements must be provided, maintained and used to prevent insertion of any part of the body into a useful beam. *IRR: 47(4)*

X-RAY CRYSTALLOGRAPHY AND SPECTROMETRY—All X-ray crystallographic apparatus, and all apparatus used for X-ray spectrometry, must be adequately shielded. *IRR: 45(2)*

Effective arrangements must be provided, maintained and used to prevent the insertion of any part of the body into the useful beam from such apparatus. *IRR: 45(3)*

When an X-ray diffraction camera or slit collimating system is in use, the useful beam passing between the X-ray tube aperture and the camera or collimating system must be completely enclosed so as to provide adequate shielding. *IRR: 45(4)*

When any X-ray crystallographic apparatus, or any apparatus used for X-ray spectrometry, is energised adequate warning must be given to all persons in the vicinity. The warning must be given by light signals or audible signals, and the signals must be arranged to work automatically. *IRR: 45(5)*

RADIOGRAPHY, FLUOROSCOPY, ETC.—The requirements quoted below apply to the following processes:—

(*a*) The use of ionising radiations in radiography or in fluoroscopy;

(*b*) The testing of machines and apparatus intended to produce ionising radiations (other than the X-ray machines and measuring apparatus mentioned earlier in this item);

(*c*) The use of ionising radiations in the irradiation of materials for the purpose of inducing chemical, physical or biological changes, including the irradiation of materials for the purpose of sterilisation, disinfection or disinfestation, or for the purpose of preserving food (but not including changes induced solely for the purpose of measuring ionising radiations). *IRR: 40*

Unless a scheme of work approved by the Chief Inspector of Factories is in operation, the processes just mentioned must be carried out in a walled enclosure or cabinet which provides adequate shielding. (A modification of this requirement is allowed when ionising radiations are being used in radiography and the provision of a walled enclosure or cabinet is not reasonably practicable. *IRR: 4 and 43(3)*

When a machine or apparatus producing ionising radiations is used inside a walled enclosure or cabinet, the control panel must be placed outside. Doors and openings in a walled enclosure or cabinet must be fitted with a device to ensure the energising of the machine or apparatus is automatically prevented while the door, etc., is open. *IRR: 42(1)*

To protect any person who may be accidentally shut inside an enclosure or cabinet there must either be exits so designed that they can easily and quickly be opened from inside, or means whereby persons shut inside can quickly control all sources of radiation, or appropriate shielding within the enclosure or cabinet. *IRR: 42(2)*

Where necessary, suitable means of communication must be provided and maintained to enable persons shut inside an enclosure or cabinet to summon help. *IRR: 42(3)*

When any machine or apparatus intended to produce ionising radiations is energised within an enclosure or cabinet, all persons must be excluded. Adequate warning, by light signals or audible signals, or both, must be given when a machine or apparatus is about to be energised and a different signal must be given once it actually is energised. (In the case of X-ray machines and apparatus the warnings must be arranged to operate automatically.) *IRR: 41 and 43*

When any sealed source is exposed within an enclosure or cabinet all persons other than authorised persons must be excluded. Adequate warning, by light signals or audible signals or both, must be given when a sealed source is about to be exposed and a different signal must be given once it actually is exposed. *IRR: 41 and 45*

In radiography, the radiographic set-up must be completed before any machine or apparatus is energised or any sealed source is exposed. No changes in the set-up must be made while a machine or apparatus is energised; changes while a sealed source is exposed must be made by the use of remote controls. *IRR: 44(3)*

When processes other than radiography are carried out inside a walled enclosure or cabinet, and it is necessary to bring material into the beam of radiation while a machine or apparatus is energised or a sealed source is exposed, this must be done by means of mechanism operated from outside the enclosure or cabinet. *IRR: 44(2)*

Whenever practicable, fluorescent screens must be viewed indirectly, by the use of inclined mirrors or other suitable means. *IRR: 44(4)*

Sealed sources must be moved only by the use of a handling rod or tool, or by an automatic or mechanical method, or by some other suitable method of remote control. *IRR: 44(1)*

257 – Medical Examinations and Supervision

No person must be employed as a classified worker, as defined in item 251, unless he has been medically examined within the 14 months preceding the start of such employment and unless he has, at some time or another, undergone a suitable blood test of which the results are known to the employment medical adviser. The employment medical adviser must, by signed entry in the health register, state if the person is fit for employment as a classified worker and he must not be so employed unless such an entry has been made. *IRR: 25(1)*

As part of the medical examination the employment medical adviser may, at his discretion, require a blood test or any other special examination. If a blood test is required it must be made by an approved laboratory or an approved person and a report of the test must be sent to the employment medical adviser. *IRR: 29*

When the dosage record shows that a worker has received, from X-rays, gamma rays, or neutrons, a dose exceeding the permitted dose by 10 rems to parts of the body other than the hands, forearms, feet and ankles, the worker must be immediately re-examined. *IRR: 27*

In all circumstances other than those just mentioned, *any* excessive dose must be followed by re-examination. *IRR: 27*

A classified worker must be re-examined once in every calendar year if it appears from his dosage record (see item 258) that during the immediately preceding calendar year he has received a sum of radiation doses exceeding three-tenths of the permitted dosage for that year. *IRR: 26*

If a person ceases to be employed as a classified worker he must be medically examined again before resuming such work, unless the resumption is within 14 months of the previous spell of such work. *IRR: 25(2)*

Except when the district inspector of factories otherwise directs or permits, medical examinations made for the purpose of the regulations must take place at the factory. (This does not apply to blood tests or other special examinations asked for by the doctor.) *IRR: 28 and 29.*

The occupier must give due notice to those who are to be examined, and the latter must submit themselves to the examination and to any special examination required by the employment medical adviser under the regulations, including blood tests. *IRR: 28*

On occasions when employees are to be examined, the occupier of the factory must provide a room for the exclusive use of the employment medical adviser. The room must be properly cleaned and adequately warmed and lighted, and must be furnished with a table and writing materials, chairs, an examination couch, a screen, and a washbasin supplied with running hot and cold, or warm, water. *IRR: 24(1)*

SUPERVISION AND POWERS OF SUSPENSION—The occupier must make arrangements for medical supervision of classified workers by the employment medical adviser. This must always include the periodical medical examinations prescribed by the regulations and must also include any other arrangements which may be considered necessary. *IRR: 23*

The occupier must give the employment medical adviser adequate facilities for inspecting any process, operation or work in which persons examined, or about to be examined, have been employed or are to be employed. *IRR: 24(2)*

The employment medical adviser has power to suspend, from employment as a classified worker, or in a radiation area, any worker examined by him under the regulations. No person so suspended must thereafter be employed as a classified worker, or in a radiation area, without the approval of the appointed doctor. *IRR: 30*

Suspension must be directed by means of a written certificate in the health register (see item 258) and approval for a suspended worker to resume the same employment must also be given in writing in the health register. *IRR: 30(1) and 30(2)*

Whenever a worker is suspended from classified employment by the employment medical adviser, the occupier must notify the district inspector of factories. *IRR: 30(3)*

258 – Dosage Records and Health Registers

Every classified worker must wear, in a proper manner on an appropriate part or parts of his person, either an approved dosemeter or dosemeters, or a suitable photographic film or films in an appropriate holder or holders. *IRR: 18(1)*

Films, holders and dosemeters must be obtained from a laboratory approved for the purpose by the Chief Inspector of Factories and must be returned to the laboratory, identified by reference to the particular wearer, for examination and the issue to the occupier of certificates showing the radiation doses received by the wearer. *IRR: 18(2)*

The certificate issued by the laboratory must contain the approved particulars called for by the Certificate of Approval No. 1 (General) 1969, Form 2340.

A dosage record must be kept for each classified worker showing the maximum radiation dosage permitted in his particular case (see item 254) and the doses received as indicated by the laboratory certificates. The record must be kept in Forms 2065 and 2305A.

Where a dose received, as indicated in the certificate, did not fall wholly within a calendar quarter it is assumed to have been received at a uniform date during all the days of that period, and the quarterly entries are to be made accordingly. *IRR: 19(4)*

Every classified worker is entitled to examine his dosage record at any reasonable time. *IRR: 19(3)*

If any person, on being engaged or employed as a classified worker, produces a document from another employer which purports to be a record of radiation doses already received, the particulars given in the document must, so far as practicable, be entered on the dose record by his new employer. *IRR: 19(2)*

Excessive Exposure—If the dosage record shows that a worker has received more than the permitted dose the occupier must at once notify the employment medical adviser and the district inspector of factories, and must arrange for an investigation to be made. As explained in item 257 he must also, in most cases, arrange for an immediate medical examination. *IRR: 20(3)*

If any person has reason to believe that he or some other person has received an excessive radiation dose he must report the circumstances to the occupier, who must arrange for an investigation to be made. If the investigation confirms the report, or if the occupier has other reasons to believe that an excessive dose has been received, the occupier must notify the employment medical adviser and the district inspector of factories and must keep a record of the circumstances. *IRR: 20(1) and (2)*

Discrepancies in Dosage Indicated—If the occupier has reason to believe that any person has received a radiation dose which is much greater or much less than the dose indicated by the certificate supplied by the laboratory he must arrange for an investigation to be made. If the results of this investigation confirm his belief he must ask the Chief Inspector of Factories to approve a special entry in the dose record. *IRR: 21(1)*

Health Register—A health register (Form 2067) must be kept, containing particulars of all classified workers. *IRR: 31*

The employment medical adviser must enter in the health register the dates and results of all medical examinations conducted under the regulations. *IRR: 31*

If a person is employed as a classified worker at more than one factory belonging to the same employer, all particulars concerning him must be kept in the same health register and the register may be kept at any one of the factories in which he is currently employed. *IRR: 17*

Transfer Records—When a person for whom a dosage record has been kept changes his place of employment (otherwise than on transfer to another factory belonging to the same employer) he must be given a transfer record (Form 2066). A copy of the transfer record must be sent to the district inspector of factories. *IRR: 22(1)*

Before being engaged as a classified worker, an employed person must inform his new employer of his previous employment in classified work and must hand to his new employer the transfer record. *IRR: 22(2)*

If an employer knows that an employed person was formerly in classified employment but has not received the transfer record he must obtain a copy from the district inspector of factories unless the employee concerned is no longer being employed on classified work. *IRR: 22(3)*

Preservation of Records—Health registers, dose records, transfer records, and copies of transfer records must be retained for a period of 30 years. They must be kept at the factory unless the factory inspector gives permission for them to be kept elsewhere, and must be available for inspection by the inspector or by the employment medical adviser. (Alternatively, an approved copy of the documents may be retained instead.) *IRR: 10*

Records of leakage tests must be kept for 3 years; all other records required under the regulations must be kept for 2 years. (As with health registers, etc., approved copies may be kept instead.) *IRR: 10*

259 – Registration of Premises using Radioactive Material

The Radioactive Substances Act 1960, which was brought into operation on December 1st, 1963, provides for the registration of premises on which radioactive materials are used or kept. (It also regulates the disposal of radioactive waste as described in item 260.)

Definition of Radioactive Material—For the purposes of this Act the term "radioactive material" includes any substance containing one of the elements shown in the table opposite, if the number of microcuries per gramme contained in the substance exceeds the number shown in the table.

The term is also applied to a substance possessing radioactivity which is wholly or partly attributable to a process of nuclear fission or other process of subjecting a substance to bombardment by neutrons or to ionising radiations, except where such process occurs in the course of nature. *RSA 60: 18(2)*

Element	Microcuries per gramme		
	Solid	Liquid	Gas or vapour
Actinium	1×10^{-5}	2×10^{-6}	7×10^{-11}
Lead	2×10^{-5}	1×10^{-7}	3×10^{-9}
Polonium	1×10^{-5}	7×10^{-7}	6×10^{-9}
Protoactinium	1×10^{-5}	9×10^{-7}	3×10^{-11}
Radium	1×10^{-5}	1×10^{-8}	1×10^{-9}
Radon	—	—	1×10^{-6}
Thorium	7×10^{-5}	1×10^{-6}	6×10^{-10}
Uranium	3×10^{-4}	2×10^{-5}	2×10^{-9}

It will be noted that the definition of radioactive material for the purposes of this Act is wider than the definition used for the purposes of the Ionising Radiations Regulations, as given in item 249.

Registration of Premises—Except in the special circumstances mentioned in item 261, any premises on which any radioactive material is kept or used must be registered.

Application for registration of premises in England must be made to the Minister of Housing and Local Government; in Scotland and Wales it must be made to the respective Secretaries of State. The application must specify the premises to which the application relates, the undertaking for the purposes of which the premises are used, a description of the radioactive material to be kept or used, the maximum quantity of such material likely to be on the premises at any one time, and the manner in which the material is likely to be used. *RSA 60: 1(2)*

In registering premises, the Minister (or Secretary of State) may impose such conditions or limitations as he thinks fit in regard to the following matters:—

(*a*) Requirements, including requirements involving structural alterations, in respect of any part of the premises on which the materials are to be kept or used.

(*b*) Requirements in respect of any apparatus, equipment or appliance to be used in connexion with radioactive material and from which radioactive waste is likely to arise.

(*c*) Requirements governing the sale or supply of radioactive material from the premises concerned—but only in connexion with the labelling or other marking of the material or its container.

(*d*) Requirements regarding the provision of information as to any removal of radioactive material from the premises concerned to any other premises.

Except in connexion with the supply, sale or removal of radioactive material, any conditions imposed must have regard solely to the amount of radioactive waste likely to arise from the keeping or use of radioactive materials on the premises concerned. *RSA: 1(4) and 1(5)*

Before the Minister (or Secretary of State) refuses an application for registration, or attaches conditions to it, he must give the applicant an opportunity to be heard in support of the application. *RSA 60: 11(1)*

Clocks and Watches with Luminous Dials—The presence on any premises of clocks or watches with luminous dials does not in itself constitute "keeping or using" of radioactive materials. But if the manufacturer or repair of clocks or watches involves the use of luminous material the premises must be registered. Such premises are also subject to the Ionising Radiations (Unsealed Radioactive Substances) Regulations, 1968. See item 204. *RSA 60: 2(5)*

Mobile Apparatus—When mobile radioactive apparatus is used to provide any testing, measuring or other service, the person providing the service, or letting the apparatus on hire, is responsible for registering it. In these circumstances the person on whose premises the apparatus is being temporarily used need not register the premises—unless, of course, he keeps other radioactive material in addition to the apparatus. *RSA 60: 3(1) and (2)*

Applications for the registration of mobile apparatus must specify the nature of the mobile apparatus and the services in the course of which it is to be used, lent or let on hire. *RSA 60: 3(3)*

For the purposes of the Act, the term mobile radioactive apparatus means any apparatus, equipment or appliance which is radioactive material and which is constructed or adapted for being transported from place to place. *RSA 60: 18(5)*

As with the registration of premises, the United Kingdom Atomic Energy Authority is exempt from the need to register. *RSA 60: 4*

Inspection—The Minister of Housing and Local Government and the Secretary of State for Scotland have power to appoint inspectors, whose powers of entry, etc., are similar to those of factory inspectors. See item 300.

Posting of Notices—Copies of certificates of registration must be posted up on the premises so as to be conveniently read by those who may be affected. *RSA 60: 11(3)*

260 – Radioactive Waste

For the purpose of the requirements quoted in this item, radioactive waste is waste which (*a*) consists wholly or partly of a substance or article which, if it were not waste, would be radioactive material or which (*b*) consists wholly or partly of a substance or article which has been contaminated by radioactive material or other radioactive waste. *RSA 60: 18(4)*

When radioactive material is produced, kept or used on any premises, any substance arising from such production, keeping, or use is presumed to be radioactive waste if it has been retained on the premises for three months or more. If it is not radioactive, the onus is on the occupier to prove that it is not. *RSA 60: 7(5)*

Radioactive waste must not be disposed of unless the Minister of Housing and Local Government (or the Secretary of State for Wales or for Scotland) has given written authority. When the waste is on or from premises licensed as a nuclear site under the Nuclear Installations Act 1965, or is on or from any premises used by the United Kingdom Atomic Energy Authority, authorisation by the Minister of Agriculture, Fisheries and Food is also required (except in Scotland) and such local authorities as river boards, water undertakings, etc., must be consulted by both Ministers before authorisation is given. *RSA 60: 6 and 8*

Authority is also required for the accumulation of radioactive waste with a view to its disposal at a later date, except on premises used by the United Kingdom Atomic Energy Authority or licensed as a nuclear site. *RSA 60: 7*

Before refusing authorisation, and before varying the terms of an authorisation already given, the Minister (or the

Secretary of State) must give the applicant an opportunity of being heard in support of his application. *RSA 60: 11(1)*

Copies of the authorisation must be posted up in the premises to which they refer, so that they can be conveniently read by those who may be affected. *RSA 60: 11(3)*

In certain circumstances the Minister of Housing and Local Government and the Secretaries of State have power to dispose of radioactive waste and recover the cost from the owner of the premises. These powers may be exercised only when there is reason to suppose that the waste will not otherwise be lawfully removed. *RSA 60: 10(4)*

These requirements apply to all means of disposal of radioactive waste, including burial, discharge into water, air or drains, dumping and destroying. *RSA 60: 19(1)*

261 – Exemptions under the Radioactive Substances Act

The following premises, and the following forms of radioactive materials, are exempt from the requirements of the Radioactive Substances Act as regards the need for registration (item 259) or from the requirements regarding the disposal of radioactive waste (item 260) or both.

NUCLEAR SITES—Nuclear installations operated by the United Kingdom Atomic Energy Authority, and licensed sites of the kind dealt with in item 262, need not be registered under the Radioactive Substances Act but are subject to the requirements of that Act as regards the disposal of waste. See item 260.

The power of the Minister of Housing and Local Government and the Secretaries of State to impose conditions regarding the provision of information and the labelling of radioactive material (see item 259) can be extended to nuclear sites even though they do not require registration. *RSA 60: 2(3)*

CROWN PROPERTY AND GOVERNMENT DEPARTMENTS—The Act does not apply to premises occupied by the Crown, by a government department, or by the armed forces of other countries while stationed in Britain. Such government departments, etc., may make voluntary agreements whereby they undertake not to dispose of radioactive waste without the authorisation which would be necessary if they were not officially exempt. *RSA 60: 14*

Premises which *belong* to the Crown or a government department but which are *occupied* by others are subject to the Act in the ordinary way. *RSA 60: 14*

VEHICLES, VESSELS AND AIRCRAFT—Radioactive material on a vehicle, vessel or aircraft which is temporarily on any premises in the course of a journey is not classed as being "kept or used" on the premises from which the vessel operates. *RSA 60: 19(2)*

Radioactive material used for propelling a vessel, and kept in or on the vessel for that purpose, is not regarded as being "kept or used" on the premises from which the vessel operates. *RSA 60: 19(2)*

DISPOSAL OF WASTE TO AUTHORISED PERSONS—Waste closed sources are exempt from the requirements regarding the disposal of waste if they are disposed of to a person authorised under Section 6(3) of the Radioactive Substances Act to dispose of waste of the kind concerned, or who carries on a licensed installation which produces radioactive material of the same kind, and if records of the disposal are kept in the form required by the regulations. *SI 1963 No. 1831 and SI 1963 No. 1877 (S 94)*

PRECIPITATED PHOSPHATE—The requirements as to registration do not apply to substances which contain precipitated phosphate and which are radioactive solely because of the presence of actinium, lead, polonium, protactinium, radium, radon, thorium or uranium in quantities not greater than those specified in the regulations. *SI 1963 No. 1836 and SI 1963 No. 1882 (S 99)*

WASTE FROM HOSPITALS—Certain radioactive materials used for medical treatment in hospitals and nursing homes are exempt from the requirements regarding the disposal of waste. *SI 1963 No. 1833 and SI 1963 No. 1879 (S 96)*

FIRE DETECTORS—Radioactive fire detectors attached to the premises and containing no more than 100 microcuries of all the radio nuclides present are exempt from registration and from the requirements governing the disposal of radioactive waste but the loss or damage of any such detector must be reported to the Ministry of Housing and Local Government or the appropriate Secretary of State. *SI 1962 No. 2640 and SI 1962 No. 2770 (S 130)*

MATERIALS USED AT EXHIBITIONS—Radioactive materials used for purposes of demonstration at exhibitions are exempt from the requirements as to registration but not from the requirements governing the disposal of radioactive waste. *SI 1962 No. 2645 and SI 1962 No. 2768 (S 128)*

OTHER EXEMPT MATERIALS AND USES—Radioactive materials coming under any of the following descriptions, or used for any of the following purposes, are exempt both from registration and from the requirements concerning the disposal of waste:—

(*a*) Radioactive materials and radioactive waste which is on the premises concerned only because it is being temporarily stored in the course of transit. *SI 1962 No. 2646 and SI 1962 No. 2765 (S 125)*

(*b*) Illuminated instruments on which radioactive luminous compounds are used to provide a luminous dial or similar indicator. *SI 1962 No. 2644 and SI 1962 No. 2761 (S 121)*

(*c*) Natural lead (and articles made from it) which is radioactive solely because of the presence of lead and polonium, or either of them. *SI 1962 No. 2649 and SI 1962 No. 2762 (S 122)*

(*d*) The use of compounds of prepared thorium, prepared uranium, and certain related substances when used for laboratory work in quantities no greater than those prescribed in the regulations. *SI 1962 No. 2711 and SI 1962 No. 2772 (S 132)*

(*e*) Materials containing thorium-x if kept on the premises of certain hospitals and nursing homes or of authorised sellers of poisons. This exemption is subject to certain conditions set out in the regulations. *SI 1963 No. 1834 and SI 1963 No. 1880 (S 97)*

(*f*) Electronic valves possessing limited radioactivity, and articles incorporating such valves, except when they are manufactured or stored on the premises concerned. The exact limits of radioactivity are specified in the regulations. *SI 1962 No. 2642 and SI 1962 No. 2773 (S 133)* (*g*) Substances which are radioactive solely because of the presence of titanium, yttrium, zirconium, niobium, lanthanum, cerium, praseodymium, neodymium, samarium, europium, gadolinium, terbium, dysprosium, holmium, erbium, thulium, ytterbium, lutecium, or hafnium in quantities no greater than those prescribed in the regulations. *SI 1962 No. 2648 and SI 1962 No. 2769 (S 129)*

(*h*) Substances and articles which are radioactive only because they contain natural uranium or natural thorium (or both) as defined by the regulations. The substances and articles concerned include thoriated tungsten used for electric lamp filaments, certain hard metal alloys, incandescent mantles, heat-resisting ceramics and refractories, and uraniated glass used for optical instruments. *SI 1962 No. 2710 and SI 1962 No. 2766 (S 126)*

(*j*) Specified instruments of the kind used for testing the characteristics of material, except when they are made or stored on the premises concerned. The regulations define the types of instrument to which the exemption applies. *SI 1962 No. 2643 and SI 1962 No. 2764 (S 124)*

(*k*) Devices forming part of lightning conductor systems and incorporating radioactive materials in the form of one or more closed sources. The exemption is subject to the conditions set out in the regulations. *SI 1963 No. 1835 and SI 1963 No. 1881(S 98)*

(*l*) Geological specimens of natural rocks or minerals containing uranium or thorium (or both) in quantities no greater than those prescribed in the regulations. *SI 1962 No. 2712 and SI 1962 No. 2771 (S 131)*

(*m*) The use and disposal of certain radioactive material used in the training of civil defence workers, or in the testing or calibration of instruments used for that purpose. *SI 1962 No. 2641 and SI 1962 No. 2767 (S 127)*

(*n*) Prescribed radioactive substances used in certain schools, teacher training colleges, and institutions. *SI 1963 No. 1832 and SI 1963 No. 1878 (S 95)*

The figures in italics give the year and numbers of the statutory instruments under which the particular exemption is granted. Where the number includes the letter S the statutory instrument refers to Scotland; the others refer to England and Wales.

262 - Licensed Nuclear Sites

Except on premises occupied by the UKAEA, a licence from the Minister of Power (or Secretary of State for Scotland) is needed before the following are installed or operated:

(*a*) Any nuclear reactor, other than a reactor comprised in a means of transport by land, water or air;

(*b*) Any installation designed or adapted for carrying out any process involved in the manufacture of fuel elements for atomic energy production from uranium so enriched as to contain more than 0·72 per cent of the isotope 235, or from plutonium, or from any alloy or compound of such uranium or plutonium;

(*c*) Any installation designed or adapted for the carrying out of any process involved in the production, from uranium enriched as just described, or from plutonium, of any alloy or chemical compound of such uranium or plutonium (other than any such process carried out solely for chemical or isotopic assay);

(*d*) Any installation designed or adapted for the incorporation of uranium, enriched as described in paragraph (*b*) or plutonium, or any alloy or chemical compound of such uranium or plutonium, in a device designed to form part of a nuclear assembly, or designed for irradiation in a nuclear reactor, other than a device designed solely for measuring neutron flux;

(*e*) Any installation comprising a nuclear assembly designed or adapted for the production of neutrons, being plant which contains uranium enriched as described in paragraph (*b*), or plutonium, or any alloy or chemical compound of such uranium or plutonium, and in which a controlled chain reaction can be maintained with an additional source of neutrons;

(*f*) Any installation designed or adapted for the processing of irradiated nuclear fuel, other than the processing of such fuel for chemical or isotopic assay or metallographic investigation;

(*g*) Any installation designed for the storage of nuclear matter in the form of irradiated nuclear fuel or fuel elements as referred to in paragraph (*b*) above—other than storage incidental to the carriage thereof and, in the case of irradiated nuclear fuel, other than storage incidental to any process exempt by regulations. *NIA: 1(1) as amplified by the Nuclear Installations Regulations 1965 (SI 1965: No. 1825)*

LICENCES FOR NUCLEAR SITES—Nuclear site licences may not be granted to individuals; they may be granted only to corporate bodies. They are not transferable and may at any time be revoked by the Minister or surrendered by the licensee. *NIA: 3(1) and 5(1)*

A licence may be varied from time to time by the exclusion of any part of the site which the licensee no longer needs for any use requiring a licence and which the Minister (or Secretary of State) considers is not a source of danger *NIA: 3(6)*

If the Minister granting the licence thinks fit, two nuclear installations in the same vicinity may be treated as one site for the purposes of licence. *NIA: 3(2)*

Where the Minister (or Secretary of State) considers it appropriate, he may direct that the applicant for a licence shall notify the local council, the local river authority or river purification board, or any other public body or authority likely to be affected. In such circumstances the licence will not be granted until the authorities so notified have been allowed three months in which to make representations and until any such representations have been considered. (This does not apply to applications which relate to the establishing of generating stations by one of the electricity boards.) *NIA: 3(3) and 3(4)*

CONDITIONS ATTACHED TO LICENCES—The grant of a licence may be made subject to any conditions considered necessary or desirable in the interests of safety. Such conditions may deal with the following matters in particular:—

(*a*) The maintenance of an efficient system for detecting and recording the presence and intensity of any ionising radiations from time to time emitted from anything on the site or from anything discharged on or from the site;

(*b*) The design, siting, construction, installation, operation, modification and maintenance of any plant or installation;

(*c*) The dealing with any accident or other emergency, including the laying down of the measures to be taken for dealing with specific emergencies;

(*d*) The discharge of any substance on or from the site;

(*e*) The handling, treatment and disposal of nuclear matter.

Conditions which do not come under any of these headings may be imposed if they are considered necessary or desirable in the interests of safety. *NIA: 4(1) and (2)*

Conditions attached to a licence may be varied, revoked or added to during the currency of the licence. *NIA: 4(3)*

Copies of any conditions attached to a licence must be posted up on the premises in places where they can be conveniently read by persons whose duties may be affected by them. *NIA:4(5)*

PROCESSES NEEDING SPECIAL PERMITS—Even if a site is licensed, a special permit is necessary before the site is used for any treatment of irradiated matter involving the extraction therefrom of plutonium or uranium, or for any treatment of uranium which increases the proportion of the isotope 235 contained therein. Permits may be granted by the Atomic Energy Authority and by Government departments if the processes in question are to be undertaken for purposes of research or development. Fissile material produced during such processes must be disposed of only in such a manner as is approved by the authority granting the permit. *NIA: 2*

LIABILITY FOR INJURY OR DAMAGE—The licensee of a nuclear site must ensure that no occurrence involving nuclear matter, and no emission of ionising radiations, causes injury to persons or damage to property. This liability extends to nuclear matter which is not on the site but which is in course of carriage on the licensee's behalf. *NIA: 7*

If injury or damage is caused by the licensee's failure to comply with his legal obligations he may be required to meet a claim for compensation. Every licensee must make arrangements, by insurance or otherwise, for ensuring that funds are available to meet claims; such arrangements must be approved by the Minister of Power or the Secretary of State for Scotland. *NIA: 12 to 21*

If the licensee arranges for any nuclear matter to be carried on his behalf, or with his approval, he must provide the carrier with the statutory document prescribed by the Nuclear Installations (Insurance Certificate) Regulations 1965 (SI 1965: No. 1823). This document must include details of the matter to be carried and must show the amount of money available to meet claims for injury or damage. *NIA: 21(3)*

REPORTING OF DANGEROUS OCCURRENCES—Under Section 22 of the Nuclear Installations Act, 1965, and the Nuclear Installations (Dangerous Occurrences) Regulations 1965 (SI 1965: No. 824) the following dangerous occurrences must be reported to the Minister of Power or the Secretary of State for Scotland:—

(*a*) Any occurrence involving the emission of ionising radiation, or the release of radioactive or toxic substances, in such circumstances as to be liable to cause the death, or serious injury to health, of any persons, whether such persons are on or off the site;

(*b*) Any explosion or outbreak of fire on a licensed site, if of a nature likely to affect the safe working or safe condition of nuclear installations;

(*c*) Any uncontrolled criticality excursion;

(*d*) Any occurrence during the course of carriage of nuclear matter on behalf of any person other than the Atomic Energy Authority of a government department, if the occurrence is liable to cause the death, or serious injury to the health, of any person or the breaking open of any outside container on which such nuclear matter was being carried. This requirement does not apply to the carriage of what is called excepted matter i.e., isotopes prepared for industrial, medical or scientific use and certain other small quantities of nuclear matter defined in Section 26 of the Nuclear Installations Act 1965 and the Nuclear Installations (Excepted Matter) Regulations 1965 (SI 1965: No. 1826)

Reports of dangerous occurrences must be made immediately, and by the quickest means available. A written report, giving the particulars prescribed in the regulations, must subsequently be made to the Minister or the Secretary of State. Reports of dangerous occurrences liable to injure persons outside the site, and those happening during transport, must also be reported to the local authority and the chief officer of the local police force.

OTHER REQUIREMENTS FOR NUCLEAR SITES—While a nuclear site licence is in force, the Ministry of Power and the Secretary of State for Scotland must consider any representations received from trades unions or other organisations representing persons employed on the site. *NIA: 4(4)*

After a licence has been surrendered or revoked, the licensee must keep warning notices posted up, indicating the limits of the site, until he receives written notice from the Minister or Secretary of State that there is no longer any danger from radiation. In addition to posting warning notices, the licensee must take any other steps ordered by the Minister or Secretary of State to protect persons and property from injury and damage by radiation. *NIA: 5(2) and (3)*

Lists and maps of licensed sites must be maintained by the Minister of Power and the Secretary of State for Scotland and must be made available to the public. *NIA: 6(1)*

After an occurrence which may have caused serious injury to the health of any person, the appropriate Minister may make an order providing for a register to be compiled showing particulars of any persons who were within the danger area at the time of the occurrence. *NIA: 23*

Although licensed sites are exempt from the necessity of being registered under the Radioactive Substances Act, the power to impose conditions which that Act gives to certain Ministers (see item 159) may be exercised in respect of licensed sites in so far as they apply to the sale or supply of radioactive materials and the furnishing of information regarding the removal of such materials to other premises. *RSA: 2*

263 – Other matters affecting Radioactive Materials

Nuclear power stations and other premises belonging to the United Kingdom Atomic Energy Authority operate under special Acts of Parliament and are outside the scope of ordinary legislation except as regards the disposal of radioactive waste as mentioned in item 260.

The use of unsealed radioactive substances is covered by the Ionising Radiations (Unsealed Radioactive Substances) Regulations 1968, which have replaced and extended the former Luminising Regulations. See item 204.

Chapter XV

Offices, Shops and Railway Premises

As explained in item 9, offices are not covered by the Factories Act even if they are physically part of the factory premises. They are, however, subject to the Offices, Shops and Railway Premises Act, the requirements of which are set out in this chapter. The same requirements, of course, apply to offices which are elsewhere than on factory premises.

The requirements quoted also apply to shops, to certain warehouses used by wholesalers, to premises where fuel is stored for sale, and to some premises occupied by railway undertakers. Although a factory occupier will not normally be concerned with any of these, there may be occasions when they are relevant; e.g., if a factory sells any of its products by retail to the public, or if it has a service department to which members of the public bring articles for repair.

264 – Premises affected

The requirements quoted in this chapter apply to offices, shops and railway premises as defined below, unless they are covered by one of the exceptions quoted in item 265.

OFFICES—The term " office premises " is defined as any building, or part of a building, used solely or principally for office purposes, including administration, handling money, operating telephones and telegraph apparatus, writing, book-keeping, sorting papers, filing, typing, duplicating, machine calculating, drawing, and the editorial preparation of matter for publication. The term also includes premises which are occupied in conjunction with office premises and for the purposes of the activities carried on in them, such as storerooms or canteens, even if they are not physically part of the office premises. *OSRA: 1(2)*

SHOPS—In addition to ordinary shops, this term includes the following:—

(*a*) Any building, or part of a building, of which the sole purpose or principal use is the carrying on of retail trade; for this purpose "retail trade" includes the sale to the public of food or drink for immediate consumption, retail sales by auction, and the business of lending books or periodicals for the purpose of gain.

(*b*) A building or part of a building occupied by a wholesale dealer or merchant who keeps goods there for sale (this does not include a warehouse belonging to the owners, trustees or conservators of a dock, wharf or quay).

(*c*) A building or part of a building to which members of the public resort for delivering goods for repair or other treatment, or for carrying out repairs or other treatment of goods for themselves.

(*d*) Fuel storage premises, i.e., premises occupied for the purposes of a trade or business which consists of, or includes, the sale of solid fuel and which are not already covered by the Dock Regulations (see item 138) or the Mines and Quarries Act 1954.

Docks, wharves and quays on which the wholesale sale of fish is carried on are not classed as shop premises but are subject to the requirement of the Dock Regulations as quoted in items 138 to 151.

RAILWAY PREMISES—The types of railway premises covered by the Offices, Shops and Railway Premises Act are buildings occupied by railway undertakers for the purposes of that undertaking and situated in the immediate vicinity of the permanent way but the term does not include hotels or residential accommodation of any kind, nor does it include any premises which are already subject to the Factories Act. *OSRA: 1(4) and 85(1)*

265 – Exceptions and Special Circumstances

The following types of premises, even though within the general definitions outlined above are either exempt from the requirements of the Offices, Shops and Railway Premises Act or are covered by it subject to the modifications stated.

PART-TIME USE—Premises on which the total number of man-hours worked does not exceed 21 per week are completely outside the scope of the Act. *OSRA: 3*

TEMPORARY PREMISES—The Act does not apply to moveable structures (e.g. offices on building sites) in which persons work for less than 6 months, nor to permanent structures in which they work for less than 6 weeks, except that notice of occupation, as described in item 278, must be given to the factory inspector or local authority as the case may be. *OSRA: 86*

OFFICES, ETC., ON FACTORY PREMISES—Offices, shops and railway premises which are within the close or curtilage of a factory are subject to the Offices, Shops and Railway Premises Act and not to the Factories Act except in the matter of First Aid (see item 277) and except for any part which is, by definition, part of a factory as described in items 1 and 2. When such premises are in the same building as a factory they are treated as one for certain fire protection purposes, as explained in item 274.

DOCKS, WHARVES AND QUAYS—Offices on docks, wharves and quays are subject to the Offices, Shops and Railway Premises Act and not to the Factories Act.

Warehouses which are not the property of the owners, trustees or conservators of the dock, wharf or quay on which they stand are subject to the Offices, Shops and Railway Premises Act, and not to the Factories Act, if they are used for the storage of goods for sale by wholesale. *OSRA: 75(3)*

Where a dock, wharf or quay subject to the Docks Regulations (see item 138) is used for the wholesale sale of fish it is not classed as shop premises. A wholesale fish warehouse not belonging to the owners, trustees or conservators of the dock is, however, covered by the Offices, Shops and Railway Premises Act, like the other warehouses mentioned in the previous paragraph. *OSRA: 85(2)*

ELECTRICAL STATIONS—Offices at electrical stations covered by the Factories Act are nonetheless subject to the Offices, Shops and Railway Premises Act, except in the matter of First Aid facilities, as explained in item 277. *OSRA: 74(1)*

MINES AND QUARRIES—An office which is below ground in a mine or quarry is outside the scope of the Offices, Shops and Railway Premises Act. *OSRA: 85(3)*

Offices, fuel storage premises, and shops which are above ground at a mine or quarry are subject to the Act but the law is enforced by inspectors of mines and quarries (or other persons appointed by the Minister of Power) instead of by the factory inspector or the local council. *OSRA: 52(6)*

SITE OFFICES—Offices on, or adjacent to, the site of building operations or works of engineering construction, and used in connexion with those operations, are subject to the Act with certain modifications explained in item 186.

266 – Responsibility for Compliance

Generally, speaking, the occupier of any premises is responsible for carrying out the requirements of the Offices, Shops and Railway Premises Act so far as they affect those premises. When different parts of a building are used by different occupiers, each is responsible for his own part (except for certain fire protection requirements affecting the whole building) and the owner of the premises is responsible for such parts as are used in common (e.g., passages and stairs giving access to the premises, and washrooms used by more than one occupier) and for such of the fire protection requirements mentioned in items 274 and 275 as affect more than one occupier. *OSRA: 42*

When different parts of a building belong to different owners each is responsible for such common parts as he himself owns (either alone or jointly with others) and the owners collectively are responsible for fire precuations throughout the whole building. *OSRA: 43*

Where such facilities as sanitary conveniences and washing facilities are provided by the owner for communal use of several different occupiers, the individual occupiers are still responsible for ensuring that the facilities comply with the legal requirements so far as their own employees are concerned. See items 271 and 272.

The responsibilities of persons employed are referred to in item 279.

267 – Floors, Stairs, Passages and Gangways

The following requirements apply to all floors, stairs, passages, and gangways in premises covered by the Act, except as mentioned in the course of this item.

FLOORS, PASSAGES AND GANGWAYS—All floors (and steps forming part of floors), passages and gangways must be of sound construction and must be properly maintained. They must be cleaned once a week or oftener by washing or such other methods (such as sweepings) as are suitable and effective, and no refuse or dirt must be allowed to accumulate on them. *OSRA: 16(1) and 4(2)*

So far as is reasonably practicable, floors, passages and gangways must be kept free from obstructions and from any substance on which a person might slip. *OSRA: 16(1)*

Openings in floors must be securely fenced, so far as the nature of the work makes this practicable. *OSRA: 16(4)*

STAIRS—Stairs must be of sound construction and must be properly maintained. No dirt or refuse must be allowed to accumulate on them, and so far as is reasonably practicable, they must be kept free from any obstruction and from any substance on which a person might slip. *OSRA: 16(1) and 4(2)*

Every staircase must have a handrail or handhold and if, because of the construction, condition, or other special circumstances, the staircase is specially liable to cause accidents, a handrail or handhold must be provided on both sides. *OSRA: 16(2)*

The open side of a staircase must have a midrail or other means of preventing persons falling between the handrail and the stairs themselves, and if a staircase has 2 open sides there must be handrails and midrails on both sides. *OSRA: 16(3)*

PASSAGES, STAIRS, ETC., USED IN COMMON—When different parts of a building are used by different occupiers, the responsibility for seeing that passages, stairs, etc., used in common comply with the Act rests with the owner. Where there are several owners, each is responsible for his own part of the building. *OSRA: 42 and 43*

When part of a building is used for purposes covered by the Offices, Shops and Railway Premises Act and part is used for other purposes, the requirements quoted in this item apply to all passages, stairs, etc., used by those working in parts subject to the Act. *OSRA: 42 and 43*

FUEL STORAGE PREMISES—The requirements quoted in this item do not apply to such parts of fuel storage premises as are in the open air but in such places the surface of the ground must be kept in good repair, all steps and platforms must be of sound construction and must be properly maintained, and all openings in platforms must be securely fenced except in so far as the nature of the work makes fencing impracticable. *OSRA: 16(5)*

268 – Lighting Heating and Ventilation

LIGHTING—Adequate natural or artificial lighting must be provided in all parts of offices, shops and railway premises where persons are working or passing. This includes such parts of the premises as are in the open air; it also includes sanitary conveniences and places where washing facilities are situated. It is not necessary to maintain this lighting at all times, so long as it is provided when needed. *OSRA: 8*

The Minister of Labour has power to make regulations prescribing standards of lighting for various types of premises. So far no regulations have been made, but see Health and Safety Booklet No. 39 (H.M.S.O.).

All lighting fittings and apparatus must be properly maintained. *OSRA: 8(4)*

Where glazed windows or skylights provide natural lighting they must be kept clean both inside and outside, so far as is reasonably practicable. *OSRA: 8(3)*

Where parts of a building are used as office premises, shop premises or railway premises and the other parts are used for different purposes, all parts used in common must be illuminated to the same standard as other places covered by the Act. Where different parts of a building belong to different owners, the owner or owners of the part in common use is responsible for the illumination of those parts. *OSRA: 32(3) and 43(2)*

VENTILATION—Every room in which persons work, and every sanitary convenience, must have adequate ventilation produced by natural or artificial circulation of fresh air. *OSRA: 7 and 9(2)*

As from January 1st, 1966, there must be effective provision for ventilating, so far as is reasonably practicable, rooms in which washing facilities are located. *WFR: 7*

TEMPERATURE—In all rooms where people work (unless they work there for only a short period at a time) there must be effective provision for securing and maintaining a reasonable temperature. Where a substantial proportion of the work done in a room is such as is done without severe physical effort, a temperature of at least 16°C (60.8°F) must be maintained after the first hour of the working period. *OSRA: 6(1) and 6(2)*

On every floor on which there is a room where people habitually work there must be a thermometer available in a conspicuous place, so that persons employed may take the temperature in any room. If the Minister of Labour so orders it, other thermometers may have to be provided as well. *OSRA: 6(4) and 6(5)*

The above requirements do not apply to certain types of room, office, etc., because it would not be reasonably practicable to maintain the temperature stipulated, but persons working in such rooms must be given access to some means of warming themselves. The types of room, office, etc., to which this exception applies are as follows:—

(*a*) Offices on, or adjacent to, sites where building operations or works of engineering construction are being carried on. See item 186.

(*b*) Rooms, in office premises, to which the public resorts and in which it is not reasonably practicable to maintain the prescribed temperature.

(*c*) Rooms, in shop premises and railway premises, in which the maintenance of the prescribed temperature is not reasonably practicable or in which the maintenance of the prescribed temperature would cause deterioration of goods.

Persons employed in such rooms as have just been mentioned must be given reasonable opportunities to warm themselves by the means provided. *OSRA: 6(3) and 6(4)*

Premises must not be heated by any method which allows injurious or offensive fumes, gases or vapours to escape into any room. *OSRA: 6*

269 – Tidiness and Cleanliness

All office premises, shop premises and railway premises (except such parts of fuel storage premises as are in the open air) must be kept in a clean state. This applies not only to floors, walls and ceilings but also to all furniture, furnishings and fittings. *OSRA: 4(1)*

Floors (and steps forming part of them) must be cleaned at least once a week by washing or by such other means (e.g., sweeping) as may be effective and suitable. *OSRA: 4(2)*

Glazed windows and skylights used to provide natural lighting must, so far as is reasonably practicable, be kept clean both inside and outside. *OSRA: 8(3)*

Sanitary conveniences, and places in which washing facilities are located, must be kept clean. *OSRA: 9(2) and 10(2)*

Floors, passages, gangways, stairs and steps must, so far as is reasonably practicable, be kept free from obstruction and from any substance likely to cause persons to slip. *OSRA: 16(1)*

No dirt or refuse must be allowed to accumulate in any part of the premises where persons either work or pass on their way to work. (This does not apply to such parts of fuel storage premises as are in the open.) *OSRA: 4(2)*

All means of escape specified in the fire certificate (see item 274) must be kept clear of obstructions, and the contents of rooms must be so arranged that they do not prevent free passage way to a means of escape. *OSRA: 30 and 33(2)*

Where part of a building is used as office premises, shop premises or railway premises, and the rest is used for other purposes, those parts which are iused n common must be kept in a clean state. *OSRA: 42(2) and 43(2)*

270 – Other Matters affecting Environment

PREVENTION OF OVERCROWDING—Rooms in which persons are at work must not be so overcrowded as to endanger health. In deciding whether a room is overcrowded, regard must be paid not only to the number of people likely to be working in it at any one time but also to the amount of space occupied by furniture, equipment, etc. *OSRA: 5(1)*

On premises used as offices, shops or railway premises, the number of persons regularly working in any room (other than one to which the public are admitted) must be such that there is at least 40 square feet of floor space and 400 cubic feet of room space for every person. *OSRA: 5*

If, owing to particular conditions, the standard just quoted is not high enough to prevent danger to health, a higher standard must be adopted and fewer people must be allowed to work in the room concerned. *OSRA: 5(2)*

SEATING—When persons employed have reasonable opportunities for sitting in the course of their work (without detriment to that work) suitable and sufficient seating facilities must be provided so that advantage can be taken of such opportunities, and employers must permit their employees to use these facilities whenever it does not interfere with their work. For those parts of shop premises to which the public have access the Act specified that the number of seats must not be less than one for every three persons employed there. *OSRA: 13(1) and 13(2)*

Where all, or a substantial part, of a person's work can be done sitting, that persons must be provided with a seat of a design, construction and dimensions suitable for him or her and, where necessary, with a foot-rest. *OSRA: 14.* See Health and Safety Booklet No. 45 (H.M.S.O.).

LIFTING OF LOADS—Persons working in offices, shops and railway premises must not be required to lift, carry or move any load which is so heavy that it may cause injury. *OSRA: 23*

Noise and Vibration—The Minister of Labour has power to make regulations requiring that reasonable precautions shall be taken when they are necessary to protect persons employed from the effects of noise and vibration. No such regulations have so far been made. *OSRA: 21*. (See Noise Abatement Act, 1960 and item 33.)

Other Environmental Matters—A magistrate's court (or, in Scotland, a sheriff's court) may order the discontinuance of any work, or of the use of any room or plant, which is considered to involve a risk to the health of employees. Persons aggrieved by such a decision may appeal to quarter sessions. *OSRA: 22 and 72*

271 – Washing Facilities

Sufficient and suitable washing facilities must be provided at places conveniently accessible to all persons employed on the premises. Unless exempted by the Minister of Labour, or under the procedure described in item 278, the facilities must include a supply of running hot and cold (or warm) water, They must also include either soap and towels or some other means of cleaning and drying. *OSRA: 10(1)*

It is not necessary for each occupier or employer to provide washing facilities himself, so long as he makes effective arrangements for his employees to use facilities which are available elsewhere and which are available at all times during working hours. He must, however, ensure that the communal facilities so used are such as to satisfy the requirements of the law (including the requirement that they shall be properly lit and kept clean) and he must see that soap and towels (or equivalent facilities) are available to his employees. *OSRA: 10(5)*

Every place where washing facilities are provided must have efficient natural or artificial lighting. Such places must be kept in a clean and orderly condition and all basins, troughs, drying facilities, etc., must be kept clean and properly maintained. *OSRA: 10(2)*

It is an offence for any person to remove, without reasonable cause, or wilfully to interfere with or misuse, any washing facilities provided under the Act. *OSRA: 27(2)*

It is illegal to charge employees for the towels, soap, etc., provided as part of the washing facilities. *OSRA: 47*

Scale and Standard of Washing Facilities—The general requirements just quoted came into effect in 1964. The following more detailed requirements operate as from January 1st, 1966.

If the number of persons regularly employed exceeds five, and these include members of both sexes, separate washing facilities must be provided for each sex so far as this is reasonably practicable. Accommodation must be marked to show for which sex it is intended. *WFR: 3(3) and 8*

The provision of washing facilities must be on the following scale:—

Number of persons to be provided for	Number of basins, trough units, or washing-fountain units
1–15	1
16–30	2
31–50	3
51–75	4
76–100	5
Over 100	5 for the first 100 and 1 for each additional 25 or part thereof

If the premises are exempt from the requirement to provide running water, the standard is one fixed or portable washbowl for every five persons. *WFR: Schedule*

If separate facilities for male and female workers are required the number of members of each sex must be calculated separately in determining the number of basins, etc., required. *WFR: Schedule*

If the facilities are shared by the employees of several occupiers, the total number of persons liable to use them must be taken into consideration. *WFR: 4*

If more than 10 employees have to be provided for, and the facilities are also liable to be used by members of the public when visiting the premises, the number of basins or units shown in the table must be increased by one. *WFR: 5*

A trough unit means 2 feet of the trough's length or, in the case of a circular or oval trough or washing-fountain, 2 feet of circumference. *WFR: 1(3)*

Washbasins provided to meet these standards must be fixed, with a supply of clean running hot and cold (or warm) water, and with a smooth impervious surface. They must be fitted with waste-pipes and (unless the water supply is from a spray tap) with a plug. *WFR: 1(3)*

Troughs must measure at least 4 feet internally over their longest or widest part, and must have a smooth impervious surface. They must be fitted with an unplugged waste pipe and must have a supply of warm water laid on, from above the trough, at intervals of not more than 2 feet. *WFR: 1(3)*

Washing-fountains must measure at least 3 feet internally at their widest part and must have a smooth impervious surface. They must be fitted with an unplugged waste pipe and must have a supply of running warm water. *WFR: 1(3)*

The washbowl provided when premises are exempt from the requirement to provide running water may be any type of water container suitable for use as a washing facility. *WFR: 1(3)*

All the washing facilities here specified must be covered and enclosed to such an extent as is necessary to give protection against the weather to those using them. So far as is reasonably practicable, effective provision must be made for their ventilation. *WFR: 6 and 7*

Communal Facilities—When different parts of a building are used by different occupiers the provision of washing facilities is the responsibility of the owner or owners, except that each occupier is responsible for seeing that those employed in his own premises are supplied with soap and towels or other means of cleaning and drying. Where the owner provides washing facilities for the sole use of any one occupier, that occupier is responsible for keeping them clean. *OSRA: 42 and 43*

Washing Facilities for Fuel Storage Premises—When two or more fuel storage premises which are in separate occupation are established on a parcel of land which is in single ownership, the owner of the land will be responsible for providing the washing facilities. *OSRA: 44*

272 – Sanitary Conveniences

Sufficient and suitable sanitary conveniences must be available at places conveniently accessible to all persons working on the premises. *OSRA: 9(1)*

It is not necessary for each employer or occupier to provide his own sanitary conveniences if he has made effective arrangements for his employees to use those provided by others. He must, however, ensure that such sanitary conveniences are aways available when required and that they comply with the requirements of the Act. *OSRA: (9)5*

Sanitary conveniences must be kept clean and properly maintained, and effective provision must be made for lighting and ventilating them. When they form part of a building in common use by more than one occupier the owner of the building will be responsible for these matters, except that if a sanitary convenience in a common part of the building is used exclusively by the employees of one occupier that occupier will be responsible for the cleaning. *OSRA: 9 and 42*

It is an offence for any person to interfere with any sanitary convenience. *OSRA: 27 (2)*

SCALE AND STANDARD OF SANITARY CONVENIENCES—The general requirements quoted above came into operation on August 1st, 1964. The following more detailed requirements have effect as from January 1st, 1966.

Public conveniences do not constitute suitable and sufficient sanitary conveniences for the purpose of the Act, even though they may be conveniently accessible. *SCR: 3(2)*

Sanitary conveniences must be provided on the following scale, separate conveniences being provided for members of different sexes. *SCR: 3(1) and Schedule*

Number of women	Number of WC's	Number of men	Number of WC's	Number of urinal units
1–15	1	1–15	1	–
16–30	2	16–20	1	1
		21–30	2	1
31–50	3	31–45	2	2
51–75	4	46–60	3	2
		61–75	3	3
76–100	5	76–90	4	3
		91–100	4	4
Each further 25	1	Each further 25	1	1

As an alternative to the scale here laid down for men, urinal units may be dispensed with and WCs provided on the same scale as for women. *SCR: 3(1) and Schedule*

Where it is not reasonably practicable to provide drainage and water for flushing, chemical closets may be provided in place of WCs and urinals. The scale of chemical closets, both for men and for women, will be the same as that laid down for WCs for women. *SCR: 3(1) and Schedule*

Where sanitary conveniences are shared by the employees of more than one employer, the total number of persons liable to use them must be considered when calculating the number required. *SCR: 4*

Where the number of persons for whom sanitary conveniences are provided exceeds 10, and the conveniences are also liable to be used by members of the public visiting the premises, the numbers of WCs shown in the table must be increased by one. *SCR: 5*

A urinal unit consists of 1 stall or, where stalls are not provided, 2 feet of space, *SCR: Schedule*

Where the number of persons regularly working on the premises does not exceed 5, only 1 WC need be provided, and this may be used by members of both sexes. *SCR: Schedule*

A water-closet provided under these regulations must have a separate fixed receptacle connected to a drainage system and separate provision for flushing from a supply of clean water, either by the operation of mechanism or by automatic action. *SCR: 1(3)*

Urinals provided under the regulations must also be connected to a drainage system and have provision for flushing with clean water either by mechanical operation or automatic action. *SCR: 1(3)*

Chemical closets provided when drainage and water for flushing cannot be provided must have a suitable receptacle for the reception of faecal matter and its deodorisation by the use of suitable chemicals. *SCR: 1(3)*

Sanitary conveniences must not be situated in a room in which any person, other than a lavatory attendant, is employed to work. *SCR: 6(1)*

No water cl oset or chemcal closet, no accommodation containing a urinal, and nio accommodation containing an unenclosed or partially enclosed water closet or chemical closet, must be so situated that there is direct access from a room in which any person, other than a lavatory attendant, has to work. (This requirement does not apply where the closet or accommodation was installed or constructed before June 25th, 1964, and it is not reasonably practicable to comply with the requirement; there must, however, be mechanical ventilation discharging direct into the open air and this must be kept in operation whenever persons are working in the room from which there is access.) *SCR: 6(2) and 6(3)*

Any enclosed space between a water closet, chemical closet, or urinal accommodation and a room in which persons other than a lavatory attendant work must be provided with efficient means of ventilation, *SCR: 6(4)*

Sanitary conveniences must be covered to an extent sufficient to give protection from the weather to those using them. *SCR: 7(1)*

Water closets and chemical closets must be enclosed to an extent sufficient to ensure privacy and must be provided with suitable doors and door fastenings. Urinals must be so placed or screened as not to be visible from outside the accommodation in which they are situated. *SCR: 7(1) and 7(2)*

Where separate accommodation has to be provided for males and females, it must be clearly marked to show the sex for which it is provided. *SCR: 8*

MEANS FOR THE DISPOSAL OF SANITARY DRESSINGS—Where the sanitary accommodation provided for women is liable to be used by more than ten persons it must include suitable and effective means for the disposal of sanitary dressings. These must be maintained in proper condition, and where the means provided consist of, or include, bins, these must be emptied, and the contents disposed of, at suitable intervals. *SCR: 9*

COMMUNAL FACILITIES—If different parts of the premises are used by different occupiers, the owner of the premises is responsible for providing the sanitary conveniences but if sanitary conveniences in a communal part of the premises are used exclusively by the employees of one occupier, that occupier will be responsible for cleaning them. *OSRA: 42*

FOOD HYGIENE—Sanitary accommodation used by persons handling food (whether in shops or in canteens) must have a notice posted up in or near them warning employees to wash their hands after using the conveniences. *FHR: 14(5)*

273 – Other Welfare Facilities

DRINKING WATER—An adequate supply of wholesome drinking water must be provided and maintained at all times, at suitable places conveniently accessible to persons employed on the premises. It is not necessary for the employer himself to provide the supply if he has made effective arrangements for employees to have access to some other suitable supply at all times during working hours. *OSRA: 11(1) and 11(4)*

Where the supply of water is not piped it must be contained in suitable vessels and renewed at least once every day, and all practicable steps must be taken to prevent either the water or the vessels from being contaminated. *OSRA: 11(2)*

Unless water is supplied in the form of a jet from which persons can conveniently drink there must be either an adequate supply of disposable drinking vessels or else non-disposable drinking vessels with facilities for rinsing them. *OSRA: 11(3)*

It is an offence for any person employed to misuse, remove or interfere with any facilities for the supply of drinking water. *OSRA: 27(2)*

Accommodation for Clothing—Persons employed must be provided with facilities for hanging up, or otherwise accommodating, clothing not worn during working hours. So far as is reasonably practicable there must also be facilities for drying such clothing when necessary. *OSRA: 12(1)*

Where persons employed have to do work for which special clothing is required, and do not take such clothing home, suitable provision must be made for the clothing to be hung up or otherwise accommodated. Provision must also be made, so far as is reasonably practicable, for drying such clothing when necessary. *OSRA: 12(2)*

Canteens—There is no statutory requirement that canteens must be provided for persons working in premises covered by the Act. However, if a canteen is provided, either on the same premises or on neighbouring premises, it will be subject to the requirements of the Act. *OSRA: 2(1)*

Canteens are also subject to the Food Hygiene Regulations. See item 136.

When people employed in shop premises eat meals there, suitable and sufficient facilities for eating them must be provided. *OSRA: 15*

274 – Means of Escape in Case of Fire

All premises covered by the Act, except such parts of fuel storage premises as are in the open air, must have such means of escape as may reasonably be required in view of the number of persons employed, the number of persons resorting to the premises, and other material considerations. *OSRA: 28*

If the fire authority considers that the means of escape from any premises are so inadequate that the employment of persons on those premises ought to be prohibited or restricted until conditions are improved, an application may be made to a magistrates' court (or, in Scotland, to the sheriff) asking for an order prohibiting or restricting the use of the premises. *OSRA: 32*

All means of escape specified in the fire certificate issued by the local fire authority (see below) must be properly maintained and kept free from obstruction. Unless in normal use as exits they must be distinctly and conspicuously marked, by notices printed in letters of adequate size, to show their purpose. *OSRA: 30 and 33*

It is an offence for any person to do anything to interfere with a means of escape provided under the Act. *OSRA: 27(2)*

Effective steps must be taken to ensure that all persons employed on premises requiring a fire certificate are familiar with the means of escape and the route to be followed in the case of fire. The Minister of Labour may make regulations prescribing the steps which must be taken for this purpose. *OSRA: 36*

While any persons are working or taking meals on the premises, the doors through which they have to pass in case of fire must not be locked nor fastened in such a way that they cannot be readily opened. *OSRA: 33(1)*

The contents of rooms must be so arranged as not to prevent free passage way to a means of escape. *OSRA: 32(2)*

Fire Certificates—All premises, except such parts of fuel storage premises as are in the open air, must have a fire certificate from the local authority if more than twenty persons are employed, or if more than ten persons are employed elsewhere than on the ground floor. A certificate is also required, whatever the number employed, if explosives or flammable materials prescribed by the Minister are used or stored in or below the premises, but so far no such explosives or materials have in fact been prescribed. *OSRA: 29*

The fire certificate will specify the greatest number of persons who can safely be employed to work on the premises at any one time and the means of escape provided. It will also mention any particular fire risks which the fire authority thinks exist on those particular premises. *OSRA: 29(5)*

The prescribed form to be used in applying for a certificate from the local fire authority is OSR 3 except when the certificate is required for railway premises (in which case it is OSR 8) or when the offices are in the same building as a factory which is also being made the subject of an application for a fire certificate, as explained in item 26. Once an application in the prescribed form has been made the premises may be used without a certificate until such time as a certificate has either been issued or has been refused because the means of escape are not considered satisfactory. In the latter circumstances the occupiers of the premises will normally be allowed a period of grace in which to make such alterations as the fire authority considers necessary, and during that period of grace the use of the premises without a certificate may be allowed to continue. *OSRA: 29(4) and 29(8)*

If after a certificate has been granted, it is proposed to make any material structural alterations or extensions to the premises, or to increase the number of employees over and above the number allowed by the certificate, the fire authority must be notified. The fire authority will then decide what alterations, if any, in the means of escape are necessary in order to suit the changed circumstances; if the fire authority considers that the existing means of escape are sufficient the fire certificate will be endorsed to that effect. *OSRA: 30(3), 30(4) and 30(6)*

The fire authority must also be notified when it is proposed to use prescribed explosives or flammable materials for the first time, or to store such explosives or materials in quantities greater than those which the Minister of Labour has specified in regulations. *OSRA: 30(3)*

If an employer or occupier is aggrieved by the fire authority's refusal to issue or amend a fire certificate, or by any conditions imposed by the fire authority, or by the cancellation of a certificate, an appeal can be made to a magistrate's court (or, in Scotland, to the sheriff) within twenty-one days. No offence is committed if the premises continue to be used while the appeal is being heard and decided. *OSRA: 31*

When a building is used partly as office premises, shop premises, or railway premises, and partly for other purposes, the application for a fire certificate must be made by the owner. When a building is shared by several owners, the application for a certificate must be made jointly by all the part-owners concerned. *OSRA: 42(13) and 43(9)*

For the purposes of administration a " building " is regarded as extending vertically from its lowest level to roof-top, and horizontally to party walls through which there is no internal communication with neighbouring buildings and to external walls.

It is an offence, punishable by imprisonment or fine, to forge a fire certificate or to make or possess any colourable imitation of such a certificate. It is also an offence to make a false statement, or make use of false documents, for the purpose of obtaining a certificate. *OSRA: 68*

275 – Other Precautions against Fire

The following requirements apply to all premises covered by the Act except for such parts of fuel storage premises as are in the open air.

FIRE EXTINGUISHERS, ETC.—Appropriate means for fighting fires must be provided and maintained in all indoor premises and must be so placed as to be readily available. *OSRA: 38(1)*

It is an offence for any person, wilfully and without reasonable cause, to remove, misuse, or interfere with any fire extinguisher or other fire fighting equipment provided under the Act. *OSRA: 27(2)*

FIRE ALARMS—Fire alarms must be provided for all indoor premises in which more than twenty people are employed, or in which more than ten people work elsewhere than on the ground floor. They must also be provided (whatever the number employed) for premises on which explosives or flammable materials are used, or stored in quantities greater than those prescribed by the Minister of Labour, and for premises situated over places where such explosives or flammable material are stored or used. *OSRA: 34(4)*

The alarm must consist of an effective means of giving warning of fire and must be capable of being operated without exposing any person to undue risk. It must be tested or examined at least once in every period of three months, and also at any time when the fire authority ask for a test or examination to be made. The Minister of Labour may make regulations specifying the nature of the test or examination to be applied. *OSRA: 34(1) and 34(2)*

When a building is used partly as office premises, shop premises or railway premises and partly for other purposes, the fire alarm must be perceptible in all parts of the building which are in common use and the responsibility for providing it will rest with the owner of the building. When a building belongs to several owners the alarm must be perceptible in all parts used as office premises, shop premises or railway premises, and the responsibility for providing the alarm will rest with all the owners jointly. *OSRA: 42(14) and 43(13)*. (See item 274 for the meaning of " building " for administration purposes.)

It is an offence for any person to interfere with, misuse or remove any appliance which is part of a fire alarm system. *OSRA: 27(2)*

276 – Machinery

Every dangerous part of any machine must be securely fenced unless it is in such a position, or of such construction, as to be as safe to everybody working on the premises as it would be if it were securely fenced. *OSRA: 17(1)*

It will be noted that this requirement is the same as that for machinery in factories and although no cases bearing on the legal interpretation of the term " dangerous part " have yet come into court it may reasonably be assumed that what has been said in items 43 to 48 will apply to machines in offices as it does to machines in factories. If it is impossible, because of the nature of the work done on the machine, to guard the dangerous parts by means of a fixed guard, it is permissible to use an automatic guard which prevents the operator from coming into contact with the dangerous parts while they are in motion. *OSRA: 17(2)*

Fencing or guarding must be of a substantial construction and must be properly maintained. It must be kept in position whenever the machine is in motion or use, except when the parts guarded are necessarily exposed for an examination which cannot be made with the machinery at rest, or for such lubrication or adjustment as the examination shows to be immediately necessary and which cannot be done with the machine at rest. *OSRA: 17(4)*

Necessary approach to unfenced machinery, for the purposes just mentioned, may be made only by persons who have reached the age of eighteen. This applies not only to parts of a machine from which the fencing has been removed but also to such parts as have been left permanently unfenced because they are normally out of reach. *OSRA: 17(3) and 17(5)*

No person under the age of eighteen may clean any machine if it would expose him or her to danger either from that machine or from any adjacent machine. *OSRA: 18*

The following machines may be used only by persons who have been fully instructed in the dangers involved and the precautions to be taken, and who are either fully trained or are under adequate supervision:—

(*a*) Platen printing machines, whether used for printing or for cutting and creasing, and whether worked by mechanical power or not.

(*b*) Guillotine machines, whether worked by mechanical power or not.

(*c*) Power-operated wire stitching machines, loose-knife punching machines, and corner-staying machines.

(*d*) All types of power-operated machines fitted with a circular saw blade or a blade formed as a continuous band or strip.

(*e*) Power-operated planing machines, vertical spindle moulding machines, and routing machines used for cutting wood, wood products, fibreboard, plastic, or similar material.

(*f*) Power-operated garment presses

(*g*) Power-operated dough mixers, dough brakes, and pie and tart making machines.

(*h*) Power-operated worm-type mincing machines, rotary-bowl-type chopping machines, vegetable slicing machines, and food mixing machines fitted with attachments for mincing, slicing, chipping or other cutting operation, or for crumbing.

(*j*) Circular-knife slicing machines used for cutting bacon and other foods, whether operated by mechanical power or not.

(*k*) Potato chipping machines, whether operated by mechanical power or not.

(*l*) Power-operated wrapping and packing machines.

All the above are prescribed for the purposes of Section 19 of the Act, under the Prescribed Dangerous Machines Order 1964 *SI 1964 No. 971*

The Secretary of State may make regulations dealing with machinery, plant, equipment, appliance or substance. The only regulations made so far under this section are the Offices, Shops and Railway Premises (Hoists and Lifts) Regulations, 1968 (SI 1968 No. 849). These regulations are similar to those for factories, (item 78). *OSRA: 20*

277 - First Aid

When office premises, shop premises, fuel storage premises, or railway premises are within the close or curtilage of a factory. persons employed in such premises must be able to use the First Aid facilities provided under the Factories Act described in item 40. In counting the number of employees to determine whether or not a trained first-aider is required by law, those working in offices, etc., must be included but the number so included should be only one third of the actual number, e.g., if there are 100 persons working in the actual factory and 12 working in the office, the total number for First Aid purposes would be reckoned as 100 plus 4 and not 100 plus 12. Where the number of workers in offices, etc., is not exactly divisible by 3, an odd 2 is reckoned as 3 and an odd 1 is disregarded. *Offices and Shops in Factories (First Aid) Regulations 1964 (SI 1964 No. 1321)*

A similar arrangement is made as regards offices at electrical stations covered by the Factories Act and at offices used in connexion with building operations or works of engineering construction *SI 1964: 1322 and SI 1964 No. 1323*

For all other premises subject to the Offices, Shops and Railway Premises Act the requirements quoted in this item apply.

General Requirements—Adequate First Aid boxes must be provided on a scale of one box for the first 150 employees and a further box for every additional 150 or part thereof. *OSRA: 24(1)*

Each box must be in the charge of a responsible person, who must be available at all times during working hours unless the person in charge of another box is available instead. *OSRA: 24(3)*

A notice giving the names of those required to be trained in first aid treatment must be displayed in a prominent part of the premises. (On fuel storage premises which are wholly in the open air, a notice must be given to each employee, instead of being displayed.) *OSRA: 24(5) and 24(8)*

It is an offence for any person, wilfully and without reasonable cause, to remove, misuse, or interfere with any First Aid box provided under the Act. *OSRA: 27(2)*

Trained First-Aiders—If more than 150 persons are employed to work on the premises at any one time, at least one of the persons in charge of First Aid boxes must either be a state registered or state enrolled nurse or else have received, within the past 3 years, a certificate or other evidence of qualification from the St. John Ambulance Association, the St. Andrew's Ambulance Association, the British Red Cross, the Harlow Industrial Health Service, the Inner London Education Authority, the West Midlands Industrial Health Service, and the Greater London Council (in respect of its full course for civil defence volunteers). *OSFA: 4 and Form OSR 21*

Contents of First Aid Boxes (general)—Except on premises where the special circumstances quoted later in this item apply, the minimum contents of each First Aid box must be as shown in the table below. *OSFA: Schedule, Part 1*

Contents of First Aid Boxes (special)—On premises where butchery work is done, and premises where machinery is used for cutting, slicing or sawing, the standard for 1 to 10 persons is the same as the one for 11 to 50. *OSFA: Schedule, Part 1*

In warehouses where mechanical power is used, and in fuel storage premises and railway premises, the standard for **1** to 10 persons is the same as the standard laid down elsewhere for 11 to 50 persons, and the standard for 11 to 50 persons is the same as the standard laid down elsewhere for 51 to 150

	Number of employees using facilities at any one time			
	1 to 10	11 to 50	51 to 150	Each further 150 or less
Sterilised unmedicated finger dressings	3	6	12	12
Sterilised medium-sized dressings ..	2	3	6	6
Sterilised large dressings	1	3	6	6
Adhesive wound dressings in assorted sizes	12	12	24	24
Triangular bandages	1	2	4	4
One-inch adhesive plaster	5 yds	5 yds	10 yds	10 yds
Half-ounce packets of absorbent sterilised cotton wool	1	2	3	3
Sterilised eye-pads in separate sealed packets	1	2	4	4
Safety-pins	6	6	12	12
Rubber bandage or pressure pad ..	—	1	1	1
Leaflet SHW 1 giving advice on First Aid and issued by the Ministry of Labour	1	1	1	1

The quality and prescribed details of the contents of boxes are given later in this item

persons. For 51 to 150 persons, and for each 150 thereafter, the standard quantities are double those laid down for the same number elsewhere, except for the number of adhesive wound dressings, which is 36, and the number of safety-pins, which remains at 12. *OSFA: Schedule, Part 1*

Quality and Description of Contents—All materials for dressings must be those designated in, and of a grade or quality not lower than the standard specified in, the British Pharmaceutical Codex and any supplement thereto current on June 25th, 1964, or approved for this purpose since that date. *OSFA: 3*

Triangular bandages must be of unbleached calico. The longest side must be at least 51 inches in length and the other sides must be at least 36 inches in length. *OSFA: Schedule, Part 1*

Adhesive wound dressings must consist of pads fixed to pieces of plaster (waterproof or otherwise) as centrally as possible, so as to leave an adequate margin of adhesive surface all round. The pad and the margin of adhesive surface must be protected by muslin or other suitable material for removal before use. The pad must be of absorbent lint, or other suitable material, and must either be unmedicated or must contain a medication specified for surgical dressings in the British Pharmaceutical Codex or relevant supplements thereto. Each dressing must be in an individual sealed pack, marked clearly to indicate its contents. *OSFA: Schedule, Part II*

First Aid Room—If a properly equipped First Aid room is provided on or in connexion with the premises, exemption from the requirement to provide First Aid boxes may be obtained from the local council or District Inspector of Factories with whom the premises are registered. *OSRA: 24(7)*

278 – Registration, Enforcement and Exemptions

Registration of Premises—All premises which are used as offices, shops, or railway premises (as defined in items 264 and 265) must be registered with the appropriate authority. If the premises are within the close or curtilage of a factory, or are occupied by the Crown, a local authority, or the U.K. Atomic Energy Authority, the appropriate authority is the District Inspector of Factories. If the premises are at a mine or quarry the appropriate authority is H.M. Inspector of Mines and Quarries. In all other circumstances the appropriate authority is the local borough or district council. *OSRA: 49*

Registration must be made by serving a notice on the appropriate authority on the prescribed form, copies of which may be obtained from the authority to whom it is to be returned. For railway premises, including offices on railway premises, the prescribed form is Form OSR 7; for all other premises covered by the Act it is Form OSR 1. *OSRA: 49 and SI 1964 No. 533*

It should be noted that this notification to the appropriate authority is in addition to, and not instead of, the notification sent to the local fire authority as explained in item 274.

Enforcement—The authority with whom the office, shop premises, or railway premises is registered will also be the authority responsible for enforcing most of the provisions of the Act, but the requirements regarding means of escape in case of fire will be enforced by the local fire authority except in premises occupied by the Crown, a local authority, or the U.K. Atomic Energy Authority, where they will be enforced by the District Inspector of Factories. *OSRA: 46*

Penalties for Breaches of the Act—The following are the maximum penalties laid down for breaches of the Act:—

(*a*) Forgery of documents required under the Act, the use of false documents, or the making of false statements in connexion with fire certificates or certificates of exemption: £100 or three months' imprisonment.

(*b*) Unauthorised removal, damage or defacement of a notice displayed under the Act: £10.

(*c*) Failure of an employer to notify the occupier of any premises on which one of his workmen has met with a reportable accident: £10.

(*d*) Failure to notify the appropriate authority that persons are employed in premises subject to the Act: £20.

(*e*) Obstructing an authorised inspector in the execution of his duty: £20.

(*f*) Selling or letting on hire, for use on office premises, shop premises or railway premises, a machine or appliance the use of which has been forbidden by regulations of the Minister: £200.

(*g*) Using premises without having applied for a fire certificate, or after a certificate has been refused or cancelled, or contrary to the conditions contained in the certificate: £200 for the first offence and £500 for any subsequent offence.

(*h*) Other offences: £300 if the offence was likely to cause death or serious injury and £60 otherwise, with £15 per day for continuation of the offence after conviction.

Exemptions—The Minister of Labour has power, after consulting the appropriate trade unions, employers' representatives, etc., to grant exemption from certain provisions of the Act to any type of premises in which the imposition of such provisions is considered by him to be unreasonable. The provisions in question are those relating to overcrowding, sanitary conveniences, temperature, and washing facilities, and the exemption may apply to all or part of such provisions and may be for an indefinite period or for a stated length of time. *OSRA: 45*

An individual occupier or owner who considers that it is not reasonably practicable for him to comply with the requirements relating to overcrowding, temperature or sanitary conveniences, or to provide running water for washing facilities, may apply to the factory inspector or the local council (whoever is the appropriate authority for those particular premises) for a certificate of exemption. Before doing so he must display a notice in the premises concerned, announcing his intention of applying for exemption and informing persons employed of their right to make representations to the appropriate authority if they consider the exemption would be unjustified. The application of exemption must be made on Form OSR 5 and must be accompanied by a declaration on Form OSR 4 certifying that the prescribed notice to employees has been displayed. *OSRA: 46 and SI 1964 No. 605*

If the appropriate authority refuses to grant or renew a certificate of exemption, or withdraws a certificate already given, the occupier or owner of the premises may appeal to a magistrate's court or, in Scotland, the sheriff's court. *OSRA: 46*

It is an offence, punishable by imprisonment or by a fine, to forge a certificate of exemption or to make or possess any colourable imitation of a certificate of exemption. *OSRA: 68*

279 – Other Matters affecting Offices, Shops, etc.

Safety of Premises—If a magistrates court (or, in Scotland, the sheriff) is satisfied that any premises, plant or type of work provides a risk to the safety of persons employed, the court may order that the use of such premises or plant, or the performance of that work, must be discontinued until the danger has been eliminated. Persons aggrieved by such an order may appeal to a higher court. *OSRA: 22 and 72*

Information for Employees—Under the Information for Employees Regulations 1965 (SI 1965: No. 307) every employer of persons working in offices, shops or railway premises must ensure that his employees are familiar with the requirements of the Act and the regulations made under it. This can be done either by posting up the statutory abstract of the Act (Form OSR 9 or 9B) or by giving each employee a copy of the same abstract in booklet form (Form OSR 9A).

When an employer proposes to apply for exemption from any provision of the Act he must display a notice informing his employees of his intentions. Any certificate of exemption subsequently granted must also be displayed. See item 278.

Safety Training—Effective steps must be taken to ensure that all persons employed on the premises are familiar with the means of escape and the route to be followed in case of fire. The Minister of Labour may make regulations prescribing the steps which must be taken for this purpose. *OSRA: 36*

This applies to premises requiring a fire certificate (item 274).

Where more than 150 persons are employed, the person in charge of first aid boxes must be properly trained in First Aid. See item 277.

Employees' Responsibility—It is an offence for any person

on premises covered by the Act, to do anything (wilfully and without reasonable cause) which is likely to endanger the health or safety of persons employed. It is also an offence to interfere with, misuse or remove (without reasonable cause) any equipment, appliance, or other things provided to meet the requirements of the Act or regulations made under it. *OSRA: 27*

REPORTING OF ACCIDENTS—If any accident causes the death of a person employed, or prevents him from doing his normal work for three days or more, a notification must be sent to the local council or other appropriate authority by the occupier of the premises. If the victim of an accident dies after the original notification has been sent, a further notification must be sent. The prescribed form for the purpose is Form OSR 2. *OSRA: 48(1) and 48(2)*

If the victim of an accident is not employed by the occupier of the premises on which the accident occurs, the occupier is still responsible for reporting it but the actual employer is responsible for seeing that the occupier is informed of the accident and its consequences. *OSRA: 48(3)*

STRUCTURAL ALTERATIONS—If the occupier or owner of any premises is prevented, by any covenant or condition of a lease, from making any structural alterations necessary to enable him to comply with the Act, he may ask a county court (or, in Scotland, the sheriff) to make an order modifying the terms of the covenant, lease, etc. *OSRA: 73(1)*

A person who has an interest in any premises and who has to undertake structural or other alterations in order to comply with the Act, may in appropriate circumstances ask the county court to make an order for the expense to be shared by others having an interest in the same premises. *OSRA: 73(2)*

Where a local Act requires a person to make alterations to a building or its fittings or apparatus, and such alterations cannot be made without contravening the requirements of the Offices, Shops and Railway Premises Act, the provisions of the local Act will cease to be enforceable. *OSRA: 77*

DEDUCTION FROM WAGES—It is illegal for an employer to make any deductions from wages, or otherwise levy a charge on employees, in respect of anything done or provided in compliance with the Act or the regulations made under it. *OSRA: 47*

POWERS AND DUTIES OF INSPECTORS, ETC.—These are dealt with under item 300.

HOISTS AND LIFTS—Under the Offices, Shops and Railway Premises (Hoists and Lifts) Regulations 1968 (SI 1968 No. 849), all hoists and lifts in offices, shops and railway premises must comply with regulations similar to those for hoists and lifts in factories (see item 78). These requirements cover construction and maintenance, the fitting of proper enclosures and gates, the marking of lifts with the safe-working load, the fitting of over-running devices to passenger lifts, and the making of regular examinations. Reports of examinations, which must be made every six months by a competent person, must be in the form specified by the Offices, Shops and Railway Premises (Hoists and Lifts) Reports Order 1968 (SI 1968 No. 863).

Chapter XVI

Safety Precautions Required by Common Law

The safety and welfare requirements quoted in the previous chapters are all statutory obligations, that is to say, they are detailed requirements laid on the factory occupier, employees and others by Acts of Parliament and Statutory Instruments. The present chapter deals with more general duties imposed by Common Law. As will be seen, these duties have a far wider scope than the statutory requirements imposed by the Factories Act and other legislation, and often where there is no statutory duty to take precautions there is a Common Law duty to do so.

280 – Difference between Statutory and Common Law Duty

Criminal Law and the tort of negligence on which Common Law action is taken are different. Criminal Law is concerned with acts or omissions which concern us all—it is the maintenance of the Queen's Peace. Action for negligence is a matter between the parties concerned. Criminal Law is the subject of punishment by a fine or imprisonment, whereas Common Law actions for negligence are concerned with compensation.

A successful criminal action, e.g., a case by an inspector of factories for a breach of the Factories Act, cannot be used to support an action for compensation which is in a different court. Nevertheless a breach of some statutes can be proved and used in support of an action for compensation.

To establish negligence the Factories Act has been accepted as a standard of care by which negligence can be established or denied.

Where there is a statutory duty to take a particular safety precaution, failure to do so is an offence for which the occupier can be prosecuted and fined, even if no accident has occurred. If an accident does occur, the occupier can not only be prosecuted before a magistrate but can also be sued for damages by the injured workman. He may be sued even if he has satisfied the magistrates court that the breach of the Act was committed by some other person as the "actual offender", as explained in item 299.

Where a safety precaution is not required by statute an occupier cannot be prosecuted for not taking it but he can still be sued for damages if an accident occurs and the workman can show that it was due to the employer's failure to take that precaution.

The best example of this difference between statutory duty and Common Law duty is to be found in the leading case of *Franklin v. Gramophone Company Limited, 1948*. In this case a workman inhaled dust from a grinding wheel which was not provided with exhaust ventilation. As a result of continued exposure to this hazard he died and his family claimed damages. The Court found that, owing to certain special circumstances, the grinding wheel in question was not subject either to the Grinding of Metals Regulations or to Section 47 of the 1937 Factories Act, so that failure to provide exhaust ventilation was not a breach of the occupiers statutory duty. None the less, the occupiers were required to pay damages, because they had failed in their Common Law duty to safeguard an employee against a foreseeable danger.

Another example can be found in the provision of goggles or other eye protection. For certain specified processes, mentioned in items 116 and 180, there is statutory duty to provide eye protection in the form of goggles or screens. But if a process, though not among those definitely named, involves danger to eyesight there may be a Common Law duty to provide eye protection and any failure to do so, though not rendering the occupier liable to prosecution, may render him liable for damages in the event of an accident.

A second difference betweeen statutory duty and Common Law duty is that the latter applies wherever persons are employed, and not only on factory premises or other premises subject to the various Acts. Common Law duty therefore affects such places as research laboratories, etc., which are normally outside the scope of the Factories Acts.

Finally, Common Law duty differs from statutory duty in that it is expressed in general principles and not in detailed requirements. It is thus sometimes a little difficult to say what the actual duty of the employer is in a particular set of circumstances. However, the application of the principles set out below should, in most cases, enable the occupier of a factory to decide what his liabilities are.

281 – Summary of Common Law Duty

Successful action for compensation depends on the claimant establishing: (i) that he has suffered loss; (ii) that the defendant owed him a duty of care; (iii) that there was a breach of that duty, i.e., that the defendant had been negligent; and (iv) that his loss was caused by that negligence.

The Common Law duty of every employer has been summed up in numerous legal proceedings, one of the most concise definitions being the observations of Lord Oaksey in the case of *Paris v. Stepney Borough Council, 1951:* "The duty of an employer towards his servant is to take reasonable care for the servant's safety in all the circumstances of the case."

This raises the question, "What is meant by reasonable care?" The view generally taken by the Courts is that it means the taking of such precautions as are necessary and reasonably practicable to protect the employee against dangers which the employer can reasonably be expected to foresee. If the employer knows that a danger exists and yet fails to take reasonable precautions against it he fails in his duty. If he does not know that it exists, his liability depends on whether or not he ought to have known it.

In one respect the employer's responsibility has been increased by the Employer's Liability (Defective Equipment) Act, 1969. If an employee is injured because of a defect in equipment provided by the employer, the latter will be legally guilty of negligence even though the defect may be attributable wholly or partly to the fault of a third party such as the manufacturer of the equipment.

With the great developments now taking place in manufacturing techniques and with the introduction of new materials and new chemicals, it is particularly important that the factory occupier should take all practicable steps to ascertain the hazards, if any, connected with a process or substance he is introducing into his works for the first time. In the case of *Graham v. Co-operative Wholesale Society Ltd., 1957,* it was observed by Lord Justice Devlin that an employer must take reasonable steps to keep up-to-date in his knowledge of trade processes.

The extent to which precautions must be taken depends on the magnitude of the risk and the practicability of the precautions. To take an extreme example, if there is a slight danger of an employee receiving a minor injury, and if this cannot be removed without great trouble and expense, the Court will probably hold that it is not reasonable to expect the employer to go to such trouble and expense to remove so slight a risk. At the other end of the scale, if there is a fairly heavy risk of a fatal accident the employer is bound to take every possible precaution even if this involves great trouble and expense. Between these two extremes lie a wide variety of different situations and the extent of the employer's duty in a particular case can be decided only in the light of the particular circumstances. The best advice that can be given is that the employer should make himself acquainted with the precautions taken in similar circumstances by other reputable firms. Although the Courts have sometimes held, in special cases, that the customary precautions were insufficient, the general rule is that "a defendant can clear himself if he shows that he acted in accordance with general and approved practice" (Dictum of Lord Alness in *Vancouver General Hospital v. McDaniel, 1935*). But following accepted practice does not provide a defence if there has been failure to take reasonable precautions against an obvious and known danger, see *Markland v. Manchester Corporation, 1934.*

It is, of course, useless to plead that the customary precautions were taken in cases where there has been a breach of the occupier's statutory duty under the Factories Acts or other legislation. Also, it is of little value to plead that the general practice has been followed unless that practice has been followed generally for a sufficiently long period and in similar circumstances to those in question.

One factor which must be taken into consideration is the possible consequences of an accident to the particular worker concerned. For example, the leading case of *Paris v. Stepney Borough Council 1951,* arose out of an accident in which a one-eyed man lost the sight of his remaining eye. The House of Lords decided that although the risk of injury may not have been great enough to necessitate the provision of goggles or an eye screen for ordinary workers, they should have been provided for this particular worker because the consequences of an injury, if it did occur, would be so much more serious.

The employer must similarly take into account any individual peculiarities which may make an operation more dangerous for one worker than for another. For example, a means of access which may be used safely and easily by an able-bodied man in good health may not be safe for an elderly man who is less nimble.

The employer's responsibility at Common Law applies not only when the worker is doing the actual job for which he is employed but also when he is doing anything which is ordinarily and reasonably incidental to that job. For example, when a woman worker slipped on a greasy duckboard while on the way to wash a tea-cup it was decided by the Court that the employer was liable although the woman was not actually engaged on the work for which she was employed.

The above summarises the general Common Law duty owed by all employers, including factory occupiers. These duties can be divided into specific categories as follows: (*a*) the duty to provide a safe place of work; (*b*) the duty to provide proper plant and equipment; (*c*) the duty to organise and maintain a safe system of work and (*d*) the duty to employ competent workers. In the following items these are dealt with at greater length.

282 – Provision of a Safe Place of Work

The workplace, and the means of access to it, must be maintained in a safe state. To some extent this is a statutory obligation, so far as factory occupiers are concerned, but the Common Law duty is wider in its scope; it not only includes workplaces which are not normally covered by the Factories Act but it also requires precautions to be taken against many dangers not mentioned in the Act. For example, there is nothing in the Factories Act about exposure to noise. But in the case *Berry v. Stone Manganese Marine Ltd., 1971,* it was held that the employer was negligent in that he had not sought advice on the type of ear defenders to use and the type (ear plugs) provided by him were not suitable.

Where a workplace or the means of access to it is unsafe for any reason, it is not sufficient to warn employees of the danger; it is necessary to take all reasonable steps to remove or avert that danger.

The premises must not only be safe in the first instance but must be maintained in a safe condition, so far as is practicable. This not only involves the detection and remedy of defects as soon as possible after they occur but also the maintenance of a good standard of cleanliness and tidiness so as to prevent, as far as possible, the sort of accidents that may occur if floors are allowed to become greasy and objects are left in gangways where they may be tripped over.

In certain circumstances a workplace or means of access may become temporarily unsafe, e.g., while repairs are going on or after damage by fire or explosion. The occupier must then decide whether the danger is great enough to warrant putting that part of the premises out of use for the time being. In one leading case (*Latimer v. A. E. C., Ltd., 1952*) a factory was flooded by an exceptional storm and the floor was made slippery by a mixture of oil and rainwater. The Court of Appeal decided that, although the condition of the floor caused a man to slip, the danger had not been great enough to warrant a stoppage of work. The House of Lords supported this view, though one of the Law Lords added that there might be circumstances in which a temporary danger was so great as to necessitate closing down the factory.

When employees are sent to work on premises outside the control of the factory occupier, the latter cannot be expected to exercise the same degree of care as when they are on his own premises. Nonetheless, he is expected to do what he can to safeguard his workers when they are elsewhere, especially by supplying them with equipment which will enable them to do the job safely. (These observations apply mainly when the employee is sent on to premises which are not subject to statutory requirements. A builder's employees, for instance, are normally covered by statutory obligations because the place where they work automatically becomes a building site, subject to the Construction Regulations.)

283 – Provision of Proper Plant and Equipment

It is part of the employer's duty at Common Law to ensure, as far as practicable, that all plant and machinery used by an employee is in good condition and is " suitable for its purpose." Here again, this duty partly overlaps the statutory obligations, since many items of plant (e.g., cranes) are the subject of specific requirements. As in other matters, however, the Common Law duty is wider in scope; " suitable for its purpose " goes beyond the requirements of the Factories Act as injury may occur when perfectly sound plant is used which is not suitable for the work being done. This is especially the case with makeshift plant and such practice may well support Common Law action. In addition it should be noted that Common Law duty not only covers many items of plant and equipment not mentioned in the Factories Acts, etc., but it may in some circumstances impose additional duties regarding items which are already the subject of statutory requirements. For instance, safety catches for crane hooks are not compulsory under the main Factories Act (though they are required for certain cranes used in building operations) but if an accident occurred owing to the lack of such a catch the employer's failure to provide one might be regarded as a failure of his Common Law duty, if the Court considered that the risk of such an accident was great enough to warrant the taking of this particular precaution.

It is the employer's duty to ensure that proper plant and equipment is available. If the employee is left to find an item of plant for himself, and he selects something which is defective or unsuitable, the employer may be held liable, though if the employee is a skilled worker, capable of deciding for himself whether a particular tool or piece of equipment is suitable, the employer may escape liability.

As mentioned in item 281, the employer's liability in respect of the tools and equipment he supplies to his employees has been increased as a result of new legislation. In the past it had been held by the Courts that if an employer bought or hired a piece of equipment from a reputable manufacturer or supplier he was entitled to assume that it was safe to use and had no liability at Common Law if a workman was injured by some latent defect which the employer could not reasonably have been expected to know about. This state of affairs has been ended by the Employer's Liability (Defective Equipment) Act, 1969, under which the employer is liable for *any* injury which an employee sustains through being given defective equipment, even though the defect was due to the negligence of a third party. (It may, of course, be open to the employer in his turn to sue the manufacturer or supplier of the equipment.)

284 – Provision of a Safe System of Work

The system of work includes physical layout of the job, the sequence in which operations are carried out, co-ordination of departments or individuals whose co-operation is essential to safety (e.g., a shunter and an engine driver), the method of using particular machines or other equipment, the adequate supervision and instruction of workers, the provision of any necessary safety devices, etc. The employer's duty is limited to devising a safe system and ensuring that it is normally adhered to—he is not likely to be held liable if, on an isolated and unforeseeable occasion, the system is departed from though he will certainly be held liable if the system is allowed to lapse into general disuse.

It is recognised that some operations (e.g., the climbing of a tall chimney stack by a steeplejack) are inherently dangerous and cannot be made one-hundred-per-cent safe. The employer's obligation at Common Law is limited to devising a system which makes the operation as safe as can reasonably be expected.

In deciding what is a safe system for a particular job the employer can, to a great extent, rely on following the normal practice of reputable firms though there have been occasions when the Courts have held that a system, though generally accepted, was not good enough. If an employer is genuinely satisfied that the accepted method of doing a job is as safe as can reasonably be expected he will normally be justified in adopting it, but if he feels that it could be improved upon he is bound to adopt such improvements unless the additional cost is out of all proportion to the extra safety obtained.

As mentioned in item 280, the employer must consider the fact that what may be a safe system for one worker may not be safe for another. The case of the one-eyed worker has already been quoted; other physical disabilities such as deafness, poor eyesight, lameness, cardiac weakness, and even a tendency to fits must also be allowed for if the employer is aware of them. He cannot, of course, be expected to allow for disabilities of which he is justifiably ignorant, but where the efficiency of a system depends on the physical fitness of an employee (e.g., when it depends on a look-out man having good eyesight and good hearing) a check on the fitness of the employee concerned would probably be considered an essential part of the system.

285 – Employment of Competent Workers

The employer is expected to ensure that the persons he employs are competent to carry out their duties without negligently endangering their fellow workers. From the employer's point of view the need to fulfil this obligation is greater than ever because, since the passing of the Law Reform (Personal Injuries) Act of 1948 and the consequent abolition of what was called the doctrine of common employment, an employer is liable at Common Law for accidents in which one employee is injured through the negligence of another.

In most circumstances it will be sufficient to ensure that an employee knows the correct way to do his job. In some circumstances, however, it might be held that the physical fitness of a worker was part of his skill—for instance, a one-eyed man might be considered incompetent to do certain jobs properly, owing to his restricted vision. It has also been held that the employer is liable if he knowingly employs an irresponsible worker whose known tendency to skylarking (e.g., by tripping up a fellow-worker) or known disposition to disobey the orders of the supervisor makes him a source of danger (see *Hudson v. Ridge Manufacturing Company, 1957*).

286 – Liabilities to Third Parties

What has been written in the preceding items of this chapter applies to the employer's duties to his own employees. To some extent he owes similar duties to those who come into his factory, even though they are employed by someone else. Until recently such persons were legally divided into three types —invitees, licensees and trespassers—and the occupier's duty varied according to type. So far as England, Wales and Northern Ireland* is concerned, however, the position has been modified by

* For Scotland see the Occupiers Liability (Scotland) Act, 1969.

the Occupier's Liability Act 1957, which sweeps away the distinction between invitees and licensees and imposes the same Common Law duty in regard to all visitors who come on to the premises with the occupier's express or implied permission, irrespective of whether he himself asks them to come on to the premises for a specific purpose (e.g., as a contractor to do a job) or merely permits them to enter for some purpose of their own (e.g., to bring a message to a member of the staff).

Duty to Visitors—When people come on to the factory premises to work as employees of a contractor or as vanmen delivering goods or anything of that kind, the occupier's duty towards them is very similar to his duty to his own employees. He must provide them with safe access and, if he supplies them with plant or equipment, he must take as much care to ensure that it is suitable and in good condition as he would do in issuing it to his own workers. He must also take steps to protect them against any dangers to which they are liable to be exposed while on the premises and, in this connexion, it must be remembered that a danger which is recognised and avoided by the occupier's own employees may not be recognised by an invitee unfamiliar with the premises or the processes carried on.

The duty of care to visitors defined in the 1957 Act expressly mentions that the occupier must be prepared for children to be less careful than adults. However it provides some protection for the occupier against action by visiting contractors by allowing that " the occupier may expect that a person in the exercise of his calling will appreciate and guard against any special risks ordinarily incident to it ".

One matter in which the occupier is not normally liable in the case of an invitee is that of organising a safe system of work, since the way an invitee does his job is normally outside the control of the occupier. However, where the invitee works in co-operation with the occupier's employees (e.g., when a lorry driver delivers goods and helps the factory employees to unload them) the system of work may be held to be within the occupier's control.

Apart from the Common Law duty to an invitee, the presence of the latter may have an effect on statutory duties. For instance, an overhead shaft may have been left unfenced because it is considered " safe by position ". If a painter, coming into the works as an invitee, approaches the shaft in the course of his work it thereby ceases to be safe by position and the occupier will have a statutory duty to guard it, just as if it were being approached by one of his own men.

Duty to Trespassers—A trespasser is a person who comes on to the premises without the occupier's permission. This would probably include anyone who had been invited on to the premises by persons not authorised to do so though if a responsible member of the management (e.g., the works manager) invited someone on to the premises the Courts might hold that the person was a visitor.

The occupier owes no duty to a trespasser, except that he must not knowingly and deliberately carry on any activity which puts the trespasser in danger. For example, if a man is trespassing on a railway siding and his presence is known, shunting operations must not be carried on regardless of the trespasser's danger. But there is no obligation to search for possible trespassers before starting such operations.

A visitor may become a trespasser if he goes on to a part of the premises where he has no need or permission to go. Much depends, however, on the circumstances of the case. For instance, if a contractor's employee whose work was to be done in one part of the factory went off to another just to look round, or to talk to an acquaintance, he would probably be regarded as a trespasser on that part of the premises. If, however, he had to go to another part of the factory to consult his foreman, or for some other necessary purpose connected with his work he would presumably remain a visitor.

Duty to General Public—The operations carried out by a factory occupier sometimes involve danger to the general public. A common example is when a crane or teagle is used for hoisting loads over a public highway. Other familiar examples are lines of rails which run across a public highway and scaffolds erected against the street face of a building.

In these and all other circumstances where persons using public highways or other public places may be endangered by factory operations, the occupier must take adequate steps to prevent such danger. Such steps must be positive; the mere display of a warning notice or a red flag is not likely to be regarded as a sufficient precaution.

In some districts the local byelaws impose statutory requirements for the protection of the public. For example, some Local Authorities require special precautions to be taken to prevent window cleaners falling on to persons passing below. Similarly, the erection of scaffolds near a public highway is often controlled by the Local Authority.

Duty to Neighbours—Factory occupiers, like all other citizens, have a duty at Common Law to abstain from any action which may endanger the safety or property of persons occupying neighbouring premises, or which may unreasonably interfere with the interests of those neighbours. The only difference in this respect between factory occupiers and others is that, by virtue of the type of operation liable to be carried on in a factory, there is a greater need to guard against any breach of this duty.

287 – Acceptance of Risk and Contributory Negligence

It sometimes happens that an employer fails to take necessary precautions and the employee, knowing this, still takes the risk of doing the job. In such circumstances it is sometimes argued that the employee has no claim if an accident occurs. Such an argument, however, is rarely upheld. It is true that there is a legal maxim, *Volente non fit injuria,* which means that no injury is done to a consenting party. But the application of this maxim to cases arising from factory accidents is not generally supported by the Courts, chiefly because it is doubtful whether an employed person often " consents " to incur the risk as that term is understood in law. As one judge expressed it, " A man cannot be said to be truly willing unless he is in a position to choose freely; and freedom of choice predicates . . . the absence from his mind of any feeling of constraint in order that nothing shall interfere with the freedom of his will." And one recent Lord Chief Justice has said that " the maxim *volente non fit injuria* is one which, in the case of master and servant, is to be applied with extreme caution. Indeed, I would say that it can hardly ever be applicable where the act to which the plaintiff is said to be 'volens' arises out of his ordinary duty, unless the work for which the plaintiff is engaged is one in which danger is necessarily involved." It is therefore fairly safe to say that if an employer fails to take reasonable precautions he cannot afterwards plead that the injured man carried on with his work in spite of the absence of those precautions.

The defence of *volente non fit injuria* may sometimes succeed if an accident occurs to a visitor after he has been warned of a danger. Since the visitor, unlike an employee, would be a free agent, his taking of a risk—so long as he knew the nature of the risk—could really be a voluntary act. Much would depend, however, on the circumstances of the particular case.

Where an employee adds to the danger of his job through his own negligence, this provides the employer with an argument which can be urged in mitigation of damages but which does not necessarily absolve him from blame altogether. If the employer fails to take reasonable precautions and then the employee increases the risk still further by being negligent, the employer will still be liable but the Court may reduce the amount of damages awarded, the amount of the reduction depending on how the Court divides the blame between the employer and employee.

288 – Recapitulation of Common Law Liability

Many of the statements made in this chapter have unavoidably lacked decisiveness because Common Law liability, unlike statutory duty, does not consist of detailed requirements which can be expressed in hard and fast rules. Every case has to be judged on its own merits, both by the occupier when he decides what precautions to take and by the Courts if the worst happens and an accident occurs.

Two points should be kept constantly in mind. First, the precautions which a factory occupier is required to take are not confined to those laid down in the Factories Act. Secondly, the standard of safety that the employer is expected to maintain is no more than the standard that any good management will maintain as a matter of efficiency. The employer is not expected to go to fantastic lengths to protect employees against remote dangers; what he is expected to do is to run his factory efficiently, with all operations properly organised and without haphazard and makeshift ways of doing the job.

Chapter XVII

Miscellaneous Matters affecting Conditions of Employment, etc.

In this chapter will be found certain statutory requirements affecting the employment generally and particularly the employment of women and young persons, the employment of outworkers, the supervision and training of employees, the legal duties of persons employed, hours of work, and the employment of pieceworkers. Many of these matters are also subject of agreements between employers' organisations and trades unions, or of rulings made by arbitration boards, joint consultation councils, and the like. But whether such agreements exist or not, the requirements quoted in this chapter are obligatory and must be carried out in all circumstances.

289 – Contracts of Employment

The Contracts of Employment Act 1972 repealed and re-enacted the Contracts of Employment Act 1963. The term employee covers both manual and clerical work (see section 11) and employees excluded from the Act are given in section 9.

Under Section 4 of the Contracts of Employment Act 1972 every person employed (unless he is employed for fewer than 21 hours a week) must be given written notification of the following:

(*a*) The scale or rate of remuneration, or the method of calculating remuneration;

(*b*) The intervals at which wages will be paid, e.g., weekly, monthly, etc.;

(*c*) Any terms and conditions relating to hours of work;

(*d*) Any terms and conditions relating to holidays and holiday pay, sick leave and sick pay, and pensions and pensions schemes. If there are no arrangements for holidays and sick pay the fact must be stated.

It is not necessary to give each individual person employed a separate written notice of the above particulars. It is sufficient to give each individual a notice stating where the required particulars can be obtained from a general document which is reasonably accessible to all those concerned.

HOURS AND PIECEWORK—The hours of work laid down in a notification given to women or young persons engaged in manual work must not be in excess of those permitted under the Factories Act. See item 294.

The rates of remuneration for piece workers must, of course, be notified to them in the same way as any other form of remuneration would be. For certain processes there is a similar requirement which has long existed under the Factories Act; these include certain matters of detail not contained in the Contracts of Employment Act. See item 295.

TERMINATION OF EMPLOYMENT—Sections 1 and 2 of the Contracts of Employment Act provide for the minimum periods of notice to be given to a person who has been employed for 13 weeks or more. These are as follows.

Where employment has lasted for more than 13 weeks but less than two years: One week's notice.

Where employment has lasted for between two and five years: Two weeks' notice.

Where employment has lasted between five and ten years: Four weeks' notice.

Where employment has lasted between ten and fifteen years: Six weeks' notice.

Where employment has lasted more than fifteen years: Eight weeks' notice.

An employee who has been employed for 13 weeks or over must give at least one week's notice if he wishes to terminate the employment.

The periods mentioned here are, of course, subject to any agreement between employer and employed whereby longer periods of notice are agreed to, but it is not legal to specify shorter periods in a contract. It is, however, permissible for either employer or employee to waive his rights and for an employee to accept payment in lieu of notice.

The Contracts of Employment Act does not affect the right of either employer or employee to terminate a contract without notice if the circumstances are such that termination without notice would have been justified in the conditions prevailing before the Act was passed. This could conceivably cover occasions when an employee is dismissed for gross breaches of the safety regulations or when an employee refuses to work under conditions which expose him to a serious hazard.

In calculating the length of time for which a person has been employed continuously, no account is taken of breaks in employment due to industrial disputes, unless an employee has joined in a strike which is in breach of his contract of service.

REDUNDANCY PAYMENTS ACT 1965—Under this Act an employee who fulfils certain conditions is entitled to a payment if he is made redundant (see Section 1(2)). The Act covers all kinds of work and " employee " is defined. Certain employees are not eligible, e.g., an employee with less than 104 weeks employment, an employee who normally works for less than 21 hours a week etc. Furthermore a person who works under a contract " for services " (e.g., an independent contractor) is not eligible. For a person to qualify for payment on grounds of dismissal because of redundancy, the conditions in section 1(2) of the Act must be satisfied. There is no entitlement to payment under this Act if dismissal is due to inefficiency, health, etc. See the booklet *The Redundancy Payment Scheme* obtainable free from the Department of Employment.

THE TRUCK ACTS—The TA 1831 to 1940 are complicated. The series of Acts in force extend from the original TA 1831 to include the TA 1887, 1896 and 1940. All the Acts apply to a workman as defined in the Employers' and Workmen's Act 1875, i.e., one engaged in manual labour, etc., (excluding a domestic servant); but the TA 1896, which regulates deductions and payments in respect of fines for acts or omissions, also applies to a shop assistant. The Acts are enforced in factories by the factory inspector and offences may be prosecuted in the Magistrate's Court. A workman can bring proceedings to recover wages due to him under the Acts.

The law of truck stems from the TA 1832 which was to ensure that all the wages due to a workman were paid in coin of the realm. The payment of wages in bank notes is valid; so is a payment by postal order, cheque or money order, or into a bank account if done in accordance with the Payment of Wages Act 1960. The TA 1896 regulated payments by a workman (or deductions from his wages) in respect of damaged goods and materials and fines for acts of omissions. The TA 1940 protected certain transactions before 10th July 1940, which would otherwise have been illegal (see *Pratt v. Cook, 1940*) but it made no change in the law of the TA 1831 to 1896 for present-day purposes.

290 – Employment of Women and Young Persons

Most of the statutory requirements quoted elsewhere in this book apply equally whether the employees are men or women, and regardless of age. When women or young persons are employed, however, there are certain additional requirements which have to be considered. (For the purpose of the Factories Acts, a young person is a youth or girl who has not attained the age of 18.)

FITNESS FOR EMPLOYMENT—See item 42

RESTRICTIONS ON EMPLOYMENT OF YOUNG PERSONS—Young persons must not be employed as machinery attendants (item 66), must not be allowed to clean certain machinery (item 65) and must not be allowed to operate certain machines without adequate instruction and supervision (items 63 and 276).

No young person may work in a blasting enclosure (item 133) and young persons must not be employed to paint buildings with lead paint, unless they have been regularly apprenticed (item 176).

Young persons employed on building sites or on works of engineering construction must not drive vehicles or locomotives, operate lifting appliances or capstans, or give signals to operators of lifting appliances, except when they are undergoing training under the supervision of a competent person. See items 170 and 179.

No young person may drive a locomotive or operate a capstan used for the traction of wagons. See item 135.

Young persons under 18 must not be employed in operations restricted to classified workers. See item 251.

Young persons must not be employed in any nitro or amido processes in chemical works. *CWR: 24*

Young persons must not be allowed to lift or move loads which are too heavy for them (item 114). Maximum weights are prescribed in the regulations for potteries (item 203), wool textile mills (item 240), and jute spinning (item 239).

Girls under 18 must not be employed in any part of a factory where glass (other than lamp blown glass) is melted or blown or where glass other than plate or sheet glass is annealed. The same prohibition applies to places where brine is evaporated in open pans or where salt is stoved. *FA: 73*

The employment of young persons is also prohibited or restricted in certain processes involving the use of lead compounds (item 199), chromium plating (item 131), tinning hollow-ware (item 197), pottery (item 203), manufacture and repair of accumulators (item 205), vitreous enamelling (item 134), asbestos manufacture and processing (item 228), the use of horsehair (item 236), spinning and weaving (item 239), indiarubber manufacture (item 200), the manufacture of paints and colours (item 201), shipbuilding and ship-repairing (item 244), and radioactive substances (items 204 and 249).

If any young person is employed in a factory in contravention of the provisions of the Factories Acts, the parent is liable to prosecution as well as the occupier. *FA: 158*

Even when there is no definite prohibition on the employment of young persons for a particular purpose, care must be taken to ensure that the work in question is such that the young person can do it without danger of injury to himself or others. If an accident occurs through a young person being given work unsuited to his or her age and physique, this might be held to be a breach of the employer's duty at Common Law. See items 281 and 284.

RESTRICTIONS ON EMPLOYMENT OF WOMEN—Women must not be employed as machinery attendants. They are also prohibited from cleaning certain machinery (item 65).

Women must not be allowed to lift or move loads which are too heavy for them. See item 114.

Limitations on the weights that women must be allowed to lift or carry are prescribed under the regulations for potteries (item 203), wool textiles (item 240) and jute spinning (item 239).

The employment of women is prohibited or restricted in the painting of buildings with lead paint (item 176), various other processes involving lead (item 199), the manufacture of indiarubber (item 200), accumulator manufacture and repair (item 205), the manufacture of paints and colours (item 201), and certain processes in potteries (item 203).

MISCELLANEOUS REQUIREMENTS—When women or female young persons are employed, separate sanitary accommodation must be provided for them, unless all employees are members of one family. See items 38 and 272.

When the age of a person has to be ascertained or proved for the purposes of the Factories Act, a birth certificate can be obtained for a special fee of tenpence. Forms on which applications for such certificates can be made are obtainable from the local registrar of births and deaths. *FA: 178*

HOURS OF WORK—The number of hours which may be worked by women and young persons is limited by law. See item 294.

In factories subject to the Indiarubber Regulations (item 200) no person must be employed in a room in which carbon bisulphide is used for more than 5 hours in any one day nor for more than 2½ hours at a time without a rest interval of at least one hour.

291 – Employment of Outworkers

When a factory occupier employs outworkers (i.e., people who do work for him in their own homes) he is not normally responsible for the taking of safety precautions, etc., in those homes. If, however, the work given out involves the use of any dangerous material (such as a flammable substance) or of potentially dangerous machinery (such as an electric power tool supplied by the employer) the employer should ensure that the outworker is fully aware of all necessary precautions, since failure to give adequate instruction might make the employer liable at Common Law if an accident occurred.

If the district council considers it dangerous to health for certain work to be done in an outworker's home, the council may forbid the employer to give out any more work to be done there. The types of work concerned are those listed in the last paragraph of this item. *FA: 134*

An employer must not knowingly allow wearing apparel to be made in any home where anyone is suffering from scarlet fever or smallpox. *PHA 36: 153 and FA: Fifth Schedule*

The district council may forbid homework to be done in a house where one of the notifiable infectious diseases has broken out, even if the infected person has been removed. *PHA 36: 153 and FA: Fifth Schedule*

If outworkers are employed in certain specified occupations, a list of their names and addresses must be kept and must be sent to the district council every February and August. A detailed list is given in the various Home Work Orders (SRO 1911 No. 394, SRO 1912 No. 158, SRO 1913 No. 91, SRO 1929 No. 1118, and SRO 1938 No. 561) which also prescribe the form in which the list must be kept. The occupations affected are those connected with the manufacture (and in some instances the repair, alteration or cleaning) of wearing apparel; household linen; curtains and hangings; furniture and upholstery; electro-plate; files; brass and brass articles; iron and steel cables, chains, anchors and grapnels; cart gear; locks, latches and keys; umbrellas and sunshades; artificial flowers; nets other than wire nets; tents; sacks; tennis balls; paper bags; boxes made of paper, cardboard, chip or similar material; brushes; stuffed toys, and baskets. The same order also includes fur-pulling; pea-picking; feather sorting; and the carding, boxing and packeting of buttons, hooks and eyes, and pins. Later orders have added the following additional operations: the making of chocolates or sweets; the making or filling of Christmas stockings, Christmas crackers, etc.; the weaving of textiles; and the making of lampshades.

292 – Training and Supervision of Employees

In general, the duty to train and supervise employees efficiently is implied in the Factories Act and Common Law obligations, because few of these obligations can be met unless such training and supervision is given. It is thus left to the occupier to arrange for such training and supervision as he considers necessary. In a few circumstances, however, the duty to train and supervise employees is specifically laid down and failure to comply is in itself an offence.

TRAINING—Persons employed must be instructed in the route to be followed in case of fire and must be made familiar with the means of escape. See items 26 and 274.

Persons in charge of self-acting machines must be given special instructions regarding the danger of persons coming between the fixed and traversing parts. *FA: 19(1)*

Persons working at woodworking machines (see item 126) must be given adequate training unless they are under the direct supervision of skilled workers.

When more than a prescribed number of persons are employed, the person in charge of a First Aid box must have been trained in First Aid. See items 40, 149, 185 and 277.

Where work has to be done in certain confined spaces, a sufficient number of persons must be trained to use the breathing apparatus required by law. See item 120.

In building operations and works of engineering construction, experienced workmen must, as far as possible, be employed for the erection of timbering for excavations, tunnels, etc. (item 177), for the erection of cofferdams (item 175), the demolition of buildings (item 178), and the erection of scaffolds subject to the requirements for building operations (item 161). All these operations must be supervised by a competent and experienced person; see below under Supervision.

The use of explosives in building operations and works of engineering construction must be controlled by a person with adequate knowledge of the dangers. *CGP: 10*

Vehicles and locomotives used on building sites or in connexion with works of engineering construction must be given only by trained persons, or by persons undergoing training and supervised by competent instructors. See item 179.

Young persons must be given adequate training before being allowed to operate certain types of machinery. See items 63 and 276.

Persons who are required to be within sight or hearing of a machinery attendant while he carries out the operations described in item 66 must be told what to do in an emergency. *OUM: 5(c)*

Every person employed in connexion with the conveyance of petroleum spirit by road must be familiar with the appropriate legal requirements. See item 102.

Instructions for the treatment of persons suffering from electric shock must be posted up in all factories where electricity is used at over 250 volts DC or 125 volts AC. See item 76.

Special requirements regarding the training of persons for certain processes are mentioned in the regulations for the use of radioactive substances in sealed sources (item 255), diving (item 245), the opening of bales of wool and hair (item 238), power press setters (item 67) and persons mounting abrasive wheels (item 53).

SUPERVISION—When work on any electrical equipment needs technical knowledge or experience to avoid danger, it must be supervised by a person specially authorised by the factory occupier or the contractor responsible for the work. *ER: 28*

When building operations or works of engineering construction are carried out, responsible persons must be appointed to supervise the safety precautions required by law (see item 155). In addition, experienced supervisors must oversee the erection and use of cranes (items 165 to 170), the construction of cofferdams (item 175), the erection of timbering for excavations, tunnels, etc. (item 177), and the demolition of buildings (item 178). On building sites there must also be expert supervision of the erection of scaffolding and the use of boatswains chairs in lieu of suspended scaffolds (items 161 and 163).

Experienced supervisors are specifically required under the regulations for the repair or demolition of gasholders. See item 123.

The appointment of competent persons to supervise the carrying out of safety regulations is also required under the regulations for celluloid manufacture and use (item 192), film manufacture and film stripping (item 193), potteries (item 203), the boiling of textiles in kiers (item 292), shipbuilding and ship-repairing (item 244), and the use of radioactive materials (items 204 and 252).

293 – Duties of Persons Employed

GENERAL DUTIES OF FACTORY EMPLOYEES—No employee

must wilfully interfere with or misuse any means, appliance, convenience or other thing provided under the Act for securing the health, safety or welfare of employees. *FA: 143(1)*

No employee must, wilfully and without reasonable cause, do anything liable to endanger himself or others. *FA: 143(2)*

Where the law requires any means or appliance to be provided for securing health or safety, persons employed must make use of such means and appliances. (It should be noted that this applies only to safety devices, etc., required by law; if any device is supplied voluntarily by the occupier this section does not apply. Nor does it compel the employee to use such things as cloakrooms or First Aid facilities, since these are in the part of the Act which deals with welfare, not safety or health.) *FA: 143(1)*

In general, there is no compulsion on the employee to use washing facilities, since these also are provided under the welfare provisions of the Act. Certain codes of regulations, however, require employees to wash before meals, when this is necessary for health. These regulations are quoted below.

The fact that an employee fails in his statutory duty does not in itself free the employer from liability. For instance, a man who uses an unguarded machine may technically be said to be breaking the law, as he is wilfully doing something liable to endanger himself. But this would not necessarily save the employer from being prosecuted for allowing the machine to be used without a guard. The effect of an employee's negligence on the employer's Common Law duty is dealt with in item 287.

DUTIES OF OFFICE WORKERS, ETC.—Persons working in offices, shops or railway premises must not, wilfully or without reasonable cause, do anything which might endanger the health or safety of other employed persons. They must not interfere with, misuse or remove (without reasonable cause) any equipment, appliance or other things provided to meet the requirements of the Offices, Shops and Railway Premises Act or any regulations made thereunder. *OSRA: 27*

Persons handling food in shops, or in office canteens, must comply with the requirements of the Food Hygiene Regulations. See item 136.

REPORTING OF ACCIDENTS—If any person employed is the victim of an accident for which he is entitled to injury benefit under the Industrial Injuries Act 1946 he (or someone on his behalf) must notify the employer or the employer's authorised representative. *National Insurance (Industrial Injuries) Claims and Payments Regulations 1965*

SPECIAL DUTIES IN CERTAIN PROCESSES—Persons operating woodworking machines and horizontal milling machines must keep the guards in proper adjustment and, where necessary, use the push-sticks, jigs, and other appliances provided. See items 126 and 127.

Persons operating grinding wheels must use the safety and health appliances provided and must report any defects in them to a responsible person. They must not spit upon the floor or any other part of the room or fixtures. When grinding magnesium, or handling magnesium sludge or scale, they must not smoke. See items 128 and 129.

Persons loading, unloading or conveying petrol must take precautions against fire and explosion. See item 102.

Persons handling food, in canteens or elsewhere, must comply with the Food Hygiene Regulations. See item 136.

Machinery attendants, when working near unfenced moving machinery in the particular circumstances permitted by law, must wear the overalls provided in such a way as to cover all loose ends of other clothing and must make proper use of any other safety equipment or devices provided. See items 65 to 68.

Locomotive drivers and shunters must comply with the regulations laid down. See item 135.

Persons painting buildings and liable to come into contact with lead paint must wear overalls, which must be washed at least once a week and which must not be worn at meal times. Clothing taken off during working hours must be deposited where it will not be contaminated with lead paint; as far as practicable it must be placed in the accommodation provided under the Regulations. Such persons must clean and wash their hands before taking meals and before leaving the premises and they must present themselves for medical examination if so required under an order from the Chief Inspector of Factories. See item 176.

Persons rubbing down surfaces which have been painted with lead paint must observe the precautions required by regulations. See item 176.

Persons employed at chromium plating tanks must make proper use of the appliances provided and must not interfere with them without the concurrence of the occupier or manager. See item 131.

No person may smoke where highly flammable liquids would give rise to fire (item 130).

Persons engaged in the blasting of castings, or in cleaning blasting enclosures, or in any other work connected with blasting castings, must report to a responsible person any defects they find in any blasting enclosure, apparatus, plant, protective clothing or accommodation provided. See item 133.

Persons employed in building operations or work of engineering construction and in the loading and unloading of ships or barges have various statutory duties. See items 150 and 187.

Duties are also placed on employees under the regulations for grinding cutlery (item 189), file cutting by hand (item 190), vitreous enamelling (item 134), testing of aircraft engines (item 191), film manufacture (item 193), tinning of hollow-ware (item 197), bronzing in letterpress printing (item 198), lead processes (item 199), pottery (item 203), accumulator manufacture and repair (item 205), aerated water manufacture (item 221), the casting of metals (item 224), processing of refractory materials (item 227), manufacture and processing of asbestos (item 228), handling of hides and skins (item 235), use of horsehair (item 236), handling of East India wool (item 237), wool sorting (item 238), spinning and weaving (item 239), manufacture and dyeing of wool (item 240), boiling textiles in kiers (item 242), shipbuilding and ship-repairing (item 244), celluloid manufacture (item 192), work in compressed air (item 246), diving operations (item 245), indiarubber manufacture (item 200), the manufacture of paint and colours (item 201), the manufacture of patent fuel (item 226), the painting of vehicles with lead paint (item 202), chemical works (item 247), the use of ionising radiations (items 204, 254 and 255) and the use of abrasive wheels (item 53).

MISCELLANEOUS DUTIES—It is an offence for any employee to pull down, injure or deface any notice posted in a factory in compliance with the Factories Acts. *FA: 138(4)*

It is also an offence for an employee to obstruct a factory inspector in the exercise of his powers under the Acts. See item 300.

It is an offence for an employee to alter fraudulently any automatic indicator used for ascertaining piecework payments. *FA: 135(2)*

294 – Hours of Work and Holidays

Although hours of work are mainly matters for negotiation, the law lays down certain requirements affecting the hours worked by women and young persons. It also prescribes certain statutory holidays. These requirements are binding on the employee as well as the employer, and the mere fact that an employee is willing to work more than the legal number of hours does not entitle the employer to exceed that limit.

Hours worked by men over 18 years of age are not subject to control under the Factories Acts but work in bakeries, by men as well as by women, is restricted by the Baking Industry (Hours of Work) Act 1954. Because of the danger of over-exposure to radiation, there are also limits to the amount of time any person may work on processes involving radiation (items 204 and 254), but in the latter case the limitation is in terms of radiation received and not in terms of actual hours.

The requirements quoted do not apply to office workers nor to women who hold responsible managerial positions and are not normally engaged in manual work. Nor do they apply to male young persons employed as part of the regular maintenance staff, or by a contractor, to repair any part of the factory or machinery. *FA: 95 and 106*

See Health and Safety Booklet No. 23 (H.M.S.O.).

NORMAL HOURS—If the women and young persons in a factory work a 5-day week, the total hours worked by each person, exclusive of intervals for meals and rest, must not exceed 10 hours a day or 48 a week. The period of employment including intervals must not exceed 12 hours a day. *FA: 86 and 100*

For other factories, the total hours exclusive of intervals must not exceed 9 hours a day or 48 a week, and the period of employment including intervals must not exceed 11 hours a day. *FA: 86*

The period of employment must not begin earlier than 7.0 a.m. It must not end later than 8.0 p.m. for young persons over 16 and for women. On Saturdays the period of employment must end not later than 1.0 p.m. *FA: 86*

The times at which the periods of employment begin and end must be the same for all women and young persons in the factory.

No woman or young person must be employed continuously for a spell of more than 4½ hours without at least half an hour's interval for a meal or rest. The spell may be increased to 5 hours if an interval of not less than 10 minutes is allowed in the course of the spell. Male young persons over 16 may work a 5-hour spell in the morning if this is necessary to enable men working with them to carry on their work *FA: 86 and 105*

As a general rule, the times of meals and rest intervals must be the same for all women and young persons employed. An exception is made when such persons are employed in a process which has got to be carried on continuously, or when different sets of persons are employed on different processes, or when it is necessary to divide employees into sets for the purpose of taking meals in a works canteen. *FA: 86 and 102*

No woman or young person must be allowed to do any work during a period set apart for them for meals or rest. *FA: 86*

A notice (Form 11) showing the periods of employment for each day of the week, and the times of meal and rest intervals, must be displayed in the factory. Once such a notice has been posted, the times must not be changed without notice of this intention being given to the factory inspector and also displayed in the factory. Such changes must not be made oftener than once in three months without the written permission of the factory inspector. *FA: 88*

There is nothing to prevent different times from being fixed for different days of the week, so long as the various requirements respecting maximum hours, intervals, etc., are complied with and the times are duly stated on the notice displayed. *FA: 88*

Different sets of times may be fixed for different parts of the factory if the factory inspector gives his consent. This concession is subject to the conditions laid down in the Factories (Separation for Certain Purposes) Regulations, 1939 (SRO 1939: No. 1888).

OVERTIME—The hours specified above may be increased by way of overtime, subject to the following conditions.

For young persons over 16, and for women, the total amount of overtime worked must not exceed 6 hours in any week or 100 hours in any year. Overtime must not be worked on more than 25 weeks in any year. *FA: 89(1)*

The total hours worked on any one day, excluding intervals, must not exceed 10½ hours for factories working a 5-day week or 10 hours for other factories. The total period of work including intervals must not exceed 12 hours a day. *FA: 89(2)*

In calculating the hours of overtime worked, any fraction of an hour less than half an hour is reckoned as half an hour, and any fraction over half an hour is reckoned as an hour. *FA: 89(10)*

In factories where a 5-day week is normally worked, work on a sixth day must be reckoned as overtime and must not exceed 4½ hours. *FA: 100(2)*

The period of employment must not begin earlier than 7.0 a.m. and must not last later than 8.0 p.m. for young persons and 9.0 p.m. for women. On Saturdays it must not last beyond 1.0 p.m. *FA: 89(2)*

In arranging hours of overtime in any factory, different departments or groups of persons may be given different sets of hours, as if they were working in separate factories. When this is done, the occupier must comply with the requirements of the Factory Overtime (Separation of Different Parts or Sets) Regulations 1938 (SRO 1938: No. 640) which, among other things, makes it necessary to obtain a certificate from the district inspector of factories, describing the parts of the factory or the groups of employed persons into which the division is being made. *FA: 89(8)*

Notification that a woman or young person is to be employed overtime on any day must be sent to the district inspector of factories and particulars must be entered in a register. A notice giving particulars of overtime must be posted up in the factory. The official forms for this purpose are Factory Forms F 21 and F 22 and the particulars to be given are prescribed by the Women and Young Persons (Register and Particulars of Overtime) Order 1965 (*SI 1965: No. 242*)

The Minister of Labour has power to amend the hours of overtime in respect of particular industries or processes. Exceptions made by virtue of these powers are mentioned below, under the heading Special Hours for Certain Industries.

SHIFT WORK—The Minister of Labour has power to permit the employment of women and young persons, in shifts, between the hours of 6.0 a.m. and 10 p.m. on weekdays and 6.0 a.m. and 2.0 p.m. on Saturdays. Before an application to work such a shift system can be granted, the employees concerned must be given the opportunity of voting by secret ballot to show whether or not they are in favour of shift work. The procedure for organising these ballots is laid down in the Shift System (Consultation of Workpeople) Order 1936 (SRO 1936: No. 1367). The conditions to be satisfied when a shift system is worked are laid down in Sections 97 and 98 of the Factories Act.

Shift work by male young persons is permitted in certain special processes and industries. See below under Special Hours for Certain Industries.

EMPLOYMENT OUTSIDE THE FACTORY—Women and young persons must not be employed outside the factory during meal or rest intervals, nor at any other time outside the period of employment fixed by notice. (This does not prevent a woman, or a young person over 16, from being employed in a shop outside the notified period of employment, but any time so spent must be considered as employment within the factory for the purposes of maximum hours worked, overtime, etc.) *FA: 91(1)*

Young persons engaged in carrying goods or messages, working wholly or mainly outside the factory, must not work more than 48 hours a week. In addition they must not work for a spell of more than 5 hours without half an hour's rest. If their working period includes the time between 11.30 a.m. and 2.30 p.m. they must have at least ¾-hour's interval between those times. They must have a free afternoon (beginning not later than 1.0 p.m.) on one weekday in every week and at least 11 hours' rest between noon of one day and noon of the next, this 11-hour period including the time between 10 p.m. and 6 a.m. The amount of overtime each such young person works is limited to 6 hours in any one week and 50 hours a year in all. The weeks in which *any* such young persons work overtime must not exceed 12 in a year. *FA: 116 and the Factories Act (Adaptations under Section 98) Order 1938 (SRO 1938: No. 533)*

The requirements quoted in the previous paragraph also apply to young persons employed in connexion with certain work at docks, wharves, quays and warehouses. *FA: 116*

SUNDAY EMPLOYMENT—No woman or young person must be employed in a factory on Sundays, nor must women and young persons employed in a factory during the week be employed on Sunday in any other business carried on by the factory occupier. *FA: 93*

Where both employer and employees are members of a religious body which observes the Jewish Sabbath, the women and young persons may work on Sundays so long as they do not work on Saturdays and so long as the factory is not open for business on a Saturday. *FA: 109*

Certain male young persons employed on maintenance work are allowed to work on Sundays and women may be allowed to work in certain food processess on Sundays during the Christmas and New Year period. See below under Special Hours for Certain Industries.

ANNUAL HOLIDAYS—In England and Wales, women and young persons must be given whole-day holidays on Christmas Day, Good Friday and every bank holiday, unless the occupier gives three weeks' notice that he intends to substitute some other specified weekday for one of the statutory holidays. In Scotland, women and young persons must be given whole-day holidays on six weekdays a year, these days being notified at least three weeks in advance. In Scottish burghs two of the six weekdays are to be fixed by the town council. *FA: 94*

At least half of the whole-day holidays given under the Act must be given between March 15th and October 1st. *FA: 94*

In some types of industry, specified by regulations, it is permissible for different employees to have their statutory whole-day holidays on different days from other employees. The types of factory to which the regulations apply are mainly those handling perishable foodstuffs and those doing work which is inherently urgent, such as laundries and drycleaners, printing of newspapers, maintenance of vehicles, etc. *Factories Act Holidays (Different Days for Different Sets) Regulations 1947 (SRO 1947: No. 184)*

On whole-day holidays given under the Act, no woman or young person normally employed in the factory must be employed in any other business carried on by the occupier. *FA: 94*

SPECIAL HOURS FOR CERTAIN INDUSTRIES—In certain processes male young persons over 16 may be employed in shift work outside the hours normally permitted, so long as the conditions laid down in Section 99 of the 1961 Act are complied with. (But note that Subsection 99(4) which required the medical examination of these young persons was repealed by the Employment Medical Services Act 1972—item 42). These processes are the smelting of iron ore; the galvanising of sheet metal or wire (except pickling processes); the manufacture of paper and glass; the manufacture of wrought iron, or of steel, or of tinplate; and all processes in which reverberatory or regenerative furnaces are used in connexion with the smelting of ores, metal rolling, forges, or the manufacture of metal tubes or rods, when such furnaces are necessarily kept in operation day and night to avoid waste of fuel and material. *FA: 99 and Night Work of Male Young Persons Regulations 1938 (SRO 1938: 608).*

Male young persons employed as members of the regular maintenance staff of a factory, or by a contractor, in repairing any part of the factory or any machinery and plant are not subject to the legal limitations affecting hours of employment, overtime, Sunday employment and annual holidays. This concession, however, applies only to male young persons who are regular members of the maintenance staff; it does not apply to a young person who is normally employed on other work and is occasionally employed on maintenance work as well. *FA: 106*

Women employed in the manufacture of sausages and certain types of cooked or prepared meats, or in the manufacture of bread, confectionery and fruit pies, may be allowed to work on certain Saturday afternoons and Sundays during the Christmas and New Year period. It is usual for the Minister of Labour to make a special order each year, specifying the actual dates on which such work is permitted.

Many other industries and processes have been made the subject of special requirements regarding hours of normal employment, overtime, annual holidays, etc. A list of these industries and processes is given in column 1 together with the number of the Statutory Order or section of the Factories Act under which details may be found:—

If an employer proposes to avail himself of any permitted exceptions to the requirements regarding hours of work he must give 7 days' notice to the district inspector of factories and must also display a notice of his intentions in the factory. *FA: 115*

INDUSTRIES AND PROCESSES SUBJECT TO SPECIAL REQUIREMENTS IN CONNEXION WITH HOURS OF WORK, OVERTIME, ETC.
All factories in which food or drink is manufactured (including those also covered by other and more specific orders mentioned below). SRO 1940: 109. The preparation for sale of food or drink which is wholly or partly perishable or is for early consumption (including the washing or filling of bottles or other containers for such food and drink). SRO 1947: 184. The manufacture of biscuits. FA 111. SRO 1938: 607. SRO 1938: 729. SRO 1939: 510. *SRO 1938: 1528. The manufacture of bread and other flour confectionery, including meat pies and fruit pies. FA 111. SRO 1938: 607. SRO 1938: 729. SRO 1939: 510. *SRO 1939: 509. SI 1940: 109. The manufacture of sausages. FA 111. SRO 1938: 729. SRO 1939: 510. *SRO 1939: 509. The preparation of poultry for sale. *SI 1958: 1819. The manufacture of sugar confectionery and chocolates. *SRO 1938: 1245. The manufacture of ice-cream. *SRO 1939: 857. The canning or preserving of fruit and vegetables between June and September. FA 112. SRO 1939: 621. The canning, preserving, and preparation for sale of fish. FA 112. All factories in which milk powder, condensed milk, cream, butter, or cheese is made, or in which fresh milk is treated before sale. FA 113. SRO 1947: 184. SI 1949: 35. The bottling of beer, wine or spirits. *SRO 1940: 729. The manufacture of aerated water. *SRO 1938: 727.
Spinning or doubling of cotton yarn or the weaving of cotton cloth. SRO 1947: 2600. The manufacture of rayon by viscose or acetate processes. SRO 1947: 184. The manufacture, repair or renovation of wearing apparel in factories other than textile factories. SRO 1940: 109. The dyeing and cleaning of wearing apparel or made-up household articles of textile character. SRO 1947: 184. *SRO 1939: 642. Making or mending of nets. *SRO 1939: 1490. SRO 1947: 184.
Smelting of iron ore in the manufacture of wrought iron, steel or tin-plate. SI 1959: 756. Factories manufacturing a variety of light metal articles, or fittings or accessories composed wholly or largely of metal. *SRO 1938: 1228. The manufacture of glass bottles and jars. SRO 1955: 274. *SRO 1938: 1612. Factories in which the business of a florist is carried on. SRO 1940: 109. SRO 1947: 184. *SRO 1938: 1163.
The printing of newspapers, periodicals, timetables, Parliamentary papers, race cards and score cards. SRO 1947: 184. (The printing of newspapers, but not the other types of printing mentioned, is also covered by SRO 1940: 109.) The printing and development of photographs. SRO 1940: 109. SRO 1947: 184. The repair, cleaning or washing of road vehicles and cycles. SRO 1938: 607. SRO 1940: 109. (If the premises are open for at least six days a week, for the repair and cleaning of such vehicles for members of the public, they are also covered by SRO 1947: 184.) The repair of vehicles and locomotives ancillary to a transport undertaking or other commercial undertaking. SRO 1947: 184. Certain work in connexion with engine cleaning, locomotive stoking, or signal box operation on premises of the British Transport Board SI 1962: 183.
Laundries: FA 37: 92. SRO 1938: 729. SRO 1940: 109. SRO 1947: 184. *SRO 1938: 728.
Factories where the business is carried on in connexion with a retail shop on or adjoining the factory premises. SRO 1940: 109. SRO 1947: 184. (If the work includes the making of wearing apparel, the developing or printing of photographs, or the business of a florist, the premises are also covered by SRO 1938: 607.)
Film Studios and other places where films are produced or where scenery and costumes are made or adapted for film or theatrical productions. SRO 1947: 184.

* These regulations only affect overtime

295 – Pieceworkers

The rates of payment made to pieceworkers, like all other wages, are matters for negotiation and are outside the scope of the Factories Acts.

In certain industries there has long been an obligation on the employer to notify pieceworkers in writing, or by a notice displayed in the workroom, of the rates applicable to the work they are doing. Under the Contracts of Employment Act (see

INDUSTRIES AND PROCESSES IN WHICH PIECEWORK IS SUBJECT TO SPECIAL REGULATIONS
Bleaching and dyeing of cotton cloth. SRO 1909: 1370. All piecework in textile factories. FA 135. Making, altering, ornamenting, finishing or repairing wearing apparel. SRO: 1909: 1027. Making up, finishing or repairing household linen. SRO 911: 1046. Making curtains, furniture hangings or lace. SRO 1911: 1046. Printing of cotton cloth. SRO 1909: 1370. Fustian cutting. SRO 1907: 409. Making felt hats. SRO 1903: 334. Making or repairing sacks. SRO 1907: 409. Net making. SRO 1907: 410. Tent making. SRO 1907: 409. Making rope or twine. SRO 1907: 409.
Mixing, casting or manufacture of brass or of brass articles, and the electro-depositing of brass. SRO 1907: 792. Moulders' work in iron and steel foundries. SRO 1913: 1388. Making chains, anchors, grapnels and cart gear. SRO 1902: 561. File making. SRO 1911: 1292. Making iron safes. SRO 1911: 413. Making locks, keys and latches. SRO 1902: 560. Brush making. SRO 1907: 409. Pen making. SRO 1900: 52.
Tobacco manufacture. SRO 1909: 1337. Making chocolates or sweets. SRO 1912: 234. Warehouse processes in the manufacture of articles of food, drugs, perfumes, blacking and other shoe dressings, starch, blue, soda, and soap. SRO 1907: 409.
Making or decorating pottery. SRO 1922: 317. Making or repairing umbrellas, sunshades and parasols, or parts thereof. SRO 1907: 409. Making toy balloons, pouches and footballs from indiarubber. SRO: 1911: 1293. Covering tennis balls or racquets balls. SRO 1907: 409. Making lampshades. SRO 1929: 1119. Making artificial flowers. SRO 1907: 409. Relief stamping. SRO 1907: 409. Making paper bags. SRO 1907: 409. Making boxes or receptacles composed wholly or partly of paper, cardboard, chip or similar material. SRO 1907: 409.
All piecework in laundries. SRO 1911: 1294 All piecework in shipbuilding and ship repairing. SRO 1912: 1297. Cartridge making. SRO 1909: 1337. Pea Picking. SRO 1907: 410.

item 289) all employed persons must now be notified in writing of the scale of remuneration, so that earlier requirements have to some extent become redundant. The appropriate Factories Act requirements, however, contain matters of detail not contained in the Contracts of Employment Act and for this reason it is desirable that they should be referred to by those concerned. A list of processes affected is given in column 2 opposite, together with the numbers of the relevant Statutory Orders of sections of the Factories Act.

If an employer who pays piecework rates for any of the above processes fraudulently uses a false indicator for ascertaining the particulars or amount of any work he will be liable to prosecution under Section 135(2) of the Factories Act 1961. Under the same section an employed person can be prosecuted if he fraudulently alters an automatic indicator used for the same purpose.

Where the piecework rates paid for any of the above processes constitute a trade secret, it is an offence for an employed person to disclose them or for any other person to solicit or procure such disclosure. *FA: 135(4)*

Under the Checkweighing in Various Industries Act 1919 and the orders made thereunder, pieceworkers in certain industries have the right to appoint a checkweigher or to take other specified steps to ensure the accurate calculation of wages. The industries concerned are the manufacture of iron and steel, the loading or unloading of vessels, the manufacture of cement and lime, and the quarrying of chalk and limestone.

Chapter XVIII

Administrative Duties, Legal Proceedings, etc.

Factory occupiers have a number of statutory administrative duties such as the sending of various notices to the factory inspector, the keeping of certain records, etc. These are dealt with in the present chapter, as well as certain miscellaneous matters not dealt with elsewhere in the book.

296 – Notices to be given to Factory Inspector, etc.

Except where otherwise stated, all the notifications mentioned in this item must be sent to the district inspector of factories.

NOTICE OF OCCUPATION OF FACTORY—A month before any premises are used as a factory a notification on Factory Form No. 9 must be sent to the district factory inspector. This notice must state the name of the occupier or the title of the firm, the postal address, the nature of the work to be carried on, the nature of any mechanical power to be used, and the name of the district council in whose district the factory is situated. *FA: 137(1)*

If the premises were already being used as a factory when the occupier took them over, and if the new occupier proposes to use them for the same purpose without interruption and without changing the nature of the work, he need not give notice one month in advance of taking over but must give it as soon as practicable and, in any event, not later than one month after taking over. *FA: 137(3)*

The factory inspector may, at his discretion, give permission for premises to be used as a factory, or for mechanical power to be introduced, without waiting for a full month to elapse after the giving of the notice. *FA: 137(3)*

If, when the original notice was given, it was not intended to use mechanical power, one month's notice must be given of any subsequent intention to use it. *FA: 137(2)*

With the exception of certain small factories, no factory must be used until a certificate respecting fire exits has been applied for. See item 26.

NOTICE OF CONSTRUCTION WORK—For notice of a building operation or works of engineering construction see item 154.

NOTICE OF OCCUPATION OF OFFICES, SHOPS, ETC—If premises within the close, curtilage or precincts of a factory are to be used as offices or shops a notice on Form OSR 1 must be sent to the district inspector of factories. The same applies to the use of premises within the close, curtilage or precinct of an electrical station, dock, wharf or quay subject to the Factories Act and to a building which is to be used as an office in connexion with a building site or works of engineering construction. *OSRA: 49 and 52(4)*

If premises occupied by a railways undertaking and situated in the vicinity of the permanent way are to be used as offices, notice must be given to the district inspector of factories. *OSRA: 49 and 52(4)*

If any premises other than those just described are to be used as offices or shops, the notification on Form OSR 1 must be sent to the district council unless the premises are to be used by a county council, district council, fire authority, police authority, education authority, government department, or the United Kingdom Atomic Energy Authority, in which circumstances the notification is to be sent to the district inspector of factories. *OSRA: 49 and 52(4)*

NOTIFICATION OF SPECIAL EMPLOYMENT, PROCESSES, ETC.—When employing a young person under 18 notice should be sent to the local careers office within 7 days (item 42).

The intention to employ any woman or young person overtime must be notified to the district inspector of factories, See item 294.

If persons are employed in painting buildings with lead paint, their employer must send notice to the inspector unless the persons concerned are only occasionally employed for this purpose. *FA: 129(4) and item 176*

If persons are to be employed in connexion with premises where solid fuel is stored for sale, notice under the Offices, Shops and Railway Premises Act must be given to the district council unless the premises are operated by a railway undertaking in which circumstances the notice must be sent to the district inspector of factories. *OSRA: 49 and 52(4)*

If persons are to be employed in a building which is occupied by, and used for the purposes of, a railway undertaking, and which is situated in the vicinity of the permanent way, notice under the Offices, Shops and Railway Premises Act must be sent to the district inspector of factories. (In the case of a locomotive running shed notice will need to be sent under the Factories Act because, as explained in item 4, such sheds are classed as factories.) *OSRA: 49 and 52(4)*

Notice must be given to the local fire authority before any explosive or highly flammable material is stored or used, or when there is to be any appreciable increase in the amount stored or used. *FA: 41(3)*

Twenty-eight days' notice of the use of crocidolite must be given to the district inspector of factories (item 228).

Film stripping and drying must not be carried out until notice has been given and the plans of the premises approved. *CFS: 12*

Notice must be given before artificial humidity is produced in any factory in connexion with a textile process. Notice must also be given if it is desired to take advantage of certain exemptions respecting the daily reading and recording of hygrometers. *FA: 68(1) and (8)*

The district inspector of factories must be informed of the loss of radioactive substances (items 204 and 255).

The district inspector of factories must be notified before ionising radiations in sealed and unsealed sources are used or stored (see items 204 and 250). Radioactive substances subject to the Radioactive Substances Act (see item 259) must not be kept until an application for registration of the premises has been granted by the Ministry of Housing and Local Government, unless covered by one of the exemptions to that Act (see item 261).

Notice must be given to the Minister of Housing and Local Government before any premises are first used for processes subject to the Alkali, etc., Works Regulation Act. See item 247.

PERIODICAL RETURNS—An annual return must be made of the number of persons employed, together with particulars of age, sex, and occupation, etc., as directed by the Minister.

If, after the fire authority has issued a certificate respecting means of fire escape, etc., it is proposed to increase materially the number of employees, or to make any substantial structural alterations or extensions, the fire authority must be informed. *FA: 41(3)*

A list of outworkers in certain specified occupations must be sent to the district council every February and August. See item 291.

REPORTING OF ACCIDENTS CAUSING DEATH OR INJURY—Any factory accidents in which persons are killed, or incapacitated from their normal work for more than three days, must be reported to the district inspector of factories. Where an accident is reported as causing injury only, and the injured person subsequently dies his death must also be reported. The normal form on which such reports must be made is Factory Form F 43, a revised version of which was prescribed by the Factories (Notice of Accidents, etc.) Order 1965 (SI 1965: No. 867), which came into operation in April 1965. For accidents occurring during building operations or works of engineering construction the form is Factory Form F 43B. *FA: 80(1) and (2)*

Accidents which need not be reported are those for which notices are sent in accordance with the Explosives Act 1875 or the Petroleum (Consolidation) Act 1928.

If a person injured in a factory accident is not an employee of the occupier it is the duty of the person's employer to report the accident immediately to the factory occupier, who must then report it to the inspector. *FA: 80(3)*

Accidents occurring in offices, shops or railway premises are reportable if they cause death or absence for more than three days The report must be sent to whoever received the original notice of occupations—i.e., to the district council or to the district inspector of factories according to the circumstances described earlier in this item under "Notice of Occupation of offices". *OSRA: 48*

Accidents must be reported forthwith, that is to say, as soon as it is known that they have resulted in any of the consequences mentioned above. *FA: 80(1) and OSRA: 48*

REPORTING OF ACCIDENTS WHICH DO NOT CAUSE INJURY—The following dangerous occurrences must be reported even if they do not cause death or injury:—

(1) Any boiler explosion. (For the purpose of this requirement a boiler is defined as any closed vessel for generating steam or for heating water or for heating other liquids or into which steam is admitted for heating, steaming, boiling or other similar purposes);

(2) Any fire or explosion on premises registered under the Explosives Acts 1875 and 1923, or licensed under the Petroleum Acts, and any fires or explosions involving compressed gases in cylinders;

(3) The bursting of any revolving vessel, wheel, grindstone, or grinding wheel moved by mechanical power;

(4) The collapse or failure of any crane, derrick, winch, hoist, or other appliance used in raising or lowering persons or goods, or the failure of any part of such appliance (other than the breaking of a chain or rope sling);

(5) The overturning of any crane;

(6) Any electrical short-circuit, or any failure of electric machinery or plant, which is attended by explosion or fire which causes structural damage to the plant and involves its stoppage or disuse for five hours or more;

(7) Any explosion or fire affecting a room in which persons are employed, if it causes complete suspension of ordinary work there for 24 hours or more;

(8) The explosion of any receiver or container used for the storage, under pressure, of air or other gases or any liquid or solid resulting from the compression of gas;

(9) Explosions or fires resulting from the ignition of dust, gas, vapour, celluloid, or substances containing celluloid, if such fire or explosion damages places in which persons are employed and causes complete suspension of work or stoppage of plant for five hours or more.

The reports of boiler explosions must be made to the Ministry of Transport under Section 5 of the Boiler Explosions Act 1882. The reports of fires and explosions in premises registered under the Explosives Acts or Petroleum Acts must be made to H.M. Chief Inspector of Explosives, Home Office. Reports of all the other dangerous occurrences mentioned must be made to the district inspector of factories under Section 81 of the Factories Act 1961 and the Dangerous Occurrences Regulations 1947 (SRO 1947: No. 31). The prescribed form (F 43) is the same as the one used to report accidents causing injury.

REPORTS OF OCCURRENCES ON NUCLEAR SITES—Certain dangerous occurrences on sites licensed under the Nuclear Installations Act 1965 must be reported to the Minister of Power (in Scotland the Secretary of State.) The dangerous occurrences concerned are set out in the Nuclear Installations (Dangerous Occurrences) Regulations.

REPORTING OF INDUSTRIAL DISEASES—The employment medical adviser and the factory inspector must be notified if an employee is suffering from any of the following: anthrax; aniline poisoning; arsenical poisoning; beryllium poisoning; cadmium poisoning; chronic benzine poisoning; carbon bisulphide poisoning; compressed air illness; chrome ulceration; epitheliomatous ulceration due to tar, pitch, bitumen, mineral oil, or paraffin or compounds or products thereof; lead poisoning; manganese poisoning; mercurial poisoning; phosphorous poisoning; toxic anaemia; toxic jaundice; and poisoning by any organic compound of lead, phosphorous, arsenic or mercury. In most cases the obligation to report a prescribed disease includes the acute, sub-acute, and chronic forms of the disease and extends to diseases caused by compounds, alloys or derivatives of the substances mentioned. *FA: 82 as amplified by SRO 1915 No. 1170; SRO 1919 No. 1775; SRO 1924 No. 1505; SRO 1936 No. 686; SRO 1938 No. 1386; SRO 1942 No. 196 and SI 1966 No. 1400*

Doctors called in to patients suffering from these diseases

must give notice to the Chief Inspector of Factories, unless notice has already been given. *FA: 82*

If any person handling food is found to be suffering from one of the diseases mentioned in the Food Hygiene Regulations (see item 136) the Medical Officer of Health must be notified.

NOTICE OF EXCEPTIONAL HOURS OF WORK—If a factory occupier avails himself any special exceptions in the matter of hours of work, statutory holidays, etc. (see item 294) he must give at least seven days' notice of his intention to do so. *FA: 115*

When notice has been given of the hours of employment, intervals, etc., fixed by virtue of these exceptions, a further notice must be given before such hours, etc., are changed. *FA: 115*

297 – Keeping of Registers and other Records

GENERAL REGISTER — Every factory must keep a register, known as the General Register. This must record particulars of young persons employed; the periodical whitewashing, painting, etc., of the factory; particulars of all reportable accidents, dangerous occurrences, and cases of poisoning and industrial disease; details of tests and examinations of fire alarms; particulars of qualified first-aiders; particulars of any exceptions under the Factories Act of which the occupier is availing himself; particulars of the fire authority issuing the fire certificate; and particulars of all certified machinery attendants (except when these are attached to the General Register instead of being actually entered in it). *FA: 140(1)*

The General Register for a factory must be kept in the official book (form F 31), published by H.M. Stationery Office; certain sections can also be obtained separately as form F 32 (particulars of young persons), form F 33 (accidents and dangerous occurrences), and form F 34 (particulars of limewashing, painting, etc.).

For building operations and works of engineering construction the appropriate form is F 36; for docks, wharves and quays it is F 35.

The register must be kept available for inspection either at the factory or at such other place as the factory inspector may approve (where it relates to building operations or works of engineering construction it may be kept at the office of the contractor carrying out such operations or works). It must be available for inspection by any factory inspector and the appointed factory doctor, and must continue to be available for two years after the date of the last entry. *FA: 141 and 127*

CERTIFICATES, ETC., KEPT WITH GENERAL REGISTER—The following documents must be attached to the General Register, when they are not actually entered in it:—

(1) The fire authority's certificate relating to means of escape in case of fire. *FA: 140(2)*

(2) Reports of statutory examinations of other plant, kept on Factory Form 54 (hoists and lifts), Factory Forms 55, 55a, 56, and 57 (boilers, economisers and superheaters), and Factory Forms 58, 59, 60, and 62 (steam and air receivers, and steam heated ovens and hotplates).

(3) Reports of the examination of water-sealed gasholders, containing the particulars prescribed by the Gasholders (Record of Examinations) Order 1938, SRO 1938: No. 598. A record showing the age of the oldest lift of every gasholder, so far as it can be ascertained must also be kept available, though not necessarily attached to the General Register. *FA: 39*

(4) A record of inspection and examination of exhaust ventilation equipment for asbestos (item 228).

ACCIDENT BOOK—In all premises subject to the Factories Acts (and in other premises also, if more than ten persons are normally employed) a book must be kept in which an injured employee, or someone acting on his behalf, can enter particulars of any accident liable to the subject of a claim under the Industrial Injuries Act. The particulars to be entered are the name, address and occupation of the injured workman, the date, time and place of the accident, the cause and nature of the injury, and the name, address and occupation of the person giving notice of the accident, if the injured employee did not do so himself.

Under the National Insurance (Industrial Injuries) (Claims and Payments) Regulations, 1964, the employer must take reasonable steps to investigate the circumstances of every accident, and if the circumstances appear to differ from those recorded in the accident book a note to that effect must be appended to the entry.

The prescribed form for keeping this record of accidents is B.I. 510, but where an employer still has a copy of the old Workmen's Compensation Act book (Form 85) he may continue to use this.

This recording of accidents for the purpose of the Industrial Injuries Act is separate and distinct from the recording and notification of accidents under the Factories Act.

OTHER RECORDS—A record must be kept, though not necessarily attached to the General Register, of the periodical cleaning of rooms where the grinding of metals is done (item 129); the examination of ventilating plant in grinding rooms (item 129) and blasting enclosures (item 133); the monthly examinations of breathing apparatus provided for work in confined spaces (item 120), the appointment of persons to mount abrasive wheels (item 53) and record of radioactive sources (items 204 and 250).

A record must be kept of any painting of buildings with lead paint done by persons whose ordinary employment does not include such painting and whose names have not therefore, been notified to the factory inspector as mentioned in item 296. *LPR: 8*

Health registers, containing the names of persons liable to medical examination at prescribed intervals, are required to be kept under the regulations for vitreous enamelling (item 134), tinning of hollow-ware (item 197), lead compounds (item 199), indiarubber manufacture (item 200), manufacture of paints and colours (item 201), potteries (item 203), manufacture and repair of accumulators (item 205), spinning and weaving (item 239), diving operations (item 245), work in compressed air (item 246), chemical works (item 247), the use of ionising radiations in sealed sources (item 258) and unsealed sources (item 204).

A register of overtime worked by women and young persons must be kept under Section 90 of the Factories Act and the Women and Young Persons (Register and Particulars of Overtime) Order 1965 (SI 1965: No. 242)

The regulations for various special industries and processes may require certain additional records to be kept. These are mentioned under the heading of the industry or process concerned.

FALSE ENTRIES—Any person who wilfully makes a false entry in any register, certificate, or other document required under the Factories Acts is liable to imprisonment or a fine. *FA: 159*

PRESERVATION OF REGISTERS—Health registers kept under the ionising regulations (see item 258), together with radiation dose records, transfer records, and copy transfer records kept under the same regulations, must be retained for thirty years from the date of the last entry, either at the factory or in some other place approved by the factory inspector. *IRR: 5*

Registers of leakage tests of sealed radiation sources must be kept for three years from the date of the last entry. *IRR: 5*

All other records kept under the Factories Act or regulations made under it must be retained for two years from the date of the last entry. *FA: 141 and IRR: 5*

298 - Display of Statutory Notices

GENERAL REQUIREMENTS—The prescribed abstract of the Factories Act must be displayed in every factory. Copies of this abstract are obtainable from H.M. Stationery Office. The normal abstract is Factory Form 1 (a revised version of which was introduced in August 1967) but for docks, wharves and quays there is a special version (Form 2) and there is another special version for building operations and works of engineering construction (Factory Form 3). With this abstract must be displayed the addresses of the superintending and district inspector of factories; the name and address of the appointed factory doctor; and a notice specifying the clock (if any) by which statutory periods of employment and meal intervals are regulated. *FA: 138 and Abstract of Factories Act Order 1967 (SI 1967: No. 1182)*

The abstract and the other documents mentioned must be posted at the principal entrances of the factory, unless the inspector directs otherwise. They must be in such characters and in such positions as to be conveniently read by persons employed. *FA: 138*

In the case of building operations and works of engineering construction the abstract, etc., may be posted up at each office, yard or shop belonging to the employer at which persons employed in the operations attend. *FA: 127*

Unless the inspector directs otherwise, a notice must be displayed in every room in a factory showing the maximum number permitted to work in that room. *FA: 2(6)*

There must be also a notice in every room showing the name of the person in charge of the First Aid box provided for the employees working in that room. *FA: 61(5)*

Where women and/or young persons are employed, notices must be displayed showing their hours of employment, intervals for meals, etc., and any days which it is proposed to substitute for the statutory holidays. (In Scotland, where the statutory holidays are not fixed, the latter notice will always be necessary.) A notice must also be displayed if the occupier proposes to avail himself of any exceptions to the standard hours, as permitted in certain processes and industries. See item 294.

Where pieceworkers are employed, notices showing rates of payment must be displayed in respect of certain classes of work unless each employee is given an individual written notice. See item 295.

NOTICES TO BE DISPLAYED IN OFFICES, SHOPS AND RAILWAY PREMISES—Notices to be displayed under the Offices, Shops and Railway Premises Act are dealt with in item 279.

NOTICES RELATING TO PARTICULAR PROCESSES—Where any of the processes carried on are subject to special regulations (e.g., woodworking, grinding of metals, sho t-blasting) a copy of the appropriate regulations or the prescribed abstract of them must be displayed in such positions as to be conveniently read by the employees concerned. The most obvious example is provided by the Electricity Regulations, which are applicable to almost every factory. Prescribed abstracts of some of the regulations are obtainable from H.M. Stationery Office; where no abstract is available the actual text of the regulations must be displayed. *FA: 139(1)*

If electricity is used, generated, or transformed at pressures normally exceeding 125 volts A.C. or 250 volts D.C., placards showing how to deal with cases of shock must be displayed. See item 76.

A cautionary placard (Factory Form 398) warning employees of the effects of chrome on the skin must be displayed where chromium plating or dyeing by chrome solutions is carried on. See items 131 and 241.

Various other cautionary placards are also required in certain circumstances; these are mentioned under the heading of the processes concerned.

If a sanitary convenience is regularly used by persons handling food (including canteen workers) a notice must be displayed in a prominent position requesting such workers to wash their hands after using the convenience. *FHR: 16(5)*

When radioactive materials are used, and in premises which are licensed as nuclear sites, a copy of the conditions imposed by the Minister when registering or licensing the premises must be posted up where it can be read by those concerned. See item 249.

When petrol is kept in a licensed store, a notice showing the conditions included in the licence must be displayed. See item 100.

INDIVIDUAL NOTICES—In addition to displaying copies or abstracts of regulations applicable to his factory, the occupier must furnish copies of such regulations to any employee affected by them, if the employee asks for such copies. *FA: 139(2)*

When an employee is appointed as a certified machinery attendant (see item 66) he must be given a copy of the prescribed leaflet, Factory Form 280, whether he asks for it or not.

When a person is first employed in the painting of buildings with lead paint he must be given a copy of Factory Form 394 (Cause and Prevention of Painters Colic). If he continues in this employment he must be given further copies on the first pay day of each year. *LPR: 7*

Office workers must be given the official booklet explaining the effect of the Offices, Shops and Railway Premises Act, unless the prescribed abstract is displayed on the premises. See item 279.

299 - Legal Proceedings

This item refers to legal proceedings following breaches of the Factories Act and of the regulations made under it. Prosecutions of factory occupiers under the Explosives Acts,

Petroleum Acts, etc., are less common and, in order to save space, discussion of them has been omitted; reference should therefore be made to the texts of those Acts if information is required.

PROSECUTION OF OCCUPIERS—As explained in item 10, the responsibility for carrying out the Factories Acts rests, with a few exceptions, on the occupier of the factory. It is therefore generally the occupier who is liable to be prosecuted if any breach of the law occurs, even if he himself was absent from the premises when the offence was committed. A way in which he can escape liability is by successfully taking out a cross-summons against the "actual offender", as explained below.

Strange as it may seem, the term "occupier" has not been defined anywhere in the Factories Acts, but it can be assumed to mean the individual or company owning the business carried on in the factory, irrespective of whether he exercises personal supervision of the work or delegates that duty to a manager.

PROSECUTION OF FACTORY OWNERS AND CONTRACTORS—In a few circumstances, mentioned in item 10, the owner of the factory is liable to prosecution instead of the occupier. When a contractor's employees are working in a factory the contractor may be liable instead of the occupier, as explained in items 10 and 153. What is said below about the right of an occupier to take out a cross-summons against the " actual offender " applies also when an owner or contractor is prosecuted.

PROSECUTION OF OTHERS AS WELL AS THE OCCUPIER—Where a company is prosecuted as the occupier, and it is proved that the offence in question was committed with the consent or connivance of a director, manager, secretary, or other officer of the company, that person may be prosecuted as well as the occupier. The same applies if the negligence of such a person has facilitated the commission of the offence. *FA: 155*

Where the act or default for which the occupier is liable is in fact the act or default of some agent, servant, worker or other person, that person is liable to be prosecuted. *FA: 160*

An employee who commits a breach of his own statutory duties (see item 293) is liable to prosecution and in such circumstances the occupier is not liable unless it can be proved that he failed to take all reasonable steps to prevent the employee from breaking the law. This does not prevent the occupier from being prosecuted for a separate offence arising out of the same incident; for instance, if an employee wilfully removed a guard from a machine he might be prosecuted for doing something liable to injure himself or others while, if the occupier allowed the guard to remain off. he on his part might be prosecuted for allowing the machine to be unguarded. *FA: 155(2)*. See *Wright v. Ford Motor Co. Ltd., 1967.*

The parent of a young person who is employed in contravention of the Factories Acts (e.g., for longer than the permitted hours) is liable to prosecution unless such employment was without the consent, connivance or wilful default of the parent. *FA: 158*

PROSECUTION OF THE " ACTUAL OFFENDER "—If, in England and Wales a factory occupier is prosecuted for an offence which was actually committed by some other person, such as an employee or a contractor, he is entitled to have that person brought into court as the " actual offender ". If the court is satisfied that the occupier has used all due diligence to enforce the execution of the act, and that the other person committed the offence without the occupier's consent, connivance, or wilful default, the occupier can be acquitted and the "actual offender " will be convicted instead. *FA: 160(1)*

In Scotland the occupier can escape conviction without bringing the " actual offender " into Court if he satisfies the Court that he has used all due diligence to enforce the law and that the offence was committed by some other person without his consent, connivance or wilful default. *FA: 161(3)*

Where the factory inspector, at the time of discovering an offence, is satisfied that the occupier has used all due diligence and that some other person has committed the offence without the occupier's consent, connivance or wilful default and in contravention of orders, the inspector may prosecute the "actual offender" in the first instance, without bringing the occupier into court at all. *FA: 161(4)*

At first sight it would seem that there must be many occasions on which the occupier could successfully seek to transfer liability elsewhere, especially when an employee does something in defiance of orders. In actual fact, however, such circumstances are comparatively rare. The important consideration is the using of "all due diligence" by the occupier to enforce the execution of the law. Unless the court is satisfied that the occupier has done everything reasonably possible, in the way of organisation and supervision, to prevent employees or others doing things which are contrary to the law, it will probably be held that due diligence has *not* been used and the occupier will therefore be held liable.

PENALTIES FOR OFFENCES—For making a false entry in any register, certificate, etc., required under the Acts, and for making use of, or conniving at, any such false entry, the penalty may be either a fine not exceeding £100 or imprisonment for up to three months. *FA: 159*

For any breach of the Factories Act which has caused, or might have caused, death or injury to any person, the maximum fine is £75 if the offender is an employed person and £300 in other cases. *FA: 156(2)*

A parent convicted of allowing a son or daughter under 18 to be employed in contravention of the Factories Act is liable to a fine not exceeding £10. *FA: 158*

For all other offences under the Factories Act the penalty is a fine not exceeding £15 if the offender is an employed person and not exceeding £60 in other cases. *FA: 156(1)*

Additional fines may be incurred if contravention of the law continues after conviction, or after any period of grace given by the court in ordering the offender to discontinue the contravention. *FA: 156(1) and 157*

In addition to imposing a fine, or instead of imposing one, the court may order a convicted occupier to take steps to rectify the state of affairs for which he was prosecuted and may give him a specified time limit within which to take those steps. *FA 61: 157*

Penalties for breaches of the Offices, Shops and Railway Premises Act are dealt with in item 278.

CONDUCT OF PROSECUTIONS—The conduct of prosecutions under the Factories Act is regulated by Section 155 to 171 of the Factories Act. The modifications which apply in Scotland are covered by Section 182.

Two points to be noted are that a convicted occupier can

appeal to Quarter Sessions and that no one who is related to the occupier or engaged in the same trade as the occupier may sit on the Bench to hear a prosecution of this kind.

COMMON LAW CLAIMS—An action brought by an injured person to recover damages after an accident in a factory is naturally quite distinct from any prosecution arising out of the same accident. The fact that the factory inspector has not prosecuted, or has prosecuted unsuccessfully, does not necessarily mean that a claim at Common Law will fail since, as explained in Chapter 16, there may be a liability at Common Law even if there has been no breach of statute law.

On the other hand, the fact that an occupier has been convicted of a breach of the Factories Act does not necessarily mean that a claim for damages will succeed.

300 – Powers of Inspectors

FACTORY INSPECTORS—A factory inspector may enter a factory at any reasonable time by day or night if he has good cause to believe that people are at work there. By day he may also enter any place which is not known to be a factory but which he has reason to think may be in use as a factory. He may also enter any premises which he has been officially informed are about to be used as a factory. On all such visits he may take a constable with him if he has reason to expect any serious obstruction in the execution of his duty. *FA: 146(1)*

While in the factory the inspector may ask for the production of registers, certificates and other documents required by the Acts and may make copies of them. He may also make such examination of the factory itself as is necessary to ascertain whether the law is being observed. *FA: 146(1)*

He may require any person he finds on the premises to give what information he can as to the name of the occupier. He may question persons found in the factory, or recently employed there, as to any matters related to the carrying out of the Acts and, if he so desires, this questioning can be done without the presence of a third party. He may also take written statements from such persons. But no person so examined may be required to answer any question or give any information which might criminate himself. *FA: 146(1)*

He may take samples of any substance used, or intended to be used, in the factory if he suspects that it is likely to cause bodily injury or to be in contravention of the Acts. Before taking such samples he must inform the occupier or some responsible person such as a foreman. This person may insist on the sample being divided into three parts, one part to be retained by the occupier, one part to be kept for future comparison, and one part to be taken by the inspector for analysis. The occupier or other responsible person may also require the analysis of the sample to be done by a Government Depart. ment. The results of such an analysis must not be disclosed except in so far as is necessary to determine whether there has been a breach of the Factories Acts. *FA: 78*

If an inspector considers that any part of the factory or plant is in such a condition, or is so constructed, that it cannot be used without danger he may ask the magistrates' court to make an order prohibiting the use of the part of the factory or plant concerned until the danger is removed. The same power applies to any process or operation which, in the inspector's opinion, cannot be carried on without danger. *FA: 54*

If an inspector is of the opinion that the employment of any young person in a certain factory or process is prejudicial to his health, he may order such employment to be discontinued until the young person concerned has been examined by the employment medical adviser and certified as fit for that employment. *FA: 119*

An inspector may conduct legal proceedings before a magistrate and may examine witnesses at a coroner's inquest. *FA: 83(2) and 149*

If an inspector finds that the district council has failed to deal with any matter affecting drains, sanitary conveniences, etc., which the council is required to deal with under the Factories Acts or Public Health Acts, he may serve a notice on the council requiring action to be taken. If no proceedings are taken within one month of this notice the inspector may take proceedings himself. *FA: 9*

An inspector visiting a factory in connexion with matters mentioned in the previous paragraph may take with him the medical officer of health, sanitary inspector, or other official of the district council. *FA: 9*

If an inspector considers that dangerous conditions exist regarding the means of escape in case of fire he may give notice to the local fire authority requiring them to examine the factory and inform him of what action is being taken to remedy those conditions. If the fire authority does not act within one month of receiving the inspector's notice the inspector may act himself. *FA: 41(5) and 42(5)*

In the case of factories belonging to the Crown, the inspector exercises all powers normally exercised under the Factories Act by the district councils. See item 268.

Where offices, shops or railway premises are within the close, curtilage or precincts of a factory, they are subject to inspection by the factory inspector instead of by the district council. This also applies to offices, etc., on docks, construction sites, etc. See item 278.

Every factory inspector is provided with a certificate of appointment which he is bound to show on request to any factory occupier or other responsible person connected with the factory he is visiting. *FA: 150*

OTHER INSPECTORS—An officer of the fire brigade, or any other appointed representative of the fire authority, may enter a factory to examine the means of escape with a view to the granting or amending of a certificate as described in item 26. An officer of the fire brigade may also enter a factory, if requested by the factory inspector, to investigate any possibly dangerous conditions noted by the factory inspector. *FA: 148*

Officers of the district council may enter office premises to enforce the Offices, Shops and Railway Premises Act, except where the enforcement of this Act is the responsibility of the factory inspector. See item 278.

Officers of the district council may enter a factory to ensure that the requirements regarding sanitary conveniences, cleanliness, overcrowding, temperature, ventilation and drainage are being complied with. They also have powers of entry to enforce the appropriate provisions of the Public Health Acts and the Food and Drugs Acts. *FA: 153(3)*

Section 12 of the Radioactive Substances Act 1960 provides for the appointment of inspectors who have power to enter premises where radioactive materials are used or where radioactive waste is kept or disposed of. Similar powers under Section 24 of the Nuclear Installations Act 1965 provide for the appointment of inspectors for licensed nuclear sites.

Inspectors authorised under the Petroleum Acts may enter any premises licensed for the storage of petrol or on which compressed gases are kept. See items 101 and 109.

DOCTORS—The employment medical adviser for a factory has the right to inspect the General Register at all reasonable times. The Medical Officer of Health may enter a factory for the purpose of enforcing the Public Health Acts or other statutory requirements for which he is responsible. *FA: 151(4)*

KEEPING OF TRADE SECRETS—If an officer of the local council or fire authority enters a factory in the exercise of his powers he is under a legal obligation not to disclose any trade secret he may discover in the course of his visit, unless such disclosure is necessary for the performance of his duty (e.g., when the description of a process forms part of the evidence in a prosecution). *FA: 154*

Strangely enough, the Factories Act lays no similar obligation on a factory inspector but it may reasonably be assumed that they are under a moral obligation, as a matter of professional etiquette, to preserve any trade secrets.

301 - Powers and Duties of Local Authorities

DISTRICT COUNCILS—The requirements of the Factories Act respecting sanitary conveniences (see item 38) are enforced by the district council, except in factories belonging to the Crown or occupied by visiting armed forces. *FA: 8(1) and 172*

In factories in which no mechanical power is used the district council is also responsible for enforcing the provisions relating to cleanliness, overcrowding, temperature, ventilation, and drainage of floors—except for Crown factories, factories occupied by visiting armed forces, and such factories as are mentioned in SRO 1938: No. 488 and SI 1950: No. 842. (The factories mentioned in these orders are those in which special regulations have been made for the protection of health.) *FA: 8(2)*

Every district council must keep a register of the factories in which it has the duty of enforcing any of the provisions mentioned above. *FA: 8(5)*

The district council must examine the lists of outworkers received from factory occupiers in its district, and if any persons on such lists live outside the district, the other district councils concerned must be informed. *FA: 133(2)*

The district council is also responsible for enforcing the regulations regarding the employment of outworkers in houses where there is infectious disease. See item 291.

The district council must, every five years, inspect such basement bakehouses as are still permitted to be used under Section 70 of the Factories Act 1961. If not satisfied that the bakehouse is still suitable for use, the council may revoke the certificate under which it is permitted to be used. *FA: 70(2)*

If asked to approve plans for the erection or conversion of a building to be used as a cotton cloth factory, the district council must ensure that the plans are accompanied by a certificate of approval from the superintending inspector of factories for the division. *FA: 79*

In addition to their duties under the Factories Act, the district councils are responsible for licensing petroleum stores (item 100) and explosive stores (item 111), for enforcing the various provisions of the Public Health Acts and the Food and Drugs Act (including the Food Hygiene Regulations outlined in item 136).

In certain circumstances the district council has the right to be consulted by the Minister of Housing and Local Government or the Secretary of State for Scotland before either of the latter makes an order for the disposal of radioactive waste. Local authorities may be requested to undertake the reception and treatment of such waste. See item 262.

The district council is normally responsible for enforcing the Clean Air Act 1956 (see items 82 and 135), including the provisions relating to the emission of dark smoke. The emission of smoke, grit and dust from processes covered by the Alkali Works Regulation Act (see item 247) is, however, a matter for the alkali inspectorate of the Minister of Housing and Local Government, except in the few cases where the Minister has delegated the responsibility to a local council under the Clean Air Act.

The district council is also responsible for the enforcement of the Offices, Shop and Railway Premises Act, except in the special circumstances under which the responsibility rests with the factory inspector (see item 278) District councils must make an annual report on the operation of the Act, giving the information prescribed by the Offices, Shops and Railway Premises (Annual Reports) Order: 1967 (SI 1967 No. 1668)

FIRE AUTHORITIES—The Greater London Council, the county councils, and the county boroughs, as the fire authorities in England and Wales, are responsible for issuing—and revising when necessary—the certificates of means of escape required by Section 40 of the Factories Act and Section 29 of the Offices, Shops and Railway Premises Act. They are also responsible for enforcing any regulations made by the Minister of Labour in respect of means of escape from any particular factory or class of factory. Where the factory inspector so requires, the council must re-examine a factory with a view to securing the removal of dangerous conditions affecting means of escape.

In Scotland the fire authorities are the City of Glasgow and the various area fire authorities set up under the Fire Services Act.

Fire authorities must make an annual report of their work in connexion with the Offices, Shops and Railway Premises Act, giving the information prescribed by the Offices, Shops and Railway Premises Annual Reports Order 1964 (*SI 1964: No. 1247*).

The fire authorities have power to make any necessary byelaws regarding means of escape from factories in their districts, so long as these byelaws are not inconsistent with any regulations made by the Minister of Labour. *FA: 46(4)*

EDUCATION AUTHORITIES—Every education authority must furnish, on application from the employment medical adviser, particulars of the medical record of any young person. Such information will be for the confidential use of the employment medical adviser in carrying out his duties under the Employment Medical Services Act (EMAS: 1(6) and item 42).

MEDICAL OFFICERS OF HEALTH—In his annual report to his council every medical officer of health must include a report on the administration of such parts of the Factories Act as are administered by the council. A copy of this section of the report must be sent by the medical officer of health to the Minister of Labour. *FA: 153(1)*

If the medical officer of health, or any other official of the council, discovers that any factory is failing to display the required abstract of the Factories Act (see item 298) he must give written notice of this to the district inspector of factories. *FA: 153(1)*

302 – Powers and Duties of other Officials, etc.

The Secretary of State of the Department of Employment (formerly Minister of Labour) as the minister responsible for the administration of the Factories Act, has numerous powers under those Acts by which he can extend or modify the legal requirements. Her Majesty's Chief Inspector of Factories also has certain powers in regard to the granting of exemptions and the requiring of certain additional precautions or amenities. These powers are exercised through statutory instruments, certificates, etc., which may be of general application or may apply only to certain specified factories or groups of factories. Orders and certificates of general interest are normally notified in the *Department of Employment Gazette* and in the trade and technical press.

A coroner conducting an inquest on a person killed in a factory accident must notify the district inspector of factories so that the latter may be present. The coroner must also allow witnesses to be examined—subject to his right of prohibiting improper questions—by the factory inspector; relatives of the victim, the factory occupier; any accredited representative of the victim's fellow workers, trade union, friendly society, etc.; and the accredited representative of any employers' association to which the occupier belongs. *FA: 83(1) and (2)*

Where the evidence at an inquest discloses the existence in the factory of any dangerous condition the coroner must notify the factory inspector, if the latter was not present at the inquest. *FA: 83(3)*

When the Minister of Labour sets up a special court to inquire into any accident or case of industrial disease, the court has the powers and responsibilities set out in Section 84 of the Factories Act 1937.

When a doctor finds that a patient is suffering from any of the industrial diseases mentioned in item 296 he must notify H.M. Chief Inspector of Factories, Baynards House, 1 Chepstow Place, London, W2, unless he knows that a notification has already been sent by someone else. The notice must give the name and address of the patient, the disease from which he is considered to be suffering, and the name and address of the patient's present or last employer. The doctor is entitled to a fee of 12½p for every notice so sent. *FA: 82*

Chapter XIX

Health and Safety at Work Act 1974

303 – Obligations on Employers

A civil action for damages cannot be brought in respect of breach of any of the following statutory obligations. *HSW: 47(1)*

It is the duty of every employer to ensure as far as is reasonably practicable, the health, safety and welfare at work of all his employees. *HSW: 2(1)*

An employer must conduct his undertaking in such a way as to ensure, so far as is reasonably practicable, that persons not in his employment who may be affected thereby are not exposed to risks to their health and safety. *HSW: 3(1)*

In particular, he must:

(1) Provide and maintain plant and systems of work that are, so far as practicable, safe and without risks to health. *HSW: 2 (2)(a)*

(2) Make arrangements for safety and absence of risk to health in connection with the handling etc of articles and substances. *HSW: 2(2)(b)*

(3) Provide information, training etc to ensure the health and safety of his employees at work. *HSW: 2(2)(c)*

(4) Maintain the place of work, means of access and agress, in a condition that is safe. *HSW: 2(2)(d)*

(5) Provide a working environment that is safe, without risk to health, and with adequate welfare facilities. *HSW: 2(2)(e)*

Every employer of five or more employees must prepare a written statement of his general policy with respect to health and safety at work and must bring it to the notice of all his employees. *HSW: 2(3) as amended by SI 1975: No. 1584*

No person shall intentionally or recklessly interfere with anything provided as a result of any statutory provisions. *HSW: 8*

No employers shall levy any charge on his employees in respect of any requirement of statutory provisions. *HSW: 9*

The burden of proving that anything is not practicable or reasonably practicable is placed upon the defendant in any prosecution. *HSW: 40*

304 – Obligations on Employees

For the purposes of the Health and Safety at Work Act 'employees' includes directors of companies and other management staff.

Every employee must take reasonable care for the health and safety of himself and other persons at work. *HSW: 7(4)*

He must co-operate with his employer so far as is necessary to enable employers' duties to be fulfilled. *HSW: 7(6)*

305 – Obligations on the Self-Employed

Every self-employed person must conduct his business so as to ensure that neither he nor any other person is exposed to risk to their health and safety. *HSW: 3(2)*

He may be required to give certain information, if so prescribed, to anybody who may be affected by the way he carries on his business. *HSW: 3(3)*

306 – Obligations on Persons in Control of Premises

Persons who are to be treated as in control are defined. *HSW: 4(3)(4)*

Finance houses who supply under hire purchase agreements etc are 'ostensible suppliers', and are not subject to these duties. *HSW: 6(9)*

Such persons who control non-domestic premises, or access to or egress from premises, are under a duty to ensure that they are safe and without risk to health. *HSW: 4(2)*

They are under a duty to prevent the emission of offensive substances into the atmosphere. *HSW: 5(1)*

307 – Obligations on Manufacturers

Manufacturers, designers, importers and suppliers of articles or substances for use at work are required:

(1) To ensure that it is safe and without risk to health. *HSW: 6(1)(a) and HSW: 6(4)(a)*

(2) To arrange for tests and examinations to ensure this. *HSW: 6(1)(b) and HSW: 6(4)(b)*

(3) To provide adequate information to ensure this. *HSW: 6(1)(c) and HSW: 6(4)(c)*

(4) To carry out necessary research to this end. *HSW: 6(2) and HSW: 6(5)*

In the cases of substances only, the manufacturer etc is not required to repeat examination or researches carried out by others if it is reasonable for him to rely on their results. *HSW: 6(6)*

Obligations similar to those of manufacturers are placed upon those who 'erect or install' any article for use at work. *HSW: 6(2)*

308 – Creation of Instruments

Two bodies, the Health and Safety Commission and the Health and Safety Executive, are created by statute. *HSW: 10*

The constitution and duties of the Commission and Executive are set out in HSW 10, 11, 12, 13, 14 and Schedule 2.

The Commission is authorised to issue Approved Codes of Practice. *HSW: 16*

Failure to observe an Approved Code of Practice does not of itself make a person liable to either civil or criminal proceedings. *HSW: 17*

However, in criminal proceedings the approved code is admissible in evidence, and a failure to observe it in regard 'to any matter which it is necessary for the prosecution to prove in order to establish a contravention' of statutory requirements shall be taken as proved. *HSW: 17(2)*

Supplement

This supplement details amendments made under the Health and Safety at Work Act 1974 from the date it was passed until 1st January 1976.

The supplement heading numbers below relate to the item numbers which run consecutively through the text in bold type from Chapters I to XIX. Where material appears in the supplement it should be read in addition to, or in place of, existing text under the appropriate item number. Where there is no material in the supplement under a particular item number, the main text for that item still remains valid.

Note: The main text *must* always be read in conjunction with this supplement.

1(S) – General Definition of a Factory

'Factory' is given an extended meaning in The Protection of Eyes Regulations 1974 SI 1974: No. 1681, to include 'any premises to which these Regulations apply' (see item 116(S) PE 2(2)) that is to say, anywhere where the processes specified in these regulations are carried out. *PE: 2(2)*

3(S) – Factories belonging to the Crown, municipal and public authorities, institutions, etc

FA: 179 repealed and FA: 124 partially repealed by SI 1974: No. 1941.

9(S) – Offices, Canteens, etc

Add under CANTEENS:

If the canteen is outside the curtilage of a factory, it may be a factory itself. *Simmonds Aerocessaries (Western) Ltd. v. Pontypridd (1944).*

13(S) – Walls, Ceilings, Floors, Windows and Doors

Under FLOORS for woodworking delete WWM: 4 and substitute WWM: 74(11). See also item 51(S).

30(S) – Lighting

Add under SPECIAL LIGHTING FOR CERTAIN OPERATIONS:

In addition to the requirements of FA: 5(1)–(4) and FSL, any work done with woodworking machines shall be sufficient and suitable for purpose for which machine is used; and, artificial lighting shall be shaded to prevent glare and so that direct rays do not impinge on the eyes of the operator. *WWM: 74(43)*

31(S) – Heating and Ventilation (General)

FA: 3(1) does not apply where WWM: 74 applies (see 49(S)). This states that a temperature of 13°C (=56°F approx.) is required for woodworking places unless impracticable, when other 'effective means' are necessary *WWM: 74(12)(1) and (2).*

Sawmills. Temperature here to be 10°C (=50°F) unless impracticable when other 'effective means' are necessary. *WWM: 74(12)(5)*

METHODS OF HEATING—Add:

Places to which WWM: 74 applies (see 49(S)) must have heating appliances enclosed or protected against fire risk, *WWM: 12(4)*; must not use heating apparatus which result in injurious or offensive fumes, *WWM: 12(5).*

32(S) – Dust Control, Humidity, etc

Add:

Woodworking Machinery (not operative until 24th May 1976). Effective exhaust appliances must be provided and maintained for collecting from a position as close as possible to the cutters of the following woodworking machinery (see item 51(S)) material removed by the cutters: every planing machine used for thicknessing; vertical spindle moulding machine; multi-cutter moulding machine; tenoning machine; automatic lathe. *Exceptions:* combined machines for surfacing and thicknessing; high speed routing machines with device for blowing away material from cutters; vertical spindle moulding or tenoning machine not used for more than six hours a week. *WWM: 74(41)*

33(S) – Noise Abatement

Add:

Where any part of a factory is used mainly for woodworking machines and any person is liable to be subject continuously for 8 hours to a sound level of 90dB(A), suitable ear protectors must be provided and used by person for whom they are provided, and measures must be taken to reduce the noise to the greatest extent that is reasonably practicable. *WWM: 74(44)*

The Secretary of State for Employment has prepared a 'Code of Practice for the Reduction of Exposure of Employed Persons to Noise'. Although this is not an 'approved code' for the purpose of the Health and Safety at Work Act, breach of it would doubtless be held to be evidential value in a civil action for damages for personal injuries sustained as a result of an employer's breach of his common law duties (see items 280–282).

42(S) – Employment Medical Services Act

The whole of FA: 10 has been repealed by SI 1974: No. 1941.

MEDICAL SUPERVISION—Delete the sentence 'The Minister of Labour . . .' The whole of FA: 11(1) repealed by SI 1974: No.

1941 (except in so far as it enables orders to be made otherwise than by statutory instrument).

44(S) – Meaning of 'Dangerous Part'

Delete in third paragraph of item the words 'The absolute nature . . .' (FA: 76 repealed by SI 1974: No. 1941).

Insert:

The obligations under FA: 14(1) to fence 'dangerous parts' do not apply to woodworking machines specially provided for by WWM: 74 (see 51(S)).

48(S) – Other Machinery (General): Design, Construction and Fencing

Add to BASIC GENERAL REQUIREMENTS:

FA: 14(1) does not apply to woodworking machines specifically provided for by WWM: 74 (see 51(S)).

49(S) – Band Saws

Delete the whole item. *Substitute:*

The Woodworking Machines Regulations 1974 (WWM: 74) are in substitution for the requirements of S14 of the Factories Act 1961 that all dangerous parts of machinery should be fenced, and similar requirements of SB (item 244) and CGP (item 172).

The term 'woodworking machine' now includes any machine (including portable ones) for use on wood, cork or fibre board or material composed partly of any of these materials. It may therefore apply to some plastics. *WWM: 74(2)(2)*.

See item 51(S) for list of machines to which the regulations apply.

The following machines are subject to special requirements, in addition to the general requirements for all woodworking machines set out in item 51(S).

NARROW BAND SAWING MACHINES—Defined as a sawing machine designed to be fitted with a blade not exceeding 50 mm. in width in the form of a continuous band or strip, the cutting portion of which runs in a vertical direction. Excluded from the definition of 'narrow band sawing machines' are: a log band sawing machine, band re-sawing machines. *WWM: 74(2)(2)*

Saw wheels and the whole of the blade to be enclosed by a guard of substantial construction, except for portion of blade that runs between top wheel and machine table. *WWM: 74(22)(1)*

The part of the blade which is above the friction disc or rollers and below the top wheel must have a frontal plate as close as is practicable to the blade, with one flange at right angles to the plate and extending behind the blade. *WWM: 74(22)(2)*

Friction disc or rollers to be kept adjusted as close as practicable to the surface of the machine table having regard to the work being done. *WWM: 74(22)(3)*

VERTICAL SPINDLE MOULDING MACHINES—Including high speed routing machines. *WWM: 74(2)(2)*

Every detachable cutter to be of correct thickness for the cutter block or spindle. *WWM: 74(32)*

To be mounted to prevent it, so far as is practicable, from becoming detached accidentally. *WWM: 74(32)*

Where straight fences are used, gap to be reduced as far as is practicable by false fences. *WWM: 74(33)*

If it is impracticable to provide the guard required by WWM: 74(5) (see item 51(S)) but it is practicable to provide a jig or holder of such a design as to hold the material being machined firmly, the machine is not to be used without a jig or holder. *WWM: 74(34)*

If impracticable to provide such a jig or holder, a suitable back stop, to prevent the material being thrown back when the cutters first make contact with it, must be provided. *WWM: 74(36)*

The machine not to be used without a jig or holder, unless work commences at the end of a surface of the material and during the process of the cutting the material moves in the same direction as the cutters. *WWM: 74(37)*

The guard for cutters to be of such a design as to contain any part of the cutters or their fixed appliances if they are ejected. *WWM: 74(35)*

If a suitable spike or push-stick would enable work to be done without unnecessary risk, such a spike or push-stick is to be provided. *WWM: 74(38)*

Machines designed to operate at two speeds must be arranged so that the motor cannot run at the higher speed without first running at the slower. *WWM: 74(39)(1)*

MULTIPLE RIP SAWING MACHINE AND STRAIGHT LINE EDGING MACHINES—Every machine must have a device to contain as far as practicable any material ejected by the machine on the operator's side. *WWM: 74(21)(1)*

Every machine on which the saw spindle is mounted above the machine table must be fitted on the side remote from the fence with a suitable guard, which extends from the edge of the device along a line parallel to the blade at least 300 mm. towards the axis of the saw. *WWM: 74(21)(2)*

The device must be designed to contain as far as practicable any material ejected from the machine accidentally. *WWM: 74(21)(2)*

PLANING MACHINES—Defined as machines for surfacing or for thicknessing or a combined machine for both these operations. Excluded from this definition are multi-cutter moulding machines having two or more cutter spindles. *WWM: 74(2)(21)*

Not to be used for cutting any rebate, recess, tenon or mould unless the cutter is effectively guarded. *WWM: 74(23)*

Unless mechanically fed, such a machine is to be fitted with a cylindrical cutter block. *WWM: 74(24)*

Unless mechanically fed, to be designed and constructed so as to be capable of adjustment so that the clearance between the cutters and the front edge of the delivery table does not exceed 6 mm. (measured radially from the centre of the cutter block) and the gap between the feed table and the delivery table is as small as practicable, having regard to the operation. No planing machine not so adjusted is to be used for surfacing. *WWM: 74(25)(1)*

Unless mechanically fed, a planing machine is to be provided with a strong and rigid bridge guard, as long as the full length of the cutter block and at least as wide as the diameter of the cutter block. The bridge guard must be constructed so as to be capable of easy adjustment both vertically and horizontally. It must be mounted on the machine in a position which is approximately central over the axis of the cutter block, and constructed so as not to be accidentally displaced. *WWM: 74(26)(1), (2), (3)*

Unless mechanically fed, the bridge guard must be adjusted to enable, so far as is practicable, the work to be done without risk of injury *WWM: 74(27)(1)*

The regulations which follow are requirements when squared stock is being machined. 'Squared stock' is defined as material that has a square or rectangular cross section of which the dimensions remain substantially constant throughout the length of the material. *WWM: 74(2)(2)*

When a wider surface of squared stock is being planed or smoothed and, by reason of the shortness of the material, the work cannot be done with a guard adjusted as required by WWM: 74(27) (see above), a suitable push-stick with suitable handholds must be provided and used. *WWM: 74(29)*

When the planing or smoothing both of a wider and a narrower surface of squared stock is being carried out and one operation immediately follows the other, the bridge guard must be adjusted so that when the width surface is being machined, the underside of the guard is not more than 10 mm. above the upper surface.

When narrower surface is being machined, the end of the guard must be at a point not more than 10 mm. from the surface of the material remote from the fence. *WWM: 74(27)(4)*

In all other cases when the wider surface of squared stock is being machined the bridge guard must be adjusted so that the distance between the end of the guard and the fence does not exceed 20 mm. and the underside of the guard is not more than 10 mm. above the upper surface of the material. *WWM: 74(27)(2)*

When a narrower surface of squared stock is being machined, the end of the bridge guard must be at a point not more than 10 mm. from the surface of the material which is remote from the fence and the underside of the guard not more than 10 mm. above the surface of the feed table. *WWM: 74(27)(3)*

When the planing of two adjoining surfaces of squared stock is being carried out and the operations immediately follow one another, the bridge guard must be adjusted so that neither the height of the underside of the guard above the feed table nor the distance between the end of the guard and the fence exceed the width of the material by more than 10 mm. *WWM: 74(27)(6)*

Except when the previous condition applies, whenever the planing of squared stock is being carried out the bridge guard must be adjusted to comply with either WWM: 74(27)(2) or WWM: 74 (27)(3) above. *WWM: 74(27)(5)*

When smoothing of squared stock of square cross section is being carried out, the bridge guard must be adjusted to comply with either WWM: 74(27)(2) or WWM: 74 (27)(3) or WWM: 74(27)(6). *WWM: 74(27)(7)*

Unless mechanically fed, every planing machine used for surfacing must have a strong and effective guard for that part of the cutter block which is on the side of the fence remote from the bridge guard. *WWM: 74(28)(1)*

Planing machines used for thicknessing, unless they were manufactured before 24th November 1974, must have sectional feed rollers or some other suitable device on the operator's side of the feed to restrain any workpiece ejected from the machine. *WWM: 74(31)(1)*

Machines manufactured before 24th November 1974 may be used without such a device provided not more than one workpiece at a time is fed and there is a notice to that effect fixed to the machine. *WWM: 74(31)(2)*

50(S) – Circular Sawing Machines

These are defined as machines with a saw bench and a spindle below the machine table to which a circular saw can be fitted for the purpose of dividing material into separate parts.

A saw bench includes a bench in the form of a roller table and a bench incorporating a travelling table. A machine table includes any frame which supports the material being cut.

'Circular sawing machines', as defined, do *not* include: a multiple rip sawing machine, a straight line edging machine, or any sawing machine in which the blade is moved towards the material to be cut. *WWM: 74(2)(2)*

GUARDS—The part below the machine table must be guarded to greatest extent that is practicable. *WWM: 74(16)(1)*

A riving knife must be fitted behind the saw blade and in a direct line with it and must have a smooth surface, be strong, rigid, easily adjustable. In addition the following provisions must also be observed:

(1) The edge of the knife nearer the saw blade must form an arc with the radius not greater than the saw blade.

(2) The knife must be kept adjusted as close as practicable to the saw blade and not exceeding 12 mm. from it at the level of the machine table.

(3) The knife must extend upwards above the machine table not more than 25 mm. below the saw blade, in the case of saw blades of less than 600 mm. diameter; in the case of saw blades above 600 mm. the knife must extend upwards from machine table at least 225 mm.

(4) In case of parallel plate saw blade, the knife must be thicker than the plate. *WWM: 74(16)(2)*

That part of the blade which is above the machine table must be guarded, and the guard must be kept adjusted so that it extends from the top of the riving knife to a point above the upper surface of the material being cut. When squared stock is being fed by hand, the guard must extend to not more than 12 mm. above the upper surface of the material. *WWM: 74(16)(3)*

The guard must have a flange of adequate depth on each side of blade, adjusted to extend beyond the roots of the teeth. *WWM: 74(16)(4)*

This is subject to the further obligation that if machine is to be used for cutting any rebate, tenon, mould or groove, unless the part of the saw blade above the table is effectively guarded. *WWM: 74(18)(1)*

PUSH STICKS—A suitable push stick must be provided and kept available at every machine fed by hand. *WWM: 74(19)(1)*

It must be used throughout any cut of 300 mm. or less, during the last 300 mm. of any greater cut, and to remove materials which have been cut, unless either:

(a) the distance between the saw blade and the fence is too great, *or*

(b) the method of feeding allows a push stick to be safely dispensed with. *WWM: 74(19)(2)*

SIZE OF BLADES—Every machine must have a notice fixed on it, specifying the diameter of the smallest blade that can be legally used. *WWM: 74(17)(3)*

Machines with spindles capable of operating at one speed only must not be used with a blade less than six-tenths of the diameter of the largest saw blade for which the saw bench is designed. *WWM: 74(17)(1)*

Machines with spindles capable of operating at more than one speed: not to be used with a blade less than six-tenths of the largest blade which can properly be used at fastest working speed. *WWM: 74(17)(2)*

USE OF MACHINES—Apart from cutting rebates, tenon, mould and grooves, circular sawing machines are not to be used for ripping operations unless blade projects above upper surface of material being cut. *WWM: 74(18)(2)*

Not to be used for cross-cutting logs or branches unless material is firmly held by a gripping device fixed to a travelling table. *WWM: 74(18)(3)*

REMOVAL OF MATERIALS—The following regulations do not apply to:

(a) machines with a saw bench in the form of a roller table, *or*

(b) a saw bench with a travelling table, *or*

(c) moveable machine which cannot accommodate a blade less than 400 mm. diameter.

In all other cases, if a person other than the operator is employed to remove material while machine is in motion, the distance between the delivery end and the up running part of the blade must not be less than 1200 mm. *WWM: 74(20)*

The person removing cut material is not to stand anywhere except at delivery end, but this does not apply to types of machines described in (a) and (b) above. *WWM: 74(20)(1)*

51(S) – Other Woodworking Machinery

Delete section and substitute:

Woodworking Machines in General

Premises and places to which the above regulations are applicable include not only factories, but all those specified in FA: 123 (electrical stations), FA: 124 (institutions), FA: 125 (dock premises and certain warehouses), FA: 126 (ships) and FA: 127 (construction sites). *WWM: 74(3)(1)*

All such places, including those out of doors, and premises are subject to the regulations if any woodworking machinery, as defined below, is used on them even if the machine is only a portable one. *WWM: 74 Sch. I*

Machines which are woodworking machines if used on materials specified for the purpose of WWM: 74, (see item 49(S)), are:

1. Sawing machines with circular blade or blades
2. Grooving machines
3. Sawing machines with continuous blade
4. Chain sawing machines
5. Morticing machines
6. Planing machines
7. Vertical spindle moulding machines and high speed routing machines
8. Moulding machines having at least 2 cutter spindles
9. Tenoning machines
10. Trenching machines
11. Automatic and semiautomatic lathes
12. Boring machines *WWM: 74(2)(2) and Sch. I*

The Chief Inspector can exempt in writing any of above or any process or any place from provisions of the regulations if satisfied not necessary. *WWM: 74(4)*

GENERAL PROVISIONS—Applicable to all above machines:

Guards. Cutters must be enclosed by guards of substantial construction to greatest extent practicable. *WWM: 74(5)(1), (2)*

Must be kept in position, unless impracticable. *WWM: 74(7)(1)*

Adjustments not to be made while cutters in motion, unless without danger to operative. *WWM: 74(5)(2)*

Cleaning. Blade not to be cleaned by hand while machine is in motion. *WWM: 74(40)*

Machine controls. Effective devices, convenient to operator, necessary for starting and stopping. *WWM: 74(9)*

Working space. Clear and unobstructed space necessary. *WWM: 74(10)*

Floors. To be good and level, not slippery, and free from chips. *WWM: 74(11)*

Maintenance and fixing. Every part of machine to be of good construction, sound material and properly maintained. *WWM: 74(42)(1)*

To be securely fixed to floor or other substantial part of structure; if not practicable, other arrangements must be made for stability. *WWM: 74(42)(2)*

Other requirements:

lighting, see item 30(S)
heating, item 31(S)
noise, item 33(S)
training, item 292(S)

52(S) – Lathes

Delete part of item headed
WOOD-TURNING LATHES; see item 51(S).

66(S) – Examination, Lubrication and Adjustment of Machinery

For adjustments of woodworking machinery see item 51(S).

84(S) – Steam Boilers

PRESSURE GAUGES—Delete 'in lbs/sq in'.

116(S) – Processes endangering Eyesight

Delete whole item and substitute:

There is a general obligation to provide suitable goggles or effective screens for processes (to be specified by regulations) which involve a special risk of injury to the eyes from particles or fragments thrown off in the course of the process. *FA: 65*

The processes specified by the Protection of Eyes Regulations 1974, SI 1974: No. 1681 PE: Sch. 1, are:

(a) blasting of concrete by material propelled by compressed air. (*1*)

(b) cleaning of buildings by similar methods. (*2*)

(c) cleaning by high pressure water jets. (*3*)

(d) striking masonry nails with a hand tool or a power driven portable tool. (*4*)

(e) any work, including loading and cleaning, with hand held cartridge operated tool. (*5*)

(f) chipping of metal etc. (*6*)

(g) chipping or surfing of paint etc from surface of metal

(h) applying articles of metal or similar materials to a power driven tool. (*7*)

(i) use of power driven metal cutting saws.

(j) use of power driven abrasive wheel. (*8*)

(k) pouring molten metal in foundries.

(l) skimming molten metal in foundries. (*9*)

(m) working at molten salt bath. (*10*)

The following are specified processes if there is a reasonably foreseeable risk of injury to the eyes of persons engaged in the work.

(a) any operation, etc on any part of any plant which has ever contained corrosives. (*11*)

(b) handling in open vessels of corrosives, etc. (*12*)

(c) driving bolts and similar articles into any structure with hand or portable powered tools. (*13*)

(d) injection of liquids under pressure into buildings, etc. (*14*)

(e) breaking up of metal by a hammer, hand or power driven or by a tup. (*15*)

(f) drilling, etc by means of a hand or portable power tool of glass, hard plastic, brick, stone concrete, fired clay and similar materials. (*16*)

(g) use of compressed air for removing swarf, dust, etc. (*17*)

(h) work on molten metals at places other than foundries. (*18*)

(i) any process in foundries. (*19*)

(j) work on the manufacture of wire or wire rope. (*20*)

(k) all operations in connection with coiling wire. (*21*)

(l) cutting of wire, etc under tension. (*22*)

(m) glass making. (*23*)

For all the above processes approved eye protectors must be worn.

For any process involving the use of an exposed electric arc or an exposed stream of arc plasma, an approved shield or an approved fixed shield is necessary. *PE: Sch. 1(24)*

For the following processes approved eye protectors or approved shields or approved fixed shields are necessary. *PE: Sch. 1*

(a) welding of metals.

(b) hot fettling and de-seaming of metals. (*25*)

The following also constitute a specified process if there is a reasonably foreseeable risk of injury to the eyes of persons engaged in the work:

(a) the cutting, boring, cleaning, surface conditioning or spraying of materials by means of an apparatus (other than those driven by compressed air) to which any flammable gas etc is supplied under pressure. (*27*)

(b) any process with an instrument which produces light amplification by the stimulated emission of radiation. (*28*)

For the following processes, approved eye protectors or approved shields or fixed shields (not necessarily approved) are necessary, if there is a reasonably foreseeable risk of injury to the persons engaged in the work.

(a) fraying or dressing of an abrasive wheel. (*29*)

(b) work with drop or power hammers, horizontal forging machines and presses, (other than hydraulic presses) used for the manufacture of forgings. (*30*)

(c) dry grinding of materials by applying them by hand to power driven wheel. (*31*)

(d) fettling of metal castings. (*32*)

(e) production of metal castings by pressure die casting. (*33*)

(f) machining of metals. (*34*)

(g) welding of metals by electric resistance process or submerged electric arc. (*35*)

The employer of every person who is employed in a factory (see item 1) for any of his time in any of the specified processes (see above) must provide the appropriate eye protection specified above. *PE: 5(1)*

Fixed shields must be provided between adjacent positions in which persons work. *PE: 5(2)*

Protection must also be provided for persons at risk from, but not employed in, the processes specified above. *PE: 6*

Eye protectors provided must be given into the possession of each person for whom they are provided. For persons occasionally employed, a sufficient number must be provided, maintained and kept readily available. *PE: 7*

Eye protectors must be replaced by the employers if lost, destroyed or defective and the employer has obligation to keep sufficient in stock for this purpose. *PE:* 8(*1*), (*2*)

Eye protectors or shields must be suitable for person for whom they are provided, made to conform with approved specification and marked to indicate the purpose for which they are designed. *PE: 9*

Provisions are made for the fixing, construction and maintenance of fixed shields. *PE: 10*

There is an obligation on every person to use the protection provided and to take reasonable care of it, and report to the employer the loss or destruction or any defect in it. *PE: 11*

The Chief Inspector has power to exempt any factory or any process, etc from these obligations. *PE: 4*

Protection is also necessary for persons at risk from, but not employed in, the specified processes in certain cases specified. *PE: Sch. 2*

126(S) – Operation of Woodworking Machinery

Delete item and substitute:

Woodworking machinery as now defined includes machinery for carrying out certain operations on materials other than wood (see 51(S)).

For regulations regarding *lighting* in connection with such machines, see now 30(S); *heating* 31(S); *noise* 33(S); *training* 292(S).

132(S) – Foundries

Delete last section of item, NON-FERROUS METALS. After section PROTECTIVE CLOTHING AND EQUIPMENT add 'see also 116(S)'.

180(S) – Protective Equipment and Clothing

Delete part of item entitled PROTECTION OF EYES down to words 'See Item 116' in second paragraph and substitute:

CGP: 52 and Schedule are repealed and substituted by the Protection of Eyes Regulations (see item 116(S)). *PE: 1(2) and Sch. 3*

244(S) – Shipbuilding and Ship-repairing

The provisions in regulation 67(2) of the Ship Building and Ship Repair Regulations 1960 SI 1960: No. 1932 do not apply to parts of woodworking machines subject to WWM: 74—see 51(S).

247(S) – Chemical Works and Alkali Works

Various sections of The Alkali etc. Works Regulations Act 1906 have been repealed by The Clean Air Enactments (Repeals and Modifications) Regulations 1974 SI 1974: No. 2170. The whole of The Alkali etc. Works Regulations (Scotland) Act 1951 has been repealed by the same SI—see 116(S). For fuller details of particular sections, see index of statutes at the end of this supplement.

290(S) – Employment of Women and Young Persons

Add under RESTRICTION ON EMPLOYMENT OF YOUNG PERSONS:

A person who has not yet attained the age of 18 may not, unless he has successfully completed an approved course of training in the operation of the machine or is operating under adequate supervision by an experienced person, operate:

(i) any circular sawing machine—see 50(S)
(ii) any sawing machine with a circular blade
(iii) any planing machine for surfacing which is not mechanically fed
(iv) any vertical spindle moulding machine. *WWM: 74(13)(3)*

291(S) – Employment of Outworkers

Delete paragraph beginning: 'If the district council . . .' FA: 134 repealed by SI 1974: No. 1941.

292(S) – Training and Supervision of Employees

Under TRAINING delete item under:

'Persons working at woodworking machines' (see also 126(S)) and substitute:

No person shall be employed on a woodworking machine (see 51(S)) except where he works under adequate supersivion, unless he has been sufficiently trained on machines of that class. *WWM: 74(13)(1)*

Every person must be fully instructed as to the dangers connected with woodworking machines, precautions to be observed, requirements of WWM and methods of using guards, devices and appliances required by WWM. *WWM: 74(13)(2)*

Add at end of item TRAINING:

'and operating certain woodworking machines' (item 290 and 290(S)).

293(S) – Duties of Persons Employed

Under SPECIAL DUTIES IN CERTAIN PROCESSES delete item starting:

'Persons operating woodworking machines . . .' and substitute:

Every person operating a woodworking machine (see 51(S)) must:

(a) keep guards and devices provided under WWM in proper adjustment
(b) use prescribed spikes, push sticks, push-blocks, jigs, holders and back stops. *WWM: 74(14)(1)*

Every person who is employed by the occupier of a factory, and is trained in the use of woodworking machinery (see 51(S) and 290(S)) who discovers any defects in the machinery or that the floor is not good and level or is slippery must report it without delay to occupier, manager or other appropriate person. *WWM: 74(14)(2)*

Add at end of item:

It is an offence for any person in purported compliance with FA: 135 to produce or allow to be produced any document which is false in a material particular, or make any statement which he knows to be false in a material particular or recklessly to make such a statement. *FAR: 2(5)*

It is also an offence to obstruct any officer (see 295(S)) appointed for the purpose of enforcing FA: 135 or fail to comply with any requirement imposed by such an officer. *FAR: 2(6)*

295(S) – Pieceworkers

The Factories Act 1961 (Enforcement of Section 135) Regulations SI 1974: No. 1776 became operative 1st January 1975. Section 135 is the only section of the Factories Act which, under the Health and Safety at Work Act 1974, will be retained. Duties under that section have not been assigned to the Health and Safety Executive but the SoS has taken power by these regulations to appoint other officers for the purpose of enforcing the section, by adding a new section to the FA, new section 135A. *FAR: 2(1)*

Such officers will have power to enter factories, require production of documents, and require any person to give any information, in accordance with the regulations. *FAR: 2(3)*

New offences have been created in connection with FA: 135 (see item 293(S)). *FAR: 2(5)(6)*

296(S) – Notices to be given to Factory Inspector, etc

On 1st January 1975 under the HSW inspectors of factories became inspectors appointed by the Health and Safety Executive.

Add under REPORTING OF ACCIDENTS WHICH DO NOT CAUSE INJURY: Report has to be sent to Health and Safety at Work Executive. For penalties for failure to notify see item 299(S).

297(S) – Keeping of Registers and other Records

Delete section FALSE ENTRIES. FA: 159 repealed by SI 1974: No. 1941.

Add at end of item:

Further offences have been created in connection with FA: 135—see item 293(S).

299(S) – Legal Proceedings

Delete whole section under PENALTIES FOR OFFENCES and substitute:

For a breach of FA: 135 (outworkers) as amended by FAR, see items 293(S) and 295(S).

For producing a false document or making a false statement, the penalty on summary conviction is a fine not exceeding £100 or 3 months' imprisonment. *FAR: 2(5)*

For obstruction of an officer or failure to comply with instructions, the penalty on summary conviction is a fine not exceeding £20. *FAR: 2(6)*

The following offences on summary conviction carry a fine not exceeding £400:

(i) contravening any requirement imposed by regulations made under HSW
(ii) intentionally obstructing any person appointed under HSW
(iii) attempting to prevent a person from appearing before an inspector and answering any question an inspector may require answering under HSW
(iv) intentionally obstructing an inspector in the performance of his duties under HSW
(v) falsely pretending to be an inspector appointed under HSW.

Unless:

(a) the penalties are restricted in Health and Safety Regulations made by the SoS under power conferred on him by HSW: 15(6)(d), *or*
(b) the offence is in connection with the importation into the United Kingdom of any article that has been specified by regulations as one to be dealt with under the Customs and Excise Act 1952, in accordance with HSW: Sch. 3: 2(2)

then the following offences:

(i) failing to discharge a duty under HSW: 2(7)
(ii) contravening any health and safety regulations

(iii) contravening any condition or restriction attached to a licence
(iv) contravening HSW 8 and 9
(v) contravening any requirement of an improvement notice or a prohibition notice
(vi) failing to provide information required by the Commission by a notice under HSW: 27(1)
(vii) disclosing any information in contravention of HSW: 27(4) or 28
(viii) making false statements or false entries in a register with intent to deceive, or forging any document in connection with HSW
(ix) any offence under any existing statutory provisions for which no other penalty is specified. *HSW: 33(3)(a) and (b)*

carry on summary conviction a fine not exceeding £400; and on conviction on indictment, a fine.

In addition, on indictment the following offences carry a penalty of imprisonment for a term not exceeding 2 years, or a fine or both:

(i) doing anything without a licence which requires such a one under the HSW from the Health and Safety Executive or the Agriculture Minister
(ii) contravening any term or condition attached to such a licence
(iii) attempting to acquire or acquiring explosives in contravention of any enactment
(iv) contravening any requirement of a prohibition notice
(v) disclosing any information in contravention of HSW: 27(4) or HSW: 28. *HSW: 33(4)*

In addition, for the following offences if they continue after conviction; a fine of £50 for each day on which the contravention continues:

(i) contravening any requirement of an improvement notice or a prohibition notice
(ii) failing to comply with an order made by a court under HSW: 42 (see item 302). *HSW: 33(5)*

For a breach of CPA: 78(2) (which relates to cable burning) on summary conviction a fine not exceeding £400. *CAR: 10*

For producing or furnishing etc a document known to be false in material particular or for making any statement known to be false in relation to the Truck Acts 1896, or for intentionally obstructing any officer appointed under section 10(1)(7A) of the Truck Acts 1896—on summary conviction a fine not exceeding £100 and/or 3 months' imprisonment. *TA: 1896 10(3)(5) and (6)*

Add:

Where an offence has been committed by a corporate body (such as a company) with the consent or connivance of any director or manager or by his neglect he shall be guilty as well. *HSW: 37*

300(S) – Powers of Inspectors

Delete whole item and substitute:

The Health and Safety at Work Executive is under a duty to:

(i) exercise such of the Commissions' powers as the Commission directs it to. *HSW: 11(4)(a)*
(ii) give effect to any directions by the Commission. *HSW: 11(4)(b)*
(iii) give information and advice to any Minister of the Crown if requested. *HSW: 11(5)(a) and (b)*

An Inspector appointed under the HSW can:

(i) at any reasonable time enter premises. *HSW: 20(2)(a)*
(ii) take a constable with him if he has reasonable cause to fear any serious obstruction. *HSW: 20(2)(b)*
(iii) take with him any person authorised by the enforcing authority. *HSW: 20(2)(c)(i)*
(iv) take with him any equipment or materials necessary. *HSW: 20(2)(c)(ii)*
make any examination and investigation necessary. *HSW: 20(2)(d)*
direct that premises or anything on them shall be left undisturbed. *HSW: 20(2)(c)*
take measures and photographs and recordings. *HSW: 20(2)(f)*
take samples. *HSW: 20(2)(g)*
cause any article or substance to be dismantled or tested. *HSW: 20(2)(h)*

The statute specifies what must be contained in a prohibition notice. *HSW: 22(3)*

There is provision for appeal to any industrial tribunal against an improvement or prohibition notice. An appeal has the effect of suspending the improvement notice. In the case of a prohibition notice, an appeal does not suspend it automatically but the industrial tribunal can, on application, direct that it shall be suspended pending their decision. *HSW: 24*

The inspector has power to serve an improvement notice requiring remedy of a contravention within a specified period. *HSW: 21*

He can serve a prohibition notice, with immediate effect if there is imminent danger, to stop certain activities. *HSW: 22*

Persons appointed by the SoS for Employment to enforce the Truck Acts 1831–1940 have powers under S10(3) of the 1896 Act, as amended by SI 1974: No. 1887:

(i) to enter any premises at any reasonable time
(ii) to require production of and take copies etc of any entry in wage sheets etc
(iii) to require any person giving out work and any outworker to give information
(iv) to inspect and copy list of outworkers
(v) to require any person to give information. *TA 1896: 10(3)*

Imminent Danger—If an inspector considers any article or substance is a cause of imminent danger of serious personal injury, he may seize it and render it harmless by destruction if necessary. If this is done he must give a signed report to the person concerned. *HSW: 25*

An inspector, if duly authorised in writing, may prosecute in a magistrates court even though he is not a solicitor or barrister, except in Scotland. *HSW: 39*

(i) to take steps to make any article or substance available as evidence
(ii) to require any person to give information
(iii) to require the production of any entry, book or document
(iv) to require any facilities or assistance to exercise any other power necessary to bring into effect any relevant statutory provision. *HSW: 20(1) and (2)*

There are obligations on the inspector to test in the presence of persons specified, to consult, and to leave a notice if he removes any article or substance. *HSW: 20(4)*

No person is required to produce any document he would be privileged from producing in an order for discovery. *HSW: 20(8)*

301(S) – Powers and Duties of Local Authorities

Every local authority is under a duty to make adequate arrangements for the enforcement of relevant statutory provisions, and to perform their duty in accordance with such guidance as the Health and Safety Commission may give them. *HSW: 18(4)*

The SoS for Employment is empowered to make regulations to make local authorities responsible for the enforcement of parts of HSW, and to transfer enforcement authority from local authorities to the Health and Safety Executive or vice versa. *HSW: 18(2)(2)*

Under DISTRICT COUNCILS sixth paragraph, on bakehouses, note that FA: 70 was repealed by SI 1974: No. 1941 from 1st January 1975.

302(S) – Powers and Duties of other Officials, etc

CORONERS—The whole of FA: 83 was repealed by SI 1974: No. 1941 as from 1st January 1975. On the same date the Coroners' (Amendment) Rules 1974, SI 1974: No. 2128 came into force. These add two further rules to The Coroners' Rules 1953, SI 1953: No. 205:

> Where a coroner holds an inquest where death may have been caused by accident or disease, notice of which is required to be given to an inspector, the coroner must adjourn the inquest and give the inspector at least 4 days' notice.
>
> An inspector means an inspector appointed under HSW: 19.

Appendix I—Abbreviations used to Indicate Acts, Codes of Regulations, etc.

NOTE: Numerous Acts of Parliament and Statutory Orders are mentioned only once or twice in the course of the book, and these have been given their full title in the text. It is only those to which frequent reference has had to be made which have, for convenience, been indicated by abbreviations and these are the only ones included in the list below.

ABW—Abrasive Wheels Regulations, 1970: SI 1970 No. 535

AR—Acetylene Regulations 1937: SRO 1937 No. 54

AS—Asbestos Regulations, 1969: SI 1969 No. 690

AWR—Aerated Water Regulations 1921: SRO 1921 No. 1932

AWRA—Alkali, etc., Works Regulation Act 1906

BCR—Blasting (Castings and other Articles) Special Regulations 1949: SI 1949 No. 2225

CA—Certificates of approval. These are issued by H.M. Chief Inspector of Factories and are referred to by reference to the particular section of the Factories Act under which they are made. They are listed in the Stationery Office Sectional List No. 18, referred to on page 2.

CAA 56—Clean Air Act 1956

CAA 68—Clean Air Act 1968

CAR—Clean Air Enactment (Repeals of Modifications) Regulations 1974: SI 1974 No. 21070

CCF—Cotton Cloth Factories Regulations 1929: SRO 1929 No. 300

CE—Certificates of Exemption. These are issued in a similar way to the Certificates of Approval. See above.

CEL—Regulations for the Manufacture, Manipulation and Storage of Celluloid: SRO 1921 No. 1825

CFS—Cinematograph Film Stripping Regulations 1939: SRO 1939 No. 571

CGP—Construction (General Provisions) Regulations 1961: SI 1961 No. 1580

CHW—Construction (Health and Welfare) Regulations 1966: SI 1966 No. 95

CLO—Construction (Lifting Operations) Regulations 1961: SI 1961 No. 1581

CLW—Clay Works (Welfare) Special Regulations, 1948: SI 1948 No. 1547

CP—Chromium Plating Regulations, 1931: SRO 1931 No. 455, as amended by the 1973 regulations

CPA—Control of Pollution Act, 1974

CWP—Construction (Working Places) Regulations 1966: SI 1966 No. 94

CWR—Chemical Works Regulations 1922. SRO 1922: No. 731

DMO—Dangerous Machines (Training of Young Persons) Order, 1954: SI 1954 No 921

DR—Docks Regulations, 1934. SRO 1934: No. 279

EA—Explosives Act, 1875, as amended by the Explosives Act, 1923

E(FA)R—Electricity (Factories Act) Regulations 1944: SRO 1944 No. 739

EMAS—Employment Medical Service Act, 1972

ER—Electricity Regulations 1908: SRO 1908 No. 1312, as amended by the Electricity (Factories Act) Regulations 1944: SRO 1944 No. 739

ESB—Examination of Steam Boilers Regulations 1964: SI 1964 No. 781

FA—Factories Act 1961

FAB—First Aid Boxes in Factories 1959: SI 1959 No. 906

FA(MI)O—First Aid Boxes (Miscellaneous Industries) Order 1960: SI 1960 No. 1691

FA(ST)O—First Aid Boxes (Standard of Training) Order 1960. SI 1960 No. 1612

FAR—Factory Act Regulations

FCR—Order for the Process of File-Cutting by Hand. SRO 1903 No. 507

FHR—Food Hygiene (General) Regulations, 1970. SI 1970 No. 1172. (These Regulations apply only to England and Wales but similar requirements are in force for Scotland under the Food Hygiene (Scotland) Regulations, 1959. SI 1959 No. 413)

FPM—Foundries (Parting Materials) Special Regulations, 1950. SI 1950 No. 1700

FSL—Factories (Standard of Lighting) Regulations 1941: SRO 1941 No. 94

GC—Grinding of Cutlery and Edge Tools Regulations, 1925. SRO 1925 No. 1089. (As amended by the Grinding of Cutlery and Edge Tools (Amendment) Special Regulations, 1950. SI 1950 No. 370, and Abrasive Wheels Regulations, 1970)

GM—Grinding of Metals (Miscellaneous Industries) Regulations, 1925. SRO 1925 No. 904. (As amended by the Blasting (Castings and Other Articles) Special Regulations, 1949, SI 1949: No. 2225, and the Grinding of Metals (Miscellaneous Industries) (Amendment) Special Regulations, 1950. SI 1950 No. 688, and Abrasive Wheels Regulations, 1970)

HEO—Hoist Exemption Order, 1962 (SI 1962 No. 715) as amended by the Hoists Exemption (Amendment) Order, 1967 (SI 1967 No. 759)

HFL and LPG—Highly Flammable Liquids and Liquefied Petroleum Gases Regulations, 1972: SI 1972 No. 917

HMM—Horizontal Milling Machines Regulations, 1928. SRO 1928 No. 548. (As amended by the Horizontal Milling Machines (Amendment) Regulations, 1934, SRO 1934 No. 207)

HSW—Health and Safety at Work Act 1974

IRR—Ionising Radiations (Sealed Sources) Regulations 1969: SI 1969 No. 808

IRUS—Ionising Radiations (Unsealed Radioactive Sources) Regulations, 1968: SI 1968 No. 780

ISF—Iron and Steel Foundries Regulations, 1953. SRO 1953 No. 1464

LCR—Regulations for the Manufacture of Certain Compounds of Lead, 1921. SRO 1921 No. 1443

LPR—Lead Paint Regulations. SRO 1927 No. 847

LR—Regulations for the Use of Locomotives and Wagons, 1906. SRO 1906 No. 679

LSR—Regulations for the Smelting of Materials containing Lead, etc., 1911. SRO 1911 No. 752

MAG—Magnesium (Grinding of Castings and other Articles) Special Regulations, 1946. SRO 1946 No. 2107

NIA—Nuclear Installations (Licensing and Insurance) Act, 1965, as amended by the Nuclear Installations Act, 1969

OC—Order in Council. Those Orders in Council mentioned in this book are all made under the Explosives Acts

OSFA—Offices, Shops and Railway Premises First Air Order 1964: SI 1964 No. 970

OSRA—Offices, Shops and Railway Premises Act 1963

OUM—Operations at Unfenced Machinery Regulations, 1938. SRO 1938 No. 641. As amended by the Operations at Unfenced Machinery (Amended Schedule) Regulations, 1946. SRO 1946 No. 156

PCA—Petroleum (Consolidation) Act, 1928

PCCO—Petroleum (Carbide of Calcium) Order, 1929. SRO 1929 No. 992

PCGO—Petroleum (Compressed Gases) Order, 1930. SRO 1930 No. 34

PCR—Petroleum Spirit (Conveyance) Regulations, 1957, as amended by the Petroleum Spirit (Conveyance) Regulations, 1958

PHA 36—Public Health Act, 1936

PHA 75—Public Health Act, 1875

PHA(L) 36—Public Health (London) Act, 1936

P(HW)R—Pottery (Health and Welfare) Regulations, 1950. SI 1950 No. 65

PMO—Petroleum (Mixtures) Order, 1929. SRO 1929 No. 993

PMVR—Petroleum Spirit (Motor Vehicles) Regulations, 1929. SRO 1929 No. 952

PPR—Power Press Regulations 1965: SI 1965 No. 1441, as amended by the Power Press Regulations, 1972

PVR—Vehicle Painting Regulations 1926: SRO 1926 No. 299

RSA—Radioactive Substances Act 1960

SAR—Sanitary Accommodation Regulations 1938: SRO 1938 No. 611

SCR—Sanitary Conveniences Regulations 1964: SI 1964 No. 966

SI—Statutory Instrument. Normally these are referred to by name but in a few places, to save space, only the number of the order is given. This consists of two figures—the year of issue and the number of the order; e.g., SI 1964 No. 966 was issued in 1964 and was the 966th order issued that year. In ordering copies of statutory instruments it is only necessary to quote the date and number

SLR—Factories (Standard of Lighting) Regulations 1941: SRO 1941 No. 94

SMO—Order dated 8th November 1918 in regard to Ambulance and First Aid Arrangements at Saw Mills, etc.: SRO 1918 No. 1489, as amended by SRO 1925 No. 864 and SI 1961 No. 2434

SRO—Statutory Rules and Orders. This was the former term used for what are now called Statutory Instruments (see above) and the abbreviation is still used in connexion with orders made before 1948

TA—Truck Acts 1831–1940

TDN—Technical Data Notes, issued free by HM Factory Inspectorate

VER—Order for the Vitreous Enamelling of Metal or Glass 1908: SRO 1908 No. 1258

WFR—Washing Facilities Regulations 1964: SI 1964 No. 965

WSR—Order for the Processes of Sorting Wool, etc., 1905: SRO 1905 No. 1293

WWM—Woodworking Machinery Regulations 1922: SRO 1922 No. 1196. (As amended by the Woodworking Machinery (Amendment) Regulations 1927: SRO 1927 No. 207, and the Woodworking (Amendment of Scope) Special Regulations 1945: SRO 1945 No. 1227). These regulations may presently be revoked and new regulations substituted.

Appendix II—Meaning of certain Terms frequently used

Throughout this book the definitions of the terms used have, for the most part, been given as they occur, where such definitions are necessary. There are, however, a few words and phrases which constantly recur throughout the Factories Act and the various regulations and which, partly because of this wide use, are not always capable of being precisely defined. The most common of these terms are given below.

ACCESS, SAFE MEANS OF—See below under "Safe Means of Access."

COMPETENT PERSON—Whether a person is competent to carry out a particular inspection, test, etc., is a matter of fact which the occupier must decide for himself and in the event of legal proceedings he must be prepared to satisfy the Court that he has indeed chosen someone who is competent to do the work in question. There is no statutory definitions of the term but the following unofficial definition is often quoted for guidance and is worth bearing in mind: "The person chosen should have such practical and theoretical knowledge and actual experience of the type of machinery or plant which he has to examine as will enable him to detect defects or weaknesses which it is the purpose of the examination to discover and to assess their importance in relation to the strength and functions of the machinery or plant." This means that it is not sufficient for the person making an examination to be able to detect faults; he must also, from his knowledge and experience, be able to assess their seriousness.

It should never be assumed that a person is competent merely because he has worked for a long time in a particular trade. For instance, a builder's foreman who has been in the building trade for twenty years may be competent to make the periodical examination of scaffolds but this fact should not be taken for granted and the occupier should satisfy himself that the man really is competent to do this. See *Brazier v. Skipton Rock Co. Ltd., 1962*

For the examination of some types of plant, especially boilers, cranes and hoists, many factory occupiers call in outside experts employed by the manufacturers, insurance companies, or professional consultants. This is generally the best policy but there is nothing in the Factories Acts to prevent an occupier from having such examinations made by one of his own employees, if he is satisfied that the employee really is competent.

Under Regulation 21 of the Docks Regulations 1934, the Chief Inspector of Factories can give formal written notice that he does not consider a person competent to carry out the tests and examinations of lifting appliances required by those regulations, or of steam boilers (see FA: 32(9)).

DANGEROUS PARTS—Although the Acts refer to dangerous parts of machinery they do not define that term: the interpretation likely to be adopted by the Courts is given in item 44. It should be remembered that while the danger usually to be anticipated from moving parts of machinery is that of crushing or cutting part of the body, both moving and fixed parts of a machine may be dangerous because they are hot, or because they are electrically live.

EMPLOYEE—See below under "Persons employed."

MAINTAINED—For the purpose of the Factories Acts, this word means "maintained in an efficient state, in efficient working order, and in good repair" (FA 176). Therefore, if the Acts require a particular type of machine to be properly maintained there is a statutory duty to ensure that it is always in proper working order when in use. This requirement is absolute; when a man was killed owing to the unaccountable failure of a safety device on a hoist, the House of Lords decided that the occupier had failed in his duty to maintain the hoist in proper working order, even though the failure of the device could not have been foreseen (*Galashiels Gas Company v. O'Donnell* or *Miller, 1949.*)

OCCUPIER—There is no legal definition of this term. The meaning usually given to it is discussed in item 299.

PERSONS EMPLOYED—This term is not defined in the Acts. Its meaning may seem to be self-evident but for the purposes of the Acts all employees are not necessarily "persons employed." It is generally assumed that the term covers those actually employed in, or in connection with, the processes of the factory and excludes members of the administrative and executive staff. Apprentices are included (FA 176) and so are any women or young persons working in the factory (whether for wages or not) either in a process or in cleaning any part of the factory used for process, or in any other work connected with the process. This latter provision is subject to one exception; a woman employed solely to clean the factory is not a person employed unless the cleaning is incidental to or connected with a process (FA 176).

Many requirements, such as those for safe means of access, affect every person "employed or working on the premises" and are not limited to "persons employed".

PRACTICABLE—There is no statutory definition of this frequently used term but Lord Goddard, when Lord Chief Justice, accepted the Oxford English Dictionary definition which is "capable of being carried out in action" or "feasible." A safety precaution must not be regarded as impracticable merely because it would slow up production, or because it is difficult or inconvenient. (See *Schwalb v. Fass and Son, 1946*).

For the narrower meaning of "Reasonably practicable" see below.

PROPERLY MAINTAINED—See above under "Maintained."

PROVIDE—Where articles have to be provided under the Acts (e.g., goggles) they must be readily available, at some convenient place, for any workmen who needs them and all workmen concerned must have been told where to obtain them. So long as these requirements are satisfied it is not necessary for the article to be issued personally to a workman by the foreman or other supervisor. Care must be taken, however, to ensure that all workmen concerned do in fact know where to obtain the article and that they can obtain it readily—i.e., without having to go to a remote part of the works or wait till some particular storekeeper, etc., is available to issue them. Leading cases in which the above principles have been affirmed are *Finch* v. *Telegraph Construction and Maintenance Company, 1949*, and *Farquhar* v. *Chance Brothers, 1951*.

REASONABLY PRACTICABLE—The best definition of this term is the one formulated by Lord Justice Asquith in the case of *Edwards* v. *National Coal Board, 1949*. His lordship said: Reasonably Practicable is a narrower term than Physically Possible and seems to me to imply that a computation must be made . . . in which the quantum of risk is placed on one scale and the sacrifice involved in the measures necessary for averting the risk (whether in money, time or trouble) is placed in the other. If it be shown that there is a gross disproportion between them—the risk being insignificant in relation to the sacrifice—the defendants discharge the onus upon them.

SAFE MEANS OF ACCESS—This term, which is used in item 12 and elsewhere, has been the subject of much argument in legal proceedings. So far as access to places where people work regularly is concerned, there is little room for controversy; it should always be reasonably practicable to ensure that employees can get to their workplace in safety. What sometimes cause uncertainty are the occasions when a maintenance man, or contractor's employee, has to work in a place which is not a normal workplace (e.g., on a roof) and to which there is no regular means of access. Here it is the duty of the occupier to provide some safe means of access "so far as is reasonably practicable" but it may not be possible to provide a means of access which is one-hundred-per-cent safe without going to an amount of trouble or expense which is out of all proportion to the danger and in such circumstances the occupier has carried out his obligation if he takes such steps as are reasonably practicable. It should be noted that the occupier's statutory duty is fulfilled when he has provided the safe means of access; if someone uses an unsafe means of access when a safe means is available there is no breach of the Factories Acts (this was established in *Farquhar* v. *Chance Brothers, 1951*, where it was shown that the occupiers had provided adequate ladders though the person concerned had not used them.)

It should be noted that the safe means of access required under Section 29 of the Factories Act 1961 is limited to safe access to workplaces; it has been held that a passage used by a workman to reach the canteen was not covered by this Section, because the canteen was not a place at which he had to work. The same limitation would presumably apply to the means of access to a cloakroom or washroom. But these limitations only apply to the statutory obligation under Section 29; so far as passages, stairs, etc., are concerned there is also an obligation under Section 28 (see item 12) and the Common Law obligation to take reasonable care for an employee's safety (see item 281) would probably be held to include the provision of safe means of access to any place to which an employee might legitimately go, such as the canteen or washroom, as well as to a workplace.

Under the Construction (Health and Welfare) Regulations, 1966, safe means of access is required to the welfare amenities required by the regulations (washing facilities, messroom, etc.). C(HW): 16.

SAFETY BY CONSTRUCTION—Machinery is safe by construction only if it is "of such construction as to be safe to every person employed or working on the premises as it would be if securely fenced". This lays down a precise and absolute standard and nothing less is likely to be accepted as an alternative to secure fencing. The matter is discussed further in item 45.

SAFETY BY POSITION—This is also discussed in item 45.

SOUND CONSTRUCTION—This term is usually taken to mean that the article in question is made of sound material properly put together. It has been held that an item of plant, etc., can be accepted as sound if it is capable of standing the strain arising from its normal use in a factory. To satisfy the requirements of the Acts it must actually *be* strong enough for this purpose, it is not enough that it should *appear* to be sound.

YOUNG PERSONS—The Factories Act, 1961, defines a young person as one who has ceased to be a child (i.e., has reached the current school-leaving age) but has not attained the age of eighteen. It applies to members of both sexes.

INDEX OF STATUTES

The intention of the Health and Safety at Work Act 1974 is that certain statutes should be repealed, together with all statutory instruments and regulations made under them, to be 'progressively replaced by a system of regulations and approved codes of practice'. For this purpose section 15 confers power on the Secretary of State for the Employment to make regulations for any of the purposes set out in the twenty-two sections of Schedule 3, except where they relate exclusively to agricultural matters, in which case regulations can be made by the Minister of Agriculture, Fisheries and Food (section 50).
The index below serves two purposes. It details what statutes or parts of statutes are to be repealed, or have already been repealed as at 1 January 1976. Secondly where reference has been made in the text to any of the statutes, the item number is given in italic; where reference is made in the supplement, the item number is given in italic followed by '(*S*)'.

Numbers in italics refer to items, not pages. 'S' refers to supplement.

Numbers in italics refer to items, not pages. 'S' refers to supplement.

INDEX OF STATUTORY INSTRUMENTS

and other delegated legislation

Numbers in italics refer to items, not pages. 'S' refers to supplement.

Numbers in italics refer to items, not pages. 'S' refers to supplement.

Numbers in italics refer to items, not pages. 'S' refers to supplement.

Numbers in italics refer to items, not pages. 'S' refers to supplement.

GENERAL INDEX

Many machines, processes, etc., are not mentioned by name in any Acts or Regulations and therefore do not appear by name in this index. If any machine or process cannot be found, reference should be made to the appropriate general heading. For example, the term "Drilling machine" will not be found in the index, because the only requirements affecting these machines are those under the general headings of "Machinery" and "Electrical Equipment".

Numerical references are to items (not to pages). Where '(S)' appears this refers to an item in the supplement

Numerical references are to items (not to pages). Where '(S)' appears this refers to an item in the supplement

Numerical references are to items (not to pages). Where '(S)' appears this refers to an item in the supplement